A HISTORY OF MODERN HUNGARY
1867–1986

A HISTORY OF MODERN HUNGARY 1867–1986

JÖRG K. HOENSCH

translated by
KIM TRAYNOR

LONGMAN
London and New York

Longman Group UK Limited,
Longman House, Burnt Mill, Harlow,
Essex CM20 2JE, England
and Associated Companies throughout the world.

Published in the United States of America by
Longman Inc., New York

Geschichte Ungarns 1867–1983 © 1984 Verlag W.
Kohlhammer GmbH, Stuttgart, Berlin, Köln, Mainz; by
arrangement with EULAMA S.R.L., Rome
Translation © Longman Group UK Ltd 1988

First published 1988

British Library Cataloguing in Publication Data

Hoensch, Jörg K.
    A history of modern Hungary 1867–1986.
    1. Hungary — History — 1867–1918
    2. Hungary — History — 20th century
    I. Title II. Geschichte Ungarns 1867–1983.
    English
    943.9'043 DB945

ISBN 0-582-01484-0 CSD
ISBN 0-582-25109-5 PPR

Library of Congress Cataloging-in-Publication Data

Hoensch, Jörg K. (Jörg Konrad)
    A history of modern Hungary, 1867–1986.

    Translation of: Geschichte Ungarns, 1867–1983.
    Bibliography: p.
    Includes indexes.
    1. Hungary — History — 1867–1918. 2. Hungary —
History — 20th century. I. Title.
DB945.H5613 1988   943.9'05   87-4170
ISBN 0-582-01484-0
ISBN 0-582-25109-5 (pbk.)

Set in Linotron 202 10/12pt Bembo

Produced by Longman Singapore Publishers (Pte) Ltd.
Printed in Singapore

Contents

List of Maps

Abbreviations

ÁVH, ÁVO	Department of Political Police
KGB	Committee for State Security (USSR), after 1954
MDP	Hungarian Workers' Party
MKP	Hungarian Communist Party
MSzMP	Hungarian Socialist Workers' Party
MVD	Ministry of the Interior and Protection of Public Order (USSR)
NATO	North Atlantic Treaty Organisation
NKGB	People's Commissariat for State Security (USSR), 1941–1946
NKVD	People's Commissariat for Internal Affairs (USSR)
SDP	Social Democratic Party
SS	Schutzstaffel
USSR	Union of Soviet Socialist Republics
USA	United States of America

Pronunciation Guide

Hungarian words are invariably stressed on the first syllable.

The accents denoting length, frequently encountered on the longer vowels (*á, é, í, ó, ú*) or extra-long vowels (*ä, ö, ü*) do not refer to stress, but simply denote the long pure vowels. Their pronunciation corresponds roughly to the following English sounds: *á* = a in 'father', *é* = a in 'gate', *í* = e in 'equal', *ó* = o in 'foe', *ú* = u in 'rude'.

The unlengthened vowels are always pronounced short and distinctly: e.g. *e* as in English 'get'. The Magyar *a*, in contrast, corresponds to the short, open o in the English word 'hot'.

The consonants are also distinctly short or pronounced long if written double. In the case of double consonants like *cs* or *ny* only the first letter is written twice to show length.

The consonants *b, d, f, g, h, k, l, m, n, p, t, z* are pronounced similarly to English.

j is pronounced y
c is pronounced ts
cs is pronounced ch
sz is pronounced hard s
s is pronounced soft s = sh
zs corresponds to the j in the French word 'journal'

Before the spelling reform of 1903 the double consonant *cz* was used for the sound ts. Nowadays it appears only in surnames.

r is pronounced as a strongly rolled r
y is used phonetically in conjunction with g, l, n and t:
e.g. *gy* = dje as in during

ly = English y as in yet
ny = English nj as in new or French ng as in cognac
ty = tje as in tureen

If y appears in a surname without any of these four terminating consonants it is pronounced like a short i (as in English eat).

Preface

Perhaps an art will come which, without words or even gestures, can convey the experiences of a people by looks alone.

Stanislav Jerzy Lec

Behind the widespread cliché which views Hungary primarily in terms of romantic steppes, grazing cattle herds, village wells, operetta melodies, gypsy ensembles, *csárdás, paprika* and *tokajer* lies a country whose historical development has witnessed a number of breaks in continuity and contradictions since the abortive revolution of 1848–49, while at the same time displaying an astonishing capacity for regeneration. The Compromise of 1867, which regulated the status of the historic kingdom of St Stephen in the Austro-Hungarian monarchy, the collapse of the Habsburg Empire and the effects of the 1920 Trianon Treaty, Hitler's attempts to incorporate Hungary into his vision of a 'New European Order', its integration into the Socialist Bloc after the catastrophe of the Second World War and Kádár's independent 'Hungarian path towards Socialism' are generally known, although a detailed knowledge of these developments and their context tends to be lacking. Although the past few years have seen a number of western tourists to the country straddling the Danube steadily increase, its history, ongoing traditions and the motivating factors behind the 'Hungarian model' of the present tend to remain obscured from view on these holiday trips.

Since 1956–57, when Gyula Miskolczy's lectures first introduced me to nineteenth-century Hungarian history during a year spent studying at the University of Vienna, I have repeatedly occupied myself with specific aspects of Hungarian history. This interest has been nurtured and strengthened by my own family's connections with Hungary on my paternal side. Since the thirteenth century the family enjoyed the right of abode in the relatively isolated German-speaking area of Zips in the High Tatra mountains in the Kingdom of the Holy Crown of St Stephen. Towards the end of the nineteenth century some members of the family became fully assimilated into Magyar culture and after the Second World War my paternal uncle, together with his wife and children, felt obliged to take Hungarian citizenship. Hungarian was used quite naturally as a normal means of communication within the family circle.

With this personal background as my starting point, but also aware of the inherent pitfalls, I gladly embarked upon the task of writing a history of Hungary over the past 125 years. Unfortunately, owing to lack of space, I have had to neglect most of Hungary's cultural history. Alongside the account and interpretations of Hungary's political development, the book's main focus of interest is, above all, the country's frequently neglected social and economic history. Over the past thirty years, Hungarian scholarship has produced a number of valuable historical studies, some of which have appeared in translation in the West. Highly illuminative accounts have come from the pens of both Hungarian émigrés and western specialists, who have covered both long-term developments over a substantial period of time and more detailed issues of historical interest. Since, however, a factually accurate, informative account, free of ideological or apologetic tendencies, has not been available recently, I felt justified in embarking upon the task of writing this book, for the English edition of which the final chapter has been updated and expanded.

I am indebted to my colleagues at the School of Eastern European History at the University of the Saarland in Saarbrücken for their help in overcoming the technical problems involved in producing this volume, to Kim Traynor for his translation and to Dr John Leslie for his helpful comments on the latter. My wife constantly helped in the preparation of the manuscript. Without her participation and active assistance I could scarcely have managed to complete this task over and above my normal teaching duties. I alone am aware of the extent to which I am indebted to her. To my father, who lived through most of the events described in this book, and who also suffered to some extent, this book is dedicated with the warmest affection.

Nothing brings nations closer together or separates them more than contemplation of the past. The purpose behind this history of

Hungary will have been served, if it succeeds in helping dispel clichés and prejudices, and if, across borders which are fortunately becoming less impenetrable, it arouses a sense of our shared responsibility for maintaining the peace.

Saarbrücken, 4 November 1986,   Jörg K. Hoensch
the thirtieth anniversary
of the crushing of the
Hungarian Uprising

CHAPTER ONE

Hungary under the Habsburgs up to the Compromise of 1867

THE HISTORICAL BACKGROUND UP TO THE REVOLUTION OF 1848–49

Dressed in the uniform of a Hungarian general, the Habsburg Emperor, Francis Joseph I, was crowned Apostolic King of Hungary in Buda on 8 June 1867. In the course of a solemn religious ceremony, conducted in accordance with traditional mediaeval custom, the Hungarian Primate placed the holy crown of St Stephen on the Emperor's head to the rapturous acclaim of the crowd. This splendid act of reconciliation between a political nation and its ruler had come about not least through the mediating efforts of the Empress Elizabeth, who enjoyed great popularity in Hungary; and was an event which, on the basis of a compromise agreement negotiated in the previous weeks, brought to an end a crisis which had been smouldering in Hungary ever since the revolution of 1848.

To this day the Emperor has remained a controversial figure. But, given his bitter personal experiences from the time the Hungarian diet deposed the House of Habsburg-Lorraine on 14 April 1849, the many failures in domestic and foreign policy following subsequent attempts to re-establish absolutist rule, unsuccessful experiments at constitutional centralism and Old Conservative federalism and especially Austria's shock defeat at Königgrätz, it says a great deal for his political vision that he was not blind to political realities, but instead deliberately instigated the Austrian Empire's transformation into the Dual Monarchy of Austria-Hungary. Although the advocates of a unitary Empire thought that the dualistic solution contained in the so-called 'Compromise' of 1867 set the wrong course for the future and that the obstruction of a genuine federal structure for the Empire would inevitably contribute to the break-up of the multi-national state, the Compromise – soon to be fiercely attacked also in Hungary – offered the only real chance of preserving the Habsburg Empire's great-power status and ending the prevailing conflict between the central imperial power and nationalist aspirations for independence which had existed in Hungary since before the 1848 Revolution.

Following the annihilation of a small and badly led army under the young King Louis II (1516–26) by the army of Sultan Suleiman II at Mohács on 29 August 1526, Hungary fell under the rule of King Ferdinand I of Habsburg (1526–64) by the terms of a double marriage contract of 1515. Internal conflict between the Habsburg monarch and the Prince of Transylvania, John Zápolyai, whom the lesser nobility had crowned king, diverted attention from the need to defend the country against the Turks, so that, with the exception of a narrow strip of territory in the west and north-west, the main part of the old mediaeval kingdom of Hungary was incorporated into the Ottoman Empire. Only the Principality of Transylvania, though liable to pay tribute to the Turks, managed to preserve some degree of internal autonomy. Economic mismanagement under the Turks, constant fighting on the frontier and the long drawn-out Turkish wars exacted a high price. Whole areas were depopulated, trade and commerce suffered and Hungarian intellectual and cultural life stagnated. Buda, the ancient capital of mediaeval Hungary, was not wrested from the Turks by the imperial armies until 1686, and at a price. The Hungarian estates agreed to acknowledge the Habsburg succession, renouncing the right to the monarch's free election and the right to resist a ruler's illegal actions, as guaranteed in the Golden Bull of 1222. The country's reorganisation, carried out in a spirit of absolutism by the Emperor Leopold I (1657–1705), inspired the rebellion led by the prince of Transylvania, Ferenc II (Rákóczy). The diet convoked at Ónod in 1707 declared that the Habsburgs had forfeited the throne and proclaimed Hungary's independence. A compromise was finally reached in 1711 with the signing of the Treaty of Szatmár which secured for the nobility the unlimited possession of their estates, their traditional privilege of tax exemption, the self-administration of the counties, the right of the Hungarian diet to legislate and unlimited seigneurial powers over their peasant labour. Following their acceptance of the Pragmatic Sanction in 1723 the Hungarian estates also acknowledged the Habsburg succession in the female line and accepted the principle that Hungary, like the monarchy's other territories and possessions, formed an integral and indivisible part of the Habsburg dynasty's domains.

Despite all attempts to unify and modernise the Habsburg Empire in the eighteenth century, Hungary, thanks to its self-conscious maintenance of its special traditions, its nobility's feudal landownership and its retention of many independent political institutions, succeeded in maintaining its special position within the Empire on the basis of a distinct nobility and national identity. Even Joseph II (1780–90) only partially succeeded in transforming Hungary from a constitution based on estates to a modern bureaucratic state and absolute monarchy. Hungary's estates, comprising some 200 magnates, approximately 8,000 wealthy landowners and about 135,000 families of the lesser nobility with 330,000 members, sought to preserve the old constitution, not for its own sake, but as a means of safeguarding the existing social order and aristocratic way of life from any major changes. Although Hungary retained its representative assembly and constitution based on estates, these institutions did not guarantee independence or autonomous government, since its main political institutions – the Royal Hungarian Chancellery, the Royal Hungarian Council of Governors and the Royal Privy Council were in practice under the direct control of the imperial central government in Vienna.

The first decades of the nineteenth century witnessed the earliest attempts to modernise the country. In the wake of the French Revolution the nobility attempted to liberalise the constitution and promote a greater sense of Hungarian nationhood. During the so-called 'Reform Era' in the quarter century preceding the 1848 Revolution demands were made to replace the old estates-based constitution with a democratic constitution on the French or Belgian model, in other words, to replace the diet and its estates with a popularly elected representative assembly and responsible ministerial government. These demands were accompanied by efforts to institute land reform, emancipate the peasants, reform the judiciary, and introduce such civic rights as equality before the law, freedom of the press and the right of free assembly. Economic demands, such as the improvement of the infrastructure through the improved regulation of the Danube, the construction of roads and railways, general industrialisation and increased productivity in the backward agricultural sector were accompanied by concrete measures to raise the extremely poor standard of education and generally promote intellectual life in the fields of literature, the press and the theatre. Every traditional area of life, customs and behaviour witnessed dramatic change, intended to place Hungary with its traditional mediaeval character on the road to modern socio-economic conditions and parliamentary government. This comprehensive process of modernisation also affected the Hungarians' previously unpolitical national consciousness which gave way to a Magyar nationalism and its political aspirations for a nation state. The long-held desire to see the power of the monarchy replaced by the creation of a nation state was combined with the wish to see the Magyar language predominate in the schools and public life, even to the point of fully assimilating the non-Magyar majority. As a result of the demographic effects of Turkish rule and the extensive settlement of foreign immigrants during the eighteenth century, Hungary, in 1842, comprised a colourful mixture of races. The country's 5.57 million Magyars were confronted by a majority of non-Magyars (2.47 million Rumanians, 1.72 million Slovaks, 1.32 million Germans, 1.26 million Croats, 1.05 million Serbs, 0.46 million Ukrainians, 45,000 Slovenes and 288,000 of other ethnic origin). Since no nationally conscious Magyar middle class existed, in the modern sense of the term, it was the aristocracy in Hungary which gave impetus to reformist demands grounded in the liberal and nationalist spirit of the time.

The originator and main advocate of a programme of evolutionary reform was Count István Széchenyi. He wished to see urgent reforms cautiously and gradually introduced in consultation with the dynasty. However, the suspicion of reform harboured by the ageing Emperor Francis I (1792–1835), together with Metternich's repressive policing measures during the reign of the weak Emperor Ferdinand I (1835–48), encouraged the growth of radical ideas among the lesser nobility, plagued as it was at ths time by financial hardship. From 1841 onwards, its spokesman was the young lawyer and writer, Lajos Kossuth. His ironical and pointed articles, which appeared in his newspaper, *Pesti Hirlap* (Pest Journal), argued passionately for major changes in the existing social structure. He also argued increasingly openly for Hungary's complete independence from the Habsburg monarchy – or, at least, for parity alongside Austria in the framework of a confederation. Hungary's rigid tariff barriers, which had never been ratified by the Emperor, and the Language Decree promulgated by the Hungarian diet of 1843–44, which made Magyar the official language in almost all areas of national life, added to existing tensions. Although it was widely believed that the national language, more than any other factor, would guarantee the unity of Hungary's emergent 'bourgeois democracy', the imposition and spread of Magyar in those parts of the country inhabited by national minorities fuelled existing racial tensions and resulted in open conflict between the various ethnic groups and Magyar nationalism.

The successes of the opposition movement, which finally formed itself into the party of 'opposition' (*Ellenzék*) at a national congress in Pest on 15 March 1847, caused the central government in Vienna to take counter-measures. The energetic Count György Apponyi took over as head of the Royal Hungarian Chancellery and filled the key positions in the county administrations with men who worked energetically against this 'opposition' which drew its support from the liberal and educated middle class. When, in November 1847, a new diet was convened in Pressburg (now Bratislava), not far from Vienna, the pro-government elements were in the majority. However, they were unable to prevent the opposition's demands, formulated by Kossuth, from becoming the main focus of debate. These included the demand for national self-determination, abolition of the nobility's exemption from taxation, removal of the peasants' feudal status and obligations, the extension of the franchise beyond the aristocracy and the appointment of a ministry for Hungarian affairs, responsible to the assembly. The government was obliged to promise an end to corrupt administrative practices which flouted the law. Although it became clear in the course of the proceedings that most of the nobility shrank from any major radical reforms, the revolution, which spread throughout the Habsburg Empire in mid-March 1848 brought about a completely new phase of development which was to have a profound affect on Hungary's relationship with the monarchy.

The revolution broke out in Vienna on 13 March 1848 and by the 15 March had spread to the university town of Pest, Hungary's intellectual and cultural capital. Bad harvests had given rise to peasant disturbances in the countryside and the still comparatively small industrial proletariat which numbered around 150,000 was suffering from the effects of what was a general European economic crisis. Members of the intelligentsia and the student body began to stir up opposition to the monarchy's absolutism and joined the aristocracy in demanding greater political rights and a share in government. The unrest escalated into armed uprisings in the provinces inhabited by national minorities. Against this background, the Twelve Point programme proclaimed in the Café 'Pilvax' in Pest on the morning of 15 March 1848 found widespread support. This programme surpassed the aims of the nobility's reformist policies.

It called for the abolition of hereditary serfdom, civic and religious equality before the law, universal taxes from which the nobility would no longer be exempt, the convocation in Pest of annual diets based on limited suffrage, the creation of a ministry with parliamentary responsibility, press freedom, the release of political prisoners, the introduction of trial by jury, the creation of a national militia, an army oath of allegiance to the constitution and, finally, union with Transylvania.

On the same day a deputation sent from the diet in Pressburg to meet Emperor Ferdinand managed to exploit the favourable situation at this point. By 17 March 1848, the delegates had pressed home their demands and managed to secure the appointment of the magnate, Count Lajos Batthyány, as Hungary's first prime minister responsible to a Hungarian parliament. Shortly thereafter, the representatives of the nobility in the diet drafted in quick succession the necessary laws for the annual summoning of a popularly elected representative assembly, the creation of a national bank, the introduction of press freedom, the formation of a responsible ministerial cabinet, compensation for landowners affected by the commutation of servile tenures and labour services and, finally, the abolition of entailed estates. Because of their fear of peasant revolution even the conservative elements voted for the immediate and unconditional emancipation of the peasants, especially since the liberated peasant masses were seen as the main guarantee for wresting and subsequently maintaining Hungary's newly-won independence. It was probably for this reason that, on 28 March, the court in Vienna refused at first to sanction the draft laws for the emancipation of the peasants or create a council of ministers. However, in view of the revolutionary situation developing in Italy and Germany it eventually felt obliged to accept the draft proposals in their original form on 11 April 1848.

Despite the court's panic and impotence, which lasted through to June and July 1848, the central government in Vienna was not prepared in the long term to honour concessions forced upon it by the pressures of the hour, especially since many issues remained unresolved in the rush to pass all thirty-one laws and Hungary's relationship to the Empire as a whole had not been properly clarified. Although the moderates in Batthyány's ministry, led by Count Széchenyi (labour and transport), Baron Jozsef Eötvös (religion and public education) and Ferenc Deák (justice) were in the majority, and Kossuth had to content himself with the thankless job of minister of finance, they were scarcely able to influence developments. The emancipation of the peasants gave rise to so many problems that a growing dissatisfaction was noticeable not only among the nobility, which was heavily burdened by the loss of feudal dues and labour services, but also among the peasants who had had to settle for barely 50 per cent of the country's cultivated land. Their discontent could be contained only by military intervention and a declaration of martial law. Since the the national minorities' demand for cultural autonomy within the framework of the Hungarian kingdom was completely rejected, the non-Magyar population turned against the Hungarian revolution. Attempts by the Croats, Rumanians, Slovaks and Ruthenes to take their own independence by force were brutally suppressed and gave the dynasty in Vienna a welcome opportunity to use the minorities which acknowledged the Habsburg Empire but objected to the idea of a Magyar nation state to help contain Hungarian revolutionary fervour. The gradual return to normality in western Europe encouraged Vienna to attempt Hungary's forceful subjugation.

A rebellion had already flared up in Serbia in June 1848. On 11 July, the new diet, elected on the basis of a new census-based electoral law, and in which the 'opposition' comprised nine-tenths of the deputies, felt obliged to agree to Kossuth's demand for 200,000 soldiers and 42 million guilders to organise the country's defence. The 40,000 recruits which the government in Vienna called for to put down the Italian liberation campaign was agreed to, but would involve a drastic rise in taxes, whereas a growing number of people supported the demand to establish a Hungarian national army, the *Honvéd*, as a sort of militia. Since there was a distinct shift to the left in the ranks of the diet's liberal majority in August, the government in Vienna, encouraged by its successes in Bohemia and Italy, thought the time had come to put an end to Hungary's constitutional aspirations and struggle for independence. Although Batthyány's ministry was prepared to make concessions in order to avoid any punitive military action, even at the expense of Hungarian self-government, Vienna complained that the diet's military and fiscal measures had violated the Pragmatic Sanction and demanded that the April Laws be reduced in scope. In a dramatic speech before the diet, Kossuth spoke openly of the failure of Vienna's policy of pacification and called for emergency measures to be taken in defence of the country. On 10 September 1848, the Batthyány ministry resigned.

When news reached Pest on 12 September that the provincial governor of Croatia, Field Marshall Jelačić, had begun military operations on the previous day, Hungary's different social classes joined together to form a united front. It included not only liberal but radical landowners, not only peasants won over by generous concessions, but townspeople, too, all prepared to defend their national independence. Although in Transylvania the peasant leader, Avram Iancu, also staged an armed uprising and Slovakian irregulars took up arms against the Magyar authorities, the National Army comprising regular troops, the national militia, reserves and volunteers, was able to inflict a decisive defeat on Jelačić's troops on 29 September. Whereas the moderates now withdrew from the government, and the Committee for National Defence, dominated by Kossuth and the Left, became the real decision-making body, a combination of confused orders and hesitancy on the part of the Hungarian commander-in-chief, General Móga, prevented any joint action taking place with the revolutionaries in Vienna who had forced the court to flee post-haste to Olmütz on 6 October. On 30 October 1848, General Windischgrätz forced the Hungarians to retreat at Schwechat, just outside Vienna. However, the first cracks were already beginning to appear in Hungary's national effort, which was still united in the face of external threat. The more moderate politicians around Baron Z. Keményi, L. Kovács and G. Kazinczy, the nucleus of the later 'peace party' (*Békepárt*), were not prepared to go along with Kossuth's increasingly radical policies, nor with General Artúr Görgey's preparations for a final military reckoning with the Austrians. When, on 2 December 1848, Emperor Ferdinand I abdicated in favour of his nephew, Francis Joseph, these politicians called on Hungarians to accept the new monarch and argued for the need for a negotiated solution to resolve the conflict. The peasants also displayed a mood of growing disillusionment, since their demands were to be discussed only after the military operations had been concluded. Hungary's nationalities, for their part, had placed themselves firmly on the side of the young Emperor.

The imperial army's initial successes over Hungary's revolutionary army strengthened Vienna's belief that the status quo could be completely restored in Hungary. When, in the spring of 1849, however, the Hungarians succeeded in pushing back the government troops, the Hungarian diet, which had since removed itself to Debrecen on 14 April, announced the deposition of the royal house of Habsburg-Lorraine and proclaimed an independent Hungarian Republic. Kossuth was chosen as its first 'acting governor', thus effectively assuming the position of Regent. While the Republic's army marched on to further victories, the 'peace party' succeeded in increasingly curtailing the authority of Kossuth with his left-wing sympathies and substantially paralysed the revolutionary government. The news, which was made public on the storming of the fortress at Buda on 21 May 1849, that Tsarist Russia would join Austria in its war against the Hungarian revolutionaries, caused profound demoralisation and a growing mood of defeatism in a country which was now politically isolated and militarily exhausted. From the middle of June onwards, the 150,000 or so soldiers of the poorly equipped and ill-trained army of the beleaguered Republic faced over 200,000 and 170,000 men in the Russian and Austrian imperial armies respectively. The government, which moved to Szeged at the beginning of July, tried desperately to mobilise the nation. However, the increasingly frequent reports of defeats meant that it was no longer possible to mobilise the disillusioned peasants to sacrifice themselves in the further defence of the country, despite promises of a major land reform which would solve their problems. The Nationalities Law, passed by the diet during its last sitting on 28 July 1849, granted the country's non-Magyar peoples substantial rights in the use of their native languages and a limited autonomy. But these concessions came much too late in the day to bring about an improvement in Hungary's dreadful situation. At Világos, on 13 August 1849, General Görgey was forced to surrender unconditionally to the Russian commander-in-chief, Field Marshall Paskevič. Kossuth, who up to the last moment had urged the Hungarians to continue the fight, escaped to Turkey with a number of the revolution's military and civilian leaders.

Thanks to Russian support, the Habsburg Empire had survived its revolutionary upheavals. The Hungarian experiment had been a heroic struggle which had lasted eighteen months. Its failure was the result not only of its enemies' superior strength and an unfavourable international situation, but of Hungary's own internal weaknesses and contradictions. The upheaval, which had its origins in the pre-1848 'Reform Era', had exposed the inadequacies of Hungary's social and economic structure but at the same time failed to produce and establish a new social and economic order. As the social class most identified with the state, the nobility had taken an active part in the political decisions of the day. It had subscribed to a passionate nationalism which had falsely assessed the real possibilities of integrating and assimilating the country's majority of non-Magyar peoples, themselves in the grip of their own nationalism. It had also overestimated the economic capacity of a country which was still strongly agrarian in character. The missed opportunities which resulted from these misjudgements meant that the basic problems posed by the nationalities and the peasants could not be solved sufficiently quickly and decisively to ensure that national solidarity which was essential for the successful defence of the bourgeois-democratic revolution. In particular, the conflicting aims of the radical minority, the liberal nationalist majority and the conservative monarchists of the greater nobility and clergy, had quickly checked the revolution's momentum. The revolution had also proved abortive because its leaders failed to recognise the true nature of the power relationships and interests involved, and because there was a lack of compromise and moderation on the part of those who had assumed political responsibility. The desire for revenge on the part of the triumphant Habsburg dynasty, its strict policy of restoring the status quo and its refusal to acknowledge any changes which had taken place, ruled out any collaboration based on trust and, thus, obstructed the Habsburg Empire's development towards a modern constitutional state based on a western European-type of social structure and solid industrial middle class.

THE FAILURE OF NEO-ABSOLUTISM, 1849–67

Following the Republican Army's surrender at Világos, Hungary was subjected to a period of military rule which lasted until 10 July 1850. The government acted without restraint in carrying out savage reprisals against the rebels. While many tried to escape the punishment of the courts by fleeing abroad, thousands of patriots were given long prison sentences and had their property confiscated. The majority of officers of the defeated army were forced to serve as ordinary privates in punishment batallions. The overt dictatorship of Field Marshall Haynau, who had made his reputation as the 'hyena of Brescia' on account of cruelties committed under his command in Italy, reached its apogée on 6 October 1849, one year to the day after the working-class uprising in Vienna had taken place. In order to 'set an example', he ordered the execution in Arad of thirteen *Honvéd* generals as well as that in Pest of Hungary's first prime minister, Count Lajos Batthyáni, who had been appointed by the Emperor Ferdinand I. These men were to be followed to the scaffold by numerous army officers, revolutionary activists and government officials. Haynau's tough and vengeful measures forever remain a disgraceful episode in the history of the Habsburg monarchy. They not only provided Hungary with martyrs, but caused a deep divide to open up between the Hungarian nation and the Habsburg dynasty. They gave rise to anti-Austrian sentiments which were to last for decades, nourished by glorified accounts of Hungary's struggle for freedom and the heroes it had produced. The Austrian chancellor, Prince Felix Schwarzenberg, justified the 'forfeiture theory' which postulated that by rebelling and rejecting Habsburg rule, the Hungarians had forfeited their constitutional rights and their country consequently deserved to be treated as a conquered province. As early as the autumn of 1849, Baron Geringer, Hungary's newly-appointed governor-general, began to reorganise the Hungarian bureaucracy by destroying the unified administration of the old Hungarian kingdom and replacing it with five administrative districts, each under the direct authority of an army general. Transylvania, along with the Voivodina, Croatia and Slovenia with their substantial Serb populations, were detached from Hungary and placed on an equal footing with the Empire's other territories. In other words, they were reduced to the status of mere provinces. A popularly elected assembly and self-governing county administrations no longer existed. Alongside the military and a strengthened police force and gendarmerie, foreigners – mainly German and Czech civil servants, derided by the natives as 'Bach Hussars', after the new Austrian interior minister – were made responsible for maintaining internal order. As formerly in the reign of Joseph II, German became the official language of the civil service and the language of instruction in elementary and secondary schools. Under the new centralised and absolutist government, openly practised ater the suspension of the 1849 constitution by a royal decree of 1851 (the Sylvester Patent), a return to Hungary's pre-revolutionary constitution based on feudal estates, particularist interests and self-government for the nationalities was unthinkable. While the clergy's influence was considerably strengthened by the signing of a Concordat in 1855, neither the federalist Old Conservatives, nor the constitutional liberals found favour at court in Vienna. As far as Hungary was concerned, the dynasty could rely only on a few career bureaucrats who had risen to the nobility in the service of the crown and the military who had similarly inculcated monarchist values. Even the moderate representatives of Hungary's nationalities found themselves forced into opposition.

Significantly, some of the liberal achievements of the revolution remained. The law, proposed by Hans Kudlich, which emancipated the peasants in Austria and was implemented on 7 September 1848, was also extended to Hungary. This ensured the removal of the landowner's authority, patrimonial rights and police powers. The peasants' feudal services and dues were cancelled, partly through compensation, partly through commutation. The extension to Hungary of the Austrian criminal code and legal procedures was as positive in its effects as the improvements which took place in schooling. The introduction of a universal tax system, the removal of internal tariffs and the regulation of banking and commerce through uniform legal regulations produced an economic upturn and great advances. The railway network was also progressively expanded. By 1867 it already comprised over 2,000 kilometres. The favourable economic trend in the agricultural sector soon helped the larger landowners overcome the losses they had incurred as a result of peasant emancipation. The lesser nobility, on the other hand, frequently failed to hold on to its share of land and its members increasingly sought employment in the urban professions and the civil service. Favourable market conditions and a healthy employment situation helped the peasants, most of whom owned only small plots of land, to make modest economic progress, while the landless proletariat benefited from the country's gradual industrialisation and the expansion of its basic industries, financed mainly by foreign capital. The majority of Hungary's 300,000 workers, however, were still employed as small-scale tradesmen.

During this so-called 'Bach era', there was a growing readiness on the part of the conservative, anti-revolutionary aristocracy and even many members of the middle-ranking nobility to reach a sensible compromise with the monarchy. Even so, Vienna's brusque rejection of any attempt at compromise forced even the monarchist nobility, which had no wish to accept the loss of constitutional autonomy, to adopt an attitude of passive resistance. A spirit of revolt and national resistance to arbitrary rule found support only among clandestine groups. International political events also planted the hope of regaining Hungary's traditional constitutional rights. The failures of detested Russian Tsardom in the Crimea (1853–56) and Italy's anti-Austrian campaign, stirred up by Napoleon III, raised hopes that the monarchy might change its policy towards Hungary. Austria's sudden defeat by France and Piedmont in 1859 frustrated the plans of Hungarian émigrés to influence events at home by setting up a rival government in exile and a Hungarian Legion in Italy. The changes in government which resulted from the removal of the Bach ministry and half-hearted concessions by Vienna, demonstrated the temporary weakness of the central government. The Hungarians were quick to take advantage of this by staging political demonstrations to coincide with the country's traditional national celebrations. Following bloody clashes on 15 March 1860, the situation grew even more tense when news reached Hungary of Garibaldi's triumphant progress through southern Italy and the prospect of direct Austrian involvement – something Hungarian émigrés tried to encourage. In view of the difficult situation in both domestic and foreign policy the Emperor Francis Joseph soon felt obliged to enlarge the nominated imperial council (*Reichsrat*) by appointing to it some representatives of the Old Conservative Magyar aristocracy in the spring of 1860. On 20 October 1860 he also came some way towards accepting their ideas of a greater measure of federal government for the Empire by promulgating the October Diploma which reorganised the monarchy's internal governmental structure.

Faced with a dangerous situation in foreign policy, the Emperor hoped to strengthen the Empire's internal stability by partially fulfilling Hungarian demands. But this was not achieved. The high hopes for a complete restoration of the traditional prerogatives of the old Hungarian kingdom and independent government with a sufficient degree of representation and control in the imperial council were not fulfilled. As an autonomous Crown territory, Hungary was to have only equal status with the Empire's other provinces. The restoration of the diet – with albeit strongly curtailed legislative powers – the Royal Chancellery, the governor's advisory council and the county administrations did not satisfy the majority of Hungarians. Led by Ferenc Deák, they supported the idea of 'legal continuity', i.e. that the laws enacted during the 1848–49 revolution should remain effective. Since there was also fierce opposition to the attempt to strengthen the monarchy constitutionally along the lines proposed in the October Diploma from other parts of the Empire, the Emperor did a volte face and appointed Anton Ritter von Schmerling to take over in Vienna. The February Patent of 26 February 1861 now attempted to solve the problems of the Habsburg monarchy by means of a centralist liberal solution. The imperial council was now given the wider functions of a fully fledged central parliament, in whose Lower House Hungary would be represented by 85 deputies out of a total of 343, but the powers of the provincial diets (*Landtage*) were severely curtailed. By dividing the electorate into four separate classes on the basis of property qualifications, an electoral system was created which worked to the benefit of the German element and urban population.

The February Patent met with outright rejection in Hungary. The idea that a solution to the nationalities problem and a much more generous interpretation of the 1853 laws governing the commutation of the peasants' feudal obligations, which were necessary preconditions for restoring constitutional independence, would become an even greater source of conflict in future, grew not only among émigrés but in Hungary itself. The desire for reconciliation was also present among the leaders of Hungary's nationalities, although their demand to concede cultural and administrative autonomy to their virtually self-contained areas of settlement found little support among the Magyar population which continued to insist on the territorial integrity and political unity of the lands of the crown of St Stephen and on the idea of a single Hungarian political nation. An alliance of all Hungary's nationalities and a united platform in the struggle for the *restitutio in integrum*, i.e. to restore the '48 platform' was, therefore, out of the question because of the fundamental differences that existed. When the diet reconvened on 2 April 1861, two main groups of equal strength emerged. The liberal aristocrats around Deák took the view that, in keeping with the constitution, Hungary's national demands had to be addressed to the Emperor Francis Joseph, who, although not yet crowned, was their *de facto* sovereign. The so-called 'resolution party', on the other hand, led by Count László Teleki, who, having been pardoned, had already returned from exile, was not prepared to accept a situation of constitutional illegality and wanted to make its protest known through a diet decree. The conflicts of conscience which resulted from the conditions attached to his pardon eventually drove Teleki to commit suicide on 8 May 1861. Thereafter, Deák managed to obtain a narrow majority of 155 to 152 in favour of his draft petition to the Emperor. While accepting the Pragmatic Sanction as the basis of Hungary's relations with the monarchy, it also invoked Hungary's former independence in demanding recognition of the laws passed in 1848. Owing to its lack of protocol and inadequate regard for the rights of Hungary's nationalities, the Emperor Francis Joseph I twice rejected the petition and dissolved the diet on 22 August 1861. The opportunity of reaching a negotiated settlement was therefore squandered for the time being. An interim measure, the so-called '*provisorium*' abolished the self-government of the county administrations and municipal councils and ushered in a return to a new brand of absolutism.

Over the next four years the majority of the Magyar agrarian élite pursued a policy of passive resistance. The political stabilisation in Italy, the brutal suppression of the January Uprising in Poland in 1863–64, which contained the threat of expansion by Tsarist Russia, the dashing of hopes for German unification under Austria's leadership – which appeared to open the way for solving Hungary's relationship to the Empire on the basis of a personal union – and the consequences of the disastrous drought of 1863 stifled every initiative at first. Only the exiled Kossuth worked out a draft in 1862 for a Danubian Confederation of the two states, whereby Hungary, detached from the Habsburg monarchy, would form a federation in conjunction with Croatia, Serbia, Rumania and Transylvania. While respecting each state's internal autonomy based on democratic principles, this scheme envisaged that only foreign, defence and economic policies should be conducted on a common federal basis. This proposal, for which the sine qua non was an arrangement with the newly politically conscious nationalities, met with little response in Hungary itself. When, in 1864, events in the German-Danish War, fought over the Duchies of Schleswig–Holstein, highlighted Prussia's predominance in the German Confederation and Schmerling's government seemed unable to induce Hungary to accept the imperial constitution, Francis Joseph thought it was time for a change in Vienna's policy towards Hungary. After establishing informal contacts with the moderate Deák in late 1864 the government made significant concessions early in 1865 and agreed to allow the Hungarian diet to reconvene after its four-year-long suspension. Deák's celebrated 'Easter article' which appeared in the Pest daily newspaper, *Pesti Napló*, on 16 April 1865, declared Hungary's willingness to negotiate. The new Vienna government under Count Richard Belcredi took this as the occasion to annul the February Patent of 1861 and enable Hungary's partial return to constitutional rule. Apart from a small group of radicals around László Böszörményi, the representatives of the 'decree party' (*Határozati Párt*) now led by Kálmán Tisza, agreed with Deák's supporters in the diet that a compromise settlement had to be sought with a view to regulating 'common affairs'. A diet committee on which Count Gyula Andrássy, scion of a long-established and and wealthy landowning family, was soon to play a decisive part, was appointed in the spring of 1866 to work out a basis for negotiations with the central government.

Following the Austro-Prussian War of 1866, which ended in Austria's crushing defeat at Sadowa on 13 July, and the dissolution of the German Confederation, the Habsburg monarchy was reduced to its own hereditary territories. In order to preserve dynastic interests, maintain Austria's great-power status and create the preconditions for exacting revenge on Prussia, the Emperor Francis Joseph and his advisers could not avoid the political necessity of a compromise with Hungary. For this they were prepared to forego a unitary, centralised Empire. Friedrich Ferdinand von Beust, the former prime minister of Saxony, who had been appointed foreign minister and, later, prime minister in the Austrian government after 7 February 1867, worked single-mindedly for a compromise on the proposed principles on which the Habsburg Empire was to be fundamentally reorganised and – after difficult negotiations, in which the Hungarians showed their willingness to compromise – on the unresolved individual issues in the two sides' new constitutional and economic relations. On 17 February 1867, the Emperor Francis Joseph appointed a separate government responsible for Hungary, headed by Count Gyula Andrássy. This led in turn to the Hungarian diet's acceptance of the 'Compromise' on 29 May. Following his coronation on 8 June 1867, the Emperor ratified the Compromise Law four days later on 12 June. Finally, the Vienna parliament passed the 'December Laws' of 21 December 1867, which made arrangements for common affairs which took account of the changes in Hungary's relationship to the Monarchy.

THE CONTENT AND SIGNIFICANCE OF THE COMPROMISE

After 1867 the unitary 'Austrian Empire' became the Dual Monarchy of 'Austria-Hungary'. This union of the Austrian half of the Empire, the 'kingdoms and territories' of which were 'represented in the Vienna parliament' (*Reichsrat*), with 'the lands of the holy Hungarian crown' – henceforth referred to as 'Cisleithania' and 'Transleithania' respectively – was based on the Pragmatic Sanction promulgated by the Emperor Charles VI (King Charles III of Hungary) in 1722–23. Apart from the monarch's position as 'Emperor of Austria and Apostolic King of Hungary', the only areas of common responsibility within the Dual Monarchy were foreign affairs, defence policy and a common finance ministry which was responsible for providing the budgets of the other two common activities. Apart from these three 'imperial and royal' (*k.u.k.*) ministries, both halves of the Empire had their own bicameral parliaments and separate domestic government, each with a prime minister at the head of a cabinet of ministers with individual portfolios. They also had their own territorial armies and autonomous financial administration. The 'common ministry' 'could not conduct the activities of government of either half of the Empire, nor exert influence on them', except in the case of 'common affairs' (Law XII of 1867).

As well as being responsible to the monarch, the common ministry was also accountable to elected representatives from both the Austrian and Hungarian parliaments. Each parliament delegated 60 members, elected on the basis of complete parity, comprising in each case 40 from the Lower House and 20 from the Upper House who were to review the common ministry's constitutional handling of fully fledged 'common affairs'. In addition, they were also responsible for 'commonly agreed affairs' or 'affairs of common concern' – mainly in the field of economic policy, trade and currency, taxes and customs duties. These delegations deliberated separately and sat in joint session only to vote on matters where there was general disagreement. One of their tasks was to decide on the ratio or quota in which Austria and Hungary were to share the expense of common affairs. For the first ten years this was set at 70 : 30 respectively. This arrangement, which was intended to be a flexible instrument which could be adjusted to take account of future economic development, introduced an element of political insecurity into domestic affairs. The Hungarians were to make use of it later to loosen the ties within the Dual Monarchy further. It was also the cause of the scorn heaped upon the Compromise, which was seen in terms of a 'monarchy with the right to give notice to quit'. The Customs and Trade Agreement of 1867, which established a common external customs barrier remained in force for only a decade. It had to be renewed every ten years, but usually only after difficult negotiations which Hungary used as an opportunity to put forward fresh demands. The Hungarians threatened to terminate the community of Austro-Hungarian trade, customs, economy and currency if these were rejected.

Broadly speaking, however, the Compromise was a contract which could not be terminated unilaterally without jeopardising the independent existence of both halves of the Empire. As Emperor and King, the monarch reigned supreme in this undeniably complicated and cumbersome political structure. It was he who determined foreign policy. As 'Supreme War Lord', he enjoyed unlimited control of the army in which German was the language of command. He alone had the right to approve in advance draft laws brought before the legislature and he also had the final say in all controversial matters on which the governments of Austria and Hungary failed to agree. Francis Joseph had taken an active part in the initial deliberations which led to the Compromise and did not conceal his disappointment that he could neither use the common ministry to exert his political will, nor implement his plans for a just solution to the nationalities problem whose explosive potential he clearly recognised. Nevertheless, he stuck to the basic idea of establishing a German–Magyar condominium, even though it soon became obvious, however, that a policy of German centralisation was impracticable in the Austrian half of the Empire because of its complex ethnic structure and the fact that the German minority was numerically relatively weak. In contrast, it was relatively easier to maintain the fiction of a Magyar nation state on the western European model in the 'territories of the Holy Crown of Hungary', since its greater internal political cohesion and sense of purpose, together with its livelier Magyar nationalism and intolerant nationalities policy, meant that many were prepared to sacrifice even the Empire's unity for the sake of Hungarian desires for total self-government.

The Great Powers, especially Bismarck's Prussia – though it was also true of Britain and France – welcomed the new-found solution as a guarantee for the Dual Monarchy's function of keeping order in east central Europe. The Compromise, which had been so strongly influenced by the 'national sage' (*a haza bölcse*), Ferenc Deák, and first so named by him, soon aroused criticism despite the rejoicing which took place at the restoration of Hungary's constitutional rights and the final defeat of neo-absolutism, centralism and the 'forfeiture theory'. It also gave rise to the call for a purely personal union, indeed, even unlimited sovereignty as the main priority and ultimate goal of Hungarian nationalism. From exile Kossuth spoke out to warn of the dangers posed by the agreement, as long as no internal solution was found to the problem of the nationalities. The danger would be that Hungary would become 'the target for the competing ambitions of hostile neighbours in the European conflicts about to surface'. While the German advocates of centralism in the Austrian half of the Empire mourned the loss of their power basis, the Czechs and the Poles of Galicia initially welcomed the Compromise in the hope that the concessions to the Magyars could not be withheld from them in the long term. Only after attempts to transform the multi-national Empire into a federation of free and equal nations had failed, was the Compromise criticised on the grounds that the other nationalities – above all the Slavs – had been simply handed over to the rule of the Hungarian nobility and subjected to its policy of forced magyarisation.

After the break-up of the Dual Monarchy in November 1918, the

Compromise of 1867 was generally condemned on the grounds that it had made the collapse of the Empire inevitable and finally ruled out any exemplary restructuring of the Austrian kingdom into a federation based, not on historical provinces but national groups and their autonomous districts. At the same time, however, the idea of an independent Magyar nation state in the central Danube basin had to remain a utopian dream. Hungary's cooperation in the Habsburgs' imperial and great-power policies was held partly to blame for the disastrous mistakes which led to the First World War. It was not until the discussion sparked off by the centenary of the Compromise that there was room for a more positive judgement and general agreement with the Hungarian historian Gyula Miskolczy's statement that 'The Compromise of 1867 was not the best solution for the Habsburg dynasty and monarchy, but the only possible one by which it could preserve its great-power status'.

Hungary under the Dual Monarchy, 1867–1918

THE POLITICAL, SOCIAL AND INTELLECTUAL BACKGROUND

The development of the political parties

Following the long period of crisis, which had its origins in the pre-1848 period, the Compromise of 1867 marked the beginning of almost half a century of peaceful development for the Dual Monarchy upon which many were later to look back in a romantic and nostalgic light as 'the age of Francis Joseph'. Although the new political system required a period of consolidation, Hungary suddenly experienced an economic upturn and a sustained period of cultural progress. Though fundamentally a backward east-central European agrarian country, by virtue of its belonging to the Habsburg monarchy, Hungary enjoyed particularly favourable preconditions for modernisation in all areas. This development affected the country's economic structure much more than its social and political order which the landowning aristocracy and gentry continued to dominate. Although Hungary's negotiated autonomy of 1867 was not, of course, without its limitations, the Compromise restricted Hungary's internal administration only indirectly, to the extent that any state's domestic policy is influenced by the international situation at any given moment and the diplomatic and military measures which inevitably result from this. The principle of legal and constitutional sovereignty, which had figured prominently in Law XII of 1867, also included the autonomy of the Hungarian government in internal affairs, something Andrássy's new government was soon to

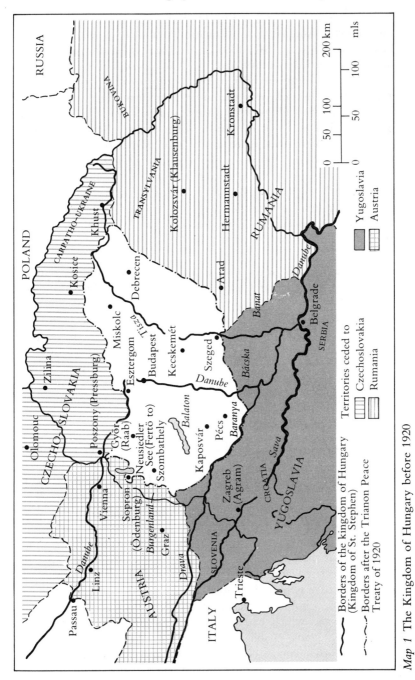

Map 1 The Kingdom of Hungary before 1920

make extensive use of. After Deák refused a post in the new government Andrássy, a former revolutionary, who had been hanged in effigy in 1848, formed a cabinet consisting of members of the propertied nobility and the haute bourgeoisie. The liberal minister for education and religion, Baron Jozsef Eötvös (d. 1871), a progressive writer, was the most prominent figure in the new cabinet. The difficult post of finance minister was filled by Count Menyhért Lónyay, that of minister of justice by Boldizsár Horvát. The new government relied on a bare two-thirds parliamentary majority of around 250 votes out of a total of 409 deputies. These were liberals who were held together on the strength of Deák's personal prestige (and thus often referred to as the Deák Party – *Deákpárt*), ranging from Old Conservatives to former advocates of a liberal centralism. Their newspapers, like the *Pesti Napló*, the *Budapesti Közlöny* and especially the *Pester Lloyd*, were held in high esteem.

These supporters of the 1867 Compromise were initially opposed by Kálmán Tisza's Left Centre Party (*Balközép*), which numbered about 100 deputies. The landowning nobility of the middle-sized and smaller estates and the aristocratic intelligentsia were its chief supporters. Its deputies, most of whom were similarly drawn from the middle ranks of the nobility, approved of the Compromise as such, but objected to its form and what they believed were its over-generous concessions on the question of common affairs. Politically, they aimed at obtaining a 'more favourable' compromise and regaining their former position of having the decisive say in government over Hungary's wealthiest landowning families. They accused the latter of betraying the 1848 Revolution's most important achievements for the sake of holding on to their own position of political and economic predominance. On 2 April 1868, the Left Centre published its new party programme, 'The Bihar Points' (*Bihari pontok*), which not only supported political independence and the abolition of the common delegations, but opposed the popular movement beginning to emerge in the Lower Danube region. The demand that there should be no change in the existing social order and the declared aim of pursuing a constitutional reform of the Compromise was bound to appeal equally to the lesser gentry and middle classes, both of which were hostile to the government. These political goals, which had popular appeal and were pursued with nationalist slogans, enabled the Left Centre to win several seats in the 1869 parliamentary elections from a government party, weakened by internal factions and policy disagreements. In all, a total of

110 Left Centre deputies were returned to the new parliament which met on 20 April 1869.

Disgusted by opportunism, attempts at personal enrichment, the strong drift to conservatism and internal party squabbles, Deák retired from politics. After Eötvös's death, and since Andrássy was no longer a possible candidate for prime minister after his appointment as common minister of foreign affairs on 14 November 1871, the office of Hungarian premier fell to the common finance minister, Count Menyhért Lónyay. His acute business acumen and close contacts with the conservative aristocracy meant that he failed to command much respect. He was able to remain in power only by resorting to brutal measures against the nationalities and arbitrary actions in internal politics. Opposition to him grew rapidly, especially when, on the approach of the 1872 elections, he proposed to narrow the franchise based on the curia system, which, in any case, benefited only 7.1 per cent of the population and advocated extending the life of parliament to five years. The elections, which were as usual rigged and characterised by administrative corruption, resulted in the government winning 245 seats. However, the premier, accused of corruption, was no longer able to hold on to office and was forced to resign on 30 November 1873.

The subsequent succession of short-lived transitional governments failed to prevent the collapse of the government party or put the state finances back in order after the disastrous effects of the 1873 economic crisis. The threat of national bankruptcy was avoided only by the government's acceptance of a loan of 150 million guilders on extremely unfavourable terms from a foreign consortium of bankers headed by the Rothschilds. The government and its supporters, already weakened by the thankless task of having to defend the increasingly unpopular Compromise against exaggerated Magyar nationalist feelings, continued to lose respect as many firms went into liquidation and the prospect of paying off the impending financial deficit and of effecting a revival of the economy was slight. To avoid complete disintegration and at the same time hold on to its share of power, the government party entered into negotiations with the Left Centre with a view to merging the two parties. After its poor showing in the 1872 elections, the latter was more willing to compromise and had no wish to let slip the opportunity of coming to power by legal means. Kálmán Tisza, who remained uncompromising on questions of social policy and the treatment of Hungary's nationalities, particularly rejected the idea of organising a broadly-based mass opposition movement in order to help bring his party to power on the grounds that this more radical course involved too many risks. Following the enactment of a new electoral law based on existing census returns (Law XXXIII of 1874) on the 1 March 1875, Tisza thought the moment had come to drop the 'Bihar Points' and merge the majority of his Left Centre with the fragmented and unstable government party. Relying on this new Liberal Party (*Szabadelvii Párt*), supported by the landed nobility and the still relatively insignificant middle class, he was appointed Hungarian prime minister on 20 October 1875 – an office which he held until the 13 March 1890.

This merger led to a significant strengthening of the pro-1867 Compromise element in Hungary and was to guarantee the Liberal Party a monopoly of power for the next thirty years. The other rival parties found their scope for effective action seriously curtailed. The social classes which formed the main pillars of the state and which rejected any moves towards .greater democracy were ready to give their full support to this single party of government, so long as it opposed radical social reform of any kind and supported, at least in its rhetoric, an improvement in Hungary's constitutional position within the framework of the Dual Monarchy. The introduction of a parliamentary system along the lines of the western European model, involving a regular change of party political direction in the exercise of governmental responsibility, was thus effectively ruled out.

The weakness of the opposition contributed to this development. At the outset those who were completely dissatisfied with the Compromise were represented by only twenty deputies, including those of the extreme Left, and were, moreover, divided into several factions. They included Kossuth's radical supporters, who, as loyal defenders of the achievements of the 1848 Revolution devoted their energies to restoring the 'undiminished constitution' and establishing a greater measure of democracy in public affairs through the National Army Associations, founded in 1861. As a result of a violation of the press censorship law of 1868, their spokesman, László Böszörményi, was imprisoned by the government and died soon after. The popular movement led by the lawyer, János Asztalos, which demanded a fairer distribution of land and greater rights of political participation for the lower classes, was brutally crushed in March 1868 and Asztalos arrested. Despite its many repressive measures, the government's bureaucratic and legal attempts failed to prevent the rise of this '1848 party', which József Madarász formed into a parliamentary opposition on 2 April

1868 (*Közjogi Ellenzék*). It still managed to win 40 seats at the 1869 elections and added a further 36 seats in the 1872 elections. Although prepared to acknowledge in principle a personal union under a common monarch, the '48ers advocated complete Hungarian independence based on democratic principles, together with full civil rights and a progressive franchise. They did not, however, take up the peasants' demands for a radical land reform, but instead supported only the realisation of the main points contained in the Liberals' agrarian programme of 1848. In the spirit of Kossuth, they were prepared to make concessions to the nationalities. A further reorganisation and, shortly thereafter, a change of name to the Independence Party (*Függetlenségi Párt*) can be attributed to the influence of Kossuth, who was seen as the party's spiritual mentor. The party programme, which was confidently addressed to the 'Citizens of Hungary!', held firmly to a position basically opposed to the Compromise. However, party defections and an increase in the Liberal Party's membership, saw the political importance of the Independence Party decline towards the end of the 1870s. Only after joining several breakaway groups in 1884 could the opposition, now renamed the Independence and '48 Party (*Függetlenségi és 48-as Párt*), count on the support of nationalist landowners dissatisfied with government policy, some members of the intelligentsia and urban population and the wealthier peasants. Closely following the programme of 1848, the party demanded Hungarian independence, a loose personal union with the Austrian half of the Empire and middle-class liberal reforms. But endemic internal disagreements and personal intrigues prevented this programme's political realisation and damaged the party's public image. Nevertheless, the Independence Party deputies could feel that their aims were endorsed by the Linz programme of the German National movement in Austria led by Georg Ritter von Schönerer which on 1 September 1882 demanded a purely personal union with Hungary and called on the latter to annex Bosnia-Herzegovina and Dalmatia.

The right-wing conservative opposition, holding tenaciously to the legacy of feudalism and supported by the magnates and court aristocracy, had a hard time with premier Tisza's policies, even though these were generally hostile to progress. Their United Opposition Party (*Egyesült Ellenzék*), founded on 12 April 1878, and renamed the Moderate Opposition three years later, had no programme of clearly defined aims under Count Albert Apponyi. It favoured strengthening the idea of a Hungarian state and constitutional power, defended the Compromise of 1867 and with its anti-liberal slogans advocated conservative reforms. It failed to encounter any significant response in Hungary, for its parliamentary strength fell from 105 deputies originally toonly 46 in 1887.

Hungary's political parties were not at first organised on the basis of ideological positions or social class loyalties. Their opposition to each other did not result from differing social programmes, but differing constitutional views and aims. It was only the unresolved social and political issues resulting from the country's transition to a bourgeois industrial society – and growing potentially more explosive towards the end of the nineteenth century – that introduced change to the traditional structure of Hungarian political life and gave rise to ideologically-based parties pursuing social and democratic reforms. But the new political tendencies expressed in political Catholicism, Socialist workers' parties, agrarian Socialist asociations and also much later by the organised political representation of the urban intelligentsia, failed to change political issues and behaviour fundamentally, or effect even modest democratic and social reforms.

Although a General Workers' Association was founded on 9 February 1869, there were still no successful attempts at organising the steadily growing working class. The government acted firmly against its organisers and, following a wave of strikes in the spring of 1871, had the ringleaders sentenced on 1 May 1872 in the first political trial to be held against workers. New attempts to create a single Workers' Party for the whole of Austria-Hungary, undertaken with the support of the Austrian labour movement, received fresh impetus with the adoption of a programme in Neudörfl in April 1874. Sickness benefit fund associations and the newspaper *Népszava* (Voice of the People) provided Leo Frankel, an erstwhile minister in the Paris Commune who had subsequently returned to Hungary, with the opportunity of furthering the establishment of a new party. The Non-Voters' Party, founded on 21 and 22 April 1878, later to become the General Workers' Party of Hungary (*Magyarországi Általános Munkáspárt*) on 16–17 May 1880, based its programme on Marxist teachings. Demands for a ten-hour working day, a ban on child labour and a guarantee of equal wages for women were accompanied by support for basic civil rights and the need for state control of the means of production. This resurgence of the labour movement, viewed with mounting mistrust by Tisza's government, suffered a serious setback with the arrest and imprisonment of Frankel in 1881, especially since after serving his sentence he went abroad as a result of constant police surveillance and internal party squabbles. Thus it was not until the founding of the Hungarian

Social Democratic Party (*Magyarországi Szociáldemokrata Párt*) in December 1890 that the labour movement had a permanent organisational structure and effective representation.

Hungary's electoral laws, which were tightened up on several occasions, excluded the industrial workers, peasant farmers, domestic servants and urban lower classes from actively participating in the country's constitutional parliamentary system. Only 6 per cent of the population, i.e. 800,000 people, were entitled to vote. Like the gerrymandering which was necessary to protect the government's interests, the electoral laws had a built-in property qualification which also ensured that the discontented, though enfranchised, peasants, middle classes and nationalities entitled to vote were practically unrepresented in parliament. Following numerous changes in the number and size of constituencies the Lower House eventually had 453 members of whom 40 were delegates from the Croatian diet. Up to the late 1870s, 80 per cent of Hungary's parliamentary deputies were drawn from the landed aristocracy and gentry. In 1910, the figure still stood at 50 per cent. The number of deputies of middle-class origin – civil servants, lawyers and intellectuals – never exceeded a third of the total. Parliamentary deputies of peasant origin were rare. The workers, on the other hand, had no representation at all. The 1885 reform (Law VII of 1885), which abolished hereditary seats in cases where the member's land tax amounted to less than 3,000 guilders per annum, resulted in a fundamental change in the composition of the Upper House, although the greater nobility continued to occupy three-quarters of the seats. In addition, the monarch had the right to appoint as life peers to the Upper House fifty persons of merit nominated by the Hungarian cabinet. These appointees had a seat and voice in the Upper House alongside holders of high ecclesiastical offices, a few elevated representatives of the bureaucracy and the judiciary as well as the wealthiest landowners, who had held on to their great wealth. The government's rigging of elections and commissions in charge of drawing up the electoral roll, together with bribery, the falsification of votes, intimidation of voters and the open ballot were normal practice and ensured the government a majority in the Lower House of the new parliament. The corruption which had also spread through the bureaucracy and judiciary helped the ruling élites not only to defend but to further their position of social and political predominance. Tisza's skilful use of patronage involving positions in government, commission appointments and honours, helped him to create within his party and in the inflated but ineffective government apparatus a body of organised supporters on whose gratitude and loyalty he was able to build.

Magyar nationalism and the failure of the nationalities policy

In 1867, following the renewal of the union with Transylvania and the abolition of the special 'military frontier' areas, the territorial integrity and political unity of the historic 'territories of the holy crown of Hungary' was restored. Some 15.5 million people inhabited a total area of 325,411 square kilometres. Approximately 40 per cent of the total population were Hungarians, 9.8 per cent were Germans, 9.4 per cent Slovaks, 14 per cent Rumanians, 14 per cent South Slavs and 2.3 per cent Ruthenes (Carpatho-Russians and Carpatho-Ukrainians). One of the first tasks facing the new independent Hungarian government was to find a speedy settlement of the future constitutional position of Hungary's nationalities, a problem which demanded an immediate solution. The Emperor Francis Joseph had already stressed the need for a just settlement of this problem during the negotiations which had led to the 1867 Compromise and had received Deák's assurance of his desire to deal with the problem. But after initial contacts were established with the spokesmen of the non-Magyar nationalities and during the so-called 'mini-Compromise' negotiations with the Croats, the Hungarian view that 'in accordance with the fundamental principles of the constitution, all Hungarian citizens [constitute] a nation in the political sense, the one and indivisible Hungarian nation, in which every citizen of the fatherland is a member who enjoys equal rights, regardless of the national group to which he belongs' (Law XLIV of 1868) proved to be an insuperable obstacle to any agreement which would do justice to the needs and expectations of both parties. Right up to the Habsburg monarchy's dissolution the uncompromisingly defended fiction of a Magyar nation state on the western European model led to a denial of the political existence of the non-Magyar nationalities. This short-sighted attitude prevented any transfer of rights of self-government to the nationalities which constituted the majority of the population before 1890.

Negotiations were based on the Nationalities Law which had been passed during the state of emergency in Szeged in 1849. Despite the earlier promises by the Hungarian Liberals during the negotiations in 1868 on the matter of 'equality of the nationalities', only Hungarian citizens 'of a separate mother tongue' were formally recognised and nominally accorded equal civic rights, the unrestricted use of their native language in the lower levels of the administration, the judicial system, and elementary and secondary schools. Only the neighbouring territory of Croatia-Slavonia, designated as 'a neighbouring territory of the Crown of St Stephen', received in a 'mini-Compromise' a measure of autonomy in the bureaucracy, the judicial system, culture and education, which was exercised by a government of provincial governors subject to the control of the Croatian diet. All other areas of activity were regarded as 'common affairs' and subject to control by the government in Budapest, enlarged to include a minister without portfolio for Croatian affairs. Forty of the deputies delegated from the Croatian diet were to ensure the defence of Croatian interests in the Hungarian parliament. These blinkered arrangements destroyed the attempts of Deák, Eöstvös and even Kossuth to institute a more sympathetic nationalities policy in Hungary, the principles of which, so strongly nationalist in spirit, could only be implemented eventually by force on account of the open opposition of the country's non-Magyars.

Despite Deák's warning to avoid an abuse of state power for the sake of Magyar nationalism and Magyar domination of Hungary's non-Magyar population, the ruling élites held neither to the letter nor the spirit of the nationalities agreements. Over the years a nationalism which had been originally liberal in character began to identify itself wholly with the traditional Magyar sense of national mission, according to which the Magyars' historic task in the second half of the nineteenth century was to work as pioneers of the new bourgeois economic, social and cultural progress in eastern Europe and the Balkans and to transmit the achievements of western European civilisation to its peoples. The aristocratic majority within the ruling élite dreamt of a Hungarian Empire which would arise when multi-national Hungary had become a Magyar nation state which would eventually become the main element in the Habsburg monarchy. Based on arguments of historical legitimacy a rampant nationalism developed which aspired to a nation state, recognising only one nation, i.e. the Hungarian 'political nation', within the frontiers of historic Hungary. Hungary's territorial integrity, political unity, the Magyar character of the state and Magyar supremacy, or at least that of the Magyar ruling class, remained a categorical imperative for all political parties and groupings up to 1918. All other aspects of modernisation and democratisation, even the extent to which national self-determination should be achieved, came second. The Hungarian ruling élite thus ignored the national, political individuality of the country's non-Magyar peoples and believed that neither collective rights for the nationalities nor the slightest degree of compromise on the question of administrative territorial independence were compatible with the 'idea of a Hungarian nation state'. They believed that recognition of individual equality for non-Magyar citizens, modest concessions in the use of their native languages and the guarantee of autonomy for the minority churches had already reached the limit of what the Hungarian nation state could reasonably concede.

In the Liberal Party, which emerged after the merger of Deák's party with the Left Centre Party, the tone was set by the county aristocracy who, in calling for the inevitable development of the Hungarian nation state, demanded complete Magyar supremacy in national life and the curtailment of the politically and culturally privileged position of the non-Magyar peoples. The protests of the national minorities against Magyar unwillingness to acknowledge their distinct national identity and the refusal to grant them self-government gave the government the welcome opportunity to intensify its magyarisation policy and expel from political life any non-Magyar citizens unwilling to be assimilated. The Elementary School Law of 1868 – still the product of the liberal spirit of 1848 – introduced compulsory schooling for all children from the age of six to twelve and provided for subjects to be taught in the language of the local population. However, the Education Laws of 1879, 1883 and 1891 made the teaching of Hungarian compulsory in nursery and the elementary and lower secondary school, since the view prevailed that complete linguistic assimilation would also lead to total political integration, i.e. allegiance to the Hungarian nation. The aims behind the legislation were determinedly and successfully implemented by the administration which was dominated by the gentry. The result was that an important linguistic and demographic shift took place on a major scale in Hungary between 1867 and 1918.

The Rumanians, Ruthenes and Slovaks, in particular, suffered from this intolerant policy towards the country's minorities. As early as 1875–76, several Slovak high schools were closed down and the Adult Education Association (*Matica Slovenská*) was banned. All teachers in minority schools had to provide proof of their ability to teach the Hungarian language and other subjects in Hungarian. The influence of Hungarian was energetically promoted in all areas of public life, while the public use of non-Magyar languages rapidly declined. Whereas approximately 10 per cent of all civil servants belonged to the population's non-Magyar groups in 1910, Hungarian was spoken as a first language by 96 per cent of civil servants and 91.2 per cent of all state employees. About a fifth of citizens registered as a 'native Hungarian speaker' may well have been in fact bilingual, having been only recently assimilated and still in the process of being integrated. Whereas, in 1880, only 14 per cent of Hungary's population could speak Magyar and at least one other of the country's languages, by 1910 the figure had risen to as high as 23.4 per cent.

Since the peoples of the Carpathian Basin occupied areas of settlement which considerably overlapped, it was not only the magyarisation measures ordered and encouraged by the state which resulted in a spontaneous process of assimilation, but Hungary's economic growth and the accompanying changes in the social structure wrought by urbanisation and greater mobility. Between 1880 and 1910 some 2 million people were drawn into the Hungarian orbit. Since positions of importance in Hungary's political, economic, cultural and social life were still dominated by the Magyar ruling élites, considerable advantages were to be gained if one acknowledged one's Hungarianness. After 1880, Hungary's 700,000 Jews, who had been granted full and equal civic rights as late as 1849 and 1867, thought of themselves as Hungarians. The same was true of 600,000 Germans, 200,000 Slovaks and 100,000 Croatians, whose common religion and similar cultural and historical traditions facilitated the process of assimilation. However, the social cohesion of the Rumanian and Ruthenian peasant communities, which still lived a very traditional life, formed an effective protection against magyarisation measures. The higher a citizen climbed on the social ladder, the more likely he was to change his nationality. A significant number of the middle class, especially the intelligentsia and the majority of businessmen in trade and industry, were assimilated citizens who played a crucial role in the development of Hungarian bourgeois society and made an essential contribution to the country's economic development, the adoption of western civilisation's achievements and the development of urban life. In literature and the arts, science, politics, the economy and the church the newly assimilated citizens, accepted without reservation by the government and a nationalist-minded society, found great scope for participation and, by their efforts, contributed to the strengthening of a sense of Magyar national pride.

Hungary's Jews, in particular, were especially rapidly assimilated. At the time of the 1787 census during the reign of Joseph II, they had numbered 83,000, i.e. just 1 per cent of the total population.

But, as a result of rapid immigration from Galicia and Moravia their number increased to 253,000 by 1850 (1.9 per cent) and 552,000 by 1869 (3.6 per cent). By the emancipation laws of 1849 and 1867 the Jews had recently been freed from political and economic discrimination. They were no longer excluded from owning property, holding public office or forming guilds. They were also now accorded full civic rights. From humble beginnings as moneylenders, grocers and retailers of livestock and agricultural produce, they used the generously offered opportunities for earning money, which the gentry had ignored, demonstrated their willingness to be integrated and consequently underwent linguistic assimilation from Yiddish to Magyar via German. Zionist ideas were relatively uncommon. The desire to advance socially by joining the emergent middle class, their gratitude for the law's protection and the wide scope for activity available to them turned them into convinced supporters of the idea of a Hungarian nation state. Since most of the impoverished gentry and those of the nobility, who were now forced to earn a living, viewed the civil service as the only respectable form of employment, the Jews, who were concentrated in the rapidly growing cities, did not represent competition for their positions and livelihood. In the absence of a Hungarian middle class, they provided a kind of surrogate middle class of small and large-scale businessmen, lawyers, doctors and intellectuals. The Jews also made their mark on the country's economic development as directors of banks and large enterprises. In 1910, they numbered 932,000, i.e. 4.5 per cent of the population, of whom over 75 per cent spoke Hungarian as their first language. The percentage of Jews in the urban population amounted to as much as 12.4 per cent; in the bigger cities they comprised over 20 per cent of the population. Budapest with 23 per cent had the largest Jewish community.

Whereas a vociferous antisemitism dominated Austrian public opinion at the turn of the century, the Hungarian government tried to suppress any anti-Jewish movement from the beginning. Early in the 1880s, the growth of nationalism was accompanied by the appearance of an antisemitism which spread rapidly among sections of the gentry and the petty bourgeoisie. It found its release in 1883 in the Tiszaeszlár ritual murder trial. The court rejected the entirely unfounded allegation that the Jewish community was responsible for the disappearance of a Christian girl. Outbreaks of anti-Jewish violence, vigorously opposed by the government, occurred in several counties, fuelled by superstition and other sinister motives. A National Antisemitic Party (*Országos Antiszemita Párt*) founded by

Gyözö Istóczy on 6 October 1883, succeeded in winning seventeen seats at the parliamentary elections of 1884. But by 1890 this party had again disappeared from the political scene. Although there continued to be a groundswell of antisemitism, particularly among the peasantry, which, encouraged by the poorer Catholic clergy, made its appearance on several occasions, it found no response in the majority of the population. The spread of a pro-Magyar nationalism among Jews in recognition of the government's attitude and in gratitude for their protection in no way arose from a sense of opportunism – as was the case with other assimilated groups. Instead, it was fostered by a doubtless genuine sense of allegiance to their adopted country which was often enthusiastically expressed.

The greatest opposition to the policy of magyarisation came from the Rumanian inhabitants of Transylvania. Initially led by the Orthodox archbishop, Andreiu Şaguna, they wanted a guarantee that the rights of the Rumanian Church would be protected. They also desired recognition of their equal status with the principality's Magyar and German settlers, especially since the latter were always represented in the Budapest parliament by twelve or thirteen deputies. Disagreement became more acute after 1881 when the Rumanian National Party (*Román Nemzeti Párt*) in Transylvania demanded that the principality be once more restored as an autonomous Crown territory, thus abolishing the union with Hungary. This led Magyar political leaders to accuse the Rumanians of irredentism. Magyar desires for greater centralisation, which subsequently became more noticeable in Transylvania, caused the Rumanians to put forward even more radical demands. Two possible schemes for separation from Hungary were discussed by the Rumanian Cultural League, founded in Bucharest in 1891. The preferred solution of the union of Transylvania with the Rumanian kingdom, did not, however, appear feasible in terms of foreign policy. The alternative proposal was that submitted by the Transylvanian Rumanian deputy, Dr Aurel Popovici. He wished to see Transylvania incorporated into an envisaged 'United Federation of Greater Austria' as a separate federal state. Further federalisation of the Dual Monarchy appeared to offer the only prospect of success against growing Magyar pressure. It also seemed to be the only way to defuse the national conflicts which were swelling up in the Habsburg Empire and thus guarantee the continued existence of Austria-Hungary. But, after the plans of the Austrian government under Hohenwart and Schäffle to reorganise the Dual Monarchy on a trialist basis by granting the Kingdom of Bohemia 'fundamental laws' had failed on account of Hungarian intransigence, Budapest's support for the plans for a federation as a precondition for the realisation of the nationalities' equality of rights could not be expected.

By the internal Hungarian–Croatian Compromise of 1868 the Kingdom of Croatia-Slavonia, which had initially wanted to regulate its position in the monarchy on the basis of a personal union, was accorded far-reaching constitutional autonomy and special status within Hungary. As a result the Hungarian government's magyarisation measures were not implemented here to the same degree as in other areas inhabited by national minorities. It was thanks to the patient labours of Bishop Josip Juraj Strossmayer, for many years leader of the Croats and imprisoned on account of his 'Illyrian' patriotism on religious, political and cultural matters, that, with the founding of the university and a science academy in Zagreb, centres had been established to defend national and spiritual independence. When, in 1883, the growing pressures of the government's magyarisation policy sparked off demonstrations, the new Croatian governor, Count Károly Khuen-Héderváry, successfully brought calm to Croatia in line with the ideas of the Hungarian government. By supporting the Serbian nationalist movement and the Serbian parties he skilfully exploited the rivalries between the different South Slav groups in order to play them off against each other. By these means he succeeded in wrecking the plans of Ante Starčević's Croatian State Party and its successor, Josip Frank's Pure Right Party, to transform the Dual Monarchy into a triple monarchy by creating a Kingdom of Croatia-Slavonia enlarged by the acquisition of Dalmatia and Fiume.

When the conflict between the Habsburg monarchy and the Hungarian right-wing parties escalated in 1903, the Croatian political leaders showed that they were prepared to cooperate more closely with Vienna. But when the Emperor rejected their offers, the Croatian opposition, led by Ante Trumbić and Frano Supilo, completely swung round, largely accepting as its own the demands of the Hungarian Independence Party contained in the Fiume Resolution of 4 October 1905. The Monarchy's Serbs now rushed to support the new policy of the Croatian opposition in the Resolution of Zara. In contrast, against a background of growing conflict between Hungary's nationalities, the Croatian People's and Peasants' Party (*Hrvatska Pučka Selječka Stranka*), founded in 1904 and led by Stepan Radić – without doubt the most important Croatian politician of the period – came out further in favour of a federal system for the Monarchy, without, however, being able to effect any change in the long-entrenched positions or in Hungary's policy towards the Croats, which was conducted with growing intransigence amid an atmosphere poisoned by the Austrian annexation of Bosnia in 1908, the high treason trial in Zagreb (Agram) and the Friedjung trial in Vienna. The anti-Austrian movement, encouraged by Serbia, which aimed at destroying the Dual Monarchy by creating a pan-Slav empire in the Balkans could appeal, however, only to a section of the relatively small intelligentsia, in particular the student youth. The loyalty of the vast majority of Croatia's predominantly agrarian population towards the Empire and its ruling dynasty remained undiminished until the end of the war.

Around 1880, Hungary experienced a wave of emigration. This was not simply motivated by economic conditions, but by the desire to escape the government's repressive measures against the country's minorities. By 1913, over 2 million people had gone overseas. The number of Magyars who emigrated was far fewer than the average for the whole country, especially since many returned home to the old country at a later date. On the other hand, many Slovaks, Ruthenians and South Slavs, who were proportionately overrepresented among emigrants – mainly small peasant farmers and craftsmen – hoped to escape for ever the material distress and limited scope for social mobility in Hungary. Since many of the immigrants who came to settle in Hungary, mainly from Moravia, Bohemia, Galicia and Italy, belonged to the second or third generation to be fully magyarised, these major population movements eventually led to an increase in the number of Magyars and their number relative to the size of the total population.

Despite all its shortcomings, it is still possible to describe the treatment of national minorities in Hungary before the First World War as relatively liberal and tolerable compared with contemporary conditions in eastern and south-east Europe. Despite the pecking order imposed by Magyar national supremacy and the repression of the national minorities, Hungary offered reasonably good opportunities for development and a degree of security before the law to all the ethnic communities settled on its soil – provided they were prepared to respect the principle of the unity and indivisibility of the 'Hungarian political nation'. The quarrel between the nationalities grew more acute around the turn of the century – above all the conflict between the ruling Magyar nation and Hungary's non-Magyar population – to the extent that the Habsburg Empire collapsed, not least because of its failure to solve the problem of the nationalities.

Social stratification and economic development

Until the middle of the nineteenth century Hungary's social order was, like Poland's, dominated politically, socially and economically by a large nobility and distinguished by the presence of an exceptionally large rural proletariat within the peasant class. The undeveloped urban bourgeoisie was relatively unimportant in terms of its size and role in society. Although the 1848 Revolution had witnessed a change from a feudal society based on estates to a constitutional monarchy, and had brought about the abolition of traditional obligations and the establishment of full civic equality, the dissolution of the feudal social structure proved to be a long and slow process. The legislature and the executive remained in the hands of the aristocracy and landowning gentry which saw itself as the only social class capable of governing.

According to careful estimates, 6 per cent of the population were members of the nobility; among the Magyars the figure was 12–13 per cent. Some 200 aristocratic and wealthy landowning families, together with approximately 3,000 wealthy families of the middle-ranking landowners, who as 'thousand *hold* men' owned estates of over 575 hectares (the so-called *bene possessionati*), dominated public life by virtue of their education and income. Their mentality and system of values, their liberal, nationalist politics and their aim to bring about what they saw as necessary democratic reforms in Hungary, in a manner that would preserve their own social and political position of predominance, dominated attitudes, thinking and Hungary's way of life well into the twentieth century. The section of the landowning élite, which was able to retain and modernise its property of 100 to 500 hectares, saw itself as the true representative of the Hungarian nation and custodian of the Hungarian national identity. Comprising around 5,000 families, this gentry class had a firm social basis and exerted a crucial influence in the government, parliament and the county councils. Its chief preoccupation was managing its estates which comprised in all more than a third of the country's cultivable land. Those of their number who were more skilled in business invested their capital profitably in banks and industry.

Most members of the old landed nobility, however, failed to adapt to the new economic conditions which followed peasant emancipation. They ran up debts, became impoverished and lost their estates entirely or in part. The economic decline of the former middle-ranking and petty nobility, referred to as the 'gentry' from the early 1870s onwards, forced many of its 500,000 or so members to earn a living in the country's expanding bureaucracy, from the legal system, municipal councils and county administrations to government posts, the army officer corps, gendarmerie and police force. Here they were able to preserve their aristocratic lifestyle and position of social predominance. The members of the gentry, many of whom were related by marriage, controlled about half the posts available in the government ministries and three-quarters of those in the county administrations. In order to maintain their positions they supported the system of the Dual Monarchy and the policies of the government party. In the absence of a broad, economically independent and self-confident middle class, the gentry formed the nucleus of an emergent urban bourgeoisie comprising assimilated groups and Magyar social climbers of petty-bourgeois or peasant origin.

After 1848 the peasants with noble status merged with the free peasantry and emancipated serfs to form a single social class of peasants.

In the early modern period the population of Hungary's towns was mainly made up of non-Magyar immigrants, of whom the Germans formed the largest single community. In the course of the nineteenth century they were increasingly joined by the Czechs and the Jews, who were being rapidly assimilated. This petty bourgeoisie, which earned its living from the craft industries and small trades took decided advantage of the opportunities for social advancement opened up by economic progress after 1850 and looked to the gentry as their social ideal. But only in exceptional cases did they succeed in acquiring great wealth. Hungary's Jews soon distinguished themselves as entrepreneurs by their enterprise and willingness to take risks. They were involved not only in the marketing and export of agrarian produce, but invested their capital in industry, railway construction and the banking system. By the turn of the century a financial oligarchy had developed which consisted of about fifty families. These families controlled all the key positions in a rapidly developing economy, but did not challenge the social predominance of the aristocracy. Indeed, they tried to ape their lifestyle in external appearances which went as far as the enoblement of 346 Jewish families of the haute bourgeoisie. Twenty-eight were made barons and many acquired large estates, with the result that before the First World War Jews owned a fifth of Hungary's major estates. But although some Jews were represented in the Upper House, the financial bourgeoisie from which they emerged was content to share power only indirectly. The strong Jewish element in the middle class and university-educated intellectual élite contributed to the fact that the increasingly confident city dwellers began to turn away from modelling themselves on the gentry in the twentieth century and developed their own bourgeois way of life, value system and codes of behaviour. The town dwellers' political views tended to be liberal–nationalist. The greatest possible measure of Hungarian independence within the framework of a monarchy transformed into a purely personal union, economic freedom, the guarantee of universal, equal suffrage and the secret ballot headed their list of demands.

The lower classes in the towns, poor craftsmen, downwardly mobile petty nobility and rapidly growing industrial proletariat were nationalistic in outlook and therefore anti-Austrian in their attitudes. They supported the movement for Hungarian independence. For a long time the state bureaucracy's repressive and coercive measures succeeded in preventing the spread of radical ideas which sprang from the social misery and denial of civic rights, but it did not feel obliged to take effective measures to remedy the miserable conditions. The social class of industrial workers living in the urban areas which attracted migrants rose from 182,000 in 1857 to 955,000 in 1910, but the specific character of Hungary's industrialisation meant that the nucleus of this class was provided by skilled workers from abroad. The ruthlessly exploited unskilled workers and day-labourers were often only seasonal workers, of whom more than half worked in large factories and a third in Budapest. Women and children supplied two-fifths of the workforce. Workers from the districts inhabited by the national minorities, mainly Slovaks and Germans, were also quickly caught up in the process of magyarisation, so that the proportion of Hungarian employees in industry rose to 60 per cent (in Budapest to 80 per cent) within the space of a few years. Since real wages failed to grow adequately, the workers in the twentieth century were increasingly prepared to form trade unions and organise themselves politically. This development and their readiness to back their demands by the use of strikes could not be halted despite minor concessions in labour law, the introduction of a social insurance system and sickness benefits and a shortening of the working day by one to two hours.

Urbanisation on a major scale began in Hungary in the second half of the nineteenth century. Growth benefited the capital, Budapest, which came into being in 1873 as a result of the original German settlement of Buda merging with Pest and the old mediaeval town of Óbuda. Of its 880,000 inhabitants in 1910, 86 per cent spoke Hungarian as their first language. The city's elevated position as Hungary's economic and cultural capital was underlined by the fact that Greater Budapest with its ribbon development of suburbs contained only 5.1 per cent of the country's total population but 28 per cent of its workforce and two-thirds of its major industry. Hungary's provincial centres suffered as a result of the capital's dynamic growth. Only Szeged had a population exceeding 100,000. A third of Hungary's towns, including half of its major cities with over 50,000 inhabitants remained typical market towns with a pronounced village character, especially in the outlying areas. The majority of the country's inhabitants continued to earn their living from agriculture. By 1910, however, a good third of the population already lived in 145 urban settlements of over 10,000 inhabitants. As a result of the rapid process of assimilation 78.6 per cent of them spoke Hungarian as their first language.

Over 50 per cent of the population, however, lived in small villages, a further 15 per cent in isolated farmsteads and in farms on the open Puszta grasslands belonging to the large estates. As a result of rapid economic growth, the number of persons employed in agriculture showed a sharp and steady decline from 75 to 60 per cent between 1869 and 1910. At the same time, however, the proportion of the workforce employed in mining, crafts and industry rose from 10 to 18.3 per cent, that of white-collar workers in commerce and transport from 4 to 6 per cent and in the services sector from 13 per cent to 15.6 per cent. Hungary contributed almost half the Dual Monarchy's total agricultural production, i.e. 47.8 per cent. Although the redistribution of common land and forest after 1849 was often accompanied by peasant unrest, the majority of small tenants acquired a farming strip of a few furrows (1 *hold* = 0.5754 hectares). By 1910 the size of the rural proletariat, the most populous class of poor peasants with diminutive holdings, grew to almost 4 million as a result of the division and parcelling out of land. During the decades of major railway construction, which witnessed impressive improvements in flood and drainage control in the Tisza and Danube valleys – increasing the available land for cultivation from 8.7 to 12.8 million hectares – and rising grain prices, they were able to earn a modest living as seasonal workers and day-labourers. But after 1890 they became gradually impoverished and many were forced to emigrate. After 1910, the introduction of imported threshing and reaping machinery, together with a more efficient iron plough, meant that the lowest category of peasantry who owned less than 5 hectares and depended on secondary earnings, could at best find secure employment for only 88 days of the year. The result was that this group, which constituted two-thirds of the peasantry and owned about a quarter of the land and two-fifths of the country's livestock, also experienced increasing hardship. Only the quarter of a million or so middle-sized farms of up to ·10 hectares were able to survive to some extent through stubborn and persevering efforts to cultivate the land, switching from extensive animal husbandry to intensive wheat or maize growing or specialised areas of production like market gardening, viticulture, poultry-keeping and tobacco growing. Between 1851 and 1895 the number of farms of less than 50 hectares, which were managed not only by major producers but by the impoverished and declining middle-ranking aristocracy, trebled from 65,800 to 188,300. Despite the immense changes in farming methods and rural society, the traditional structure of village life continued into the twentieth century. Traditional ways of earning a living by farming, together with a traditional mentality and way of life continued in the prescribed manner of feudal society.

Although 99 per cent of Hungary's landowners were peasants, they owned only 56 per cent of cultivable land, barely half of the available farming machinery and 80 per cent of the country's live-stock. The state owned between 6 and 7 per cent of the land, but 33 to 35 per cent of cultivable land remained in private or church ownership, estates sometimes equalling whole English counties in their extent. Great landed estates were often organised as indisposable entailed estates which always passed to a male member of the landowning family according to fixed rules of inheritance. This had enabled the Esterházys, the Counts of Schönborn, the Prince of Coburg-Gotha and Austrian archdukes to avoid the break-up of their estates. Among the episcopacy, the Bishop of Nagyvárad, and Archbishops of Esztergom and Kalocsa controlled the largest estates on which thousands of day-labourers and servants lived. They worked as agricultural wage-labourers in a hierarchically organised system of managed estates, often completely cut off from the outside world. This inequitable distribution of landed property remained essentially unchanged before 1918, although some changes were effected by 1945.

After the upward economic trend in agriculture in the 1860s, when Hungarian grain and cereal sales to western Europe and Austria produced substantial profits, the economic crisis of 1873 caused an initial price fall. Competition from cheap imports of foreign grain and protectionist policies meant that this lasted until the 1880s and reduced profits by two-thirds. High production costs caused by the backwardness of farming methods, natural disasters and the almost wholesale destruction of viticulture caused by the spread of phylloxera ruined many a landowner. The number of holdings which owners were forced to sell and parcel out showed a worrying increase as did the collapse of farms, which soon numbered 10,000 in all. With the help of state subsidies and protective tariffs, support was given to the introduction of modern farming methods which benefited the large estate owners in particular through the use of machinery and increased productivity. The introduction of intensive crop rotation, improved seedlings and the increased use of artificial fertiliser resulted in the doubling of the yield per hectare, although this still lay well below that of western Europe. The gradual return to cereal production, the switch to hoed crops and plants for industrial uses and the spread of dairy farming and livestock fattening led to an increase in the profits of the larger farms while the smallholders and smallest peasants could barely survive and were often reduced to the status of landless labourers. The new economic conditions in agriculture in the twentieth century, especially after the imposition of high agricultural tariffs in 1906 also benefited middle-ranking and large-scale farmers, but at the same time consolidated the dominant position of the vast estates and ruled out any redistribution of land which might do justice to the peasants' land hunger and the claims of the destitute rural population.

The period between 1867 and 1914 was particularly characterised, however, by the rapid growth of industry, commerce and transport in relation to agriculture, resulting in a profound transformation of Hungary's socio-economic structure. Thanks to an annual average growth rate of 2.8 per cent, Hungary was gradually able to close the gap with Austria and by 1914 already accounted for 28.2 per cent of the Habsburg Empire's total industrial output. But Hungary also had to accept an increase in its share of the Dual Monarchy's common expenditure by 6.4 per cent to 36.4 per cent, while Austria's contribution was reduced from the original figure of 70 per cent to 63.6 per cent. Although agriculture still accounted for two-thirds of Hungary's national income in 1913, the share contributed by industry and trade had more than doubled since 1870. This was due not least to the foreign capital which had flowed into Hungary for investment in railway construction, mining, large-scale estates and the creation of banks, and which later, together with the increasing availability of Hungarian capital, benefited large-scale industry. About half the foreign capital of 800,000 crowns invested in the Hungarian economy was Austrian. Access to the Dual Monarchy's wider domestic market greatly benefited Hungary's economic development because only this common market could absorb the increased production, given the Hungarian market's low level of demand. In addition, about 80 per cent of Hungary's trade was transacted with the Austrian half of the Empire.

Railway construction was an important factor in the modernisation of the Hungarian economy. The railway network grew from 2,200 kilometres in 1867 to 22,000 kilometres in 1913. Freight and passenger traffic developed extremely rapidly with the growth of Budapest as a major railway junction. The building of railways also benefited the domestic iron industry and manufacture of machinery, and guaranteed employment for countless railway navvies. The food industry, in particular the flour industry, attained a leading position in Europe. In the timber, paper and leather industries the trend towards large-scale production also forged ahead. Coal and iron-ore production showed a dramatic growth-spurt and encouraged the expansion of the machine industry, which continued to do well with its traditional products, the manufacture of agricultural and milling machinery. Thanks to considerable state subvention the textile industry also experienced a marked boom, although, faced with superior Austrian competition, it could only cover a third of the needs of the domestic market.

The economic trend towards larger-scale enterprises continued unchecked. Industrial concentration was encouraged by foreign capital which in 1880 owned two-thirds of Hungarian industry, in 1900 a half and in 1913 about 35 per cent. The biggest firms, which accounted for only 0.5 per cent of all enterprises, employed 44 per cent of the workforce and produced two-thirds of the country's total manufacturing output. Business consortia and cartels, formed in various branches of industry, strengthened the influence of the new banks and industrial monopolies. The craft manufacture of consumer goods, in contrast, showed a marked decline. Craftsmen and small tradesmen found themselves living through a period of crisis. Hungary failed to attract the manufacture of more modern and future-orientated products, because Austria-Cisleithania's more advanced industry, shielded by high tariffs and well attuned to its own level of demand and price structure within the monarchy as a whole, managed to forestall Hungary's innovations and thus prevented any major structural changes within Hungary's established industrial structure. This conduct resulted in a less balanced and less favourable industrial development in Hungary, but did not justify the supposition of Magyar historians that Hungary had been completely exploited because of its imbalance of trade with Austria. During the initial phase of investment-intensive modernisation, Hungary was able to rely on the Monarchy's large market and the import of Austrian capital. It could sell its agricultural exports to Austria during the agricultural crisis, and, thus secured, hasten the dynamic growth in the leading sectors of the Hungarian economy, namely agriculture and foodstuffs. Hungary was by no means an economically exploited country held in a condition of dependence on Austria, but as it was modernised had to adapt to prevailing conditions in the Monarchy and accept a delay in its socio-economic transformation and the prolongation of its traditional economic structure. Although the gap with the western industrial nations could, therefore, be only slightly reduced, Hungary in 1914 still stood on the threshold of the changeover from a purely agrarian-based economy to an industrial nation.

Religion, education and culture

Hungary, which was often referred to as 'Mary's Kingdom' (*Regnum Marianum*), was regarded as a typical Catholic country from the time of its successful Counter Reformation under the cardinal-primate, Péter Pázmány (1570–1637). In fact, only 56.14 per cent of its population in 1880 were practising Catholics. In 1910 the figure was 58.95 per cent. But, since the Catholic bishops had also exercised temporal power, Roman Catholicism had long been the established state religion and the monarch had been accorded the right of patronage, appointment of archbishops and bishops, the creation of new dioceses and the general promotion of the Catholic faith well into the twentieth century. Subject only to papal approval, the Catholic Church exercised a disproportionate influence. It was only after the Emperor Joseph II's tolerance edict of 1781, which first permitted freedom of worship and allowed non-Catholics to hold public office, that the last remnants of the state's attempts at recatholicisation came to an end. Catholicism was also able to salvage its position of predominance beyond the 1848 Revolution. Since many of the 'insurgents' had been non-Catholics, the Church enjoyed the special protection of the central government in Vienna until 1867. Although the position of the state with regard to church affairs was somewhat weakened by a Concordat concluded in 1855, no attempt was made at the complete separation of church and state. In 1868 this Concordat was ruled to be invalid for the territories of the Hungarian crown and the *Placet regium* was reintroduced. All administrative and religious affairs which affected the future relationship between church and state became the responsibility of the minister for education and religion.

These measures resulted in attempts to establish lay-control of the Church in Hungary, a development which gradually led to an erosion of the Catholic Church's privileges and brought about genuine equality of status for the country's other denominations. It especially benefited the Calvinists and Lutherans, who in 1880 made up 30.75 and 4.04 per cent of the population respectively. Although only three-tenths of the country's Magyars were Calvinists, Calvinism was regarded as the 'Magyar religion' since the significance and part played by its adherents in political and cultural life, and thus their scope for shaping the structures and behaviour patterns of Hungarian life, far outweighed their numbers as a percentage of the population. Adherence to the Lutheran faith (based on the Augsburg Confession), which was especially widespread in Transylvania, Slovakia and the German community caused it to be referred to as the 'German religion' in everyday speech. Already in possession of the equal rights accorded to legally recognised denominations, as decreed in 1848 (Law XXI of 1848), the protestant churches tried to build on the increased autonomy granted them after 1867. They created a modern church organisation and began to take an active part in public life which was increasingly dominated by liberal values. From 1885 onwards, their dignitaries had seats and a voice in the Upper House. As a result of substantial Jewish immigration, the proportion of Jews in the population also increased from 5.69 per cent to 7.2 per cent between 1880 and 1910. The Jews consequently exerted a growing influence on Hungary's economic and spiritual life. A clear majority of Rumanians, Serbs and Ruthenes adhered to the Greek Orthodox Church and a smaller number to the Greek Catholic or Uniate Church.

After 1867 the Catholic bishops were unwilling to concede their powerful position without a struggle. The liberal Education Law of 1868 expressly allowed denominational schools, although at the same time it increased state control of education. The church authorities continued to be responsible for marriage ceremonies, the recording of births, marriages and deaths and adjudication in all questions concerning marriage. The Catholic clergy consistently ignored the government's directive that the sons of mixed marriages should be allowed to follow the father's religion and the daughter the mother's religion. Growing frictions and annoyance regarding the splendid life-style of the bishops, drawn mainly from the petty-bourgeois peasantry, caused the Szápáry government to take measures against the 'irregularities' in church politics in the summer of 1892. In this, the government could rely on the support of broad sections of the middle class and intelligentsia among whom religious indifference had become widespread and who, in keeping with the liberal values of the period, favoured reorganising church politics which had come down the centuries unchanged from the time of the Middle Ages. Although the petty-bourgoisie and the peasantry still unhesitatingly obeyed their priests, a growing number of people sought to satisfy their religious needs outside the framework of official religion. Since the clerical camp even opposed the introduction of the citizen's right to choose a civil marriage and the liberals wanted to see marriage ceremonies and the recording of births, marriages and deaths become the exclusive preserve of the state authorities and, alongside religious toleration, to accord equal rights to orthodox Judaism and other denominations, church affairs became the subject of open conflict between 1892 and 1894.

Mobilised by the clergy and conservative aristocrats, the masses resisted any move towards reform and 'persecution of religion'. In this, they were supported by the papal encyclica *Constanti Hungarorum*, specifically issued by Pope Leo XIII. However, the new government, led by Wekerle and supported mainly by the protestant community, the Jewish bourgeoisie, supporters of a secular nation state and the majority of the Liberal Party, was able after lengthy parliamentary debate to push through the new legislation which sanctioned compulsory civil marriages, the state's right to keep public records and civic equality for the Jews. The devoutly pious Emperor Francis Joseph made no secret of his rejection of the new laws whose finalisation he postponed until 10 December 1894. Wekerle's government, which he viewed as much too liberal, was dismissed on 14 January 1895. Two weeks later Count Nándor Zichy and Count Miklós Móric Esterházy founded the Catholic People's Party (*Katolikus Néppárt*) with the aim of defending the Catholic Church's position and rights in Hungary while at the same time creating a political mouthpiece for Catholicism.

Of even greater significance was the movement for spiritual renewal within Catholicism initiated by the Professor of Theology and later Bishop of Székesfehérvár, Ottokar Prohászka. By adapting pastoral work to modern conditions and addressing urgent social problems, this movement took account of the changes wrought by industrialisation. The Church's return to its pastoral and socio-political tasks was also accompanied by a readiness on the part of some sections of the urban middle classes and the intelligentsia to embrace Catholicism actively once more. The protestants also experienced a similar movement of renewal at this time.

Even if, as a result of state legislation and liberal attitudes of the day, the earlier social and political influence of the Hungarian churches was, therefore, to some extent in decline in the years before 1914, their say on important matters and their opportunities for influencing political and cultural life remained largely unaffected.

It was thanks to the personal involvement of Hungary's first minister for education and culture, the respected writer, Baron József Eötvös, that Hungary was given an Education Law imbued with liberal values as early as 1868. This law not only made education compulsory for all six to twelve-year-olds, but provided for state-controlled elementary schools alongside the existing denominational schools. By 1914, the number of elementary schools increased from approximately 10,000 to almost 17,500, of which 5,000 were state-run or local government schools, each with one teacher or, in the case of 7,000 schools, several teaching staff. The number of children attending school rose from 729,000 to 2,621 million. As a result of the government's use of schooling in its forced policy of magyar-isation the number of elementary schools in which Hungarian was the language of instruction almost doubled from 7,300 to 14,200. The number of grammar schools also rose by 87 to 213. Lessons were taught in Hungary's five non-Magyar languages in only forty-one of the grammar schools. Instruction in the country's ninety-two teacher training colleges was exclusively in Hungarian. Thanks to the improvement in basic education which benefited around 90 per cent of all schoolchildren, illiteracy among the population over six years of age fell from 55 per cent in 1867 to 31 per cent in 1914 and to 41.8 per cent for the total population in the same period. The national minorities had to pay dearly for this dramatic improvement in the education system with the loss of their own languages as the language of instruction. All subsequent laws, for instance the 1883 reform of middle school instruction based on proposals drafted by Ágoston Trefort, disadvantaged the non-Hungarian languages. Little wonder, therefore, that 84.5 per cent of candidates with university entrance qualifications and 89 per cent of those attending university lectures were Magyars or spoke Hungarian as their first language.

Hungary's system of university and technical education was also systematically expanded. In 1851 Hungary had only 810 students, most of whom studied at the university in Pest. By 1914, the number had risen to 16,300. Students could now also study at Budapest's Technical University (founded in 1872), in Kolozsvár (Cluj) (founded 1872), Debrecen or Pressburg (Bratislava) (founded 1912). Legal (33 per cent), medical (19 per cent), humanities (10 per cent) and divinity (10 per cent) studies enjoyed particular popularity. Only 22 per cent of undergraduates chose to study the natural sciences, technical studies or economics. Since the proportion of students from working-class and peasant families was below 3 per cent, the majority of students were the sons of the wealthy nobility (around 50 per cent) and the urban bourgeoisie (over 40 per cent). Jewish students were overproportionately represented amongst graduates.

The period of 'national revival' had already created the preconditions for the growth of Magyar national culture before 1848. The National Museum in Budapest, whose benefactors were the father and son, Széchenyi, the National Library (1802) and the forerunner of the Hungarian Academy of Sciences (1825), which concentrated on the study of languages in the interest of creating a sense of national identity, had been followed by the establishment of a National Theatre in 1837. After the Compromise of 1867 the so-called 'national' disciplines, now freed from romantic dilettantism, were able to build on these foundations. Collections of historical source materials, the first compilations of Hungarian history and a history of the Hungarian language and its literature began to appear – although still mainly conceived in a conservative nationalist spirit. With the opening of research institutes and science laboratories, involving considerable financial outlay, the natural sciences and technical disciplines underwent rapid growth stimulated by international developments, whereby the study of physics and the Budapest school of mathematics achieved particular distinction.

The period of the 'national classicism' of the patriotic school between 1840 and 1860 saw Hungary's national literature reach its first apogée which was linked with names like Sándor Petöfi, József Eötvös and János Arany. Following a period of relative academic stagnation and derivative works a general revival took place from the beginning of the twentieth century onwards, which, parallel to general European cultural developments, embraced all areas of culture. Endre Ady and Zsigmond Móricz set new standards in literature which were reflected in the paintings of the Nagybánya school and later in the post-impressionist, avant-garde work of the so-called 'Eight'. Béla Bartók and Zoltán Kodály, who returned to traditional folk melodies for their inspiration, brought new life to Hungarian music and made a significant contribution to the development of modern music. Theatre, opera and operetta found an enthusiastic and knowledgeable public. Around 900 daily newspapers, numerous public libraries and many publishing houses catered for an interested readership.

If art and culture in Hungary had been dominated by Austrian and German influences before the turn of the century, the new liberated currents of Hungarian intellectual life in the years before 1914 turned increasingly to British and French examples. As well as the national element, there was a strong sense of social and political commitment which sought to influence the intellectual creative process in a radical and democratic spirit.

THE BEGINNINGS OF NATIONAL SELF-GOVERNMENT UNDER ANDRÁSSY AND TISZA

The consolidation of internal politics

The vociferous and resolute objections which many Magyars and most national minority leaders raised against the Compromise of 1867, forced Andrássy's government to exercise extreme caution in dealing with Hungary's outstanding political problems and show all parties a desire to compromise. The introduction of a unitary centralist administration had priority, but could expect to meet with resistance from the county administrations which held on firmly to their feudal legacy and mostly opposed the government. Since every attempt to pass parliamentary legislation was also subject to the monarch's prior consent, the government and parliament were left with a relatively limited scope for innovation, although new legislation was required in almost every sphere and draft proposals had to be submitted in advance to the Emperor. The organisational principles and legal norms to be applied had to observe the principle of the monarch's absolute rights. Since, moreover, Ferenc Deák and his immediate colleagues pursued more liberal views than the majority of the Compromise party, and the Hungarian nobility stubbornly defended its traditional prerogatives, the expansion of the Hungarian state apparatus and codification of the legal system came about only very gradually.

At the lowest level, particularly in the villages, both judicial and administrative powers were, as previously, combined in the person of the all-powerful local magistrate. As early as 10 April 1867, the government passed a decree containing its principles for regulating the areas of competence of the municipal councils. This subordinated the right of municipal self-government to national interests and set out the principles to be observed in the election of judges and public officials. Legislation subsequently passed between 1870 and 1872 on the administration of the counties and urban and rural districts plainly revealed the government's desire to curtail local self-government and encourage greater centralisation. The situation was complicated by the fact that the legal norms observed in Croatia and Transylvania differed from those in the rest of Hungary. The county administrations and their elected officials continued to exist, but had to surrender some of their autonomy to central government. In future, each county was to be administered by a governor with extended powers, to be nominated by the government and appointed by the monarch. Over the years the various departments of experts were placed under increasingly tight supervision by central government. In 1876, administrative committees of nominated civil servants were also created whose job was to supervise the administration in keeping with the government's policy of centralisation.

The expansion of the judicial system was characterised by the application of progressive bourgeois–democratic principles. The judiciary was made independent of the executive, state prosecutors were appointed and the new arrangements focussed in particular on the judicial independence and appointment for life of judges nominated by the King and confirmed by the minister of justice (Law IV of 1869). Since there was no codified legal system, the modernised *Corpus iuris* remained in force. A new civil law code was introduced in 1868, which laid down extremely cumbersome procedural rules for trials. After several amendments, however, this was replaced in 1911 by a new system of rules which took more account of the needs of bourgeois society and remained in force until 1 January 1915. No modern legal code existed for the private sector. A new penal code was introduced after 1880, followed by a uniform code of criminal trial procedures after 1900.

The development of the fiscal administration and introduction of a new tax system culminated in the setting up of a new Government Audit Office in 1870 which had the power to check the records and financial affairs of all government ministries as well as those departments entitled to make transfer payments. The government's increasing tendency to depart from the elective principle in developing new administrative institutions and extend the influence of central government was everywhere apparent.

The largely unjustified claim by opponents of the Compromise that Hungary was dependent on Austria in a semi-colonial sense was usually supported by the argument that Hungary did not exercise its due influence on the shaping of defence policy and decisions concerning the army. Apart from approving the size of the regular levée of recruits, sharing in defence expenditure and enjoying limited participation in decision-making, the Hungarian government and parliament could bring practically no influence to bear on the leadership, organisation and deployment of the common army or on the leadership and policies of the ministry of war. Although according to the terms of the Compromise the Hungarian parliament was not allowed to concern itself with the costs of the common army, which in keeping with the procedures on the respective expenditure quotas was a task reserved for the parliamentary delegations, Hungary's share of the defence budget had to be incorporated into the national budget. This meant that the Budapest parliament was able to have a certain say on defence matters, however indirectly, since it could pass a vote of no confidence in the government or oppose defence arrangements. Moreover, the taxes which had to be raised to cover defence requirements could not be collected on the basis of Hungary's own internal administrative laws, nor could recruits be conscripted without the parliament's advance approval. This interpretation of the Compromise, which to some extent contradicted the King's expressly acknowledged right to the sole command of the armed forces (Law XII of 1867, para. 11) not only caused friction between Vienna and Budapest, but occasioned increasingly acrimonious internal quarrels within Hungary about the nature and role of the army. The mutual antipathy which existed between the Hungarians and the army, whose officers often displayed offensive anti-Hungarian attitudes and the mentality of an occupying force, was the cause of continual conflicts which weakened the cohesion of the Dual Monarchy.

Satisfaction felt at the creation of a separate Hungarian ministry for the Hungarian territorial army (*Honvéd*) and the creation of purely Hungarian reserve regiments could not compensate for discontent with the unpopular and omnipotent common army, in which German was the sole language of command. Magyars occupied only 6.8 per cent of the available posts in the ministry of defence and never supplied more than 10 per cent of the generals. It was only after difficult negotiations that Andrássy's government succeeded in 1868 in overcoming the opposition of the Emperor and the military experts to the creation of a separate Hungarian force, arguing that such a militia was a necessary prerequisite for upholding internal public order. Although its leadership was derived from a common Austro-Hungarian army, the *Honvéd* was a national army modelled on the Austrian territorial army. However, it had no artillery or technical units and was intended to provide a supply of reserve manpower for the Austro-Hungarian common army. Like the gendarmerie stationed in Transylvania and Croatia–Slavonia, it was at first used chiefly as a means of intimidating the Empire's national minorities and crushing peasant discontent.

To some extent, its tasks of guaranteeing the government's executive power and maintaining internal order became of secondary importance in 1881 following the introduction of new regulations for the rural gendarmerie. In place of the old system of county constables a reorganised 'national' gendarmerie was created directly under the ministries of defence (the *Honvéd* minister) and the interior. As well as pursuing ordinary criminals, it was given responsibility for combating political activities. In 1882, the Budapest police force was reorganised. Following this example, the forces of law and order in the other self-administering municipalities were subsequently reorganised on the basis that they could call on the assistance of the national gendarmerie. The consolidation of the state apparatus, the extension of the powers of central government and the desire to be armed against possible sources of unrest – whether nationalist or Socialist – were the immediate motives behind these highly costly reorganisation measures.

The opposition's dissatisfaction with the 'alien, dynastic and absolutist' common army, most of whose officers had little understanding of the Magyar mentality and Magyar sensibilities, was strengthened in 1886 when General Ludwig Janszky laid a wreath at the grave of General Heinrich von Hentzi who had been killed fighting Hungarian insurgents in 1849. The response to this piece of tactlessness and provocation, which seemed quite outrageous in Hungarian eyes, was a long series of demonstrations which rendered military intervention necessary. In this tense atmosphere Tisza's government felt obliged after a great deal of pressure from both the crown and the military leaders in Vienna to propose a new army law which approved the size of recruitment intakes for the next decade, something especially close to the heart of Francis Joseph. It also proposed more up-to-date methods in officer traiing and a restructuring of the army. Above all, the rule that reserve officers would also have to sit a German language examination aroused fierce opposition from Magyar nationalist groups opposed to the government. During the winter session debates of 1889–90 in parliament they joined forces for the first time in a common cause and stirred the masses to action through their chauvinist appeals. Demonstrations were held not only in the capital but in the provinces, too, and had to be violently dispersed by the military. Although the government defused the conflict to some extent by conceding tests in Hungarian and Croat to take place alongside that in German and managed to push through the army law against parliamentary opposition, the prime minister, Kálmán Tisza, his experience and skills put to the test, could no longer hold on to power and was forced to resign on 13 March 1890.

It was mainly thanks to Tisza, however, that Hungary's internal political condition had stabilised during the so-called 'period of calm'. Relying on a parliamentary majority which was safe as long as elections were rigged and the administration filled with his supporters, he had succeeded not only in defusing the problems inherent in the dualistic political system, but had bolstered the social and political order by constitutional means in a multi-national Hungary increasingly subject to class divisions. Although he lacked the stature of a great statesman, he showed a keen political awareness and a capacity to use people and institutions for his own ends. These qualities, together with his ability to evade problematical issues, his pragmatism and a solid political desire and ability to maintain his position, had helped smooth out differences and retain the Emperor's goodwill. Although he had promised in his first election campaign in 1875 that he would try to obtain better conditions for Hungary in the impending negotiations by the Delegations on the prolongation of the Compromise and the customs union, during the three-year-long discussions he was only able to get his way on the pure formality of renaming the National Bank of Austria the 'Austro-Hungarian Bank'. The ensuing disappointment which spread throughout Hungary and led to political defections from the government camp, resulted in the government often relying on an extremely slender parliamentary majority. It also accelerated the founding of new opposition parties such as the United, later Moderate Opposition (1878–81), the 'Independence and '48 Party' (1884) and the Party of Non-Voters (1878). However, Tisza soon made use of the political reshuffles to reorganise his own government support to his benefit and adopted ostensibly liberal economic and education policies which took account of Magyar nationalist aspirations.

Hungary's political forces and struggles were thus kept within the strict bounds of constitutionalism while economic competition was given free reign. After the great stock exchange crash of 9 May 1873 the agricultural proletariat, which grew rapidly as a consequence, followed the workers in finding itself the object of the state's mistrustful surveillance. The Agricultural Labour Law of 1876, which covered male and female farmhands who made up almost 15 per cent of all agricultural employees with a minimum one-year wage contract, not only curtailed their legal equality and personal freedom, but placed the often inadequately accommodated, low-paid labourer, who was usually paid in kind and devoid of insurance protection under the 'authority of his master'. Henceforth, the latter was allowed the right to discipline his workers with mild corporal punishment and could call on the gendarmerie to help him restore order if necessary. An improvement in the social conditions of the agricultural and industrial workers was certainly deemed necessary. But the liquidation of the government's debts and the drafting of social welfare legislation, which had been prepared in 1889 following the government's enlargement to include ministries of trade and agriculture did not take effect until 1892.

Hungary's influence on the foreign policy of the Habsburg Monarchy

In contrast to its influence on defence policy Hungary was able to play a significant, indeed decisive part in the shaping of the Monarchy's foreign policy. Three of the common government's ten foreign ministers were Hungarians (three and a half, in fact, if one includes Count Leopold Berchtold). In 1914, Hungarians accounted for 27.5 per cent of foreign ministry officials and members of the diplomatic corps. Since para. 8 of Law XII of 1867 stipulated that the common Austro-Hungarian foreign minister required the agreement of both prime ministers including, therefore, that of the Hungarian government, the Hungarian parliament was able to influence foreign policy beyond its say in approving the budget. The direction of the Habsburg Monarchy's foreign policy, as pursued by Count Gyula Andrássy after 1871, was largely in keeping with the interests of the Magyar ruling élites who carried partial responsibility. No detailed research has yet been undertaken for the years preceding the First World War to find out how far and to what extent Hungarian demands and the Empire's relevant internal power relationships within the dualist structure influenced and – in the perception of foreign public opinion – burdened foreign policy in the long term.

There was little support in Hungary for the dreams harboured by members of the the upper nobility, sections of the bureaucracy and army leaders after the defeat of 1866: *revanche* against Prussia, a foreign policy in which Austria took the lead in German affairs, the recovery of the lost territory of Silesia, the setting up of an Austrian protectorate over the South German states and even the restoration of the old unitary Habsburg Empire. Against this line, which was also pursued by the flexible Chancellor Beust in early summer of 1870, the then Hungarian premier, Andrássy, demanded that the monarchy stick to a policy of neutrality and prepare for an armed struggle against Russia. At a crown council meeting on 18 July 1870 the Emperor Francis Joseph decided against immediate mobilisation, but at the same time agreed to military preparations and an announcement of Austrian neutrality. The rapid German victories and Napoleon III's decisive defeat at Sedan put an end to revanchist plans for once and for all. Hungary was also not interested in a future extension of the Dual Monarchy's power, nor – as was demonstrated by Budapest's veto of trialism in 1871 – in attempting a federal reorganisation internally which would reduce its own relative political importance. Instead, it was determined to defend and as far as possible extend the influence it had already attained in determining the Monarchy's destiny.

Count Gyula Andrássy, who replaced the discredited Count Beust as foreign minister on 14 November 1871, was soon presented with an opportunity for just this. In a detailed memorandum of May 1871, Beust himself had argued for a change of direction in Austro-Hungarian foreign policy. His main points were that Austria should restore its good relationship with the Prussian-dominated German Empire – something Bismarck also desired – and expand its influence in the Balkans which would require the cooperation of Russia. The first meeting of the Emperors Francis Joseph and William in Salzburg in August 1871 had produced considerable agreement on foreign policy, for it was in the interests of Prussian-dominated Germany to divert Austro-Hungary's great-power ambitions to the Balkans, given the Ottoman Empire's inexorable decline and the intensification of Russia's Policy in the East under its foreign minister, Gorčakov. Andrássy, who was keen to bring about an alliance between Vienna and Berlin had somewhat different priorities from his predecessor, Beust. As far as he was concerned, combating the 'threat of pan-Slavism', thus limiting Russia's sphere of influence, was a top priority. Since the founding of the Slav Welfare Society in Moscow in 1858, the second Slav Congress of 1867 and the publication of Danilevskij's famous book, 'Russia and Europe', in 1869, (which proclaimed the goals of a Russian-led pan-Slav federation and the acquisition of Constantinople), fears of Russian and Russian-backed Slav nationalism had grown out of all proportion in Austria-Hungary. Because of Berlin's friendly relations with St Petersburg, Austria-Hungary could not rely on Bismarck's support for an anti-Russian shift in foreign policy. Andrássy could never quite rely on the Emperor's unreserved support during his time in the Vienna foreign ministry. Against his better judgement he had to go along with a policy which, after the meeting in September 1872 between Francis Joseph, the German Emperor William I and Tsar Alexander II, eventually led to the Three Emperors' League in the following year. By this agreement the signatories undertook to consult each other in the event of an attack by another power. Russia and Austria-Hungary pledged themselves to guarantee the maintenance of the status quo in the Balkans. They acknowledged a mutual obligation not to intervene in conflicts in the Balkans and undertook to hold prior discussions in an emergency. This consultative agreement did not clash with the Monarchy's other foreign policy aims, namely the maintenance of its traditional friendship with Britain and the preservation of Turkish supremacy over the Slav nations of the Balkans.

As a direct result of the Emperor Francis Joseph's tour of Dalmatia, revolts against oppressive Turkish rule broke out in Bosnia and Herzegovina in the summer of 1875 and spread to Bulgaria in the spring of 1876. The Great Powers had no wish to escalate the conflict and the risings were brutally crushed by the Turks. Their appeal to the Sultan and the insurgents to reach a negotiated settlement, contained in the Berlin Memorandum of 13 May 1876, had no effect. However, the cruel pacification measures carried out by the Turks after an internal political power struggle outraged the whole of European public opinion against the Turks and encouraged the small independent states of Serbia and Montenegro to declare war with Russia's backing on 2 July. Andrássy had up until now maintained a policy of benevolent neutrality towards the Turks since he feared that a successful rebellion would lead to the emergence of a major Slav state and the expansion of Russian influence as far as the Bosphorus and the Aegean. Tsar Alexander

II subsequently visited Emperor Francis Joseph at Schloss Reichstadt in Bohemia on 8 July 1876 and proposed the break-up of the Ottoman Empire and a division of the Balkans by which Austria would acquire Bosnia and Herzegovina. The Hungarian fear, which Andrássy expressed, concerning the incorporation of more Slav-populated regions and the danger of Slav predominance in the Monarchy, was something Francis Joseph refused to consider.

Since the Serbs could not resist pressure from the Turks for very long, Russia felt obliged to intervene directly in the Balkan conflict in the autumn of 1876. In a secret agreement it was firmly agreed in Budapest on 15 January 1877 and again on 18 March that Austria-Hungary should be compensated for maintaining neutrality in the Russo-Turkish war by the acquisition of Bosnia and Herzegovina, in return for which it would agree to Russia's annexation of Bessarabia and certain Armenian territories. In keeping with the reservation that no major pan-Slav state should be allowed to emerge, both parties agreed to guarantee Serbian, Rumanian, Bulgarian and Albanian independence. During the fighting between the Russians and the Turks, which broke out on 24 April 1877, the Sultan was able to hold out against the Tsarist troops only until late autumn. The preliminary Treaty of Adrianople on 31 January and the Treaty of San Stefano on 3 March 1878 placed the seal on Turkey's complete defeat. Thereafter, Russia no longer felt bound by the secret Budapest agreement and acquired for itself not only substantial territorial gains in the Caucasus region, but also an impressive power base in the Balkans in the form of an enlarged Bulgaria stretching to the Aegean coast and under Russian control, as well as an expanded Serbia and Montenegro. Austria-Hungary was expected to go empty-handed since Bosnia and Herzegovina were to be given autonomous status, though still within the Ottoman Empire.

This arrangement, which completely disregarded Austro-Hungarian interests, caused Andrássy to call on 28 January 1878 for a congress of the guarantor powers of the 1856 Paris Peace Conference to be held in order to examine the Russo-Turkish peace terms. Both the Emperor and the army rejected his recommendation of military action against Russia. But in collaboration with Great Britain Austria-Hungary managed to achieve the summoning of the Berlin Congress (from 13 June to 13 July 1878) at which Russia, despite Bismarck's loyal support, was forced to make significant concessions in the peace settlement. For Austria-Hungary, the sanctioning of the annexation of Bosnia and Herzegovina was important, as was the separation of Eastern Rumelia and Macedonia from Bulgaria, which

Russian troops were allowed to occupy for nine months. Austria was permitted to garrison troops in the Sanjak of Novibazar which separated Serbia from Montenegro. Thus, the Austro-Hungarian Empire, which had steadily lost territories since 1859, had become a Balkan power, able to exert economic and military pressure on Serbia and Montenegro. It had also found itself moving forward towards the Aegean at Salonika.

Despite the fact that the Habsburg monarchy had maintained its great-power status, there was little sign of enthusiasm in Hungary at the unlimited occupation of the two South Slav provinces. After reservations had already been expressed concerning Andrássy's apparently pro-Russian policy, passionate nationwide protests took place against the occupation once the decisions taken in Berlin became known. The weakening of Turkey and the increase in the proportion of the Monarchy's Slav population caused considerable anxiety. Andrássy was just as anxious as Bismarck to build further on the goodwill which had emerged between Vienna and Berlin during the Balkan crisis and Congress of Berlin. The resentment felt in St Petersburg at Bismarck's 'honest broker' role, which found expression in a letter of complaint from Alexander II to William I (the 'box on the ear' letter) in August 1879, prepared the way for the signing of the Dual Alliance on 7 October 1879. This was a defensive pact directed against potential Russian aggression. In the event of an attack by a third power the contracting parties were obliged merely to maintain a position of benevolent neutrality. The secret neutrality agreement, finally signed in 1881 and due to run for three years between the German Empire, the Austro-Hungarian Empire and Russia (The Three Emperors' League) obliged the other two members of the alliance to maintain a benevolent neutrality in the event of an attack by a fourth power on a member. Italy's joining of the Dual Alliance in 1882 secured for Austria-Hungary Italian neutrality in the event of a Russian attack and even committed the contracting parties to provide armed support in the event of a combined attack by two or more powers.

This policy of alliances, which stabilised Austria-Hungary's influence in the Balkans and guaranteed a maximum degree of safety against external enemies, was initiated by Andrássy. He was unable to implement it personally, however, since the Emperor Francis Joseph had already dismissed him on 10 October 1879 after a long period of speculation about his imminent, albeit temporary, resignation. It remained to his successors to build upon the Monarchy's great-power status through a series of bilateral treaties with neighbouring Balkan states. On 28 June 1881, Serbia signed a treaty agreeing to orientate its foreign policy according to Austria-Hungary's interests and promised to take action to prevent any anti-Habsburg agitation in its territories. On 30 October 1883, Austria-Hungary, the German Empire and Rumania formed a defensive alliance. Relations with Bulgaria, which was ruled after 1887 by the former *Honvéd* officer, Ferdinand of Saxe-Coburg-Koháry, also began to improve after the crisis of 1886–87 once again conjured up the danger of military confrontation with Russia. Hungary profited as much as the rest of the Monarchy from this period of stable foreign relations and expanding influence in the Balkans. But with the growth of Magyar nationalism the Habsburg state's foreign policy, focussed as it was on the German Empire, remained unpopular in Hungary and was always fiercely criticised when protective tariffs hampered or blocked the export of Hungarian agricultural produce and industrial manufactures. Anti-Russian sentiments which remained latent since 1849 were further stirred up by the Slav nationalist movement supported by St Petersburg. After shifts in the alliance system became apparent after 1892 these grew into an unconcealed fear of Russia and 'Austro-Slavism' which was often conjured up by the press.

THE CRISIS OF DUALISM AND LOSS OF INTERNAL POLITICAL STABILITY

The effects of internal conflict on Hungary's relationship to the Empire

The resignation of prime minister Kálmán Tisza in March 1890 marked the beginning of a period of instability in internal politics which saw the collapse of the Liberal Party. It was a period characterised by frequent changes of government, the intensification of political, social and national conflicts and growing tension between the two halves of the Empire. Only after the election of Count István Tisza to President of the Chamber of Deputies (Lower House) on 22 May 1912 and his second appointment as prime minister in July 1913 did the opportunity for a long-term consolidation present itself, although this came to nothing as a result of the outbreak of the First World War. The Hungarian politicans and political parties failed to take adequate account of the dynamic socio-economic changes taking place in Hungarian society. They failed to recognise the significance of the country's modern economic development, underestimated the explosive force of nationalism and thoughtlessly provoked the dangerous growth of division between Austria and Hungary and thus inexcusably ignored the possible effects of this on coexistence within the crisis-ridden Dual Monarchy. By the eve of the First World War and during the subsequent conflict it was too late to undertake the necessary changes and basic reforms.

The government of Count Gyula Szápáry, which held office from 13 March 1890 to 17 November 1892, scarcely differed from Tisza's cabinet in terms of its personnel. The energetic finance minister, Wekerle, primarily devoted his energies to consolidating the state finances and introducing a currency reform by which the silver forint was replaced by the gold crown. The first social policy measures, such as the prohibition of Sunday working and the introduction of compulsory sickness insurance did not, however, bring Hungarian politics any nearer to a solution of the 'labour question' which was causing mounting concern. The completion of waterway regulation improvements at the Iron Gate on the Danube led to a rise in unemployment in the following years and a dramatic increase in emigration.

After prime minister Szápáry had encountered stiff opposition to his attempt to overcome the 'irregularities' in church politics in the autumn of 1892, Dr Sándor Wekerle became the first representative of the middle class to take over as head of government. After he had succeeded in having the law on compulsory civil marriages and the state keeping of public records passed by parliament (see p 45f), he had to hand over the premiership to Baron Deszö Bánffy on 14 January 1895, despite his undisputed qualities, at the express wish of the Emperor. His successor had a reputation as a capable administrator who had made a name for himself in the senior levels of the county administration in Rumanian-inhabited areas of Transylvania as an obdurate defender of Magyar supremacy and a 'devourer of Socialists'. As head of government he continued to suppress the Socialist movement and the national minorities with a strong hand and a provocative chauvinism, especially since the latter were now increasingly self-confident in putting forward their demands for autonomy. The organisation of the Millenium Celebrations, held amid a frenzy of nationalism in 1896 to celebrate 1,000 years of Magyar settlement in Hungary, was solely intended to demonstrate Hungary's historical greatness and, under the aegis of a narrow-

minded Magyar nationalism, to show Hungary's growing importance within the Austro-Hungarian Monarchy – especially in the
period pending renegotiation of the decennial economic Compromise.
During the festivities in May and June the Empress Elizabeth, Queen
of Hungary, became the centre of attention. The nation expressed
its thanks at a *Te Deum* at which the Hungarian Primate declared
that 'her tender maternal hand had woven the golden band by which
the Magyar nation and its dearly beloved king are inextricably bound
to one another'.

The euphoric speeches at the Millenium Celebrations had scarcely
died away when internal political disagreements raised emotions as
acutely as ever. Lajos Kossuth had died in exile in Turin on 20 March
1894. After his spectacular funeral, which was accompanied by
nationalist demonstrations, the nationalist opposition which had
degenerated into squabbling factions over the years but was still
popular among sections of the middle nobility and gentry, well-to-
do peasantry and petty bourgeoisie received fresh impetus. Although
he possessed none of his great father's charisma and insight, the
Independence Party found a new leader in his son, Ferenc Kossuth,
who had returned home from abroad after having being pardoned.
The Catholic People's Party, founded on 28 January 1895 to
represent the interests of political Catholicism, also participated in
the coming parliamentary elections with strong backing from the
clergy. As a result of the usual electoral abuses the Liberal Party
emerged in a stronger position with 60.1 per cent of the vote and
287 seats, but had to face a united parliamentary opposition which
was determined to bring down the unpopular Bánffy.

The immediate cause of renewed internal political conflict was the
successfully concluded 1896 Compromise negotiations, at which for
the first time the Hungarian delegation wrested significant economic
concessions. The coining of the malicious epithet 'Judaeo-Magyars'
by the new Mayor of Vienna, Karl Lueger, so mortally offended the
Hungarian Liberals that the Austrians were forced to compromise
in order to conciliate them. Against the background of prevailing
parliamentary anarchism in Austria, the central government, led by
the Polish landowner, Count Kazimierz Badeni, believed it could
win the Vienna parliament's agreement to the accord reached with
Budapest only if it could win the support of the Czechs by passing
legislation guaranteeing generous treatment for the Czech language
in public affairs. Badeni was defeated by the opposition of the
German-Austrian parties. His successor, Gautsch, was defeated by
Czech obstructionist tactics. The rapid succession of governments

in Vienna failed to win acceptance of the new economic Compromise. Thus, in 1898 a provisional arrangement was agreed to and approved by the Emperor. The terms of the Compromise, which had been valid until 1896, were extended until the end of 1903. If by then the requisite parliamentary majority for its passage was not forthcoming, the terms of the 1887 economic Compromise were to remain in force until one or other of the parties repudiated it. This so-called 'Ischl clause', which was seen in Hungary as a limitation on the country's constitutional rights, gave rise to a heated debate set in motion by the Independence Party which caused uproar in parliament and resulted in the adoption of obstructionist tactics. Public opinion was greatly impressed by the opposition's stance. The government was accused of 'party absolutism' and the opposition called increasingly for the replacement of the unpopular Bánffy. When the magnate faction, led by Count Gyula Andrássy Jnr., left the government camp Bánffy had to ask the Emperor to accept his resignation on 26 February 1899.

Ferenc Deák's son-in-law, Kálmán Széll, who came from a respectable old landowning family and was president of a major bank, now emerged as the saviour of the hour. His formula, that Hungary should voluntarily prolong the old economic arrangements until 1903 'in the legal framework of the autonomous customs area', went some way towards pacifying the opposition. Since he was able to entice the thirty-two 'dissidents' grouped around the younger Andrássy back into the Liberal Party, and since the Moderate Opposition, led by Count Apponyi, also joined the government camp, he could rely on a firm parliamentary majority of 320 deputies. The price he had to pay for holding this majority together was to make far-reaching concessions to the large landowners. When Széll negotiated new Compromise terms with the Austrian government under Koerber at the end of 1902 full account was taken of the interest of the agrarian élite in securing the imposition of high tariffs on agricultural imports. Although the Hungarians could not avoid conceding an increase of 3 per cent in their share of the common expenditure quota, and this encountered stiff opposition, the Magyars nevertheless felt flattered that their economic development was making visible progress and was reflected in the Monarchy's common budget. But this agreement, too, never received legislative sanction.

The country's relative calm, achieved as a result of Széll's skilful handling of the rival factions within the government party, quickly evaporated when a draft law to reorganise the army was laid before parliament in January 1903. Although the need to increase the troop strength of both the common army and the *Honvéd*, and thus Hungary's financial quota, by 25 per cent was not challenged, the opposition, in return for their agreement, demanded the introduction of Hungarian as the language of command, Hungarian insignia and a reduction in the length of compulsory service. By obstructing the bill, the opposition attempted to lay further stress on its attacks on the common nature of the army. The criticism of the army, which was concealed behind the opposition's demands, was equally popular with both the nobility and the workers. Since Széll could not bring himself to come down heavily on his political opponents he was dismissed in disgrace by the Emperor on 27 June 1903.

He was replaced as prime minister by the former governor of Croatia, Count Károly Khuen-Héderváry, to whom the Emperor Francis Joseph eagerly gave his support on 16 September 1903 when he issued a general army order from the manoeuvres in Chlopy, Galicia. In this order, which took the Magyars by surprise, he stressed that the army should remain 'as it is', a common and uniform force, adding that he would never surrender his rights as commander-in-chief. The storm of protest which subsequently overtook Hungary swept Khuen-Héderváry from office. The King now entrusted Count István Tisza, the son of the long-serving prime minister, Kálmán Tisza, with the formation of a new government on 3 November 1903. Tisza was widely regarded as a supporter of the Dual Monarchy and could be expected to take energetic measures against the opposition.

Tisza was regarded as a taciturn, unfriendly and stubborn man. With a sense of vocation born of his Calvinist convictions he had become a parliamentary deputy at the early age of 25, had gone on to become a successful president of a major bank and had successfully managed his estate of over 6,500 hectares before rising to prominence in national politics at the turn of the century. In his view Hungary depended on close ties with Austria and needed the alliance with the German Empire to ensure that Hungary could retain its territorial possessions intact. These beliefs, together with his desire to keep Socialist and nationalist movements in check, predestined him in the eyes of the Emperor to lead Hungary out of the crisis. In March 1904, he broke the obstruction of the nationalist opposition by enforcing a more rigorous application of the procedural rules of the Lower House and increasing the use of compulsory measures. In return for the withdrawal of these measures, which would have seriously hampered their parliamentary work, the opposition parties approved the budget and voted for the regular annual intake of recruits. But the precarious truce between the parties failed to calm the excited mood of the country. Tisza, who placed no importance on the unpopularity of his determined strong-arm tactics nor agreement with them, revived the crisis during the autumn session of parliament when he insisted on revising the standing orders of the Lower House and provoked the opposition to renew its obstruction of legislation. When he employed dubious methods to push through his draft proposals in parliament on 18 November 1904, the Andrássy faction again left the government which was also faced with the merger of Apponyi's party with the Independence Party to form the National Party (*Nemzeti Párt*). On 19 November, all the opposition parties – the Independence and '48 Party, the Catholic People's Party, National Party, New Party and Bourgeois-Democratic Party – joined in close cooperation to form a 'Coalition'. Although Ferenc Kossuth was to be its main spokesman, in reality, this coalition had to rely entirely on instructions from Apponyi and Andrássy.

This cooperation between the opposition parties, which Tisza had brought about against his will, led to a visible hardening of positions. After the clamour in parliament had reached its climax on 13 December with substantial damage to the chamber of deputies, and the political conflict had spilled over to the population at large, Tisza was forced to dissolve parliament and call new elections. The Coalition, supported by all the various opposition groups, was agreed on only one point: to end Tisza's 'rule by force'. The masses, who were excluded from the democratic process by the franchise system, shared this view. Since the civil service also joined the new constellation of forces, the traditional methods of electoral rigging did not benefit the government camp in the usual manner. The Liberal Party suffered a serious reverse in the election held in January 1905, winning only 37.9 per cent of the vote and 159 seats. The Independence Party managed to win 33.3 per cent of the vote and 165 seats in its own right. In all, 254 Coalition deputies were returned. An era which had lasted 30 years thus came to an inglorious end. The opinion spread, even among the defeated Liberals, that it was time to take more account of the political structures created by Hungary's new socio-economic conditions, together with the appearance of new political forces and methods.

Believing that the events of the 1905 Russian Revolution would be more likely to cause the Emperor to satisfy Magyar aspirations for a fully fledged nation state, the triumphant Coalition offered a radical programme which demanded considerable autonomy for the

Hungarian army. However, Francis Joseph brusquely rejected the idea of any concessions. After all, he saw 'his army' as the only intact and firm instrument for holding together his disintegrating empire. Since he wished to entrust Andrássy Jnr with the formation of a new cabinet only on condition that the latter forgo any reorganisation of the army, the Coalition refused to participate in the government. Only when, in the wake of the 1905 Russian Revolution, a wave of strikes by agricultural and factory workers made the need for a government capable of handling the situation increasingly obvious and the Coalition continued to refuse acceptance of the Emperor's conditions, did Francis Joseph entrust a loyal and trustworthy general, Baron Géza Fejérváry, a *Honvéd* minister of close on 20 years standing, with the formation of a caretaker government. The Coalition responded by proclaiming a state of 'national resistance', calling upon the counties and municipal authorities to boycott taxes and recruitment levées, and voted in parliament against any proposals by a 'puppet government'. The government crisis was not overcome, but instead escalated into a crisis of the entire system. Since Tisza and his Liberal supporters withdrew from the fray, Fejérváry could rely only on the confidence of the monarch, the army and the loyal civil service. The Coalition, mainly through its defence programme and desire for more Hungarian independence, but otherwise incapable of firm action on account of internal conflicts and jealousies, soon exhausted itself with its ill-defined policy of blocking tactics.

The interior minister, József Kristóffy, found a way of breaking the impasse by proposing the introduction of universal suffrage in order to secure the support of the lower social classes. When the leaders of the Coalition, summoned to a 'five minute audience' in the Hofburg, refused Francis Joseph's final demand to abandon their destructive policies and grandiose aims, the Emperor approved a draft bill proposing universal suffrage and reappointed Fejérváry, who had meantime resigned, to the post of prime minister. In response, the Coalition's leadership committee tried with varying degrees of success to mobilise opposition to the 'absolutist government' in the counties. However, when the demonstrations by advocates of electoral reform spread and the government blocked funds to the hostile county administrations and refused to pay the salaries of their officials who had been suspended, the opposition was forced to give in. The *Honvéd* general, Sándor von Nyiri, whom the Emperor had appointed 'Royal Commissioner', ordered the military to clear the parliament building on 19 February

1906 and thereupon dissolved the parliament. The Coalition's leadership committee suspended its sittings in March. Since, to the disappointment of the nationalist opposition, the urban masses remained passive, the will to resist rapidly diminished. Resigning for a second time on 8 April 1906, Fejérváry cleared the way for the formation of a new government in which the Coalition participated through the mediation of Ferenc Kossuth out of a sense of 'a higher patriotism'. In return for the Coalition forsaking its defence programme the monarchy withdrew its electoral reform proposal, feared equally by the Old Liberals and Coalition deputies alike. The way was now left open for the opposition politicians to participate in the new government. Under the premiership of Sándor Wekerle, who supported the 'Compromise', Andrássy joined the Coalition government as interior minister, Kossuth as minister for trade and Apponyi as minister for education. Thus, the government crisis which had lasted more than a year was resolved by an arrangement in the interest of the all-important class of magnates and large-scale landowners. It had been achieved without having to concede any fundamental social and political reforms to the majority of the population and without having produced a clear solution to the problem of Hungary's status within the Monarchy.

The new government's policies took special account of the wishes of the large-scale landowning class and at the same time attempted to support the country's banks and entrepreneurs with a law of 1907 designed to encourage industrial growth. It also attempted to contain the workers' discontent by introducing several social policy measures. Since the Liberal Party had collapsed and been dissolved by Istvan Tisza on 11 April, the government had no serious opponent to face during the May 1906 elections. The Independence Party captured 59.9 per cent of the vote, giving it 253 seats. The Slav and Rumanian parliamentary deputies joined together to form the Club of National Minority Deputies. Previously they had never attained more than ten seats. Now, for the first time they had been able to obtain twenty six, while the Agrarian Socialists were represented for the first time by two members. In the 1907 negotiations on the decennial economic Compromise terms the Hungarian delegation succeeded only in winning several concessions over the wording of the agreement. The 'Customs Union' was now called a 'Treaty' and the 'common tariff' now an 'autonomous tariff'. But the delegation had to pay for these conciliatory gestures with a further 2 per cent increase in its share of the common expenditure quota, which was now raised to 36.4 per cent. Disappointment that none of the nationalist aims had been realised caused several leading members of the Independence Party to turn their back on the party and reveal details of the secret terms agreed between the crown and the Coalition in 1906. The nationalists were compensated only by the 1907 Education Act, introduced by the minister of education, Count Albert Apponyi. This ordered the use of Hungarian as the language of instruction in the elementary schools of the national minorities and allowed a further intensification of the government's magyarisation policy. An increasingly apparent national chauvinism also put an end to the short-lived cooperation with the 'New Course' of the Croats under their leaders, Supilo and Trumbić, who, especially after the Bosnian crisis of 1908, sought to achieve national self-determination by restructuring the Dual Monarchy on a trialist basis or within the framework of a unitary South Slav state.

In 1909, already, there were noticeable signs of a break-up in the government camp, set in motion and accelerated by the agreement on the Austro-Hungarian Bank which was due to run out at the end of 1910. The nationalist wing of the Independence Party insisted instead on the creation of an independent Hungarian Bank licensed to issue its own banknotes and, since the government and the other Coalition parties dragged their feet on this demand, 115 deputies led by Gyula Justh broke away from the party on 11 November 1909. Details of Ferenc Kossuth's shady financial dealings published in the Vienna Christian-Social newspaper, the *Reichspost*, further undermined the government's already tarnished image, with the result that Wekerle had to hand over the premiership to the Old Liberal, Count Károly Khuen-Hedérváry, on 17 January 1910. The latter, who had already failed once as prime minister in 1903, could rely on the former Liberals who had reorganised themselves on 19 February 1910 under the name of the Party of National Work (*Nemzeti Munkapárt*) led by István Tisza who had now re-entered politics. The main support for the Party of National Work came from the land-owners and influential haute bourgeoisie, who saw holding on to the principles of the Compromise as the only way of overcoming the increasingly threatening internal and external political tensions which they perceived. In June 1910 the electorate, which still numbered fewer than a million voters out of a population of 20.9 million, showed its disillusionment with the Coalition and gave the new government party 47 per cent of the vote and 258 seats. This gave it a comfortable two-thirds majority which was achieved mainly at the expense of the Independence Party factions which suffered heavy losses: the Justh wing taking 15.8 per cent of the vote and forty one seats, the Kossuth wing 14.3 per cent of the vote and fifty-four seats. The period of consolidation in internal politics was, however, already over by the spring of 1911, since the disintegrating opposition which was once more united on account of a draft army bill, made necessary by the worsening international situation, now no longer demanded merely constitutional concessions but also put forward anti-militarist demands alongside electoral reform. Since Khuen-Hedérváry again refused to crush the growing number of demonstrations by force, Francis Joseph appointed László Lukács, Hungary's second middle–class politician to become prime minister, to head the government on 22 April 1912.

The most influential politician in the years that followed was, however, Count István Tisza, who had himself elected President of the Chamber of Deputies on 22 May 1912. Unimpressed by an abortive attempt on his life, he sent in the army against the demonstrating masses and protesting deputies outside the parliament building on 'Bloody Thursday'. The votes of the government party were sufficient to pass not only the new army bill, but a draft bill giving the government emergency powers in the event of war and new conscription proposals. The opposition which boycotted the parliament, of whom Gyula Justh, leader of the group which had split from the Independence Party in 1909, and Count Mihály Károlyi enjoyed the greatest esteem, used the new electoral reform bill submitted by the government at the end of 1912 to stir the population to action again. The new legislation contained only cosmetic changes and made no real concessions. When a corruption scandal resulted in Lukács' resignation, Tisza, who had won such considerable respect in Vienna as a result of his energetic stand against the opposition was entrusted by the Emperor with the formation of a new government for a second time on 10 June 1913, despite the serious objections of the heir apparent, Archduke Francis Ferdinand. Tisza's main objective was to conciliate his opponents by making limited concessions. By this means he hoped to a great extent to win over not only the Catholic People's Party but the nationalist Old Conservative faction of magnates around Apponyi and protestant church leaders as much as the Catholic clergy, big liberal capitalists and the antisemitic gentry. The continued pursuit of a narrow-minded and militant nationalities policy ensured that his attempts to win over the national minorities remained unsuccessful and the urban and rural proletariat, increasingly self-confident and convinced of its political importance, also refused to be drawn into his nationalist and reactionary united front.

The organisation and struggles of the labour movement

Despite the gradual progress of industrialisation the Hungarian labour movement largely stagnated in the 1880s. Although the absence of social welfare rights, the long hours demanded of employees and the denial of legal rights for the workers had produced unrest, this had been easily crushed. Thus a Congress of the relatively small General Workers' Party of Hungary met in 1889 to discuss the causes of their ineffectiveness to date and decided upon a programme of reorganisation which, with the active help of fellow Austrian Socialists, led, after over a year's preparations, to the founding of the Hungarian Social Democratic Party (*Magyarországi Szociáldemokrata Párt*) on 7–8 December 1890. Modelling its own programme on the Hainfeld programme of the Austrian Social Democratic Party, the new workers' party announced in its 'declaration of principle' its affiliation to the Second International and its aims of liberating the working class, abolishing private property and transferring the means of production to public ownership. The party also aimed at the complete democratisation of political life through the introduction of universal suffrage and the extension of basic bourgeois-democratic rights to the proletariat, demanding also a solution to Hungary's pressing social problems and a reform of work safety regulations. Following the first big demonstration of 60,000 workers on 1 May 1890, the years that followed saw the growth of trade unions and modern workers' associations throughout the entire country. The unscrupulous deployment of the army, gendarmerie and police to combat unrest and workers' strikes, the inadequate labour protection laws and a labour surplus helped produce a situation in which, in 1912 for example, the Social Democratic Party could claim only about 4,000 workers in Budapest, whereas almost 32,000 employees belonged to Social Democratic trade unions. The party's tendency to undergo splits and defections paralysed the young party for two years. The party congress of 1894, which was chaired by Ignác Silberberg and intended to unite the party failed to overcome the problem. The SDP's professed aim of abolishing private landed property won little support from the small and dwarf-holding peasantry or workers who had originally belonged to the peasant class. They were much more interested in dividing up the great estates among the peasants. When, in the summer of 1897, strikes broke out among seasonal workers employed to gather in the harvest and the more moderate wing of the party refused to support the demands of the day-labourers, the disagreements which had been smouldering since 1895 on which policy to adopt towards rural problems, broke out anew and caused the former rural labourer, István Várkonyi, to found the Independent Socialist Party of Hungary (*Magyarországi Független Szocialista Párt*) in Cegléd.

Peasant Socialist ideas had already appealed earlier to the oppressed rural day-labourers, who faced a constant struggle for survival. Their discontent had been expressed in the spring of 1891 in the Tisza and Maros basin when they had demanded higher wages and improved working conditions. Várkonyi's call to nationalise landed property of more than 50 hectares and divide it up into small-holdings of 3 hectares fulfilled the expectations of the poor peasantry and rural proletariat. The sharp rise in the membership of the new party and the land reform movement started in 1898 made the government resort to coercive measures. Várkonyi was arrested and the Social Democratic Party banned from holding congresses. The government's measures of parcelling out auctioned estates, resettling uncultivated land and guaranteeing loans to farmers were inadequate to ameliorate the distress effectively or create social and political calm. The passage of the so-called 'Slave Law' (Law II of 1898) which laid down the duties of day-labourers, also allowed draconian measures to be taken against strikers and the gendarmerie to be used against workers withholding their labour or changing their place of employment. But this measure failed to suppress the widespread discontent and the workers' readiness to organise and cooperate in their fight against social injustice, although the hard struggle of the workers and the rural poor was indeed curtailed by the state's increasing use of coercion.

While conflicts between Hungary and Vienna increased and the internal power struggles within the government party and the opposition, and between the Magyars and the national minorities, became more acute, social tensions spread to the bourgeoisie, since those sections of the gentry, forced into earning a living, had to defend their superior economic, social and cultural position against the newly advancing and only recently assimilated urban bour-geoisie. The potential for conflict also increased among the lower classes in the population. An economic recession, which caused problems particularly in mining, heavy industry and the construction industry, resulted in demonstrations by the unemployed, strikes and struggles for higher wages after 1901. By 1903 more than 40,000 workers were organised into twelve branch unions. The Reorganised Social Democratic Party (*Újjászervezett Szociáldemokrata Párt*), founded in 1900 by the journalist, Vilmos Mezöfi, defended the special interests of the rural workers and poorer peasants, while the Social Democratic Party, in its new programme of April 1903, written with the assistance of Karl Kautsky and borrowing from the 1891 Erfurt programme of the German Social Democrats, continued to pay little attention to rural problems, but on the other hand demanded all the more determinedly the guarantee of 'self-government' and 'equality' for the national minorities and the introduction of universal suffrage. When István Tisza's government broke up the first national railway strike in April 1904, which paralysed traffic across the entire country for a week, by using military units which applied relentless force, calm was apparently restored but the situation remained tense. In the wake of the revolutionary events in Russia new unrest and strikes in the pursuit of political and social demands flared up throughout the country in the spring of 1905. The strike by almost 30,000 metal workers in Budapest between the end of May and the beginning of July won considerable attention and was accompanied by a rising of 25,000 rural labourers and day-labourers demanding higher wages, improved conditions of work and more humane treatment. Only the extensive use of the military and the gendarmerie, a massive wave of arrests and the compulsory conscription of many strikers restored temporary calm to the situation. The Fejérváry government's surprising offer to the Social Democratic Party, to introduce electoral reform proposals in return for the support of organised labour did not meet, however, with the unanimous agreement of the SDP's 1905 party congress. Despite this, the campaign for universal suffrage developed into a mass movement, as part of which an estimated 100,000 demonstrators besieged the parliament building on 15 September. The increasingly frequent bloody clashes with the military, the imposition of a state of siege in numerous counties and the understanding reached in April 1906 between the monarch and the internal Hungarian opposition, now united in the Coalition, discredited the movement for electoral reform. The proposed law to introduce universal, equal, direct and secret suffrage was withdrawn by the Crown out of consideration for the traditional ruling élites, who were again ready to cooperate more closely with Vienna and whose power base would have certainly been reduced had democratic elections taken place.

Even after this disappointment, the rural proletariat, whose interests were now represented by the new Agrarian Workers' Association founded at the beginning of 1906, followed the urban workers in refusing to resign itself to the situation. The social policy measures announced by Wekerle's second government, such as the extension of a state-supervised and centrally administered sickness fund and the introduction of compulsory accident insurance helped reduce tensions at a time when the economy was entering a boom period. Railway workers, who now had to prove they could speak Hungarian, had to pay for an improvement in their wages by renouncing the right to strike and forgoing membership of Socialist organisations. The so-called 'whipping bench law', which served the interest of landowners gave rural workers a greater degree of legal security and protection against exploitation, but also sanctioned the use of disciplinary measures, including corporal punishment, by the landowner with the help of the gendarmerie. Selective state subsidies helped large-scale industry, especially the textiles industry, and led to the creation of new jobs. High agricultural tariffs resulted in a considerable level of mechanisation and the introduction of intensive cultivation methods in agriculture, although this did not lead to an improvement in social and political injustice.

The landowning peasantry had also created political organisations to represent its interests. The starting point here was the Count Sándor Károlyi's Landlords' Federation and the credit and consumer cooperatives which it established. Employing an anti-capitalist and barely concealed antisemitic and anti-Socialist propaganda, this organisation's objectives were cheap loans and state subsidies for farmers in debt and, most of all, even higher protective tariffs. The Independent Socialist Peasants' Party of Hungary (*Magyarországi Független Szocialista Parasztszövetség*), founded by wealthy peasants and the parliamentary deputy, András Áchim, on 25 March 1906, was the first genuinely political organisation to combine the call for universal suffrage with the demands for land reform, progressive taxation, an autonomous Hungarian customs area and welfare protection for agricultural labourers and smallholders. Its campaign, supported by The Peasant Journal (*Paraszt Ùsjág*), to reduce the size of holdings to at most 1,000 *hold* (= 575 hectares), made Áchim numerous enemies. Following his murder by the sons of a landowner in May 1911 his party rapidly disintegrated.

More successful in the long term was the attempt by the wealthy peasant, István Nagyatádi Szabó (i.e. Szabó from Nagyatád), who led the split from the Independence Party on 21 November 1909 which resulted in the founding of the Independence and '48ers Landlords' Party (*48-as és Függetlenségi Országos Gazdapárt*). The new party's democratic programme demanded universal suffrage and the abolition of inherited feudal privileges. This moderate peasant opposition, whose short name was the Smallholders' Party rose to national political significance only after 1918–19.

The Social Democratic Party, however, viewed peasant attempts to organise politically and demands for land reform as a regressive tendency. It also could not clearly decide whether it should support Hungarian demands for a nation state or a federal structure for the Monarchy or autonomy for Hungary's national minorities. Thus it, too, failed to become a rallying point for a united opposition movement and could not prevent regular defections by members unhappy with parts of its programme. An example of this was the group led by Ervin Szabó and Gyula Alpári which broke away in April 1910. The SDP received a certain amount of ideological support from bourgeois radicals gathered around Oszkár Jászi, the editor of the sociological periodical, *Huszadik Század* (Twentieth Century), mainly in Budapest. Its members aimed their scholarly criticism at abuses in public life, which they hoped could be overcome by a greater measure of political democracy, the abolition of the vast landed estates and the granting of extensive linguistic and cultural autonomy to the national minorities. Their unsparing analysis of Hungary's social and political conditions was taken up by the Galileo Circle, an organisation of university students, and the Hungarian Society of Free Thinkers, which admittedly had only limited contact with the organised labour movement and none at all with the peasantry or the national minorities. Only six weeks before the outbreak of war on 6 June 1914, Oszkár Jászi united these groups in the Bourgeois-Radical National Party (*Országos Polgári Radikális Párt*). Their demands focussed on the extension of political freedoms, especially a more democratic franchise, administration and legal system, together with the implementation of a radical land reform, the creation of an autonomous customs area and state control of education. From the middle of 1915 the new party supported the pacifist movement and called for the founding of a federation of states for the whole of Europe, a kind of forerunner of the League of Nations, aimed at maintaining peace.

The demonstrations organised by the Social Democrats, in which, for example on 10 October 1907, 200,000 participants again protested against the withholding of universal suffrage and in 1908 expressed their displeasure at the annexation of Bosnia and Herzegovina, had little effect on the direction taken in social policy by the rapid succession of coalition governments. On 23 May 1912 the political disagreements reached their culmination once more during another 'Bloody Thursday' when again the advocacy of electoral reform and opposition to a proposed new defence bill led to street fighting. The electoral reform, eventually passed in 1913 (Law XIV of 1913) would have increased the number of registered electors on the basis of the tax census and schooling qualifications and to some extent allowed secret ballots – but the Hungarian ruling élites were still a long way from recognising universal and secret suffrage. Even after a later electoral law (Law XVII of 1918) which was never in fact implemented, the workers, small peasants and rural poor were still excluded de facto from political participation. The growing crises in the Balkans and the increasingly discernible threat of war appeared to justify the view, which was widely held by the ruling classes, that in view of the unrest that it might cause, it was preferable to delay the introduction of greater democracy and social and political reforms for the time being.

Nationalities policy and foreign policy

As a direct result of the intensification of the government's magyarisation policy, the growing pressure to assimilate and the increasing intolerance in national affairs during the 1890s, Hungary's national minorities felt obliged to cooperate more closely and try to win the support of both the Emperor and their co-nationals living outside the Monarchy's borders. Most of their leaders subscribed to the ideal of a 'Greater Austria' aimed at abolishing Hungary's special status within the Monarchy and transforming the Dual Monarchy into a federation of free peoples or restructuring it as a Triple Monarchy. The Magyars viewed the supporters of a 'Greater Austria' and its advocate, the heir apparent, Archduke Francis Ferdinand, as the most dangerous enemies of a Hungarian nation state. Ignoring the many criticisms and admonitions provoked by their narrow-minded nationalities policy they were generally agreed, whatever their differences, to resist stubbornly any limitation of their special status. The most insoluble problem appeared to be that posed by the South Slavs, since this involved both internal and external political problems affecting the domestic affairs of both halves of the Empire, as well as 'common affairs', in an inextricably linked complex of issues excessively difficult to disentangle.

However, it was in Transylvania that unrest first appeared. The Rumanian National Committee had listed its grievances concerning national and economic discrimination in a Memorandum sent to the Emperor in 1892. When Francis Joseph I rejected the complaints as constitutionally improper, the Memorandum was published abroad in several languages and the government used this action as a pretext to have its authors sentenced to several years' imprisonment in the infamous 'Memorandum trial' in Koloszsvár (Cluj), The Rumanian National Party was banned and the National Committee dissolved in 1895. Since the activities of the political and cultural organisations of the other national minorities were also curtailed, their representatives adopted a common programme at a congress in August 1895, which demanded national autonomy within Hungary. The then prime minister, Bánffy, rejected the demand as 'federalistic hotchpotch'. Despite warnings from those who pleaded for reconciliation and a more realistic approach, he embarked upon a programme of magyarisation, carried out mainly through cultural associations and promoted by the impressive but highly chauvinistic Millenium Celebrations of 1896. The vociferous agitation of the nationalities opposition, together with inadequate employment and earning opportunities, especially in those parts of the country inhabited by minorities, made many Hungarians choose the more convenient option of assimilation. Many more people, however, sought to escape from the social misery and harassment by emigrating overseas.

The South Slav problem became the focus of interest after the change of ruling dynasty in Serbia in 1903 when the pro-Austrian Obrenović family was ousted by a military coup. The increasingly voiced demand for a union of the South Slav peoples of the Balkans under Serbian leadership and the strong appeal this programme had for the Croats and Serbs within Hungary gave the government in Budapest cause for concern, especially since national passions had already been considerably aroused by Hungary's internal political conflicts. In 1903, Russia had reaffirmed its role as guarantor of the status quo in the Balkans but following its defeat in the Far East against Japan, was again showing a much greater interest in the fate of its Slav cousins. Russia attempted to forge an alliance with Britain and France, which was bound to restrict the Dual Monarchy's good relations with Great Britain. Since Italy also was trying to detach itself from the Triple Alliance, the Habsburg Monarchy had to rely increasingly on its alliance of friendship with the German Empire. Although this alliance was not particularly popular in Hungary, the German Emperor, William II, pledged his fraternal loyalty ('*Nibelungentreue*') on several occasions. However, the surge of nationalist feeling among Austria's Slavs made it appear doubtful whether the decaying multi-national Habsburg Empire with all its social and political conflicts could prove at all determined enough or capable of defending itself.

After the rifts between Vienna and Budapest had been temporarily repaired in the spring of 1906, a tariff war broke out against Serbia in the following summer. The 'pig-war', as it became known, not only led to the banning of Serbian pig imports into the Monarchy, which had been causing problems for the large-scale agrarians; economic pressure was to be applied in order to force Serbia back to its earlier position of dependence on Austria-Hungary. When this policy failed to achieve its objective, the military leadership suggested a preventive war against Serbia. On account of the incalculable risks involved and the fact that territorial expansion in the Balkans would endanger the dualist system, this idea found no advocates in Hungary. The half-way solution, which was eventually agreed upon after the success of the Young Turks' revolution, i.e. the annexation of Bosnia and Herzegovina, conjured up the threat of war which lasted until March 1909 and caused Russia to step up its Balkans ambitions. Despite the Hungarian government's many reservations against annexation and worries about resulting foreign policy complications, it remained committed to pursuing a hard, imprudent policy toward the minorities.

The Ápponyi government's Education Law of 1907, which further restricted the use of native languages in instruction in the lower classes of the national minorities' few remaining elementary schools was especially significant in sparking off protests. By sentencing political activists from the national minorities on charges of 'incitement' or illegal canvassing, the Magyar authorities merely created martyrs and succeeded in tarnishing the image of the Monarchy abroad because of the widespread storm of protest against the oppression of Hungary's non-Magyar population. When, for example, the Slovak village priest, Andrej Hlinka, sentenced to two years' imprisonment in 1907, wished to consecrate a new church in his local parish of Černová, despite his suspension from office, the gendarmerie's intervention resulted in the loss of fifteen lives. This 'massacre' prompted the British historian, Seton-Watson, to criticise Hungary's nationalities policy in a widely-read book. While the few nationally conscious Slovaks, influenced by Tomaš Masaryk and grouped around the periodical *Hlas* (the Voice) (Vavro Šrobár, Milan Hodža *et al.*), hoped for support from their culturally, socially and economically more advanced Czech neighbours, some leaders of the Rumanian minority, such as Aurel Vlad and Octavian Goga, began to support the Kingdom of Rumania's unification efforts. The propaganda for South Slav unification increasingly gained support from the Croats, especially when the governor, Banus Eduard Cuvaj, appointed political commissar by the government, suspended the Croatian constitution during 1912 and 1913 in order to defeat the policy of blocking magyarisation measures in the administration, state enterprises and schools. Even when the heir apparent, Archduke Francis Ferdinand, promised the nationalities certain federative concessions and the abolition of Hungary's special status within the Empire on assuming the throne, most of the minorities' politicians, who now advocated the ideal of separate nation states, were no longer prepared to give their unreserved support to a programme aimed at restoring the centralist unity of the Empire.

The Balkan Wars of 1912–13 highlighted the fact that the efforts of the Balkan Slavs to carve up Turkey's European territories among themselves also affected the interests of the Great Powers. The question of the Straits, forced by Russia, Serbian expansion in the Second Balkan War, which was noted with concern in Austria-Hungary, and the increasingly popular Rumanian demand for union with Transylvania, indicated the new areas of conflict which would inevitably conjure up threats to Hungary maintaining its territorial possessions intact. The sense of relief and hope that this danger was once more averted after the signing of the Peace of Bucharest (10 August 1913) did not last long. The belief that a certain weariness had entered into the conflict of the national minorities as a result of the government's consistently oppressive measures also proved deceptive. While the vast majority of non-Hungarians remained steadfastly loyal to the dynasty and were also prepared to take up arms in defence of Hungary and the Monarchy, they were no longer prepared to accept national, political, economic, social and cultural discrimination. In view of the spread of ambitious radical nationalism to Hungary's neighbours and Russian-backed neo-Slavism, the unsolved nationalities problem contained more explosive power for Hungary and the Monarchy than all the other political and social contradictions which beset the Habsburg patrimony.

THE FIRST WORLD WAR AND THE COLLAPSE OF THE HABSBURG EMPIRE

On 28 June 1914, the heir apparent to the throne of Austria, Archduke Francis Ferdinand, and his consort, the Countess Sophie

Chotek, were assassinated in the Bosnian capital of Sarajevo by the Serbian student, Gavrilo Princip, a member of the pan-Slav 'Black Hand Society'. The event led almost inevitably to the outbreak of the First World War which imposed the greatest sacrifices on Hungary and led to the collapse of the Austro-Hungarian Monarchy. The Austro-Hungarian plan for a military showdown with Serbia to be followed by Balkan expansion, often considered since 1906, was much more seriously discussed from the summer of 1913 onwards, Vienna relying on its German ally and hoping to persuade Bulgaria and Rumania to join its side. However, in the crisis of early June 1914 the Hungarian prime minister, Count István Tisza, expressed reservations. Realising the danger of an escalation of the conflict and the uncertainty of the relative strengths of the two sides which would be involved, he sought to avoid even a localised Balkan War. However, on 12 July 1914, he bowed to the decision to attack and agreed to the ultimatum to the government in Belgrade on condition that the Monarchy would not annex a defeated Serbia.

When, in the early days of August 1914, the planned punitive military action against Serbia escalated into a world war there was an outpouring of national passions in Hungary as elsewhere. The possibility of evening the score with 'Russian barbarism' for the disgrace of 1849 caused an outburst of enthusiasm, even from the Social Democratic Party. The political parties, the churches and the people were firmly united. Despite its many different national groups, languages, religions and cultures, the common army generally displayed a high level of morale and a remarkable ability to resist the enemy. The efforts of the national minorities to participate in public affairs and gain a share of political power receded. Amongst them propaganda in favour of secession into separate nation-states met with little response and was taken up only by emigrants living in the Allied countries or by small groups of radical nationalists living in exile. Even the failure to achieve a rapid victory against Serbia and the major defensive battles on the Galician front which proved so costly in human life could not dampen the Hungarian population's enthusiasm for war and willingness to make sacrifices. The surrender of the fortress at Przemyśl on 23 March 1915 and the heavy fighting for the Carpathian passes soon placed Hungarian territory under direct threat. Relief came only with the Central Powers' successful joint breakthrough in the Gorlice and Tarnow areas. Italy's entry into the war on the side of the Entente on 23 May 1915 was seen as a betrayal of its former allies and led to an increased willingness to fight the war not only on the part of the Germans and Magyars, but the Croats and Slovenes, who inevitably felt threatened by Italian designs on the eastern Adriatic. The number of desertions from the army remained few, although after 1915, Czech and, for a time in 1916, Ruthenian units, influenced by enemy propaganda, laid down their arms without putting up any significant resistance. The unfortunate tone of Germany's propaganda, that the world war was a 'decisive struggle between Germandom and Slavdom', together with an outbreak of spy fever, increasingly poisoned the civilian population's relationship with the military authorities in the Monarchy's Slav-populated districts.

After Turkey and Bulgaria joined the Central Powers Serbia was successfully occupied in the autumn of 1915 and Montenegro captured early in 1916. When, on 27 August 1916, Rumania felt that conditions were favourable for its troops to invade Transylvania the Central Powers were able to repulse the enemy quickly and occupy almost the entire country. But the temporarily rejected Rumanian demand for the annexation of Transylvania, the campaign for an independent Czecho-Slovakian republic, disseminated among the western Allies especially by Professor Tomáš Garrigue Masaryk, the leader of the small Czech Realist Party, and his highly gifted colleague Edvard Beneš, and the campaign led by the South Slav politicians, Trumbič and Supilo, to create a united kingdom of Serbs, Croats and Slovenes, was bound to threaten Hungary's territorial integrity in the event of an Allied victory. The distress experienced by the hard-hit civilian population in the third year of the war as a result of currency depreciation and food shortages, together with the growing realisation of the war's futility, gave rise to growing discontent and caused the cooperation born of patriotic unity to fall apart. Following the Social Democratic Party's lead, other opposition groups also expressed doubts in the military leadership, questioned the government's attempts to justify the high cost in human life and complained of the disruption to Hungary's economic life. On 9 July 1916, a new breakaway Independence Party came into existence, led by Count Mihály Károlyi, which demanded basic internal political reforms and a peace without annexations.

On 21 November 1916, the 86-year-old Emperor Francis Joseph died. Public life lost a personality who had ruled for 68 years, had been an important focus of emotional loyalty for the Monarchy's various nations and had been identified with the multi-national state. His successor Charles I (King Charles IV of Hungary) tried to accommodate the desire for peace among the Monarchy's peoples by instigating fresh initiatives and replacing unpopular politicians in order to bring about a change of direction in internal politics. The principle of 'peace without victory', proclaimed by America's President Wilson in January 1917, and the outbreak of revolution in Petrograd in March 1917 showed clearly that war-weariness and the desire for peace had spread among all the belligerent nations. The Emperor Charles' peace initiatives of 1917 were not only intended to save the Monarchy from collapse as a result of military defeat, but to help liberate Austria-Hungary from the oppressive dominance of its ally, Germany. Since the Russian army was in the process of complete dissolution, a consolidation of the military situation on the Eastern Front at least proved possible in the summer of 1917. The Brest-Litovsk peace negotiations which began in December following the success of the Bolsheviks in the October Revolution (7 November 1917), and which were concluded as a result of German military pressure on 3 March 1918, brought no essential relief to Hungary. Since the many prisoners of war who subsequently returned from Russia were, however, in many cases infected by revolutionary ideas, their notions of an inevitable radical transformation of the state and society quickly combined with the dissatisfaction of a population worn down by hunger to produce a potentially dangerous revolutionary situation. True, the military's takeover of the most important sectors of the economy had tried to stem these currents, but the internal political situation had already grown more tense during the course of 1917.

After large numbers of Hungarian workers demonstrated on 1 May 1917 and trade union membership exceeded 200,000 for the first time, the Emperor Charles felt obliged to dismiss the premier, Count István Tisza, who stubbornly held to the established system, on 5 June. After an interlude lasting only until the 18 August, during which Count Moric Esterházy headed the government, the Emperor entrusted the experienced Sándor Wekerle for a third time with the formation of a government. An immediate electoral reform law did little to dampen the revolutionary atmosphere, which expressed itself in mass labour demonstrations and the formation of new left-wing groups like the Revolutionary Socialists. The Vienna munition workers' strike, which broke out in mid-January 1918, also spilled over into Hungary. It took three days to force the half a million or more participants back to work and the government tried to restore order by the use of repressive measures, a ban on left-wing publications and associations, the creation of special armed squads to maintain internal order and the arrest of the 'ringleaders'. Following the lead given by the sailors of the fleet at anchor in Cattaro,

Hungarian army units also mutinied on 20 May 1918 in Pécs and were disarmed only after heavy fighting. A wave of strikes subsequently paralysed production with greater frequency and for longer periods of time. The deployment of the army on 20 June 1918 led to a general strike, lasting nine days, which was finally ended, not by the government's declaration of martial law, but by the mediation of the Social Democratic Party.

Now the discontent also spread to the national minorities which had remained loyal and supportive of the state up to the end of 1917. The slogan of their political representatives in exile, '*détruisez l'Autriche-Hongrie!*', won increasing support at home. The Croats were the first to demand constitutional autonomy for the South Slavs. The representatives of the other nationalities demanded at first that the Monarchy be restructured on a federal basis. President Wilson's Fourteen Points, which cautiously aimed at granting the peoples of Austria-Hungary at least 'autonomous development', met with enthusiastic approval, especially after the treaty signed in May 1918 in Spa between William II and Charles I had revealed the threat of a Central European Customs Union (*Mitteleuropa*) dominated by the German Empire. Also, the subsequent increasing willingness of the Entente Powers to give their active support to the political ideals of the nationalities' politicians encouraged hopes on the home front that the increasingly obvious military defeat of the Central Powers would eventually lead to the separate nationalities' gaining their independence and autonomous government. New nation states on the western model appeared to be a better guarantee of political stability in eastern Central Europe than the rotten Habsburg Empire which had become so subservient to German imperialism. The breakthrough was achieved in the summer of 1918 with the Allies' decision to recognise the Czechoslovak National Council in Paris as a belligerent ally. The territorial aspirations of the South Slav and Rumanian National Committees were also approved, a move which sealed the fate of not only the Habsburg Monarchy but Hungary as well.

All that remained for the Emperor Charles and the governments of Austria and Hungary to do in the autumn of 1918 was to end the war and dissolve the existing state. The revolutionary overthrow of the Dual Monarchy by the proletariat was successfully prevented – not least by its disintegration into western-style democratic nation states. When Bulgaria's surrender in September 1918 signalled the impending military defeat, the Emperor Charles tried to bring about an immediate cessation of hostilities. In his Peoples' Manifesto of 16

October 1918 he did not, however, yet infringe upon the territorial integrity of the 'territories of the Holy Crown of Hungary'. On the same day the Hungarian government for its part proposed transforming the Dual Monarchy into a purely personal union, but continued to resist the demands of the nationalities, the social and political demands of the population and the need for outright democratisation which was being demanded mainly by the forces gathered around Count Károlyi. In the belated realisation that the war was lost Wekerle tendered his government's resignation on 23 October 1918. The Hungarian National Council, formed under Károlyi's leadership on 25 October, in which his own party, the Social Democrats, and the radicals participated, was ready to assume political responsibility on the basis of his twelve-point programme, largely conceived by Oszkár Jászi. Expecting that the principles set out in Wilson's Fourteen Points would not only not endanger 'Hungary's territorial integrity' but 'place it on the safest foundation' the National Council was prepared to respect the right of self-determination for 'the Kingdom of Hungary's nationalities'. Its other aims were the achievement of independence from Austria, the immediate conclusion of a separate peace and the introduction of universal suffrage and a land reform.

There was now no preventing the collapse of the Dual Monarchy and the break-up of Hungary at this late stage. On 27 October, the Rumanians in the Bukovina announced their secession from the Austro-Hungarian Monarchy to be followed by the Czechs on 28 October, the Croats on 29 October, and the Slovaks and Galician Ukrainians on 30 October. Meanwhile in Budapest, more and more people demonstrated for Count Mihály Károlyi's appointment as prime minister and for his programme to be implemented. When, on the 28 October, the police fired on demonstrators at the Chain Bridge, their brutal action signalled the start of the bourgeois-democratic 'Chrysanthemum revolution'. Urged on by the old ruling élite, King Charles IV appointed Count János Hadik prime minister and Count Andrássy Jnr common foreign minister, but this short-lived government no longer had an effective power base since the soldiers were also expressing their solidarity with the the National Council's demands. During the night of 31 October Territorial Army (*Honvéd*) units which had aready sworn allegiance to the National Council occupied public buildings, the post office, the telephone and telegraph exchanges and the railway stations. In view of the general revolutionary mood and the realities of power Hadik's government resigned. On 31 October 1918, the King entrusted Károlyi with the formation of a new government which included members of the new prime minister's Independence and '48er Party, bourgeois-radicals and Social Democrats who still swore an oath of allegiance to Charles IV. The government announced as its main priorities the proclamation of independence of the 'territories of the Holy Crown of St Stephen', the introduction of equal and secret suffrage, constitutionally guaranteed democratic rights, social welfare measures and the implementation of the long overdue land reform. Appeals to maintain law and order, surrender weapons and stop the looting and spontaneous occupation of the great estates and factories were accompanied by the creation of citizen militias. Democratisation was to be implemented in an evolutionary manner within the framework of existing laws. The murder by soldiers of Count István Tisza, seen as an advocate of the war and one of the politicians who bore the main guilt for Hungary's confused situation, underlined the need for this approach.

The signing of the armistice in Padua on 3 November 1918 signified the end of the First World War for Austria-Hungary. Since, however, the allied Balkan armies of the western Allies took no notice of this agreement, their advance placed Hungary in an extremely difficult situation. After the Emperor Charles I had renounced taking 'any part in the affairs of government' on 11 November and the Republic of Austria had been proclaimed on the following day, the Károlyi government also released itself from its oath of allegiance to the Crown and proclaimed Hungary a republic on 16 November 1918, thus finally sealing the collapse of the Habsburg Empire. However much the military defeat of the Central Powers in the First World War had contributed to this development, the break-up of the Monarchy resulted primarily from a failure to act in the political, economic, social and cultural spheres, together with an unwillingness to implement long-overdue democratic social reforms and allow the unrestricted development of its nationalities. The traditional Magyar ruling élites, the magnates, landowning nobility, liberal haute bourgeoisie and upper clergy, all shared some of the responsibility for this development as a result of the policies pursued since 1867. They had failed to recognise the full importance of socio-economic problems and nationality aspirations which had emerged during the period and had hence found no satisfactory solution of these problems. Their policies, shaped by an increasingly narrow-minded national chauvinism, had not only cheated the country's non-Magyar peoples, but undermined the relationship of trust between the two main nations which upheld the Habsburg

Monarchy. The negligence and mistakes of the reign of Francis Joseph, which was soon to assume an almost mystic significance, were to have a decisive and painful influence on Hungary's future history as an independent state.

CHAPTER THREE
Hungary Between The Wars

THE STRUGGLE FOR INTERNAL POLITICAL STABILITY AND TERRITORIAL INTEGRITY, 1918–20

From Károlyi's Bourgeois-Democratic Revolution to Kun's Soviet Republic

The Károlyi government's last-minute attempt to persuade the Entente Powers to conclude a separate peace with an independent Hungary and make generous concessions to persuade the non-Magyar peoples to remain within Hungary failed during the first days of November 1918. Despite the agreement of the Allies to leave a final settlement of the new east central European frontiers until after the Peace Conference to be held in Paris the Czechs, Slovaks, Ruthenes, Rumanians, Croats, Serbs and Slovenes now seized those parts of Hungary to which they laid claim with the help of the French military. Ignoring the armistice signed by the commander of the French Balkan army, Franchet D'Esperey, and the Károlyi government in Belgrade on 7 November 1918, the Rumanian National Council in Arad notified the Hungarian authorities on 10 November of the takeover of the administration in twenty-three counties and parts of three other counties. Rumanian troops advanced into Transylvania whose annexation was unilaterally proclaimed by the Bucharest government on 11 January 1919. The Serbs had already taken over the administration of the Bácska, the Baranya and the western Banat on 24 November 1918, presenting the Hungarians with a well-nigh irreversible *fait accompli*. Czech troops advanced into Slovakia, or 'Upper Hungary' as it was previously called, and were poised to occupy the districts of Ung, Ugosca, Bereg and Máramaros with their Ruthenian population, to which the Rumanians also laid claim. On 3 and 23 December 1918, the Allied Supreme Command agreed to the takeover of the civilian administration by the Czech authorities. On 29 October, the diet of the Kingdom of Croatia and Slavonia had announced an end to its ties with Hungary and the Habsburg monarchy and joined Serbia. In view of the realities of the situation the Hungarians were unable to take any effective measures to prevent the break-up of their country.

This dismemberment of the Monarchy, which the Hungarians were powerless to resist, caused a growing sense of bitterness among the Hungarian population and increasingly undermined the prime minister's prestige. Károlyi was regarded as relatively pro-Entente and a politician who enjoyed good relations with western statesmen. As early as 1914 in the USA and again in neutral Switzerland in the autumn of 1917 he had made a case for his belief in the need for an evolutionary change in Hungary's socio-economic and political conditions. The tough actions taken by the emerging nation states, tolerated, though not always approved of by the allied governments, showed that, contrary to expectations, Hungary could not hope for more considerate treatment. The Károlyi government was particularly disappointed by the Entente Powers' growing readiness to depart from the principles set out in Wilson's Fourteen Points, which those groups willing to introduce reforms had been in the end prepared to use as a basis for the necessary restructuring of an independent Hungary. The argument that Hungary's premier, Istvan Tisza, like the Hungarian population in general, had opposed the unleashing of the First World War in the summer of 1914 failed to persuade the Allies to grant more favourable peace terms.

With the growing willingness of the Allied governments to allow a ring of territorially well-endowed successor states to emerge, confining Hungary to a relatively narrow area of Magyar settlement, the progressive idea of the new minister for nationalities, Oszkár Jászi, aimed at making Hungary a kind of 'eastern Switzerland', became untenable. As well as analysing and condemning former policies towards the nationalities, Jászi proposed attempting a new form of coexistence between the nations in the Danube Basin on the basis of extensive political and cultural autonomy. However, during the course of the discussions with Slovak and Rumanian representatives it soon became clear that even the most generous concessions could not overcome their desire to join their conationals in the new or already existing nation states which had been greatly enlarged by the acquisition of new territories. The increasingly obvious impossibility of breaking out of Hungary's foreign policy isolation and preventing the country's territorial disintegration prior to the terms of the Paris Peace Conference being made known also increasingly limited Károlyi's room for manoeuvre in domestic politics.

The first new government measures were infused with a progressive spirit and met with broad approval. A new electoral law extended the franchise to all men and the majority of women over 21 who had been Hungarian citizens for a period of at least six years. Future elections were to be conducted by secret ballot. In a similar liberal and generous spirit the government guaranteed by law freedom of the press, assembly and speech. The Ruthenian population was granted autonomy and preparations made to introduce a land reform. The workers won the acceptance of their demand for an eight-hour working day, first raised by them a decade previously, although there was still insufficient work available and food shortages. The effects of the Allied blockade, the disruption to Hungary's close economic ties with Austria, together with the military occupation of major territories in the north, south and east of the country, all contributed to a general situation which brought factory production to a standstill. Shortages of raw materials and fuel, together with the disruption to freight traffic, produced a maximum of economic chaos. The unemployment figures rose daily. Returning prisoners of war and demobilised soldiers swelled the flood of refugees from the occupied territories who were often homeless and incapable of making ends meet. The country's finances had been completely ruined by the war and could not be used to alleviate the widespread distress. Appeals for voluntary donations showed people's willingess to help, but donations of clothes and money were inadequate to provide effective long-term relief. A feeling of growing bitterness spread as people faced basic food shortages in the towns, since they suspected landowners and wealthy peasants of deliberately holding back deliveries to the starving towns. The refusal of many landowners to cultivate their fields in view of the impending land reform and the growing impatience of the rural proletariat, which saw no sign of the promised redistribution of cultivable land, heightened tensions and created an explosive atmosphere.

Because its proposals for a democratic reform of society were increasingly criticised and condemned by the political Right as too radical and partisan, the Károlyi government felt obliged to take steps against developments assuming a more radical direction. The minister of defence, Bartha, who had been behind the setting up of special armed units to defend the government and the property of the state, was forced to resign from his post as a result of public pressure. But the minister of the interior, Count Tivadar Batthyány, also tendered his resignation on the grounds that the measures taken against the threats from the Left were too lax. Government officials were very hesitant about pushing through laws which ran counter to their own political beliefs. Members of the army officer corps founded secret organisations committed to the defence of the fatherland which Gyula Gömbös, a general staff captain and future prime minister, tried to unite in the Hungarian Militia Association.

The political Left was also in the process of organising itself. A small nucleus of political activists had been formed from among the half a million or so Hungarian soldiers who had ended up in Russian captivity and had in many cases been influenced by Marxist-Leninist ideology. After their release from captivity they had spread the message of Socialist revolution and had made their mark as organisers and speakers at mass demonstrations both before and after the revolution of 1918. Some, like Béla Kun, had also taken an active part in the Russian revolution and had fought in the ranks of the Red Guard. On his return to Budapest Kun, who derived great authority as one of Lenin's former colleagues, had immediately made contact with the Social Democratic Party's left wing and the Revolutionary Socialists. The latter had played a major part in the preparation and execution of the 'Chrysanthemum revolution', but were dissatisfied with the official line of their parties who were content with a bourgeois-democratic revolution. The Soldiers' and Workers' Councils which had appeared spontaneously in the capital, but also in the provinces, had not grown as dynamically as had been hoped. It was felt that it would be impossible to implement a political programme or gain a say in government without first developing a strict party organisation. On 24 November 1918, therefore, the Communist Party of Hungary (*Kommunisták Magyarországi Pártja*) was founded and soon published its own newspaper the *Vörös Újság* (Red News).

The new party, which at first concentrated its activities on the big factories in Budapest and on the soldiers garrisoned in the capital, soon tried to whip up support for its programme in the provinces too. Its aims were varied. Its propaganda concentrated on crushing the 'counter-revolution', exposing the betrayal perpetrated by the 'right-wing' leaders of the Social Democratic Party and creating a system of

Soviets on the Bolshevik model. It also put forward concrete demands for a 'complete break with the remnants of feudalism', an end to cooperation with the bourgeoisie and their corrupt politicians, a change in Hungarian foreign policy away from the Entente and towards an alliance with the new Soviet Russia. Although the nucleus of the Communist Party remained relatively small in size, Communist slogans had an effective appeal in a situation of growing social distress and widespread dissatisfaction. They helped weaken popular support for the Social Democrats and thus for the government coalition. Revolutionary Soldiers', Workers' and Peasants' Councils were now also formed in the provincial towns and pursued policies very close to the Communist Party programme. As early as late December demonstrators organised by the Communist Party demanded the proclamation of a Hungarian Soviet Republic. The entire country was engulfed by a wave of strikes as infuriated workers took over their factories together with transport and communications installations. When the government sent in the army to restore order numerous factories were occupied between the 1 and 5 January 1919 and control of production passed to the Communist-dominated Soviets.

The government turned out to be no match for this deeply motivated revolt. After lengthy discussions the internal argument within the Social Democratic Party, whether, in view of the masses' action and the Communists' growing influence, it would not make more sense to withdraw from participation in the government in order to retain some of their influence with the workers, or whether the Social Democrats could better defend their positions in the crisis by assuming an even more prominent role in government, was decided in favour of those who supported continuing the policy of shared governmental responsibility. The party's National Council hoped that Count Mihály Károlyi's appointment as President of the Republic on 11 January 1919 and the entrusting of the former minister of justice, Dénes Berinkey, with the formation of a new government would bring about greater stability. The Social Democrats occupied five posts in the new government, including Vilmos Bőhm as minister of defence. The Smallholders' Party nominated the popular István Nagyatádi for the new government as a man who could be expected to speed up the land reform for which the peasants were becoming more impatient. The Social Democrats tried to tame the left wing of their own party at first. After an emergency party conference had approved tough measures on 28 January 1919 the Budapest Workers' Council expelled the

Communists from its membership and that of the trade unions. Following the dissolution of the spontaneously elected workers' councils which had proved impossible to control, workers' participation was to be guaranteed by elected shop committees in all factories with more than 25 employees. The Law for the Protection of the Republic gave the minister of the interior the power to order the internment of persons considered dangerous to the state. However, it was members of the right-wing opposition who proved to be the first victims of this preventive measure. The government undertook a thorough purge of the bureaucracy, dismissing the lord-lieutenants of the county administrations. The dissolved county commissions were replaced by elected People's Councils. The Militia Association was banned and measures carried out against the conservative elements around the president's older brother, Count József Károlyi, and Count István Bethlen, who tried to unite their supporters in the county administrations in a new right-wing opposition party. By announcing the law on land reform on 16 February 1919 the government hoped to calm the revolutionary mood in the countryside. All estates of over 300 hectares were to be expropriated and compensation paid to their owners. These were then to be parcelled out with the aim of creating a new economic structure based on small peasant farms allocated to the small and dwarf-holding peasantry. The new president, Mihály Károlyi began personally to redistribute the land on his great estates in Kálkápolna on 23 February.

However, this land reform sparked off a new conflict in Hungary's internal politics. The large-scale landowners showed little inclination to support the passage of the proposed legislation and offered stubborn resistance. The rural proletariat reacted bitterly at the government's completely inadequate upper limit on the size of individual allocations. They also criticised the lengthy and cumbersome process of redistribution which prevented the transfer of ownership in time for the spring planting of crops and complained at the amount of compensation they were expected to pay, sums which the poor rural population could not in fact afford. When the government refused to halt the work of the land distribution committees and satisfy the reformist desires, voiced with increasing bitterness by the beneficiaries, the number of land seizures by the peasants began to rise from the beginning of March 1919 onwards as attempts were made to cultivate the land collectively. Even the newly-appointed government officials who were supposed to take over the leading positions in the county administrations were not always able to take up office and had to watch helplessly as makeshift committees, dominated by landless peasants and workers, usurped the administration's functions. In some provincial towns such as Szeged the town council was controlled by workers' committees set up by the left-wing Social Democrats and the Communists.

Even the arrest of the Communist Party's leaders on 21 February 1919, which the Social Democrats also agreed to after considerable hesitation, failed to reduce the mood of revolution. The arrests had come about as a result of a demonstration organised by the Communists outside the editorial building of the Social Democratic daily newspaper *Népszava* (The Voice of the People), where several policemen had been killed the previous day. Since, at Károlyi's request, the fifty or so defendants were granted the status of political prisoners, they were also able to lead the Communists from inside prison and create more difficulties for the government whose image was completely tarnished, not least because of its lack of success in foreign policy.

As early as November 1918 the Károlyi government had tried to establish closer contacts with Italy in the hope of acquiring a spokesman at the Paris Peace Conference. The government's willingness to settle the problem of Hungary's disputed territories and develop economic relations with its neighbours was communicated to the new South Slav kingdom of Yugoslavia. In Vienna and Bern, where the Hungarian diplomats had been accredited without further ado, the opportunity presented itself of establishing the first direct contacts with the western Allies and putting the Hungarian case. An economic mission led by A. E. Taylor, followed by a political mission headed by A. C. Coolidge on 15 January 1919, renewed Hungarian hopes of being included in America's financial aid programme under the direction of Herbert Hoover. It was clear that the country's national economic recovery was bound to have an affect on the government's ability to stabilise the internal political situation. While the Allied military intervention against Bolshevik Russia was fully underway, the Hungarians felt they could also expect an acceptable settlement of the frontier problem from the Paris Peace Conference, since this appeared to be the only way of avoiding revolution and a takeover of power by the radical Left in Hungary. Thus, the measures taken to curb the influence of the Communists also stemmed from foreign policy considerations.

However, the Peace Conference decision of 26 February 1919, first intimated to the Hungarian government in Budapest on 20 March, effectively swept the Károlyi government from office. It proposed creating a neutral zone in the south-east of the country in order to separate the opposing Hungarian and Rumanian forces, which stood ready for battle on the demarcation line, and envisaged sending in more Allied troops. Acceptance of these proposals would have exacerbated Hungary's internal political crisis which had already reached a dangerous level after the Communist Party announced its intention of liberating its imprisoned leaders by holding a mass demonstration on 23 March. The Social Democrats, pressed by Károlyi to take over sole responsibility for the government, intensified their ongoing negotiations with the imprisoned Communist leaders. In view of the external political threat faced by Hungary, the Social Democrats announced their willingness on 21 March to unite with the Hungarian Communist Party to form the United Workers' Party of Hungary (*Magyarországi Szocialista Párt*) and to form a new government of both parties pledged to implementing important points in the Communist Party programme. After Károlyi had rejected the Allies' demands as unacceptable he transferred power 'on behalf of the proletarian class' to this new government, the Revolutionary Governing Council (*Forradalmi Kormányzótanaés*). Although its chairman was the Social Democratic Centralist, Sándor Garbai, it was effectively led by Béla Kun who had secured his position as head of the People's Commissariat for Foreign Affairs.

On the 22 March 1919, the new government proclaimed Hungary a republic and announced its declared aim of establishing the dictatorship of the proletariat. Proclaiming its desire to live in peace with all peoples, to maintain relations with the western powers and arrive at a just compromise with the country's nationalities, it announced that the most important tasks facing the new Soviet Republic were the construction of a Socialist society and the forging of an alliance with the Soviet Union. Kun, who soon claimed and received dictatorial powers placed his faith in the prospect of military help from the Red Army in defence of Hungarian territory, interpreted as a struggle against the imperialism of the capitalist powers. The vast majority of the population was at first convinced by this view and prepared to take up arms to defend Hungary's territorial unity, although most thought little of the Communists' utopian doctrinaire measures in internal politics. There was no opposition, nor protests, at first, since only a completely new political departure appeared to offer Hungary the chance to break out of its foreign policy isolation and take the heat out of the confused internal political situation. Although the number of organised Communists remained few, the majority of Social Democrats, many bourgeois radicals and even reformist liberals supported the changes introduced by the new Soviet government. There followed a rapid succession of decrees which in the course of time revealed the dominant influence of the Communists.

On 25 March 1919, the government officially announced a reorganisation of the armed forces and the creation of the Hungarian Red Army. This was to be recruited from the organised workers and political commissars were to be attached to each unit in order to counteract the influence of the old officer corps and ensure that the troops were ideologically successfully re-educated. The Red Guard, in which Communist supporters occupied all the key positions, was charged with upholding internal law and order instead of the police and the gendarmerie. The courts were replaced by revolutionary tribunals on which lay-judges, loyal to the party line, were given the final say. On 26 March, mining and transport were nationalised along with industrial concerns employing more than twenty employees. These were to be managed in future by production commissars and controlled by elected workers' councils. Banks, insurance companies and home ownership were likewise placed under state control. By placing accommodation under public ownership an attempt was made to overcome the housing shortage caused by the flood of refugees. Social policy measures – wage increases, sexual equality, the prohibition of child labour, improved educational opportunities – met with widespread approval, as did the nationalisation of major commercial concerns, the introduction of food and consumer goods rationing and the supervised distribution of food by the trade unions. On 29 March 1919, it was announced that schools and educational institutions were also now the property of the state. Up to 80 per cent of elementary schools and 65 per cent of middle-schools had previously been run by the Church. It was envisaged that members of the Church's teaching orders would continue to be employed on the condition that they were prepared to enter the state service. György Lukács, People's Commissar for Education, also proposed a progressive reform of the universities and the entire range of cultural activities, and began a campaign against illiteracy.

The government's most radical measure was the land reform decrees of 3 April. Middle and large-sized estates together with their deadstock were expropriated without compensation and taken into state ownership. The Church's landed properties were also subsequently nationalised, although some land was spared in order to provide for the support of the clergy. The division of land into individual plots was forbidden. Estates were to be collectively managed by agricultural cooperatives, whereby the previous owners, tenants and managers had to take charge as 'production commissars', who would be subject to control by the People's Soviets, comprising former rural labourers and farmhands, i.e. the so-called 'collective farm workers'. In the belief that large-scale enterprises would effectively produce more to cover food requirements than small peasant farms lacking capital, machinery and seed stocks, the rural poor's spontaneous land seizures, hitherto encouraged by the Communists, were now reversed. However, dissatisfaction with this measure was so great in some districts that the government was soon obliged to allow the creation of small plots or allotments.

In order to acquire political legitimacy and popular support for their far-reaching measures, which resulted in considerable social change and unforeseeable changes in the production and administrative apparatus, Soviet elections were held between 7 and 10 April on the basis of the extended suffrage granted by the provisional constitution of 2 April 1919. Since there was only a single list of candidates, the Revolutionary Governing Council could be sure of winning a majority for its programme which was increasingly modelled on Soviet-Russian organisational principles. But in both the Socialist Party and the Revolutionary Governing Council the former Social Democrats, who harboured growing reservations towards Kun's new direction in foreign policy, began to raise objections to the flagrant violation of existing legal norms and ruthless persecution of opponents, whether actual or potential.

To increase pressure on the Hungarian Soviet government to change its policies or perhaps even resign, the Peace Conference, which perceived the Soviet Republic as a threat, had decided on 28 March to maintain its economic blockade of the country. Hungary could, therefore, cultivate diplomatic and economic contacts only with Austria. Soviet Russia, itself imperilled by civil war and Allied intervention, had immediately recognised the Hungarian Soviet régime, but could not provide effective help. On 24 March, Kun had asked the Peace Conference to help settle the points at issue by sending a diplomatic mission to Hungary and entering into direct negotiations with the Soviet government. Since America's President Wilson and Britain's prime minister, Lloyd George, interpreted the radical turn of events in Hungary as primarily a result of protest against the violation of Hungarian national interests and excessive French demands, they argued for the acceptance of Kun's proposal. Afraid that the Hungarian Communist virus might also spread to Austria and Germany, they thought it desirable to show a readiness to make some form of compromise. But Clemenceau's already mooted idea of establishing a *cordon sanitaire* in east central Europe appeared a better guarantee for holding feared German revanchist designs in check, while at the same time preventing the export of the Russian revolution and isolating Hungary internationally. The decision to withdraw the French interventionist troops from the Ukraine and the Crimea and hand over their weapons to the Rumanian army was motivated by the idea of using Czechoslovakia and Rumania, as directly affected neighbours, to exorcise the red spectre in Hungary. After long discussions the 'Big Four' finally agreed to send General Smuts to Budapest to sound out the Hungarians' willingness to negotiate. The talks, which began on 4 April, failed to produce any concrete results, since the Allies insisted on the creation of a neutral zone, albeit reduced, in southeast Hungary and Kun was unable to have his proposal accepted of holding a conference of the powers directly involved to settle the problems of the Danube region.

The Rumanian Crown Council, in a decree of 10 April 1919, decided, therefore, to insist on a military solution of its territorial claims against Hungary. Although the newly-formed Kingdom of Serbs, Croats and Slovenes refused to join in any common action, Czechoslovakia also made military preparations. At first the Hungarian Red Army failed to halt the Rumanian advance which began on 16 April, with the result that Hungary had to surrender its territories east of the river Tisza. Earnest appeals and a wave of patriotism did, however, result in a rush of volunteers, especially after Czech units joined the campaign. A Committee of Public Safety, organised by Tibor Szamuely, increased the pressure on the civilian population and soon · practised open terror against all suspected sympathisers of the Society for the Liberation of Hungary, founded by Count István Bethlen in Vienna on 13 April 1919. Against the background of a steadily deteriorating military situation and the failure of Hungary's increasingly anxious appeals to the Peace Conference and neighbouring governments, the Social Democratic People's Commissars showed at an emergency sitting of 1 and 2 May 1919 that they were prepared to create the conditions to end the military intervention through the resignation of the Revolutionary Governing Council and the appointment of a transitional government. With the help of the Budapest Soviet, however, Kun was able to drum up a majority in favour of continuing the fighting. The Red Army, which was quickly doubled in strength, began its offensive against the Czech units in Slovakia and Ruthenia in the middle of May. Hoping to create a direct land corridor to Soviet Russia and greatly improve the Soviet Republic's military and political situation, it managed to achieve a series of quick successes and by the beginning of June had already succeeded in driving a wedge between the rather ineffective Czech and Rumanian forces. A short-lived Soviet Republic was even proclaimed in the Slovak town of Kassa.

This unexpected recovery by the Hungarians led to various forms of intensified activity which eventually contributed to the fall of the Hungarian Soviet regime. In Szeged, which was under the control of French occupation forces, an anti-Bolshevik Committee was formed in which bourgeois politicians and members of the bureaucracy, together with some aristocrats and ex-servicemen, prepared to set up a rival government on 3 June 1919 under Count Gyula Károlyi's chairmanship. This counter-revolutionary government was to include Count Pál Teleki as foreign minister and the last commander-in-chief of the Austro-Hungarian navy and former aide-de-camp to the Emperor Francis Joseph, Rear-Admiral Miklós Horthy de Nagybánya as minister of war. At the same time, Horthy took over the command of the National Army which had been mainly organised by Gyula Gömbös. Dissatisfaction with the Communists expressed itself in revolts in the countryside and refusals to cooperate. In the towns also, tensions were again heightened by the crisis of shortages in fuel and basic food supplies. The Revolutionary Governing Council tried to blame the peasants for the lack of food, thus exacerbating the already strained relationship between town and country, and increasingly resorted to coercion in order to maintain discipline and keep work going in the unpopular agricultural collectives. A Central Economic Council was eventually put in charge of the country's entire economic life with the task of overcoming the supply situation. However, the discontented rural population increasingly refused to cooperate. Resistance spread and was merely fuelled further by the government's counter-measures. In the western counties, in particular, riots and strikes, organised by ex-army officers and civil servants, flared up repeatedly, especially since the brutality with which the Red Guard units, charged with the maintenance of internal order, tried to crush the disturbances, led to a continual increase in the numbers of those opposing the government.

At the first party congress of the Hungarian Socialist Party, held on 12–13 June 1919, a head-on clash took place between groups whose opinion differed on the government's handling of domestic and foreign policy. Many Social Democrats obviously no longer agreed with the partisan direction of the Communists' policies and sharply condemned the radical measures against the population. As a result the party changed its name to the Socialist-Communist Party of Hungarian Workers (*Szocialista-Kommunista Munkások Magyarországi*). At the opening session of a new kind of parliament, the National Congress of Councils (Soviets) which lasted from 14 to 23 June, the Communists succeeded in passing a draft constitution which was entirely dominated by their ideas. They also demonstrated their dominating influence in the elections to the Central Executive Committee, whose task was to control the work of the Revolutionary Governing Council between the sittings of the National Congress. The deliberations were interrupted by the news that a major uprising involving the rival Szeged government had broken out between the Danube and the Tisza. The unrest spilled over to Budapest on 24 June as ex-servicemen gave their support to the government's opponents. By deploying Red Guard units, the government was once more able to crush the disturbances, not least because the industrial workers refused to join the ranks of insurgents. But, since the workers were also not prepared to continue supporting the Soviet régime, the position of the Revolutionary Governing Council became increasingly precarious.

The actions of the Entente Powers also contributed to the crisis. True, the hastily-conceived plan for an allied military intervention was soon dropped in favour of diplomatic and economic pressure, but this made little impression on the Governing Council. The demand, communicated to the Budapest government on 7 June 1919, to stop the further advance of the Red Army to the north-east in order to begin peace negotiations in Paris with the participation of Hungarian delegates was ignored. On 13 June, an offer arrived from Paris that if the Hungarian troops retreated to the former demarcation line, the Rumanian army would be pulled back from the Tisza to its original positions. In view of the Hungarian army's logistical problems and the growing internal resistance this proposal was accepted, though with some reservations. The Red Army began to pull back. Many of its generals and officers, who up until now had fought in order to fulfil their patriotic duty and defend their country, protested at this climb-down. The commander-in-chief, Vilmos Bőhm, and the chief of the general staff, Aurél Stromfeld, joined others in resigning their commissions in protest. It was also announced on 2 July that the

Rumanians were refusing to withdraw their troops from the line of the Tisza until the Hungarian army had been completely disarmed.

When Kun wanted to force the evacuation of the territories beyond the Tisza by launching a surprise attack on 20 July 1919, the Red Army managed to achieve some initial victories, but was forced to fall back in disorderly flight when the Rumanians launched their counter-attack. In the final days of July Rumanian troops crossed the Tisza along a broad front. By 31 July, only 100 kilometres separated them from Budapest. Trade unionists and former Social Democrats had already expressed their view more openly that the occupation of the entire country by foreign troops could be prevented only by expelling the Communists from the Governing Council and forming a new government which the Entente Powers would recognise as a negotiating partner. This view was reinforced by reports from Vienna where Entente diplomats had presented the Hungarian negotiator, Vilmos Böhm, with a list of eight points setting out their conditions for ending the Rumanian advance and beginning peace negotiations. The first condition demanded the voluntary resignation of the Governing Council and the creation of a caretaker government under the leadership of the trade unions. Although the Communists still refused to open the way for a negotiated settlement on 31 July, they had to accept resignation of the Governing Council which was forced by the Budapest Central Workers' Council on 1 August 1919. After a period of 133 days Hungary's experiment in Soviet dictatorship had collapsed. It had ended, not only because of its total rejection by the Allies and the military superiority of its enemies, but because of internal opposition which had derived its strength from the government's errors of political judgement, economic problems and blind terror. Its leaders fled to Austria where they and their families were granted political asylum. A transitional government, headed by Gyula Peidl, had to try to minimise the damage caused to Hungary by Soviet rule.

The 'White Terror' and the Trianon Peace Treaty

In the weeks following the collapse of the Soviet dictatorship Hungary faced complete chaos. On 3 August 1919, Rumanian troops marched unopposed into Budapest where a succession of helpless and impotent governments rapidly wore themselves out. Peidl's 'government of the trade unions', which was supported only by the Social

Democrats, immediately began to repeal and annul the unpopular decrees and measures of Soviet rule. Private property was restored, a functioning state apparatus was recreated and what remained of the 'Red Terror', i.e. the revolutionary tribunals and the Red Guard, was eliminated. On 6 August, however, Peidl's government was overthrown in an armed coup. A new government led by the factory owner István Friedrich took over the running of the country. Although the rival Szeged government acknowledged the authority of the new government, the former's war minister and commander of the small counter-revolutionary 'National Army', Miklós Horthy, refused to carry out its instructions. Since the Entente Powers also refused to recognise the new government, its orders carried no weight and could not put an end to the killing and the looting. In the meantime, Horthy's troops had advanced into the areas between the Tisza and the Danube which were not under Rumanian occupation and soon extended its control over areas west of the Danube which were now free of foreign military occupation. Real and alleged Communists were ruthlessly persecuted along with workers and peasants who had played an active part in implementing the Soviet government's social programme. The same fate was shared by the Jews who suffered considerable loss of life in punitive actions reminiscent of mediaeval pogroms. The officer detachments responsible for the 'White Terror' were actively supported by such newly-formed paramilitary organisations as the Hungarian National Defence Force Association and the Association of Vigilant Hungarians, whose members were drawn mainly from the ranks of the reserve officers, students, civil servants and those Magyars who had been socially and economically uprooted following their expulsion from the former nationality territories now lost to Hungary's new neighbours. This 'White Terror', which raged throughout the countryside until the autumn of 1919 and died away only slowly in the spring of 1920, bore no semblance of legality. It claimed around 5,000 lives, put 70,000 citizens behind bars or crowded them into hastily erected internment camps and forced many suspects to flee abroad.

A mission of the Entente Powers, which arrived in Budapest on 5 August 1919, did little to stop the unbridled persecution and chaos. Whereas the various Hungarian governments tried in vain to maintain internal order and political stability, most of the government commissars in the counties, who were appointed from among the wealthy landowners, had sufficient power and means at their disposal to restore traditional authority and property relations while at the same time reversing the principles of democratic liberal reform. They were fully supported by those groups in the towns and countryside who were horrified at the extent of the Soviet government's democratisation measures and the 'Red Terror'. These were the aristocracy, civil servants, the military and middle and small-ranking property owners in the towns who had no sympathy for the appeals of the intelligentsia – itself implicated in the failure of democratic reforms – not to let Hungary depart from the principles of parliamentary democracy. The visit of the British diplomat Sir George Clerk in October 1919 was evidence of the western Allies' interest in seeing a liberal parliamentary democracy established in Hungary. The Allies also urgently demanded that a general election, based on the secret ballot, should be held for a national assembly, conceived as a single chamber parliament with a two-year period of office. The only reason that the Hungarians reluctantly agreed to these proposals was that they were the only means by which they could secure the withdrawal of the Rumanian troops from Budapest. After 16 November 1919, when Horthy entered the capital at the head of his National Army, now swollen to 25,000 men, a government of national concentration led by the Christian Social leader, Károly Huszár, was formed on 25 November. The post of social welfare minister was filled by Károly Peyer, the leader of the Social Democratic Party, newly reorganised in August. But the new government was unable to satisfy expectations that it would bring stability to the dreadful political and economic situation. It could not and would not take vigorous action against the 'White Terror' at large throughout the country. As a result, the Social Democrats left the government on 15 January 1920 and decided to boycott the elections due to be held on 25 January. The other political factions displayed a lack of unity and instability. Many influential politicians of the pre-war period like Gyula Andrássy, Albert Apponyi and István Bethlen initially held back from joining any of the parties, but instead created independent dissenting groups. Newly-created parties like the National Civic Party, the National Liberal Party or the Democratic Party lacked popular support and primarily represented business interests and high finance. In contrast, the Christian National Unity Party (*Keresztény Nemzeti Egyesülés Pártja*) which was the result of a merger on 25 October 1919 between the Christian National Party, the Christian Social Economic Party and several smaller groups, was able to rely on the support of both the petty bourgeoisie and the wealthy landowners who remained loyal to the Habsburgs and supported their restoration. In the meantime the

National Smallholders' Party, led by István Nagyatádi Szabó, had become an important political factor. After its merger with the Party of Arable Farmers and Rural Labourers (*Országos Kisgazda és Földműves Párt*), founded by Gyula Dann, it could count on the support of the majority of the rural population. Despite the continuation of the 'White Terror' the freest elections in Hungary's history – free, because they were mainly conducted by secret ballot – produced a majority for the Smallholders' Party which won 40 per cent of the vote and seventy-nine seats, while the Christian National Union won 35.1 per cent of the vote and seventy-four seats. Three further splinter groups returned ten deputies to the new parliament. The workers, however, still had no representation in the new National Assembly. When, on 15 June 1920, further elections were held in the territories which had been under foreign occupation, the Smallholders' Party succeeded in strengthening its leading position even further.

The Smallholders' demand to introduce land reform legislation in the interests of its supporters and the problem of the king were the key issues to which the new parliament had to address itself. All the parties acknowledged that Hungary's 'indivisible and indissoluble' connection with the Habsburg crown lands had been severed; but were agreed that the monarchy should continue to exist beyond the 13 November 1918, although the Crown's prerogatives had been terminated as of that date. A quarrel now broke out between the 'legitimists', who, drawn mainly from among the ranks of the wealthier magnates and the Catholic episcopacy, considered King Charles IV, who had not yet abdicated, to be the country's legitimate ruler and those who supported an elective monarchy based on popular support, i.e. the middle-ranking landowning nobility and leaders of the Calvinist Church who held that the monarch's claim to the throne had been forfeited and demanded the nation's right to choose a new king on the basis of free elections. Since both sides were unable to reach a compromise on the questions of whether King Charles was still Hungary's rightful ruler or how they should otherwise determine the succession, the government fell back on an institution of the late Middle Ages which Lajos Kossuth had revived in 1849: they proposed appointing a regent for the duration of the interregnum (Law I of 1920). On 1 March 1920, Miklós Horthy de Nagybánya was elected Regent in a parliament building occupied by the military at the time.

As commander-in-chief of the Szeged National Army, which had grown to almost 50,000 men in Transdanubia after joining up with

Baron Antal Lehár's units at the beginning of 1920, Horthy, who was not a particularly talented military commander or politician, exhibited an astonishing need to legitimise his authority. Thanks to his sincere manner in dealing with others, his ability in several languages and the troops under his command, he was able to win the support of the Entente representatives stationed in Budapest. His active tolerance of the 'White Terror' had made him acceptable to the enemies of reform as well as those opposed to revolution. They hoped they could install this reputedly malleable and arrogant professional soldier as a figurehead to help them achieve their own aims. Horthy knew how to give both the legitimists and those who supported an elective monarchy the impression that he supported their respective positions. He also cultivated the image of a leader who, on account of his good personal contacts with leading Entente politicians, could obtain improved peace terms for Hungary. But as soon as he was made Regent, Horthy increasingly pursued his own policy, primarily in the interests of his own family. The result was that the suspicion soon grew that he had his eyes on the crown for himself or his eldest son.

On 14 March 1920, the Huszár government made way for a new cabinet led by Sándor Simonyi-Semadam, whose priority was to seek an improvement in the harsh peace terms. On 25 November 1919, the Hungarian government had been invited to send a delegation to Paris to receive the peace terms. This delegation, headed by Apponyi, Bethlen and Pál Teleki tried to have the draft of the peace treaty, which was handed to them on 20 January 1920, changed to more favourable terms on the basis of historical, economic and legal arguments. They not only pointed to the geographical unity of the Danube basin up to the natural frontier of the Carpathians in the north and east and to the fact that the territories recently seized by Czechoslovakia and Rumania had for a thousand years, since the beginning of the 11th century, constantly formed part of the crown lands of St Stephen. They also argued that, despite the intermingling of populations of different nationalities it would be difficult, though not impossible, to draw a more equitable frontier. Their arguments did not, however, succeed in gaining any concessions. The Hungarian government also tried in vain to prevent the inclusion of a war-guilt clause by pointing out that the Hungarian population and the prime minister, Tisza, had been opposed to war in the summer of 1914, and suggested changing the proposed terms stipulating a reduction in the size of armed forces to allow a system of conscription for a standing army of 100,000 men in place of the permitted strength of 35,000. When this also was rejected, broad sections of the Hungarian population were already bitterly opposed to the proposed peace treaty even before it was signed in the Trianon on 4 June 1920, believing that a major revision of its terms was inevitable.

The independent 'Kingdom of Hungary', which emerged as a result of the Trianon peace treaty comprised only 92,963 square kilometres compared with the original 325,411 square kilometres of the old pre-war Kingdom of Hungary. According to the 1920 census, its population now numbered 7.62 million inhabitants compared with the earlier figure of 20.9 million. Under the terms of the Treaty the new Kingdom of Serbs, Croats and Slovenes, later to be named Yugoslavia, received the Bácska, the Baranya and the western Banat, amounting to 20,956 square kilometres, i.e. 6.44 per cent of pre-war Hungary, involving the loss of 1.5 million inhabitants. Hungary was obliged to cede 102,787 square kilometres, i.e. 31.59 per cent of its entire territory and 5,265,000 inhabitants to Rumania, the latter obtaining the whole of Transylvania including the Szekler region, the eastern Banat, most of the counties of Körös and Tisza and the southern part of Máramaros. Of the 62,937 square kilometres or 19.34 per cent of pre-war Hungary ceded to the new Czechoslovakian Republic, Slovakia received 48,994 square kilometres, Ruthenia 12,639. Of the 3,250,000 inhabitants affected by these changes, 2,950,000 were settled in Slovakia and 571,000 in Ruthenia. More than three million Magyars now lived under foreign rule: 1,063,000 in Czechoslovakia, 1,700,000 in Rumania and 558,000 in Yugoslavia.

Thanks to Italy's support, Hungary was at least able to push part of its claim through against the weak Austrian government on the question of the Burgenland when a somewhat dubious plebiscite held on 14 December 1921 resulted in the return to Hungary of the area around Sopron.

Although no exact figure was set, Hungary had to agree to pay reparations. The armed forces permitted under the treaty, comprising a professional army of 35,000 men on a long period of service, but minus heavy artillery, armoured corps and an air force, was intended exclusively to maintain internal order and the defence of Hungary's frontiers. An Inter-Allied Control Commission was given the task of seeing that these armament limitations were observed.

Every section of the Hungarian population felt disappointment at the scale of losses demanded by the peace treaty, which came to be regarded as a dictated settlement. The historic Kingdom of Hungary had possessed a geographical unity without parallel in the rest of Europe. In the second half of the nineteenth century the national economy had been a coordinated whole in which the different parts of the country had been mutually dependent on each other and the capital, Budapest. This economic unit had been destroyed by the territorial terms of the peace. The effects of the world economic crisis in 1931–32 made the problems resulting from the destruction of the Habsburg Empire's unified economy very apparent and these proved impossible to overcome satisfactorily in the period before 1938. As a semi-industrialised country with an inadequately developed manufacturing industry Trianon Hungary began to fall behind other countries economically. Since its bauxite and oil resources were yet to be exploited, the government had to give priority to agricultural production. The war and the period of Soviet rule had done little to reduce the social tensions which resulted from the partisan redistribution of landed property, and these played a crucial part in determining the direction taken by Hungary's internal and foreign policies during the inter-war period. The influx of 350,000 immigrants from the territories of the successor states, comprising mainly civil servants, teachers and soldiers, also added to the problem of achieving social cohesion, since they represented a politically aware group which could not be so quickly and easily accommodated in a country that had been reduced so much in size. The only problem solved by the imposition of the Trianon peace treaty terms was that of the national minorities. According to the 1920 census, only 833,475 people, i.e. 10.4 per cent of the population, including 552,000 Germans (6.9 per cent) and 142,000 Slovaks (1.8 per cent), did not speak Hungarian as their mother tongue. According to the same census, the number of Jews living in Hungary was 473,000.

Despite the sacrifices imposed by the treaty, Hungary's government and people continued to identify their dismembered state firmly with the Hungary of the pre-war period. Deliberately shunning any compromise with the new circumstances, they remained incredibly inflexible, rejecting even the possibility of any constructive developments within the new frontiers. They carefully nurtured the Magyars' sense of an historically-based national identity, looking back to the founding of the state, the Hungarian Kingdom's thousand years of history and their belief in the Magyar cultural mission to spread their superior civilisation. They kept alive the sense of humiliation at Hungary's defeat, the experience of economic privation and despair at the injustices of the peace settlement. In an eruption of national patriotism which permeated all social classes they argued for a revision of the peace treaty, invoking the symbol of the crown of St Stephen to argue for the restoration of the territories lost to their despised neighbours. Although differences of opinion soon emerged regarding the extent of the desired revision, the treaty's failings were pilloried. Its unrealistically high reparations demands, war-guilt clause, territorial and military terms and unjust treatment of the Magyar minorities in Hungary's neighbour states all became a focus of resentment. The slogan, '*Nem, nem, soha!*' (no, no, never!) summed up the attitude of every Magyar to the peace treaty. Diplomatic, artistic and economic contacts with other countries were cultivated with renewed intensity with a view to eventually revising the treaty's terms. 'The world's conscience' was not to be allowed to rest 'in view of the injustices done to Hungary at the Trianon and the consequent danger to peace'. Whereas at first demands were made to restore to Hungary its pre-war territories, implying a total revision of the treaty, which could not be achieved peacefully but only by a victorious war, from 1930 onwards more enlightened circles worked for a revision of the treaty's territorial terms within the framework of national self-determination: 'Hungary would recover those citizens seized from her whose first language is Magyar, although plebiscites would be held in territories whose inhabitants' native language was not Hungarian'.

Hungary's revisionist policy was, however, primarily intended to divert attention away from the country's internal social and economic problems. The traditional upper classes, the aristocratic representatives of the governments and parties of the period before the Soviet republic, which quickly rose to prominence once more, were interested only in preserving what remained of feudal rule, in resisting any genuine land reform and in obtaining compensation for their extensive holdings which now lay in the territories seized from Hungary. It was thanks to their influence that a subtle combination of democratic elements was incorporated into the new constitution of 28 February 1920 which did much to perpetuate social injustices. The traditional middle class, recruited mainly from members of declining middle nobility, who had become gentry and earned their living as civil servants or professional soldiers, tried increasingly to curb the influence of the upper nobility and secure their political and economic position. They were able – especially in their unbridled campaign against the Jews – to count on the complete support of petty bourgeoisie which was also imbued with the conviction that it was ordained to rule politically and economically. Despite a large

influx of Jewish immigration before the First World War, Hungary's
Jews, in fact, formed only 6 per cent of the country's population,
but controlled major areas of industry, banking and commerce as
well as dominating several liberal professions like medicine, the law
and journalism. Although the Jews had not posed a threat to any
social class and had created many positions for the first time in their
role as a substitute bourgeoisie, they were used as a scapegoat in
order to release the pent-up dissatisfaction of the middle classes.
Even in the officer corps, which was initially the only stabilising
factor in the state and which exerted considerable influence on
Horthy during his period as Regent, a groundswell of antisemitism
combined with anti-liberal ideals. Above all, it was Hungary's
professional soldiers who rejected democratic institutions and a
liberal state based on the rule of law. Their growing chauvinism and
demands for a complete revision of the peace treaty were
accompanied by the call to establish naked authoritarian rule in the
form of an overt military dictatorship. Hungary's governments and
political parties had to resist these tendencies before they could even
begin the long overdue process of consolidation.

THE HORTHY ERA

The successes and failures of the Bethlen government

With Count Pál Teleki's appointment as prime minister at the head
of a cabinet of distinguished personalities on 19 July 1920, the new
government could no longer simply be seen as a transitional government in the style of its short-lived predecessors. Lóránd Hegedüs,
director of the Commercial Bank, one of Hungary's largest finance
institutions, and director of the Association of Savings Banks and
Banking Companies, was appointed finance minister. His task was
to put the national budget in order and halt the depreciation of the
currency, whose value had fallen to less than a six-thousandth of its
pre-war level as a result of galloping inflation. The government's
main priorities were, however, finally to carry out a more just
distribution of land for the peasants, end the lawlessness and brutality of the 'White Terror' and resist the virulent spread of
antisemitism. The 'White Terror' and antisemitism had become
linked in the minds of many Hungarians, since Bolshevism and the
Jews were to some extent identified with each other. Béla Kun and many

of the Soviet régime's prominent personalities came from Jewish families and were equated with the Bolsheviks. Right-wing military execution squads had sworn to eliminate the last traces of Communism and, since the industrial workers and their organisations were held partly responsible for the Soviet dictatorship, they, too, became objects of persecution and repression.

However, Teleki's government had no interest in seeing the law continuously weakened; nor did it have anything to gain from the uncontrollable and arbitrary retribution of the army and sympathetic right-wing circles which spread paramilitary, quasi-facist ideas, especially since the mood of the population was still potentially explosive. Around a third of Hungary's workers were unemployed. Industrial production reached only 30 per cent of its pre-war level. The yield for the wheat harvest of 1920 was half that for 1913 and the entire country was suffering from acute food shortages. Despite major attempts to cut government spending, the number of state-employed officials almost trebled. While the Teleki government gradually achieved a situation in which constitutional principles were observed, it did not shy away from reintroducing corporal punishment on 26 September 1920 (Law XVI of 1920) or placing a ceiling on the number of university admissions in order to reduce the proportion of Jews entering the universities (Law XXV of 1920). This law, which did not mention Jews explicitly, helped bring about a situation in which the proportion of Jewish students fell from 34 per cent in 1917–18 to only 8 per cent in 1935–36. Deliberate measures were also introduced to eliminate the Jews completely from the state bureaucracy and there was widespread discrimination against practising Jews, who were eventually no longer allowed to conduct businesses in which the state had a monopoly, like tobacconists, the alcohol retail trade and cinemas. Their land was also frequently expropriated by the state. The policy of land redistribution had been stepped up following the territorial losses incurred under the Treaty of the Trianon, with the result that the relatively small number of estates of more than 50 hectares of arable land made up 44 per cent of all land under cultivation. The family of the Princes Esterházy still controlled 110,000 hectares of landed property, the Counts of Festetics 48,000 hectares and the Cathedral Chapter of Eger 45,000 hectares. As was the case with all other decrees passed under the Károlyi and Kun governments, the radical land reform laws of 1919 were repealed, although the lesser peasantry and landless peasants were promised a 'more equitable distribution of the land' in return.

Count István Bethlen, who, at Horthy's behest, was negotiating with the leadership of the Smallholders' Party, should be credited with having won over István Nagyatádi Szabó, leader of the strongest party, to join Teleki's government and support a very modest land reform. In view of the danger that the lesser peasants, comprising 95.6 per cent of the rural population, and the rural proletariat, who owned less than 3 hectares and often no arable land, might resort to land seizures, the large-scale landowners eventually agreed to offer for distribution 450,000 hectares of mainly inferior land out of the remaining total area of 8.5 million hectares. Included in the 411,000 people who benefited from this reform were some 300,000 landless peasants with next to no land, who were given on average one *hold* (i.e. 0.5754 hectares) of arable land subject to paying compensation. 100,000 smallholders were also included in the redistribution (Law XXX IV of 1920).

These measures did nothing, however, to ameliorate the basic conditions of poverty in the villages. The peasant's economic distress was barely reduced, since the repayment rates were so high that some 80 per cent of the peasants who had benefited from the reallocation had been forced to surrender their new land again within three years of the reform. At the same time, some of the applicants – army officers, civil servants, notaries, etc. all pillars of the Horthy regime – were, as members of the newly created Order of Heroes (*Vitézi Rend*), awarded farms of up to 50 hectares. Any interested applicant who had served at the front and been decorated in the First World War, and who could be proved to hold genuinely patriotic values, could be admitted to this order. By 1940 its 18,000 members, including 4,000 army officers, had at their disposal some 450,000 hectares of land. The government's promise to implement a radical land reform following the return of political stability and to make available cheap agricultural loans once the economy had stabilised consoled the smallholding peasant who had been initially disappointed by the first round of redistribution. However, the large-scale landowners knew how to fend off every new initiative on land reform in future by arguing that any further division of land would reduce Hungary's agricultural competitiveness even further and result in a serious economic crisis. Owing to the collapse of the Monarchy, Hungary had lost its most important markets for agricultural produce which still accounted for 62 per cent of the national income. Protectionist policies in the rest of Europe, high agricultural tariff barriers and competition from foreign overseas grain imports made it more difficult to find a market for Hungary's agricultural produce. Although the use of artificial fertilisers and machinery slowly increased, production remained relatively low compared with pre-war levels. Livestock figures stayed static; the number of cattle and sheep declined. The Smallholders' Party, which was coordinated and brought into line by the future prime minister, Count István Bethlen, continued to look after the interests of its former electoral support inadequately. After 1925, the newly-formed Hungarian Socialist Workers' Party, founded as a Communist cover-organisation, tried to fill the vacuum. It developed a 'new land reform' programme based on Hungarian conditions, which aimed to expropriate all holdings of more than 50 hectares and reallocate the land to the rural proletariat free of compensation. Concrete measures to improve the unsatisfactory property and income distribution in the countryside were not, however, introduced at this juncture.

Hungary's workers suffered particularly badly from the policy of turning the clock back to the political situation of pre-war Hungary. The Soviet dictatorship's achievements in the field of social policy were entirely eliminated at a stroke, and, despite growing unemployment – in Budapest alone, 150,000 people were jobless – unemployment benefit was stopped, wages were held down despite rising inflation and the working day increased to 10 hours (12 hours in the mines). Since supplies of fuel and raw materials were exhausted, foreign trade with neighbouring countries was stagnating and the rapid currency depreciation was discouraging investment, it proved extremely difficult in the period before 1921 to switch production, previously geared to military needs, to peacetime commodities and the needs of the smaller domestic market. In 1922, production output reached only 52 per cent of its pre-war levels and in 1924 stood at about 60 per cent.

The scope for action by the political parties and workers' organisations, compromised by their part in the Soviet Republic, was systematically eliminated. The Communist Party was banned (Law III of 1921). Its exiled leaders, initially in Vienna and later in Moscow, did not succeed in creating a properly functioning underground organisation, although small clandestine groups did establish contact with each other after 1921 in Budapest's main factories, in the mining area of Tatabánya and the industrial region of Borsod. The authorities obstructed the work of the Social Democratic Party, which had been reorganised in August 1919, and restricted the public gatherings of the trade unions. The Christian Social trade unions, encouraged as a counterweight to their Socialist counterparts, together with state-funded 'substitute' parties, like the Hungarian National Workers' Party and the Hungarian Socialist Party were unable to mobilise much support. The 'White Terror', wage reductions and government discrimination lead to a massive decline in the membership of the more traditional workers' organisations. Nevertheless, it was still clear that the workers and their representative organisations could not be left out of any attempt to stabilise the system.

It was not the terrible economic situation nor Hungary's unresolved and widespread social tensions that led the prime minister, Count Teleki, who belonged to the Legitimist camp, to resign on 13 April 1921, but the attempt by traditional conservative circles to force the restoration of King Charles IV to the throne. Encouraged by the Legitimists under the leadership of Count Gyula Andrássy Jnr, King Charles had returned from his Swiss exile to Szombathely in western Hungary on 26 March, subsequently entering into negotiations with Horthy, who up until this point had been keen to stress his loyalty to the king with the aim of reclaiming his vacant throne. When Horthy, however, proved unwilling to relinquish his power, for which he had in the meantime acquired a taste, and Hungary's neighbours threatened military intervention if a restoration took place, Charles, who was reputedly prepared to carry out radical social reforms, returned to exile. Count István Bethlen who had previously sympathised with the Legitimists, but now crossed over to those who supported a freely elected monarch, formed a new government on 14 April 1921.

Bethlen, who was to play a prominent part in deciding Hungary's fate over the next decade, had been born into a wealthy family of Transylvanian landowners in 1874. As a member of the Upper House of Parliament in the period before the First World War, he had maintained an attitude of critical distance both from the policies of the Independence Party and, subsequently, those of Count István Tisza's Party of National Work. After 1919 he had formed the Anti-Bolshevik Committee in Vienna which contributed to the overthrow of the Soviet dictatorship. He was one of the leading personalities, who, on account of their considerable personal prestige, had been able to exert considerable influence on political life from a position outside the existing parties and who, as early as the summer of 1920, had tried to create a united bloc of government supporters by bringing about a merger of the Christian conservative parties, i.e. the Smallholders' Party and the Christian National Unity Party. He was able to rely not only on the complete confidence of the great landowners and capitalists, but also on the sympathies of the middle class, which, still dominated by the gentry ethos, looked to him for help in reducing the power of the magnates so that they could take control of the levers of power. His general adroitness, broad vision, diplomatic skill and sense of tactics predestined him for the post of prime minister at a time when Hungary had to continue with a policy of achieving internal stability while at the same time breaking through its foreign policy isolation by way of a revision of the post-war peace treaty. The entire character of the 'Horthy Era' was strongly influenced by his personality and politics.

Bethlen soon faced his first major test as prime minister in October 1921. On 20 October, King Charles IV returned to Hungary for a second time. After the troops stationed in the western half of the country had sworn a personal oath of allegiance to him, he announced the formation of a new government and marched on Budapest. Relying on the Great Powers to protest against his actions and on the threatened military sanctions of Hungary's neigh-bours, Horthy and Bethlen mobilised the army which had the good fortune to win a minor victory against a royalist batallion on 23 October 1921 at Budaörs, west of Budapest. During the fighting the former army captain and secretary of state in Horthy's Szeged War Ministry, Gyula Gömbös de Jáfka, distinguished himself as the commander of a paramilitary force of right-wing radical organis-ations by turning the scales in the government's favour. Against his own sense of honour – after all, Charles had been crowned King of Hungary with the crown of St Stephen and Horthy had been among those who had sworn an oath of loyalty – the Regent had the defeated king taken prisoner to the castle at Taba-Tavaros and arranged for him to be exiled to the Portuguese island of Madeira where he died not long after on 1 April 1922. Bethlen lost no time in submitting new legislation to parliament which proclaimed the dethronement of the House of Habsburg on 6 November 1921 (Law XLVII of 1921).

The removal of the Habsburgs from the throne was a serious defeat for the Legitimists. Their political arm, the Christian National Unity Party, never recovered and rapidly disintegrated into several insignificant splinter groups. Also, the fact that the legitimists recognised Otto von Habsburg, born in 1912, as the rightful king after his father's death, and that the debate on the legitimacy of the Habsburg-Lorraine family's claims to the throne continued to grow in Hungary, gave Horthy and Hungary's governments no cause for concern. The anti-Habsburg elements among those who supported a freely elected king, consisting mainly of the gentry and the petty bourgeoisie, interpreted their success as having also broken the influence of the magnates and the plutocracy, and sought to exploit the opportunity of stabilising the régime to broaden their own power-base.

Bethlen continued to act vigorously against the excesses of the 'White Terror' which still broke out occasionally and greatly surpassed in cruelty and numbers of victims the 'Red Terror' of the Soviet régime. The outrages perpetrated by right-wing extremist groups, who enjoyed Horthy's protection and were never brought to justice, no longer suited the times and were a barrier to establishing and improving diplomatic relations with the outside world. The return to constitutional and legal norms was accompanied by an expansion of the police force, the gendarmerie and the courts, whereby measures to 'ensure the political and social order more effectively' were in future not only carried out against the remnants of the extreme Left like the Communists, but against the political Right. especially those groups of demobilised officers and ex-civil servants who propagated fascism. Bethlen, who felt more attached to the conservative-aristocratic political views of the large land-owners and grande bourgeoisie, and who would have welcomed a return to the established tradition-bound institutions of the Dual Monarchy, restored public order and put an end to the privileged position previously enjoyed by the armed forces. He removed the control they had usurped over the state apparatus and the military intelligence service, established the government's command of the army and the general staff and divested the paramilitary forces of their power in favour of the police force and gendarmerie. Since extreme nationalist military circles began to use great tactical skill in defying the implementation of these measures, Bethlen, with Horthy's support, had to try to begin creating his own party-political support.

On 22 December 1921, negotiations with the leaders of the Social Democratic Party, who were eager to reach a compromise, had led to the government securing an extremely favourable secret agreement in the shape of the Bethlen–Peyer Pact. The Bethlen government undertook to release imprisoned workers and trade unionists, legalise their political activities and allow them to stand for parliament, although this would be of limited effect because of the franchise system and the restriction of secret ballot to elections in the towns. In return, the Social Democrats, led by Károlyi Peyer, announced their willingness to support the government's attempts at consolidating its power. They agreed to help prevent politically motivated strikes, cease campaigning for a republic, stop canvassing agricultural, railway and civil service workers and use their international contacts to overcome the country's diplomatic isolation. The difficult economic situation, high unemployment and inflation, combined with the strict policing of political meetings, resulted in pacifying and politically taming the disheartened workers. After the collapse of the Legitimist Christian National Unity Party, only the Smallholders' Party, which had by now split into two wings, remained a political factor beyond Bethlen's control.

With the active parliamentary support of the great landowners in the Agricultural Party and the Hungarian National Economic Association, led by the agriculture minister, Gyula Rubinek, Bethlen succeeded in outmanoeuvring its wing of smallholders and middle-ranking farmers led by István Nagyatádi Szábo. He infiltrated the party with his own supporters and, after officially joining the party himself on 5 January 1922, a group of former non-party sympathisers emerged and soon took over the key posts at the party headquarters, displacing Szábo's supporters who fought against being forcibly deprived of power and subjected to threats of exposure. A change in the electoral law, which still restricted the franchise to only 27.3 per cent of the adult population (39.2 per cent in 1920) and the reintroduction of the open ballot – except in the major towns – ensured that the Christian Social majority bloc, now renamed the Unity Party (*Egységes Párt*) received 45.4 per cent of the vote and 143 out of 245 seats in the May and June elections of 1922. Of the new government party only 19 deputies were former Smallholders. Thus the old ruling class, the impoverished gentry and nationalist non-Jewish middle class had created a political grouping which could assert itself comfortably against the Social Democrats, the bourgeois-democratic parties, the new opposition Smallholders' Party and National Socialist groups which later experienced a marked upsurge of support in the 1930s. The Social Democrats, in the first ever election they had fought, succeeded in gaining 39.1 per cent of the vote in Budapest and 15.3 per cent in the country as a whole, giving them a representation of 25 seats in parliament. On the strength of the Budapest vote several representatives of the liberal-bourgeois opposition were also returned. The government, however, made sure that the new parliament remained powerless and reduced it to a forum for approving government policy.

The programme of the Unity Party, which was supported by the influential daily newspapers, *Pesti Hirlap* and the German language newspaper *Peser Lloyd*, called for the remodelling of Hungary on the basis of national and Christian values and the creation of religious and social harmony for the sake of a revisionist policy. It also promised a new electoral law and press law, the continued and speedier implementation of land reform, improved insurance protection for the workers, new legislation to enable the trade unions to play a greater role, the reintroduction of the magnate-dominated Upper House and a regressive municipal reform. Under Bethlen's unchallenged leadership, the reappointed agriculture minister, István Nagyatádi Szabó (d. 1924) took over as chairman of the new party, while the actual running of its affairs fell to its vice-chairman, Gyula Gömbös.

Some of the military and right-wing extremist organisations had influential sympathisers among the new government party's leaders in Gömbös, Tibor Eckhardt and Endre Bajcsy-Zsilinszky, but no way of preventing the undermining of their previous bastions of power. These groups began to show their dissatisfaction with the government's attempts to consolidate its power, imposed by Bethlen from his position of strength. Their attempt to revive the controversy on the continuation of the land reform, which had been stifled by the great landowners, in order to win mass support from among the disillusioned rural proletariat, misfired, as did the strike of civil servants and white-collar workers which they initiated. Bethlen was able to forestall preparations for coups against him at an early stage with the help of the loyal police force. Since Horthy, who was slowly gaining in prestige, also distanced himself from his former supporters and close colleagues, Gömbös and his right-wing associates left the Unity Party on 2 August 1923 and founded a right-wing opposition Party of Racial Defence (*Fajvédő Párt*) which never succeeded in becoming an important political factor. It became intoxicated with 'Turanianism' (the fact that the ancestors of the Magyars had come from Asia) and established contacts very early on with other European fascist and National Socialist parties. Since, however racism and a narrow-minded nationalism were also cultivated in the government camp, the right-wing opposition's ties with the Unity Party, which Gömbös rejoined in 1928, were never completely ruptured. The breakaway by the Party of Racial Defence resulted in a strengthening of the Unity Party's liberal-conservative wing. Even the left-wing opposition felt obliged to support the government party in its fight – or rather shadow boxing – against the radical Right.

During these years the political contours of Horthy's rule, which did not conceal its anti-liberal authoritarian and dictatorial character, became increasingly apparent. Hungary's parliament, which had been substantially stripped of power and influence, was elected mainly by the members of a small upper class. The relatively small opposition could, it is true, voice its criticisms and demands and disseminate them through its own party newspapers; but it could not achieve their redress, since the government party had virtually gained absolute power over the legislature, executive and the judiciary. Bureaucratic practices and arbitrary police methods ran roughshod over a number of constitutional principles and democratic freedoms. The rapidly expanding state bureaucracy was a particularly important influence in its own right on government and represented a real power factor. Racist and chauvinistic slogans, which were closely bound up with aggressive revisionist and irredentist thinking, not only contributed to an overestimation of all things Hungarian and an unwarranted cultural arrogance, but resulted in a militant rejection of liberalism, democracy and socialism, all of which were viewed as 'alien to the Hungarian spirit'.

The Jewish population, in particular, but soon also the national minorities left within Hungary's new frontiers, had to suffer this Magyar intolerance. Although the fringe groups which held fascist ideas lacked political influence, they were able to propagate their ideas openly and rely on the support of broad sections of the population, especially for the introduction of antisemitic measures. It would be wrong, however, to describe Horthy's stable régime which came to power by means of the 'White Terror' as fascist, for, despite its anti-liberal, conservative-authoritarian political system, it never attempted to employ demagogic methods to mobilise the masses or, under the cloak of revolution, to overthrow the system which was still strongly feudal and aristocratic in character. The social and political order under Horthy could more readily be compared with that of Hungary's neighbours – with the exception, of course, of the democratic Czechoslovak Republic.

Only the slowness of the economic recovery threatened the successful consolidation of political power. The government raised the expenditure necessary to expand the state, police and military apparatus by issuing unguaranteed banknotes, a measure which caused an even greater inflation and ruined the country's finances. Since the inflation helped the large-scale landowners pay off their mortgage debts more easily, they, like the industrialists, had little to say against the rapid increase in the money supply, which hit the workers especially hard. The demand for manufactured goods combined with a ban on imports encouraged an inflationary boom-period. Even so, industrial production figures for 1924 were still only 60 per cent of their pre-war level. The holding down of wages, the unavoidable lowering of living standards – which made the workers even more discontented – and the insurmountable problems of developing international economic relations made it imperative for the government to halt the inflation. When, in the spring of 1924, the conversion rate of paper crowns to one gold crown reached 16,300, Bethlen's government decided to act. The League of Nations was the only organisation prepared to make the necessary funds available for this financial operation.

Bethlen had already applied for Hungary to join the League of Nations in September 1922 and it formally joined on 31 January 1923. After some hesitation the government Budapest was granted a credit on 2 July 1924 on the basis of Hungary's promise of fulfilling the terms of the Trianon peace treaty. The loan, which amounted to 250 million gold crowns at a 7.5 per cent rate of interest on receipt of 88 per cent of the sum, was intended to bring about rapid stabilisation of the currency and economy under the financial supervision of the League. At the same time, Hungary had committed itself eventually to paying back its share of the Austro-Hungarian Empire's debts to the tune of one thousand million gold crowns. Despite the high rates of interest and heavy burden of capital repayments the following years witnessed a steady economic upturn which the government supported with a currency reform introduced on 1 January 1927. A new currency unit, the Pengö, was issued, equivalent to 12,500 paper crowns. The customs tariff already in force since 1 January imposed an import duty of 30 per cent, thus offering some protection for home industry, which underwent particularly rapid growth in the textile, paper and leather industries, while the important area of food production continued to stagnate. The value of production output in 1929 showed an increase of about 12 per cent over the figures for 1913. Compared with the USA's economic growth rate of 70 per cent and France's 40 per cent, Hungary made only very modest economic progress during the 1920s.

About 10 to 15 per cent of the workers, i.e. about 100,000 people, continued to be unemployed, even during the economic boom. The workers, who still worked a nine-hour day, earned real wages which still stood at only 80 per cent of their pre-war purchasing power. Their protests against social hardship and the suppression of political rights were clearly expressed in a wave of strikes which spread after 1926 and reached its climax in 1928 with a hunger march by mineworkers from Sálgótarján and Pilisvörösvár. The Communists, who were active underground, attempted to operate legally again by joining the defecting left-wing Social Democrats in the new Hungarian Socialist Workers' Party (*Magyarországi Szocialista Munkáspárt*), founded on 24 April 1925 under the leadership of István Vági. The attempt failed, however, because the new party did not attract sufficient support from the workers despite its popular demands for a return to pre-war wage levels, the introduction of an eight-hour day, unemployment benefits, a system of progressive taxation and elections conducted by secret ballot on the basis of universal suffrage. The tough police measures taken in the autumn of 1925 and a show trial held in the summer of 1926, which resulted in Mátyás Rákosi, who would later rise to prominence, being sent to prison, meant an end to most Communist-influenced legal and illegal working-class activity.

Hungary's slow and uphill economic recovery continued to be financed by raising further loans. Only a fifth of the total amount borrowed was used for investment in manufacturing industry, about a half was allocated to capital and interest repayments and the rest used to fuel consumption. When, in 1929, the amount of outstanding payments exceeded that of the approved loans for the first time, the Hungarian economy, which had become so dependent on foreign finance, revealed the instability which was to render it incapable of surviving the turmoil of the world economic crisis in 1931.

During these years of modest prosperity the bourgeois liberal opposition hoped to put pressure on the Bethlen government to introduce at least a modest democratisation and a more liberal application of legal norms. The National Bourgeois-Democratic Party (*Polgári Demokrata Párt*), whose chairman was Vilmos Vázsonyi (d. 29 May 1926), became the mouthpiece of the liberals, drawing its support from the liberal middle class and the Jewish petty bourgeoisie in Budapest, and fighting latent antisemitism which now employed racist arguments and economic discrimination against the Jews. But even when legitimist groups and the Social Democrats joined forces with the liberals to form a loose 'Democratic Bloc', Bethlen managed to hold his political opponents in check without much difficulty. His decree of 11 November 1926, which revived the feudal house of magnates as an upper house of the Hungarian parliament, helped him increase the government's majority in the prematurely held December elections, in which his government party won 60.1 per cent of the vote and 170 seats, thus condemning the opposition in future to political insignificance.

Equipped with wider legislative powers than in the pre-war period, the Upper House, as a result of its composition, helped guarantee the survival of Horthy's authoritarian reactionary régime. Comprising hereditary members of the upper aristocracy, Habsburg archdukes, delegates from the country's self-governing institutions, representatives of major pressure groups, members of the church hierarchy and prominent people from the upper bourgeoisie and the army nominated by Horthy, it also documented the growing political influence of Hungary's traditional ruling class. The cult of the crown of St Stephen and the growing tendency to indulge in traditional rituals and the display of splendid and sometimes fantastic historical costume on ceremonial occasions testified to the Magyar desire to escape the unpleasantness of the present and identify with the historical greatness of the defunct Hungarian kingdom.

The realisation that the necessary consolidation of political power and the socio-economic order could be attained only with the aid of foreign capital persuaded Hungary's premier to respect the terms of the Treaty of the Trianon, at least in his dealings with other countries. He thought that the right time to pursue an active revisionist policy would be when Hungary, relying on a strong and modern army and on trustworthy allies, could overturn the status quo in the Danube area imposed by the Paris peace treaties. The noticeable restraint shown by the Hungarian government in supporting the vocal revisionist demands of all sections of the population no doubt stemmed from the consideration that this was the only way to dispel the distrust of Hungary's neighbours and exhaust every possibility for securing a revision of the settlement as foreseen in Article XIX of the League of Nations' charter, whose economic assistance Hungary also wished to secure. But while the Bethlen government got to grips with measures to help the country's recovery, secret preparations were also undertaken to increase the size of the army beyond its manpower strength of 35,000 soldiers permitted under the treaty. As Horthy's prestige rose the longer he remained in office, his views on foreign policy increasingly influenced Hungarian diplomacy. These included rejecting any redrawing of the border according to ethnic criteria, restoring Hungary's prewar frontiers and gaining secure access to the sea. Horthy's offensive arrogance, with which, like so many Hungarians, he dealt with the politicians and peoples of Hungary's neighbouring states, viewing them as inferiors, certainly did not increase the prospect of a thorough revision of the harsh terms of the Trianon peace treaty.

Although Czechoslovakia was Hungary's only neighbour to make several vague offers in 1920–21 to redraw the disputed frontiers, and although its Magyar minority of around 1.06 million was doing relatively well economically, the Czechs and their foreign minister, Edvard Beneš, the architect of the Trianon treaty, were seen as the main obstacle to Hungary's revisionism. Because of the widespread existence in the 1920s of suspected pro-Magyar sympathies among the Slovaks and Ruthenes of what was formerly Upper Hungary, it appeared only a matter of time before the territories up to the Carpathian mountain range would be restored to Hungary and a common frontier with Poland thus gained. Hence Bethlen put no special emphasis on improving Hungary's political and economic relations with Prague, giving credence neither to Beneš's speeches before the League of Nations nor to President Masaryk's reconciliatory overtures. After it by chance became known that Magyar propaganda activity among the Slovaks and Ruthenes had been financed with excellently forged Czechoslovak banknotes, a much more far-reaching operation being prepared with the sanction of Bethlen and ex-premier Teleki to finance Hungary's entire revisionist policy abroad with forged French francs was suddenly revealed in early December 1925. Although the Czechoslovaks, Yugoslavs and especially the French were greatly outraged and an anti-Magyar mood to some extent prevailed, the European Great Powers had no interest in overthrowing Bethlen's government. The result was that the Democratic Bloc's demands to replace the Regent, the prime minister and senior police officials, as well as increasing parliamentary control over government affairs, proved unsuccessful.

In the case of Rumania, precise revisionist demands were not made at first, since there was initially no prospect of an amicable settlement concerning the return of Transylvania, whose loss was especially painfully felt. However, Bethlen still hoped to secure benevolent non-intervention by the Bucharest government, if a crisis over or within Czechoslovakia provided an opportunity of re-annexing Upper Hungary without risk. The blood-letting, of land and people, which was easiest for the Hungarians to reconcile themselves to, had benefited Yugoslavia – so named after 1929 – since Hungary's politicians hoped, with Belgrade's help, to break the iron ring of Little Entente states around Hungary created by Beneš as a result of King Charles IV's restoration attempts. This alliance, which posed a constant military threat, virtually ruled out even loose cooperation between Hungary and its neighbours. Since the dispute over Burgenland caused relations with Austria to remain tense for years and since contacts with Germany were initially limited to a dialogue between the Hungarian Right and circles around General Ludendorff on the prospects of overturning the status quo, Hungary was only able to break out of its diplomatic isolation to some extent when it joined the League of Nations on 18 September 1922 and took its seat in the General Assembly on 31 January 1923. Hungary's initially very close contacts with Poland had fizzled out after the failure to achieve a common border in Ruthenia and after the signing of the Polish-Rumanian alliance treaty on 3 March 1921. It was not until May 1929, when the foreign ministers of the Little Entente states met in Belgrade, that the Polish foreign minister, Zaleski, visited Budapest and contributed to overcoming the foreign policy constraints, lamented by the Hungarian government, with the signing of a friendship and arbitration treaty.

It was only the need to bring about the orderly return of Hungarian citizens from Russian captivity that induced the government in Budapest to conclude three reparations agreements with the Union of Soviet Socialist Republics in 1920–21. These were followed on 15 July 1922 by an agreement on the exchange of political prisoners. Despite the government's tough anti-Communist line at home, an agreement establishing diplomatic and consular relations with the government of the Soviet Union was signed in Berlin on 5 September 1924. In view of the distrust felt by all of Hungary's neighbours, prime minister Bethlen did not manage to find the courage to have this agreement ratified and accept Soviet diplomatic representation in Hungary in the face of widespread general opposition at home.

In contrast, the Hungarians hoped for active Italian support of their revisionist demands following Mussolini's March on Rome in 1922. But as long as the *Duce* still competed with France for the support of the Little Entente states and hoped for eventual Italian domination of the Danube basin, he had no wish to reduce Italy's chances by openly siding with the Hungarians in their disputes. Only after relations between Budapest and Belgrade had been sufficiently normalised in 1926 for Bethlen to offer the Yugoslavian government a friendship and non-aggression arbitration pact – and the Yugoslavs after lengthy negotiations had rejected closer relations with Hungary – did Mussolini come out into the open. By a 'Treaty of Friendship and Cooperation', signed in Rome on 5 Apil 1927, Hungary acquired a valuable ally, while Mussolini was able to strengthen the Italian position in the Danube basin and further his Albanian policy, now directed against Yugoslavia.

The press campaign in support of Hungary's revisionist demands, launched in June 1927 by Lord Rothermere in the *Daily Mail* under the headline 'Justice for Hungary', caused great enthusiasm in

Hungary and encouraged the hope of achieving at least partial success in obtaining the return of the lost territories inhabited by Magyar majorities. Alongside the intensified activities of the reorganised Hungarian Revisionist League (*Magyar Revíziós Liga*), at first supported by 101 economic and social organisations, but soon by over 500 corporate bodies, county administrations and towns, the government concentrated on cultivating foreign diplomatic, artistic and academic contacts in the interests of achieving a revision of the treaty. This enthusiasm, which Mussolini's encouraging declarations aroused still further, caused the increasingly anxious foreign ministers of the Little Entente states to agree on 21 October 1929 to renew automatically every five years the mutual alliance treaties chiefly directed against Hungary and to instruct their general staffs, who agreed on regular consultations, to prepare all measures necessary for combined military intervention in Hungary or Bulgaria. Although Hungary, which since 1927, had violated more deliberately and frequently than ever the treaty's military clauses, had signed a secret military agreement with Italy and come to an arrangement with the opposition Croat leader, Maček, the Hungarian army would not have been capable of resisting a combined operation by the troops of the Little Entente states. Thus, a full ten years after the war, when the world economic crisis which also affected Hungary began to undermine the social and economic consolidation thus far achieved, the Bethlen government had still failed to make any progress with its revisionist policy.

After the First World War the technical innovations which had spread slowly but surely in Hungary ensured that most towns were connected to a water supply and provided with a sewage system, electricity supply and telephone system. The countryside, however, was almost entirely bypassed by these developments. By 1939, two-thirds of Hungary's villages were still without electricity. Thus, the cinema boom after the advent of 'talkies' and the expansion of national broadcasting for the country's 400,000 available radio sets were developments which were restricted to the towns. Hungary's highly developed newspaper industry, concentrated mainly in Budapest, hardly touched the poor peasants and rural labourers, since almost a million adults were still illiterate. After 1926, the long-serving minister of education, Count Kunó Klebelsberg, was responsible for the fact that some 5,000 classrooms were established in rural areas along with accommodation for teachers. However, despite his orders that adherence to the principle of six-years' compulsory elementary education should be more strictly monitored, approximately 10 per cent of children of school age were still able to avoid schooling. Also, most children from peasant and working-class families left school after four or at most six years and could only exceptionally enter and complete a secondary school education which involved great material sacrifice and numerous difficulties. Legislation belatedly passed in 1934 and 1938 tried to standardise the educational system by merging the grammar schools with those secondary schools placing more stress on technical and vocational subjects. During the school year of 1937–38 only 52,000 pupils were taught in grammar schools or in secondary vocational schools. There was no properly developed system for vocational training, with the result that apprentices were entirely subjected to the conditions laid down by employers. Of the 11,700 students attending universities and institutions of higher education, only 2.7 per cent came from peasant and working-class families. In the 360 or so schools for national minorities, subjects with a national bias like history, civic studies and geography were taught in Hungarian. Other subjects were taught in the vernacular, whether German, Slovak or Serbo-Croat.

Cultural activities encouraged by the state also remained tied to the traditional conservative outlook of Hungarian society. Literature was especially dominated by the superficial popular novels of writers like Ferenc Herczeg or Zsolt Harsányi as well as reactionary and nationalist writings which ignored the treatment of social tensions. After the overthrow of the Soviet Republic many committed writers and academics emigrated, although they remained tied to the problems of Hungarian society in their choice of themes. The literary circle centred on the newspaper *Nyugat* (The West), which had already been influenced by bourgeois-democratic ideas at the turn of the century and which included Gyula Juhász, Árpád Tóth, Mihály Babits and Zsigmond Móricz, lost much of its fighting spirit in the Horthy era, although it continued to attempt a critical, realistic portrayal of Hungarian society and painted an unflattering picture of the social misery and material distress of village life. Under this influence, the popular, or so-called 'village writers', took up the peasants' demands for an extensive programme of land reform and state aid. Their scholarly-based and convincing portrayals, like Imre Kovács' 'The Silent Revolution' or Géza Feja's 'Thunderstorms', were banned and the authors sent to prison charged with inciting hatred of the great landowners, campaigning for social revolution and damaging the prestige of the state and society. The works of writers close to Communism, like the powerful poetry of Attila Jószefs or academic works such as those of

György Lukács, were banned from publication in Hungary. The composer, Béla Bártok, eventually preferred to emigrate rather than suffer the increasingly reactionary cultural climate.

In Trianon Hungary 62.8 per cent of the population belonged to the Catholic Church, a fact which allowed its bishops to exert a substantial political influence. The leading politicians of the inter-war period, like Horthy and Bethlen, were, however, Calvinists, who, together with members of the other protestant churches, accounted for only 27.8 per cent of the population. Of the remainder of the population 6.2 per cent were professing Jews and 2.2 per cent were Catholics who observed the rites of the. Greek Uniate Church. One per cent of the population belonged to other religious groups. Although Catholicism was no longer the established religion, the Catholic Church and clergy, operating within the ethos of a Christian and national state and society, stood solidly behind the policies of the Horthy régime and had no reservations about supporting its revisionist policies. The industrial workers, however, were largely alienated from practising religion. The number of baptised Christians who did not attend church regularly increased rapidly, although it was still the practice, even in the towns, to attend church on major holidays and personal or family occasions such as christenings, confirmations, first communions, weddings and funerals. Thanks to its large press, which included 13 daily newspapers and 33 weeklies, its landed property of some 5,400 square kilometres and its strong support in the countryside, the Catholic Church was able to resist the process of secularisation more successfully than the other denominations. This was not least a result of the efforts of Cardinal Archbishop Dr Justinián Serédi who, as Primate of Hungary, also exercised certain state functions. The son of a carpenter, co-author of the revised version of the book of Canon Law, *Codex Juris Canonici*, and reluctantly appointed head of the Hungarian clergy, he constantly kept his distance from the Horthy régime and knew how to use his moderating influence, especially during the Second World War and the persecution of the Jews.

The period of political consolidation, which was accompanied by a slow but steady rise in economic prosperity and the hope of achieving a revision of the Trianon treaty by peaceful means in accordance with Article XIX of the League of Nations or by agreement with Hungary's Little Entente neighbours, was abruptly interrupted by the world economic crisis and the ensuing internal conflicts and deteriorating international situation. It soon became clear that Hungary had to seek a closer relationship, both militarily and economically, with one of the Great Powers with interests in the Danube basin. Because of its strategic position Hungary was to assume an exceptional importance for the expansionist foreign policy of the Third Reich. Increasing economic, political and military contacts with Germany brought the country more and more into the orbit of Nazi Germany and also led to a far-reaching transformation of its socio-economic and political structure.

The effects of the world economic crisis

'Black Friday', the day when the New York stock exchange crashed on 24 October 1929, had an immediate effect on the system of international loans and ushered in a world economic crisis of considerable proportions which resulted in all payments under the system being stopped. Hungary was, of course, affected by the recession and in 1931 was plunged fully into the economic turmoil. The drastic fall in the price of agricultural produce was bound to hit Hungary particularly badly, given that the majority of its population still earned its living from agriculture and agricultural produce remained its chief export. Although the price of wheat dropped from 33 pengö per quintal to only 9, Hungarian wheat still found it difficult to find a foreign market. Small farmers, in particular, who had taken on loans to modernise or enlarge their holdings, could no longer find the money to repay their debts and shoulder increased tax burdens. Many were ruined as a result of the forced sale of land which now began to be auctioned. Some 60,000 farms of under 2 hectares were affected. Over half a million rural labourers were made destitute and a further half million forced to hire their labour for starvation wages which were inadequate to feed their often large families. Despite an unexportable surplus of agricultural products, many people in the countryside starved and perished. The towns suffered equally in terms of hardship. Industrial production fell on average by almost a quarter; 15 per cent of Hungary's factories ceased production and 30 per cent of the labour force was laid off. The unemployed found themselves facing terrible hardships, since there was no provision for unemployment benefit or public assistance. The rest were forced to accept painful wage cuts and longer working hours. State employees had similarly to accept salary reductions and dismissals. As a result, graduates entering the job market were joined in suffering extreme hardship by 2,500 unemployed teachers and 2,000 engineers without work, despite government-promoted retraining schemes. From 1932 onwards, the general decline in living standards also began to affect small tradesmen and retailers, many of whom were forced to close down or sell their businesses.

At first the Bethlen government tried to overcome the financial crisis by arranging further foreign loans. This was only made possible by the scaling down of Hungary's reparations debt in January 1930, which was intended to make 10.4 million gold crowns available annually up to 1944 and, thereafter, 13.5 million annually up to 1966. Hungary's foreign debts, which at that time had already reached the astronomical sum of 1 billion US dollars – an amount which already exceeded the national income of the economically buoyant year of 1928 and comprised mainly short-term loans, could no longer be repaid owing to a shortage of foreign exchange and rapid decline in export earnings. The situation grew worse when some of the loans were prematurely recalled after the collapse of the German banks and the payments moratorium by the Austrian *Creditanstalt* on 11 May 1931. The bankruptcy of the country's largest bank, the Hungarian General Credit Bank, was only narrowly averted. The National Bank, which had been rescued only a few years previously with the aid of British finance, now found itself on the verge of collapse.

After accepting the Hague agreements in 1930 the government still tried to divert people's attention from the deplorable economic and financial situation by holding nationwide rallies and employing nationalist appeals and revisionist slogans, but was helpless at preventing demonstrations for work and bread which were held increasingly after 1 September and resulted in serious riots involving death and injury as a result of tough police intervention. It also failed to re-establish political stability, despite proclaiming martial law. The three major interest groups, the great landowners, the upper bourgeoisie and the state bureaucracy, upon which István Bethlen's government primarily depended for its support, also increasingly pursued their members' sectional interests and advocated changing the former economic and financial system at the expense of their erstwhile partners. The representatives of the wealthy and middle-ranking peasants left the government party and founded the Independent Party of Smallholders (*Független Kisgazdapárt*), led by Bálint Szijj and Zoltán Tildy, in Békés on 13 October 1930. Bethlen indeed managed to prevent any fundamental change to the composition of parliament when he again called elections for June 1931, winning 45.3 per cent of the vote and 158 of the 245 seats for his Unity Party. However, because the financial crisis, whose effects became very apparent on 14 June, made it necessary to impose a partial moratorium and pass an enabling law for financial cuts in July, the premier felt obliged to tender his government's resignation to the Regent on 19 August 1931. In view of the deepening social divisions, the hopeless economic situation and the threat to the whole political system, Bethlen wished to 'withdraw from circulation' in order, as he put it, 'to be able to maintain and ensure the survival of the system I have created'.

Horthy now appointed the conservative Count Gyula Károlyi as Bethlen's successor on 22 August 1931. Károlyi saw no alternative but to appeal to the League of Nations for fresh help in putting Hungary's finances in order. Thanks to French financial assistance the collapse of the state finances was averted on condition that Hungary would call a halt to its revisionist propaganda and fulfil its financial treaty obligations. A repayments moratorium, approved in December 1931, offered a degree of protection for the currency, although it failed to tackle the country's real economic difficulties effectively. When the government hesitated in meeting the demands of the great landowners and the new Independent Party of Smallholders who agreed in opposing radical land reform but wanted instead more subsidies for the farming sector and agricultural exports, Károlyi, who generally sought to follow the same policy as his predecessor, aroused the enmity of the agricultural lobby. The strict financial retrenchment meant that even state employees were forced to accept further salary cuts and therefore felt impelled to maintain their distance from the new government, especially since they were convinced that the haute bourgeoisie of mainly Jewish origin would continue to enjoy its privileged position. Budapest's rejection of the plan for a German-Austrian Customs Union (Schober-Curtius Agreement), which can only be attributed to France's growing influence in Hungary, and its promise to consider positively the Tardieu plan, proposed by the French government on 1 March 1932 to help east central Europe's financial recovery, aroused opposition from financial and commercial circles. The restrictions on the Hungarian government's freedom of action, as demonstrated by its stifling of revisionist propaganda, infuriated the nationalist pressure-groups, who never tired of laying the sole blame for the effects of the world economic crisis on the unjust peace treaty.

Hungary's political and social tensions grew so acute in the summer of 1932 that a strong faction within the government party turned against Károlyi. After the prime minister's dismissal on 21

September Horthy had to bow to the pressure of public opinion and appoint the former defence minister, Gyula Gömbös de Jáfka, to take over the government on 1 October 1932. This old trusted colleague of Horthy, who had been involved in Hungarian politics from the time of the counter-revolutionary Szeged government, held views that were both anti-Legitimist and hostile to the privileges of the upper aristocracy. Since he also held openly antisemitic views, he could be seen as a representative of the self-confident new middle class which was gaining ground at the expense of the old ruling élite and the Jewish bourgeoisie. Gömbös, who thought in military categories and was the first Hungarian politician to describe himself publicly as a 'Hungarian National Socialist', had developed a foreign policy strategy which centred on German, Italian and Hungarian cooperation in the framework of an 'axis of fascist states'. Germany appeared to be the only partner in such an alliance, who would be willing and able to break Hungary's encirclement by the Little Entente and France's dominant influence in east central Europe. He was well aware of the dangers involved in helping establish German dominance in the Danube basin, but believed he could create a counterweight to this by involving Italy and, hence, lay the basis for a thorough revision of the post-war settlement. With a certain amount of naiveté and political wishful thinking he was convinced that Hungary could regain its historic frontiers with the help of its powerful allies, involving only very slight risks. For this reason he utterly rejected any notion of compromise or agreement with the governments of the Little Entente, as had been mooted in Hungary at the beginning of the 1930s.

As the former organiser of the armed counter-revolutionary squads and right-wing radical groups during the period of the Soviet Republic, Gömbös was extremely popular with the officer corps and many members of the bureaucracy. His undisguised aversion to democratic liberal ideas, hostility towards the workers, hatred of left-wing radicalism and extreme patriotism made him acceptable even to the aristocratic ruling élite, although he made no secret of the fact that his ultimate aim of breaking open the anachronistic structure of Hungarian society for the benefit of the new middle classes. The results of the 1930 census had revealed that of Hungary's population of 8.7 million, the majority, i.e. about 4.5 million, still earned their living from agriculture. Half of the country's land under cultivation still belonged to the 7,500 owners of large estates. The vast majority of the rural population, i.e. the 1.2 million holders of dwarf farms, 600,000 farm labourers, employed mainly on large estates, and 1.2

million day-labourers – in all, more than a third of the population – scratched a bare living from the soil and lived in constant uncertainty. While the number of industrial workers and small tradesmen – around 650,000 people in 1930 – had been drastically reduced as a result of the world economic crisis, they already contributed substantially to the national income. When Gömbös announced his 'National Work Plan' of ninety-five points with an unusual energy for Hungarian politics, skilfully manipulating the press and radio, he seemed to be trying to accommodate the wishes and demands of all sections of the population. He proposed land and tax reforms, generous loans and concessionary arrangements for repaying agricultural debts, the stepping up of agricultural exports and the creation of new jobs, the holding of secret elections and the introduction of social legislation which might almost be described as progressive. However, his recipe for the advent of the 'new millenium' and the dawning of an 'age of reform' could scarcely disguise his real aim of establishing a fascist-style dictatorship in Hungary.

When Gömbös tried to implement his programme for creating a fascist 'Greater Hungary', he was confronted by a country which was utterly exhausted economically. The population was disappointed and disheartened at the lack of success of the decade-long campaign for a revision of the country's borders. The economic crisis, which had resulted in mass unemployment, the loss of many civilian and government jobs and a bleak future for the country's youth, gave added impetus to a mood in favour of genuine revolutionary change. At the same time, it forced Gömbös to steer a cautious and restrained course in both domestic and foreign policy. New members of the plebeian middle class, who shared his ideas and immediate aims, were deliberately placed in key positions in politics, the administration and the army. By creating an organisation of some 60,000 'vanguard fighters' he tried to create a mass basis of support for the government camp, which had by now been renamed the Party of National Unity (*Nemzeti Egység Pártja*). An attempt was even made to incorporate workers by creating a labour section in the party. New government newspapers like the *Függetlenség* (Independence) and *Új Magyarság* (New Hungary), the creation of an efficient propaganda machine, the merging of the state apparatus with the party organisations and the establishment of strict controls over public opinion ensured that Gömbös' policies found support, despite the growing opposition of the old ruling élite, some sections of the middle class, some workers and the rural proletariat. In particular, his vociferous attacks on the aristocracy and the plutocracy, on Jews, foreigners, Social Democrats and Communists, who were accused of either obstructing radical reforms at home or promoting chaos and the collapse of national values, were widely shared and attracted many new members into the Party of National Unity.

Hungary's various groups of right-wing radicals, who had already been previously very active but never particularly united, and suffered major fluctuations in membership, felt that Gömbös's programme was an endorsement of their views. The National Socialist Hungarian Workers' Party, founded in December 1931 by the journalist Zoltán Böszörmény, which later became known as the Scythe Cross movement (*Kaszáskeresztes Mozgalom*), concealed its rabid antisemitism and extreme nationalism behind its social aims. Its urgent demands included the nationalisation of estates of more than 250 hectares, state-promoted job-creation schemes, and, especially, the exclusion of all 'non-turanic-aryan elements' from important posts, together with the restoration of the country's pre-1914 frontiers. It also demanded that the country rid itself of 'Jewish profiteers' who were blamed for the misery which had befallen the population. Other fascist groups like the Hungarian National Socialist Party (*Magyar Nemzeti Szocialista Párt*), founded in 1932 by Count Sándor Festetics, or the United National Socialist Party (*Egyesült Nemzeti Szocialista Párt*), created by Count Fidél Pálffy in 1933, tried to gain the support of the rural and urban middle classes, drawn from the gentry, who had been especially hard hit by the economic crisis through the use of Christian, agrarian, antisemitic and nationalist policies. The Party of the National Will (*Nemzet Akaratának Párt*), founded by Ferenc Szálasi on 1 March 1935, which eventually came to encompass a broad spectrum of the many right-wing radical splinter groups, was to play a greater political role only after 1937. Although the illegally active Hungarian Communist Party was still barely capable of continuing its activities after the execution of its underground leaders, Imre Sallai and Sandor Fürst, on 29 July 1932, and the Social Democrats, despite their, by 1934, 85,000-strong membership, were increasingly subjected to government pressure, Gömbös failed to emasculate the trade unions, to set up a corporate state or effectively to ban strikes, which kept breaking out as a result of adverse economic and social conditions.

Gömbös's rigorous measures, which proved only moderately successful, provoked the opposition of ex-premier Bethlen and his conservative liberal supporters. When the economy began to revive after 1934, they recommended a return to traditional government principles and wanted to place Gömbös, who was ruling with increasing self-glorification and promoting the creation of a one-party state and dictatorship, once more under their control. Personal disagreements which had already surfaced in the 'twenties between Gömbös and Bethlen now re-surfaced and further heightened the tensions already present in the government party. On 5 March 1935, Gömbös suddenly dissolved the Lower House in order to pre-empt opponents within his own party who were preparing his overthrow with the help of the parliamentary opposition. His opponents were deliberately passed over when candidates were nominated for the coming elections which were called at short notice. The election held on 11 April 1935 witnessed a far greater degree of the usual rigging, intimidation and influencing of voters and produced a distinct swing to the Right. With 43.6 per cent of the vote and 170 seats Gömbös could count on a majority of the deputies, who were drawn mainly from ex-officer circles, the gentry, civil servants and middle-rankin landowners. Two representatives of National Socialist groups also took their seats for the first time in the Hungarian parliament. His promise, given on a visit to Berlin in September 1935, that he would introduce to Hungary within two years a one-party system and political order modelled on Germany was rendered void by his unexpectedly premature death in Munich on 6 October.

Despite the grand aims of their political programmes, Gömbös and his successors scored only very modest successes with their agricultural and industrial policies. The rural population which had been won over by promises of sweeping agrarian reforms had its hopes of a generous land reform dashed. A three-year moratorium on debt repayments benefited only a relatively small number of peasants. A law on entailed estates, modelled on that introduced by the German National Socialists, represented the Hungarian variant of legislation regulating land inheritance. From 1928 onwards, students had pointed with growing emphasis to the unavoidable need for further agrarian reforms in association with the so-called 'Village Research Programme', an area in which the leading Catholic student association, *Emericana*, and the protestant Christian student federation, *Pro Christo*, had been active in Szeged on a non-denominational basis. Despite the bishops' lack of interest, young priests also participated in discussions on the position of the impoverished rural population, the majority of whom lived in simple mud and clay huts with stamped earthen floors, shared with animals under one roof. In such circumstances tuberculosis was rampant and claimed over 10,000 victims annually. After demands were made for the expropriation and redistribution of estates of more than 250 hectares during a demonstration outside the Hungarian National Museum in Budapest on the national holiday of 15 March 1934, the government felt obliged to act: Gömbös had the parliament pass a land settlement law which earmarked the great landed estates of 200,000 hectares, i.e. around 8 per cent of the area of the latifundiae, for redistribution to 37,000 families over a period of 25 years. Following payment of a quarter of the purchase price the peasants were to be given 47 years to pay off their debt. Also, in cases of compulsory purchase the government wanted in future to be able to obtain the land in advance by compulsory purchase and then lease it to its previous owners. Although the nationalist Youth Federation, *Turul* (The Eagle), which was given financial backing by the great landowners and tended to belong to the right of the political spectrum, denigrated the populist 'village researchers', who were supported by the Left, as Communists and 'Jewish hirelings', the bishops felt obliged to hold the National Catholic Day of 1936 under the 'slogan 'Christ and the Hungarian Village'. The idea of land reform was not supported in church circles, only improved social welfare for the rural poor, of whom on average some 130,000 rural labourers had no guaranteed income. The dwarfholding peasants, for their part, could not produce a sufficient surplus to feed themselves. Even somewhat improved economic conditions shortly before the outbreak of the Second World War could not prevent the fact that average daily earnings in 1938 were between a third and a quarter below their level prior to the world economic crisis.

Although the slow onset of economic recovery after 1934 was accompanied by a rise in the number of people employed in industry and the workers' situation began to improve, unemployed rural workers willing to migrate to the towns rarely found a regular source of income. Hungary was the last European country to introduce the eight-hour day. The introduction, very late on, of legislation on workmen's protection, the guaranteeing of minimum wages and family allowances did at least provide employees with more social security. But real wages in 1938 were still 10 per cent below their level for 1929. Although the governments in the latter half of the 1930s tried hard to win the support of the rural population and the workers by means of liberal-inspired social legislation, the economic, social and cultural conditions of the lower classes in Hungarian society remained behind those of the rest of east central Europe in 1939. The great landowners, in contrast, had known how to prevent the success of any measures designed to reduce the size of their estates. In 1938, over 10,000 square kilometres of cultivable land was still owned by only 80 magnate families; a further 16,000 square kilometres was in the possession of 1,000 smaller estate-owners. The process of concentration in banking had contributed to the fact that Hungarian General Credit Bank and the Hungarian Commercial Bank of Pest ultimately controlled 60 per cent of Hungarian industry. The country's economy was, in fact, controlled by a handful of families. The direct influence of foreign capital did decline after 1934, but closer foreign relations with Germany led to a considerable increase in German economic dominance and contributed greatly to the continuing growth of Hungary's dependence on Germany, especially after the annexation of Austria and the incorporation of Czechoslovakia into the Reich.

The opening up of the German market to Hungarian agricultural produce, which was having difficulty finding a market, gave Hitler the opportunity to establish a stronger political foothold in Hungary. While only 11 per cent of Hungary's exports had been sold to Germany in 1930, the figure had already risen to 24 per cent by 1937. By spring 1939, almost 50 per cent of Hungary's total exports were sold to German customers. As regards Hungary's own imports, the proportion of German goods rose from 20 per cent to 26 per cent. In the summer of 1939 half of all the foreign capital invested in Hungary was controlled from Germany, since German banks held about 14 per cent of the shares in Hungarian industry. The prime minister at the time, Count Pál Teleki, was right when he remarked that 'the German Reich has such a major and extensive stake in our country that it is able to control, and to a certain degree influence, the entire Hungarian economy'.

Hungary and the Third Reich

Before Hitler came to power German–Hungarian relations had been of secondary importance for both states. The idea that both countries had a 'shared destiny' from the time of the First World War was occasionally spoken of with a certain pride. Both had been involved in a common struggle, both had rejected the terms of the Paris Peace Treaties and both felt they had been encircled by victorious neighbours and barred from a revision of what they perceived as unjust peace terms. The Hungarians' narrow-minded nationalities policy, which gave rise to latent tensions between over half a million ethnic Germans and the Hungarian government, had already soured relations between the two countries during the period of the Weimar

Republic. Further complications inevitably arose after 1933, when the leaders of Hungary's German minority, now in receipt of financial and political support from the Reich, became increasingly self-confident and Hitler himself claimed to be the acknowledged leader of all Germans. Gömbös's willingness to secure Hitler's friendship and his efforts to realise his original concept of an international fascist axis alongside the pursuit of Hungary's economic interests, proved opportune for Hitler at a time when Germany was isolated in foreign policy. In March 1933, ex-premier Bethlen was able to explain Hungary's revisionist aims in detail to the Führer and Reich Chancellor and other leading German politicians, before Gömbös himself, in a surprise visit to Berlin on 16 and 17 June 1933, outlined to Hitler his vision of a cooperation pact between Italy, Austria, Germany and Hungary which would aim at achieving economic autarky and would serve as a counterweight to the political dominance of France and her clients in the Little Entente in the Danube Basin. But Hitler's basic dislike of the Magyars and Germany's stronger interest in forging closer ties with Rumania and Yugoslavia initially hampered the development of German-Hungarian relations. Even though they were opponents of revisionism both Rumania and Yugoslavia were more important potential allies because of the importance of their natural resources for the German economy.

Hence, Gömbös and his foreign minister, Kálmán Kánya, who became the driving force behind Hungary's revisionist policies after his appointment on 3 February 1933, developed closer contacts with Italy, especially since Mussolini was more than willing to promise his help in achieving success for Hungary's revisionist campaign. It was largely thanks to moves by Gömbös that Rome and Vienna agreed to closer cooperation in early 1933, an agreement which clearly warned Hitler not to attempt the annexation of Austria. The Hungarian general staff was, in fact, very pro-German in its sympathies, since Germany's support was seen as indispensable for secretly rearming Hungary and obtaining supplies of arms on credit. However, the fear that Germany, whose influence on Hungary's German minority was causing growing anxiety, would become a powerful immediate neighbour if Austria were annexed, led politicians of all shades of opinion to call on the government to maintain a cautious, non-commital approach in foreign policy. There were also a number of ideological reservations. Extreme reservations were felt towards the adoption of National Socialist racialist ideology. The clergy and intelligentsia advocated that, in the case of Jews, legal norms should be strictly adhered to despite the revival of antisemitism.

The programme of a 'Hungarian National Socialism', which Gömbös advocated with growing passion, encountered opposition from the liberal wing of the government camp led by the interior minister, Miklós Kozma. As a result of these objections Gömbös was forced to adopt a cautious policy.

Although the Hungarian government tried to avoid a head-on collision with the interests of the Entente Powers, and demanded only a recognition of Hungary's equality of rights instead of insisting on a minimal acceptable revision programme, the increased activities of the Austrian National Socialists forced Gömbös to adopt a clear position in the Rome Protocol, signed on 17 March 1934. Although this consultative pact between Italy, Austria and Hungary – to which economic clauses were added on 14 May 1934 – was of no great political significance, it was intended as a warning to Hitler. Following the attempted National Socialist coup in Vienna and the murder of the Austrian Chancellor, Dollfuss, on 25 July 1934, German–Hungarian relations reached an all-time low. The new organisational statute of the Little Entente states of 16 February 1933, encouraged by France to come closer together as a result of increased German diplomatic activity in the Danube area, the Balkan League of 4 February 1934 and the plans of the Czech foreign minister, Beneš, for a Danubian Federation forced Hungary to look for other partners willing to support its revisionist aims.

After a period of formal, though lukewarm bilateral relations with Hungary, Poland, which under its dynamic foreign minister, Beck, proposed the idea of a 'Third Europe' as a bulwark against Bolshevism and a barrier against the expansionist policies of German National Socialism, showed an interest in establishing closer cooperation. Neither Warsaw nor Budapest greeted the idea of an Eastern Pact, proposed by the French foreign minister on 27 June 1934, with undivided enthusiasm. Although Hungary had established full diplomatic relations with the Soviet Union on 4 February 1934, the USSR's entry to the League of Nations on 19 September caused anxiety in both Budapest and Warsaw. The assassination of the French foreign minister, Barthou, and King Alexander of Yugoslavia in Marseilles on 9 October, which provoked the unfounded accusation that Hungary had been involved in the murders and strained Hungary's relations with its South Slav neighbour to breaking-point, illustrated the importance of finding a new ally for the Gömbös government, especially since discussions in Austria concerning a Habsburg restoration also encouraged Hungarian royalists and aroused fears of foreign policy complications. For this reason,

Gömbös proposed an alliance to the ageing Marshall Pilsudski when he visited Warsaw between the 19 and 22 October 1934 in return for no more than a promise that Poland would never take up arms against Hungary but instead use its whole influence to prevent Rumania from participating in any punitive action by the Little Entente against Hungary.

When after the visit of the new French foreign minister, Pierre Laval, to Rome on 7 January 1935 Italian–French differences could be regarded as settled, and Mussolini joined the anti-revisionist powers for a time, the Hungarian government felt obliged to make a concession to the successor states. Acknowledging the improved treatment of the Magyar minorities it offered to conclude non-aggression pacts with its neighbours. However, the members of the Little Entente were not prepared to change their position towards Hungary in the slightest. The signing of the mutual assistance pact between France and Russia and Russia and Czechoslovakia on 2 and 16 May 1935 respectively worried the Budapest government so much, that more feelers were again sent out to Berlin – despite the fact that signs of closer cooperation between Germany and Yugoslavia in November 1934 had caused serious concern in Hungary. Since the foreign ministers of the Little Entente states had completely rejected Hungary's claim for military parity, a peaceful revision of the post-war settlement and improved protection for minorities at their conference in Bled on 29–30 August, the idea of creating a Danubian Confederation which would include Hungary had also become remote. Thus, after the legal position of Hungary's German minority had been improved, Gömbös met Hitler for a second time on 29 September 1935 to decide the future course of Hungarian foreign policy.

German opinion felt that Budapest should first drop its revisionist demands towards Rumania and Yugoslavia and instead concentrate exclusively on Czechoslovakia. A German loan of 100 million Reichsmark was granted on condition that the Hungarians order deliveries of German artillery and anti-tank weapons, as well as heavy Mörser artillery to supply the Hungarian army. Gömbös was also given the prospect of the return of the Burgenland if Germany were to annex Austria. After Italy invaded Abyssinia on 3 October 1935, he was also able to depend once more on Mussolini's support of Hungary's revisionist aims.

During the hectic year of 1936, when Germany's reoccupation of the demilitarised Rhineland and the outbreak of the Spanish Civil War heightened European tensions and the signing of the

German–Italian treaty on 25 October strengthened the claim of the 'Rome–Berlin Axis' to dominate east central Europe, Gömbös, on Hitler's instructions, tried for a rapprochement with Yugoslavia. However, the latter was still so closely bound to the Little Entente that it had no wish to pursue its own independent policy. On Horthy's first visit to Germany on 22 August 1936, Hitler again suggested that he should buy Rumanian and Yugoslavian goodwill, for once Germany had rearmed the Führer would force an agreement with Czechoslovakia by means of massive threatening gestures. However, the unexpected death of Gömbös on 6 October, who had not enjoyed Horthy's full confidence during his last months in power, and the appointment of the dull and undistinguished civil servant, Kálmán Darányi, as his successor on 10 October 1936, advised restraint in Hungary's foreign policy. A series of domestic political issues, such as an electoral reform, an extension of the Regent's powers, measures to deal with unemployment, the implementation of land reform and anti-Jewish legislation demanded urgent attention. Also, the mistrustful Kálmán Kánya was increasingly less prepared to tolerate interference in the conduct of foreign policy. Dissatisfied with Hungary's growing dependence on the Reich and the danger of war, deliberately cultivated by Hitler, he had no desire to place all his bets on Germany.

While Darányi, to the satisfaction of the conservative magnates and economic interests, reverted to the same methods as the Bethlen government, trying to promote consensus within the government camp and cooperating more closely with the Smallholders' Party and even the Social Democratic Party, foreign minister Kánya, in view of the consolidation of fascist with national socialist forces, again sounded out the Little Entente states on their willingness to reach an understanding. However, since the successor states rejected his proposal to link a non-aggression pact, which the government in Budapest keenly desired, with the complicated minorities problem and a complete acknowledgement of Hungarian military parity, plans for a Danubian Federation – now pursued especially by the Czechoslovak prime minister, Milan Hodža – had no chance of being realised because of their complete rejection by the Magyars. German gestures, such as the – hardly seriously intended – offer to the Czechs of a non-aggression treaty or a guarantee of Rumania's territorial integrity, caused as much annoyance in Budapest as the direct Hungarian–Czechoslovak talks in the early summer of 1937, discreetly promoted by the Austrian government, caused in Berlin. Sensing that Hungary was being manoeuvred into a dangerous

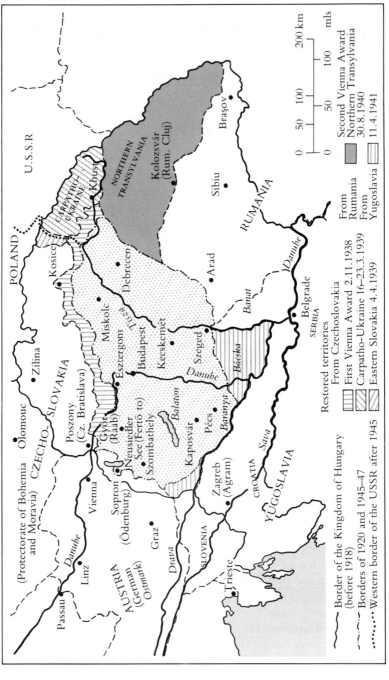

Map 2 Hungary after the First World War

collision course against Czechoslovakia without sufficient moral and diplomatic support from Germany and Italy, Kánya went all out for an agreement with the member states of the Little Entente in the autumn of 1937. However, by October the optimistic negotiations which began in late August had failed to produce any concrete result. For Kánya and the forces around Count Pál Teleki and Béla Imrédy, Gömbös' former finance minister and current president of the National Bank, this also meant the failure of the stratagem of arousing the British government's interest in the Danube area in order to stem Germany's constantly growing influence.

Although Darányi's government, which made little progress in solving the nation's urgent internal political problems, felt alienated by Hitler's methods and the risks he took in his power politics, and would rather have seen Hungary's revisionist demands settled at a conference under guarantee by the Great Powers, it had to follow Germany's course completely in November 1937 in view of its own lack of success to date. Hitler, who told his small circle of associates on 5 November of his 'unalterable decision' to smash Austria and Czechoslovakia, 'at any time, even as soon as 1938' and even at the risk of a possible war on two fronts, went on later that same month – on 25 November – to reveal to a government delegation led by Darányi the role to be allocated to Hungary. Although the Hungarians were prepared to come to terms with Germany's possible annexation of Austria in the hope of regaining the Burgenland as far as the river Leitha, Austria's invasion by German troops on 11 and 12 March 1938 took the Darányi government completely by surprise. Disappointment at the invasion was all the greater when, despite messages of congratulation and gentle persuasion, Hitler showed no desire to part with the Burgenland as a gesture towards providing Hungary with its first concrete revisionist success. German reluctance to agree to cooperation between the two general staffs and guarantee Yugoslavia's non-involvement in the event of a conflict with Czechoslovakia increased Hungarian uncertainty. However much they desired the return of Upper Hungary, Slovakia and Ruthenia, the majority of Hungary's politicians, including Horthy, who was intervening increasingly in everyday policy, perceived a threat to Hungary, if, following Bohemia's incorporation into the Reich as a German protectorate, Hitler would exploit fully his increased opportunities to influence events in the Danube region. The upright conservative, Darányi, was not regarded as the right politician to be capable of maintaining unity between the existing factions in the government camp in the event of an external threat or of stemming the danger from the extreme Right which now began to group forces around Ferenc Szálasi, the leader of the Party of the National Will. Szálasi, a staff officer, who had retired from active service with the general staff, set out as his party programme the aims formulated in his book *Cél és követelések* (Goal and Demands). Characterised by a militant anti-semitism, their only originality lay in the suggestion of creating a federal state to bring all the peoples of the Carpathian Basin together under Hungarian leadership (a solution he termed 'conationalism'). After his visit to Germany in the autumn of 1936 Szálasi stepped up his campaign among the urban population and the industrial workers, in particular. He was consequently arrested in April 1937 and his party dissolved. In the following summer László Endre founded the Racial Defence-Socialist Party, which was intended to be a broadly-based right-wing party. Eight other right-wing radical and nationalist groups joined it in Budapest on 24 October 1937 to form the Hungarian National Socialist Party (*Magyar Nemzeti Szocialista Párt*) which subscribed ideologically to the principle of 'Hungarianism', as officially proclaimed by Szálasi. Its aim of developing an advanced agrarian state with a sound industrial base was to be guaranteed by the three pillars of 'Hungarianism', i.e. moral (Christian), spiritual and material (national economy) values. Again sentenced to ten months' imprisonment at the end of November 1937, Szálasi could not prevent his new party being banned on 21 February 1938. However, Germany's annexation of Austria strengthened Hungary's National Socialists, who adopted the slogan '1938 is our year', to the extent that a new National Socialist Hungarian Party–Hungarist Movement (*Nemzeti Szocialista Magyar Párt–Hungarista Mozgalom*) succeeded the earlier party as early as 27 March 1938. Darányi's failure to take a tough enough line with the extremists, who refused to be discouraged by public order laws, bans and Szálasi's imprisonment for three years, eventually contributed to the premier's fall from power. The Arrow Cross Party–Hungarist movement (*Nyilaskerezstes Párt–Hungarista Mozgalom*), founded on 9 March 1939, tried to ensure its continued existence by adopting an emphatically moderate programme whose only radical feature was its antisemitism, and achieved substantial success in the elections of May 1939. With a quarter of the vote and 31 deputies, together with the support of a further 17 deputies from other National Socialist groups, it was able steadily to increase its influence on the course of Hungarian policy.

Darányi now tried to avoid his downfall, which, in the spring of 1938, seemed imminent. He announced a rearmament programme in

Győr on 5 March which would make 1,000 million pengö available for the modernisation and expansion of the armed forces within the next five years. Four days later, on 9 March, he announced a cabinet reshuffle of key ministerial posts. A draft of new anti-Jewish legislation which was laid before parliament on 8 April, was intended to secure him German sympathies and the support of their Hungarian sympathisers, who could hope to step into positions vacated by Jews dismissed from their posts. However, after a series of intrigues, in which ex-premier Count Bethlen had the guiding hand, Darányi was dismissed on 13 May 1938 and Horthy appointed Béla Imrédy, the capable, ambitious and devout catholic President of the National Bank, as his successor. As well as his reputation as a first-class financial expert, he owed his appointment above all to his liberal, pro-western and outright Anglophile views, which he demonstrated by giving the ex-prime minister, Count Pál Teleki, the post of education minister in his cabinet. Although this seemed to strengthen those elements critical of National Socialist Germany, after a brief and unsuccessful attempt to win Britain's support in September 1938, it was Imrédy's influence which was eventually responsible for Hungary's completely siding with Germany.

While Imrédy vigorously opposed the Hungarist movement, but at the same time eventually secured the passage of anti-Jewish legislation and the new military budget through parliament, in the field of foreign policy he attempted to use his good personal contacts with Great Britain in order to win the support of the British government for a peaceful return of the Magyar-populated districts of Czechoslovakia and at the same time boost the sale of Hungarian agricultural produce. At the same time, he established closer contacts with Poland with a view to defining mutual spheres of interest and achieving the coordination of diplomatic activities and, if necessary, military operations. Since Hungary could not rely on armed forces of any appreciable strength and greatly overestimated the strength of its potential enemies, Imrédy's cabinet tried once more to achieve a maximum possible revisionist success by peaceful means through negotiations with the Little Entente. On 22 August 1938, the foreign ministers of the Entente meeting in Bled announced that they were prepared to recognise Hungary's desire for armaments parity and were willing to consider a more conciliatory stance on the question of national minorities.

This first modest attempt at a settlement was immediately devalued by Hitler's remarks during Horthy's state visit to Germany at the end of August when Hitler expressed his annoyance at what he called the 'sloppy attitude' of Hungary's politicians and pointed out that whoever wanted to 'join the party in destroying Czechoslovakia has to do some of the cooking as well'. But during the talks held in Berlin and Kiel it became clear that even the keenest Hungarian revisionists were not prepared to rush head over heels into an uncertain adventure on Hitler's side. However, when in September 1938 the Führer set the Czechoslovakian crisis in motion and refused to relax the pressure, Hungary could not remain on the sidelines. On 20 September, Imrédy and Kánya were summoned to Berchtesgaden where they were confronted by a Hitler who was determined on world war. In a fit of generosity he informed them that he had no claims on Slovakia or Ruthenia, provided the Hungarian government – after a short interval in order to avoid intervention by Rumania and Yugoslavia – took an active part in the destruction of Czechoslovakia. Although some 200,000 inadequately trained and poorly equipped soldiers had been mobilised in Hungary in the meantime, their field strength was limited, since supplies of munitions were adequate for only some 36 hours of fighting. The news, which was eventually announced on 28 September, that a meeting of government leaders would take place at a Four Power Conference in Munich, was greeted with relief in Budapest, since there was now the prospect of avoiding armed conflict. It was entirely thanks to Mussolini's intervention that Hungary's claims were dealt with satisfactorily in the Munich agreement to the point that 'the problem of the Hungarian minorities in Czechoslovakia, insofar as this would not be settled within three months by an agreement between the governments concerned, would be the subject of a further meeting of the government leaders of the Four Powers present'.

But the sudden euphoria felt in Hungary at this first major revisionist success was soon dampened by the tough negotiations with the autonomous regional governments of Slovakia and Ruthenia (now called the Carpatho–Ukraine) in Komárom in October 1938. The opposing parties were so entrenched in their views that on 2 November 1938 the German foreign minister, von Ribbentrop, and his Italian counterpart, Ciano, were forced to give an arbitration judgement in Vienna's Belvedere Palace, which awarded Hungary the return of 12,009 square kilometres of land with 1.04 million inhabitants, including 592,000 Magyars, 290,000 Slovaks, 37,000 Ruthenes and 14,000 Germans. This increased Hungary's territory and population to 105,000 square kilometres and 10.11 million inhabitants. Splendid celebrations to mark the 'return of the occupied territories' scarcely concealed the disappointment felt at the partition of Ruthenia and the failure to secure a common frontier with Poland. Kánya, who was blamed for these failures and had to fight for his survival in the cabinet thought he could take a gamble and, without a complete assurance of Poland's backing, ordered preparations for the military occupation of Ruthenia's remaining territory, planned for the night of 19 and 20 November 1938. Because of Hitler's firm objections, the attack had to be cancelled at the last minute. As a result of public pressure the Imrédy government was forced to resign on 23 November. Since both Teleki and the chief of the Hungarian general staff, Lajos Kerezstes–Fischer, refused to accept the post of premier, Horthy once more entrusted Imrédy with the formation of a new government on 28 November. With the appointment of pro-German politicians acceptable to the German government to the leading ministerial posts in the cabinet the entire political system took a distinct shift to the right. After several candidates had turned down the post, Kánya's arrogant, ambitious and scheming secretary of state, Count István Csáky, was appointed the new foreign minister. He believed that Hungary could secure its independence and gain further revisionist successes, which as a Hungarian nationalist he thought vital to its survival, only if it followed Berlin's advice.

Csáky's belief that the 'Rome–Berlin Axis' would dominate Europe for the next quarter century and that under its protection Hungary would be restored to its former greatness within its historical frontiers led him to seek an even closer relationship with Hitler's Germany in the hope of being able to occupy the strategically important province of the Carpatho-Ukraine before the regional elections due to be held there on 12 February 1939. Because of his anxieties about holding on to his office, Imrédy may well have been the driving force behind the attempt to win Hitler's approval. Despite his new government's shift to the right and attempts to conceal the disappointing result of the Vienna Award through increased internal political activities such as a new land reform law and discriminatory anti-Jewish legislation modelled on the German example, Imrédy lost the Regent's confidence. The premier had failed overall in fulfilling the high hopes placed in him. He had been unsuccessful and had brought about a situation where – against his own wishes, not least because of Britain's lack of interest – Hungary had grown substantially more dependent on Germany. However, after Hitler had adamantly refused to tolerate any further Hungarian actions in the Carpatho-Ukraine, Horthy summoned Imrédy on 13

February 1939 and used the 'discovery' of his Jewish great grand-
mother as the excuse to dismiss him. For the second time in his
career Count Pál Teleki was appointed prime minister on 16
February 1939.

The new premier, a professor of geography, had been a former
delegate to the Paris Peace Conference and, since May 1938,
education minister. He was neither a narrow-minded revisionist nor
a cloistered academic, but a responsible full-blooded politician,
conscious of the responsibilities of his office. He did not shirk from
the effort involved in pursuing an independent Hungarian nationalist
course in domestic and foreign policy and secretly hoped that in a
conflict between the fascist dictatorships and the western democracies
– which he thought inevitable – the latter would eventually gain the
upper hand. Nevertheless, he was enough of a political realist to
recognise Hitler's current domination of east central Europe and,
since the recovery of the Carpatho-Ukraine was at stake, to support
Germany in its expected elimination of the rump of Czechoslovakia
after Munich. In the following six weeks, during which Hungary
came closer to achieving this revisionist aim, the country became
even more dependent on Germany in an irreversible development
which gave rise to the long-term danger of a complete loss of
political sovereignty. Hungary's joining of the Anti-Comintern Pact
on 24 February 1939, its breaking off of diplomatic relations with
the Soviet Union on 2 February and its subsequent withdrawal from
the League of Nations on 11 April were all signs of a willingness
to subordinate the country to Germany's leadership.

When Hitler informed the Hungarian government on the evening
of 12 March 1939 that it had 24 hours to settle the Ruthenian
problem in its own manner, Horthy and Teleki's government did
not hesitate to join obediently in Hitler's illegal action. Like the vast
majority of their countrymen, the politicians also thought only in
historical-geographical terms and were convinced of the need to
restore Hungary to its historical frontiers or else face national
decline. Disquieted by Germany's announcement that a protectorate
had been established over Slovakia, to which Hungary also laid
claim, the government ordered military operations to begin after 16
March in eastern Slovakia with the aim of extending Hungary's
common frontier with Poland. It also hoped hat it could in time
persuade the Slovak state, which was barely capable of an independent economic existence, to enter into closer cooperation or even
union with Hungary. The campaign resulted in the acquisition of
an area of 11,085 square kilometres with 552,000 inhabitants in the

Carpatho-Ukraine, of whom 70.6 per cent were Ukrainians, 12.5 per cent Magyars and 12 per cent ethnic Germans. A further 1,700 square kilometres with 70,000 mainly Ukrainian and Slovak inhabitants were wrested from Slovakia. After Poland's refusal to give in to his demands over the question of Danzig and the Polish Corridor, Hitler, who had earlier considered partitioning Slovakia to compensate its neighbours, at first showed no inclination to accommodate Hungary's revisionist demands any further. In the months that followed tensions between Hungary and Slovakia, Hitler's pseudo-sovereign vassal state which served as a model for his 'New Order' in Europe, reached the point where the threat of a military clash was only avoided as a result of major German intervention.

Although the Vienna Award did justice to an essential part of Hungary's claims and the overestimated asset of a common frontier with Poland had been achieved after the occupation of the densely afforested but economically still undeveloped Carpatho-Ukraine, Teleki's government, though breaking the encircling grip of the Little Entente, had allowed itself to become chained to Berlin, which meant in fact a much greater constraint on its freedom of action. Had Horthy and the various Hungarian governments opposed Hitler's wishes after March 1939, Hungary would have certainly suffered a similar fate to Poland. The impatient and uncompromising revisionist claims which Hungary raised against Rumania in an increasingly tense international situation from the spring of 1939 onwards aroused little sympathy. Not only did they paralyse the British and French guarantee to Greece and Rumania, announced on 13 April 1939, but by constantly stirring up trouble in the crisis-ridden area of south-eastern Europe gave Hitler the opportunity to put himself forward in the role of arbitrator and consolidate Germany's position in the Danube region. This exceptionally blinkered and dangerous foreign policy of the Teleki government, which measured its progress entirely in terms of achieving its revisionist aims and eventually made every move ultimately dependent on this goal, speeded up the process whereby Hungary became increasingly dependent on Germany in its foreign, military and economic policy. Its unhesitating alignment with Germany, which Hitler and Ribbentrop suggested to Hungary's compliant foreign minister, Count István Csáky, at Berchtesgaden on 8 August 1939, paid off a year later when the Second Vienna Award restored Northern Transylvania to Hungary. However, it involved the renouncing of Teleki's original policy of 'armed neutrality', the forsaking of genuine Hungarian independence, and eventually culminated in the catastrophe of war. Thus, Hungary's revisionist policy, which was a failure in its extent and method, also set in motion the downfall of Horthy's quasi-feudal state which was plunged by Germany's ultimate defeat into the maelstrom of social revolution and into being once more forced to accept the frontiers laid down in the Trianon peace treaty.

In domestic politics, Hungary was unsettled by the debate which lasted from December 1938 to 3 May 1939 on the second anti-Jewish law. The application of racial criteria led to the vast majority of Hungary's Jews losing their positions, especially in the educated and white-collar professions, but also in big business. A law of 27 January 1939 introducing universal conscription and the decision to build up the army reserves made it compulsory for all men and women between the ages of 14 and 70 to join the Labour Service for the sake of national defence. Yet it also served as a pretext for further restrictions on freedom of assembly and organisation, together with the introduction of summary courts and the erection of internment camps. After the Party of National Unity, led by ex-premier Imrédy, ceased its political activities and joined the modern Hungarian Life Movement on 5 January 1939, Teleki founded his own Party of Hungarian Life (*Magyar Élet Pártja*) on 7 March 1939 in preparation for the elections due to be held in March. Although representatives of the Arrow Cross–Hungarist movement continued to be persecuted, Teleki had no objections to their participating in the elections of 28–30 May 1939, which were conducted mainly by secret ballot. Together with the other National Socialist right-wing radical groups they won almost a million votes and 48 seats, of which 17 went to the splinter parties. Winning 181 of the 260 contested seats, the Party of Hungarian Life was able to rely on a comfortable majority, especially since it could count on support on national issues from the Christian Economic and Social Party (8 seats) and the National Liberal Party (5 seats). The middle ground and the left of politics, led by the Independent Party of Smallholders, did particularly badly in the election campaign which was dominated by right-wing slogans and the chicanery of the authorities. The Smallholders had only 14 seats compared with the 22 they had previously held. The Social Democratic Party, despite polling 13.3 per cent of the vote, won only 5 seats. The Hungarian Communists, whose Central Committee, which had been active underground, had been dissolved by the Comintern in 1936 and replaced by a provisional secretariat set up in Prague, tried to increase their contacts with the more left-wing elements among the extreme nationalists, but, despite attempts at reorganisation by Ferenc Rózsa in the spring of 1939, were far too weak to be able to influence political events or the majority of workers who had been won over by the National Socialists' slogans. Following internal squabbles in the 'Hungarian-German National Popular Education Association', Franz Basch founded the 'National League of Germans in Hungary' in November 1938. As a result of the financial and moral support it received from the German Nazi Party's own Department of Foreign Affairs and the SS Liaison Office for Ethnic Germans, it became the forerunner of a single party representing Hungary's ethnic Germans, who were becoming increasingly influenced by the spirit of National Socialism.

Despite the growing threat of war in the summer of 1939, the slow economic recovery, helped along by increased exports to Germany, an intensive armaments programme, first revisionist successes and growing hopes of recovering Transylvania, gave broad sections of the population the impression of standing on the threshold of a major political and economic recovery. The government attempted to play down the increasingly obvious pressures from Germany and, by staging incidents on the Rumanian border, tried to divert attention from tensions within the government and the growing political polarisation. However, the Hitler-Stalin Pact of 23 August and the German invasion of Poland on 1 September 1939, which marked the outbreak of the Second World War, shook the Magyars out of their illusory complacency and forced the country and its politicians to come off the fence.

CHAPTER FOUR

Hungary During the Second World War

The rise of Nazi Germany, Hitler's aggressive revisionist and expansionist policy aimed at acquiring 'living-space' in the East and Hungary's growing dependence on its dynamic and unpredictable neighbour caused growing disquiet in Budapest despite the government's satisfaction at regaining the territories in the north of the country which had previously belonged to the historic Kingdom of Hungary. The sharp increase in support for the extreme Right, even from among the workers, was worrying for the Magyar politicians as were the increasing claims of the leaders of the German minority which stepped up its demands and openly espoused the new 'German ideology', demanding special privileges and a degree of autonomy which Budapest could scarcely tolerate. Many Hungarians were painfully aware of their limited freedom of action in domestic and foreign policy and felt that, for better or for worse, they had been placed at the mercy of Hitler's dictates without any longer being able to represent effectively or give priority to the nation's vital interests. The existing political and social order with its anti-liberal, semi-feudal power structure and spiritual and moral values rooted in the nineteenth century appeared to be threatened if the National Socialist revolution were to spill over to Hungary and if the limited, though still existent opportunities for action, were to be eliminated under a totalitarian system. Since many Hungarians were aware that Nazi Germany would not in the long term be able to maintain military dominance over the anti-Hitler coalition, they wished to achieve the maximum possible revisionist gains in the wake of German aggrandisement at the minimum possible risk. But, at the same time, they sought to maintain contacts with the western Allies who they saw as the ultimate victors in order not to have to accept territorial losses once more in the wake of a German defeat. Most members of the upper nobility, including the increasingly influential ex-premier, Count István Bethlen, many writers, academics, some of the grande bourgeoisie and, after some vacillation, Horthy himself, took the view that despite Hungary's cautious collaboration with Germany, imposed by the situation, links with the western Allies had to be preserved. The preconditions for the development of a 'strong Hungarian Empire' had to be exploited and every means used to defend Hungarian independence.

The officer corps and the generals, many civil servants, social climbers and even younger industrial workers were convinced of the Third Reich's ultimate victory, especially after the success of German arms in the summer of 1940. Hitler's Social Darwinist views on race and the Nazi 'Lebensraum' ideology appealed to them. They were also attracted by the thought of bringing about a radical transformation of Hungary's ossified social structure, implementing social changes, completely eliminating the political Left and he Jews and restoring the historic Hungarian Kingdom to its former position of dominance in the Danube region. Although they were chauvinistically nationalist in outlook, they had little sympathy for the anti-Nazism of their internal political opponents which was based on Magyar nationalism and ethical and religious objections. Even so, both groups paid homage to the primacy of revisionist policy. Against this background of polarisation in Hungarian politics, the government pursued a vacillating policy over the next five years which was destined to fail from the outset on account of its opportunism. While Horthy and one government after another were at pains to feign unconditional loyalty towards Germany's leaders, they rapidly lost credibility with the Allies because of their complicity with Hitler and their growing involvement in the war despite the clandestine contacts they maintained with the West. Because Horthy, who was in the habit of procrastinating decisions, was personally incapable of recognising when the right moment had come to desert Germany, Hungary was forced to make immense sacrifices in the final year of the war and was handed over to the Arrow Cross' rule of terror.

When, in the late summer of 1939, German preparations for the attack against Poland could no longer be kept secret Prime Minister Teleki informed Hitler that his country, which enjoyed good relations with the Poles, would not participate in the campaign. The Führer and Reich Chancellor, who had a low opinion of the Hungarians and their military capabilities, informed Foreign Minister

Csáky on 8 August 1939 that he had no thought of asking for Hungary's military assistance, but at the same time did not expect an open declaration of neutrality. Thus, after the outbreak of hostilities Teleki declared Hungary a 'non-belligerent country', refused German troops the right of free passage and opened Hungary's borders to more than 150,000 Polish military and civilian refugees. His appeal to the political parties that they should maintain a political truce for the duration of the war was agreed to by all parliamentary factions except the left-wing deputies and the Arrow Cross. The latter demanded Szálasi's immediate release and the repeal of Ordinance No. 3400 which banned civil servants and state officials from joining the party. As a result of the truce Teleki was able with general consensus to undo many social welfare achievements, limit the freedom of the press and control the trade unions by placing them under the control of government officials. Even those directly affected did not protest. Since the wartime economy required an increasing supply of labour, and German demands – which proved increasingly difficult to fulfil – for the volume of raw materials and agricultural exports to be increased, used up every available source of labour, there was a considerable rise in wages and a noticeable improvement in living standards which made employees in all sectors of the economy initially contented. The prospect of further revisionist gains also rapidly silenced the critics.

The surprisingly easy successes of the German armies in northern and western Europe led, in the summer of 1940, to growing public pressure on the Teleki government to play an active part in the war. Arguing that even now 'a German victory' was 'by no means certain', Teleki, who had established secret contacts with the British government, refused 'to place ourselves completely and unreservedly on Germany's side'. He stepped up military preparations with the aim of forcing Rumania to return Transylvania. But since Rumania made a significant contribution to Germany's oil requirements, and since there was still a danger of British military intervention in the Balkans because of the guarantee pact still in force with Britain, the German government vetoed any unilateral Hungarian military action. Only when the sudden Soviet ultimatum of 26 June 1940 forced the Bucharest government to cede Bessarabia and the northern Bukovina and King Carol terminated the assistance pact with France and Great Britain, did Hitler and the Italian foreign minister, Ciano, give Teleki and Csáky, summoned to Munich on 10 July, permission to seek a negotiated solution of the Transylvanian conflict with Rumania. Since, however, Hungary's excessive demands ruled out a bilateral agreement, Ribbentrop and Ciano decided to impose the Second Vienna Award on 30 August 1940, giving Hungary northern Transylvania with its mainly Magyar and Szekler-inhabited districts amounting to 43,104 square kilometres and 2.53 million inhabitants. In a special agreement Germany obtained extended rights for the German minority in Hungary and, under the terms of an economic agreement signed on 10 October 1940, larger consignments of Hungarian agricultural produce.

At the same time, the German government, which was dissatisfied with Teleki's vacillating policy made renewed use of its sympathisers within Hungary to secure a domestic and foreign policy which would be unreservedly sympathetic to National Socialism. At the beginning of October Berlin encouraged Béla Imrédy, who had risen rapidly to become the spokesman of the government's increasingly stronger and bolder right-wing, to defect from the Party of Hungarian Life. Joined by eighteen like-minded colleagues, he founded the Party of Hungarian Revival (*Magyar Megújulás Pártja*) on 21 October 1940. Shortly before, on 29 September, negotiations on a merger between Count Pálffy's United National Socialist Party and the Arrow Cross had been successfully concluded. Szálasi, who had been prematurely released from prison, took over as party leader on 7 October and was soon in control of more than 300,000 members. His new programme, however, which alongside 'Hungarianism' proclaimed the unity of nationalism and socialism and aimed at a 'seizure of power', caused divisive controversies which in turn provoked several splits in the party and a steady decline in membership. With the support of German intermediaries the Hungarian National Socialist Party was refounded on 18 September 1941 and on 24 September fused with the Party of Hungarian Revival to form a new Hungarian Revival and National Socialist Alliance led by Jenő Rátz. Now the German authorities could exert influence through a parliamentary pressure group of over thirty-three deputies who ensured the satisfaction of Germany's demands up until the country's occupation by German troops on 19 March 1944 . While Teleki attempted to strengthen his position in the face of German pressure by reshuffling his cabinet, he could only curb the growth of right-wing extremism by himself adopting increasingly right-wing policies.

In foreign policy Teleki had to surrender to growing German pressure and join the Tripartite Pact of Germany, Italy and Japan on 20 November 1940. His attempts to exploit what room was left for manoeuvre led to the signing of a Treaty of Eternal Friendship between Hungary and Yugoslavia on 12 December 1940, which was formally ratified in February 1941. The new appointment of the former ambassador to Bucharest, László Bárdossy, to the post of foreign minister on 4 February – a man reputed to have little sympathy for National Socialism – could also be seen as a gesture intended to demonstrate Hungary's independence. But the fall of Cvetković's pro-German Belgrade government on 27 March and Hitler's decision to occupy Yugoslavia in preparation for the attack against Russia also demanded that Hungary adopt a clear position. Whereas Horthy was blinded by the prospect of new territorial gains and wanted to accede to German requests for the right of passage for their troops, Teleki, after sounding out the British government, decided to honour the treaty of friendship with Yugoslavia and maintain Hungary's status as a non–belligerent. Since he could not, however, make his views prevail against the opposition of the general staff, his cabinet colleagues and the Regent, he shot himself during the night of 2–3 April 1941. Teleki, who had not wanted to place himself on 'the side of the villains' had drawn the consequences from the failure of his 'vacillating policy'. The fulfilment of revisionist demands which he himself had encouraged could be achieved only if Hungary joined the Axis and violated the treaties it had signed. Subtle political arguments and the hope that the British government, realising the nature of Hungary's predicament, would continue to show goodwill, could not conceal the real power-political situation and the extent of Hungary's dependence on Germany. The new prime minister, Bárdossy, who was convinced of Germany's ultimate victory and became increasingly subservient to Berlin as time went on, ordered the Hungarian army to follow in the steps of the German Wehrmacht on 11 April 1941 by invading Yugoslavia and occupying the Bácska and parts of the Voivodina, a territory of 11,000 square kilometres with a mainly Serbian and Magyar population, but also some Slovaks and Germans. Thus, within the space of two years Germany's support had enabled Hungary to recover an area of 80,000 square kilometres with 5 million inhabitants, including over 2 million Magyars who had been living under foreign rule since the signing of the Trianon peace treaty. With a territory of 172,000 square kilometres Hungary now comprised 52.9 per cent of the old kingdom of St Stephen. Of its 14.628 million citizens, 9.78 million were Catholic, 2.79 million were Calvinist, 830,000 Lutheran and 725,000 Jewish. The government, which had failed to learn any lessons from its misguided nationalities policy before the First World War, implemented new measures of coercion and magyarisation against the national minorities, whose proportion of the total population had now grown to more than a quarter. These policies soon provoked opposition, especially in newly incorporated districts which remained under military administration. In particular, the expropriation of non–Magyar property, undertaken on the pretext of redressing the inequities of the land reform measures carried out by the Rumanians and Czechoslovaks, met with especially bitter opposition.

The new premier, Bárdossy, who had a reputation for arrogance, pride but also intelligence and a certain recklessness, had an unshakeable belief that Hungary was destined to perform a leading role in the Danube region. He had little time to familiarise himself with the work of his office before he was required to make some more momentous decisions. News of the German invasion of Russia on 22 June 1941 was welcomed by Hungary's latently anti–Communist political leaders, especially since the military put the length of the campaign at about six weeks, basing their estimate on their experience of German Blitzkrieg tactics. Nevertheless, liberal-conservative circles had reservations about acceding to Germany's request for the Hungarian army's direct participation in the Russian campaign. But after the bombing of the towns of Kassa and Munkács, which was probably carried out by German aircraft or, perhaps, by Slovakian pilots who had defected to the USSR, Bárdossy violated the terms of the constitution and pushed through a declaration of war on the Soviet Union on 27 June 1941. However, only a force of some 40,000 men were initially sent to the eastern front.

Hungary now had to place its entire economy in the service of Germany's cause. Around half of its oil production and 90 per cent of its bauxite extraction were henceforth exported to Germany. The Reich also benefited from Hungary's iron and steel production, which was increased by 30 per cent, and from the higher output from its coalmines. The expansion of Hungarian aircraft production and the manufacture of vehicles and weapons similarly benefited the German armaments industry. The export of cereals, oil seeds and meat produce had to be continually raised, with the result that growing food shortages were felt in Hungary itself from 1942 onwards, since the lack of artificial fertilisers and insufficient agricultural machinery meant that the harvest yield could not be rapidly increased. Since Germany was very slow in paying its debts and stopped making any further payments after 1943, the economy could be kept going only by a further issue of paper currency, which in turn led to high inflation. The money supply grew from 863 million pengö in 1938 to 12.3 billion in 1944. Rising prices and an inadequate supply of food and consumer goods for the civilian population led directly to a substantial lowering of living standards from 1942 onwards. Longer working hours, increased production targets, the forced subordination of the trade unions to state control, a ban on the free movement of labour and the appointment of military commissars in the factories contributed to a growing resistance which began to emerge in the course of the war and spilled over to the peasants who were forced to produce higher quotas. As against the agricultural sector, the 450,000 or more workers employed in heavy industry and 400,000 or so small tradesmen absorbed an ever larger share of national income which now exceeded 50 per cent.

Bárdossy's conscientious compliance with German demands, which sprung from his belief in an ultimate German victory, so skilfully promoted by Berlin, led to a situation in the latter half of 1941 where relations between Germany and Hungary ran 'perfectly and harmoniously', to use Ribbentrop's words. Hungary responded to Britain's long awaited declaration of war on 7 December with its own declaration of war on the USA on 13 December. When it became clear after the German defeat before Moscow that the war against the Soviet Union would continue for some time to come, Ribbentrop and the Chief of the Wehrmacht High Command, Wilhelm Keitel, forced Hungary to make a substantially greater military contribution to the war during their visits in January 1942. The Second Hungarian Army, which had around 200,000 combat troops, 50,000 occupation troops and a labour service corps of 40,000 men, was to reinforce certain sectors on the eastern front from the spring of 1942 onwards. In addition, the Waffen-SS was allowed to recruit volunteers from Hungary's German population. Hungary thus found itself increasingly involved on Hitler's side during the Second World War, the successful outcome of which began to look increasingly doubtful.

In order to lend greater stability to his régime, Horthy had his son, István, who died later on 20 August 1942 in an air-crash on the eastern front, elected Vice-Regent on 19 February and moved closer to those advocating closer ties with the Allies. Bárdossy's inability to withstand German pressure and flattery also caused the Regent to nominate a prime minister whom he found personally more acceptable. Miklós Kállay, appointed to the post on 9 March 1942, was a wealthy landowner and agricultural expert. He came from one of Hungary's oldest aristocratic families and had been minister of agriculture under Gömbös, but because of his preference for Bethlen's line in politics had already retired from public life in 1935. His reservations towards National Socialism, both in its German and Hungarian forms, were well known, with the result that he was expected to pursue a policy whereby Hungary would distance itself more from the Third Reich. Resuming Count Pál Teleki's double-edged policy, Kállay moved against both the so-called 'German Party' and the political Left. He also restored clandestine contacts with the Allied governments. The former chairman of the Small-holders' Party, Tibor Eckhardt, who had emigrated to the USA and placed himself at the head of a movement for an independent Hungary (*Független Magyarország*), tried to make his country's diffi-cult predicament comprehensible to the Allied politicians. His supporters' efforts to transform the Smallholders' Party into a western-style bourgeois-democratic Party, which induced many intellectuals to join it, facilitated increased cooperation with the Budapest government after Stalingrad. Despite these attempts to maintain a circumspect distance from Germany, Kállay's period in office failed to witness any significant reduction in Hungary's depen-dence on Hitler's Germany, although growing opposition to German domination was encouraged and cautiously promoted by the country's highest authorities.

As early as the autumn of 1941 anti-German demonstrations were held to coincide with important national festivities. The founding of the Hungarian Historical Memorial Committee in February 1942 saw the creation of a coordinating authority. On 15 March, the anni-versary of the outbreak of the 1848–49 War of Independence, a crowd of 8,000 people gathered at the Petöfi Monument in Budapest to demand an 'independent democratic Hungary'. When the insig-nificant Hungarian Communist Party, which only operated under-ground in Budapest, received fresh impetus from Germany's attack on Russia and tried to participate in the growing opposition move-ment through its sporadically published newspaper and leaflets, the police acted decisively and arrested 500 activists. The party's leaders, Ferenc Rózsa and Zótan Schönherz were executed. Following the dissolution of the Third International in May 1943, János Kádár, who took over as First Party Secretary in December 1942, also had to order that the party officially cease its activities, although it continued to operate as the Peace Party (*Békepárt*). From now on the régime's left-wing critics were frequently forced into newly formed punishment batallions.

These 'labour companies' had already been used to solve the 'Jewish question', which had been determinedly insisted upon by the

Third Reich. As a result of German pressure, a third anti-Jewish law was passed in 1941 which, despite protests from the Christian churches, led to even greater discrimination against Hungary's 787,000 citizens of Jewish origin, including 725,000 professing Jews. The new legislation prohibited marriage between Christians and Jews and prepared the way for the exclusion of more than 80,000 Jewish employees from state employment and the country's economic life. In August 1941, 12,000 Jews, who had been settled mainly in the Carpatho-Ukraine area, were, on account of their 'ambiguous' citizenship, evicted across the border into German-occupied Poland and murdered. Later deportations on a smaller scale may well have involved a further 10,000 to 15,000 Jews. When, however, large numbers of Serbs and Jews were massacred in a pogrom in the Novi Sad area in January 1942, public outrage was so great that Horthy and Bárdossy had to order a formal investigation. Those held mainly responsible by the inquiry escaped punishment by fleeing to Germany which refused to extradite them. From 1940 onwards, Jewish males eligible for military service were forcibly conscripted into 'labour companies' which amounted to little more than mobile concentration camps in which they were subjected to brutal treatment. Whereas the Jewish women, children and old men were left to continue living in increasingly difficult, but still comparatively tolerable circumstances, German pressure grew on the Kállay government to agree to German plans for a 'final solution'. Horthy was initially able to avoid fulfilling Hitler's and Ribbentrop's threatening demands, made in Klessheim on 17 April 1943, for Hungary's Jews to be sent to concentration camps or liquidated in the mass extermination camps in Poland. But the German authorities, through SS Standartenführer Mayer, subsequently established direct contacts with the 'German Party' and the more prominent antisemitic organisations in order to prepare the way for the 'final solution', as envisaged by Berlin.

From the summer of 1942 onwards, the Second Hungarian Army supported the northern wing of the German advance towards Stalingrad. Its almost complete annihilation at Voronezh on 12 January 1943 was of decisive importance for the future course of Hungarian politics. Prior to defeat 7,000 men had already frozen to death. Heavy losses suffered in smaller engagements with the enemy had sapped the soldiers' morale and, because the German High Command prevented a timely retreat, 40,000 men were killed and 70,000 taken prisoner during the Soviet counter-offensive. In the belief that the Hungarian troops had been senselessly sacrificed by the Germans and that the Axis had already lost the war, Kállay's government stepped up its contacts with the Allies via its accredited diplomats in neutral countries. In Istanbul, Madrid, Stockholm and Lisbon they attempted to discover which position and role the Allies were prepared to grant Hungary in the Danube region after the war had ended. At the same time, they hoped to receive assurances that Hungary's revisionist gains would be recognised. After the fall of Mussolini on 25 July 1943, the Hungarians stepped up their efforts to create the preconditions for Hungary to get out of the war at the earliest opportunity. In negotiations with the British government, held after the signing of the armistice with Italy on 3 September 1943, Kállay agreed to order the withdrawal of Hungarian troops from the eastern front, which were now only engaged fighting partisans. He also agreed to reduce the supply of armaments to Germany, to make personnel changes in the general staff and intro-duce social reforms in the long term, if in return Hungary were given guarantees that the territorial status quo would be maintained and no further conditions imposed in a subsequent peace treaty.

However, influential groups within Hungary's ruling circles, who continued to have faith in an ultimate German victory, rejected this programme. Kállay, it is true, no longer had to take notice of parliament whose proceedings had been suspended indefinitely on 4 May 1943. However, the Arrow Cross movement, which had been under pressure from the government and the Left because of its advocacy of a closer association with Germany, could count on the assent of the right wing of the government party and open support from Imrédy's National Socialist Party Alliance in which officers, ex-gentry bureaucrats and members of the bour-geoisie who had profited from the economic elimination of the Jews supported continuing the fight against Bolshevism and increased help for Germany's war effort. From late 1943 onwards, they established closer contacts with the German authorities and, helped by Horthy's hesitation, offered Hitler the possibility of preparing operation 'Margarethe', i.e. Hungary's occupation by the Wehrmacht. Although the Germans did not rule out a military solution, they hoped to maintain a semblance of legality when taking over control of the country. Horthy, who was again summoned to Klessheim on 17 March 1944, had to agree to dismiss Kállay and appoint a right-wing puppet government under Hungary's long-serving ambassador to Berlin, the narrow-minded Lieutenant-General Döme Sztójay, in which the representatives of the National Socialist Party Alliance would occupy the key posts. On 19 March, eight German divisions invaded the country 'at the request of the Hungarian government' and encountered no opposition. The SS and the Gestapo who followed closely on their heels immediately began their activities. SS Standartenführer Dr Edmund Veesenmayer took charge of the German embassy in Budapest as 'The German Reich's Plenipotentiary in Hungary'.

First of all, the opponents of National Socialism, including Communists, leading officials of the Smallholders' Party, Social Democrats, journalists, academics and even close colleagues of Horthy were arrested and sent to German concentration camps. With the help of the Arrow Cross and the willing assistance of the Hungarian gendarmerie, over 450,000 people, including almost all of Hungary's provincial Jews, were deported to the German extermination camps in Poland under Eichmann's supervision, despite protests by Church leaders and Horthy's hesitant attempts to halt the deportations. Only 200,000 or so Jews herded together in the Budapest ghetto were provisionally spared liquidation. The still relatively free press was banned and only a few newspapers propagating National Socialist aims allowed to appear. The country's economic resources were now openly and shamelessly plundered. On 24 August 1944 a government decree banned all political parties.

But opposition to Sztójay's new policy of collaboration steadily grew. Horthy, encouraged by the D-Day landings in Normandy, the rapid advance of the Red Army and Rumania's defection to the Allies on 23 August, still hoped to ditch the Axis and join the Allies. As a first step in this direction he dismissed the compliant German puppet, Sztójay, on 24 August after the government had been seriously weakened by Imrédy's supporters withdrawing their support on 7 August in protest at the expropriation of Jewish businesses by the SS. General Géza Lakatos, whom Horthy trusted, took over the government on 29 August and immediately tried to establish contacts with Allies, but with little success. When the Red Army crossed the Hungarian border on 23 September 1944 a delegation was sent to Moscow to enter into secret negotiations for an armistice and an agreement was reached on 11 October, under the terms of which Hungarian troops were in future to be deployed against the German occupation forces.

Believing that he could blindly trust the loyalty of his generals, Horthy wanted simply to announce an armistice and Hungary's change of allegiance without any adequate political, social or military preparations. But when he ordered the Hungarian troops to stop fighting in a radio broadcast of 15 October, without at the same time calling for action to be taken against the German armed forces, the occupying troops and the Arrow Cross had already taken their own countermeasures. Many officers who had been trained in Germany and instilled with National Socialist values were not prepared to make common cause with the Soviets. The Arrow Cross and their right-wing sympathisers had taken control of vital key positions, particularly since 19 March 1944. The lumpenproletariat now saw its chance of settling scores with the old system. As for the underground opposition, it was still not sufficiently united to be able to put up any active resistance. The hastily deployed 24th German Wehrmacht Panzer Division occupied the Royal Palace in Budapest and by threatening to execute Horthy's younger son, who had been kidnapped and taken to Mauthausen by a special unit under Skorzeny, forced the Regent to withdraw his announcement and appoint Ferenc Szálasi as prime minister. German units and armed Arrow Cross squads had occupied public buildings in the capital without encountering any resistance. The Hungarian army also announced its allegiance to the new rulers and Horthy was placed under custody before being taken to Germany.

The new 'leader of the nation', Szálasi, and his supporters established a reign of terror in the few months they were able to remain in power. This terror was directed against the new government's political opponents and Jews who had not yet been deported. During the winter of 1944/45 over 80,000 Jews, mainly older people and children, were driven into concentration camps in forced marches and perished. While most of Hungary's provincial Jews fell victim to the extermination measures carried out by the Germans and the Arrow Cross, almost 100,000 people did, at least, manage to escape death in the Budapest ghetto. As result of the régime's arbitrary rule and savage reprisals, tens of thousands of Hungarian intellectuals, civil servants, clergymen and workers lost their lives. 'Total mobilisation' meant that all citizens between the ages of 12 and 70 were forced into labour service or military service. But, as defeatism and desertion spread through the Hungarian army, it proved impossible to keep the promise given to Hitler to place 1.5 million soldiers at his disposal. Attempts at the forced evacuation of the civilian population and the holding up of the Russians' steady advance by a scorched earth policy provoked growing opposition and a complete rejection of the barbaric excesses of the Arrow Cross cohorts. On 13 February 1945, Budapest, largely destroyed after bitter street fighting, fell to the Red Army. On 4 April 1945, the last Wehrmacht units left the country which was now placed under Soviet military occupation. Szálasi's government and other leading personalities of the Horthy era had meanwhile given themselves up to American troops in Austria.

The Hungarian underground opposition had made little contribution to the military defeat of National Socialism. It was not until July 1943 that the Smallholders' Party, whose 'bourgeois section' included supporters of Communist views alongside its anti-German and radical intellectual elements, suppressed its right wing and adopted Endre Bajcsy-Zsilinszky's policy of working more closely with the Social Democrats and the Communists. A memorandum to the Kállay government on 31 July had demanded an end to hostilities and a volte face in foreign policy to join the Allies even at the price of armed conflict with the Third Reich. At the beginning of August 1943 a programme of action was formally concluded with the Social Democrats and on the 11 September a joint declaration was issued condemning the government's continuing prosecution of the war. The various opposition groups, weakened by the harsh repressive measures introduced after the German occupation and deprived of their leaders who had been mostly arrested by the Gestapo, joined forces in May 1944 in the Communist-inspired Hungarian Front (*Magyar Front*). They demanded a 'new struggle of liberation' against the German occupation forces and their collaborators and called for the creation of a new democratic Hungary after the war. The Communist Party (*Kommunista Párt*), which was reconstituted on 12 September 1944, signed an agreement with the Social Democrats on 10 October which proposed the creation of a united front and a merger of the two party organisations to form a united revolutionary and socialist workers' party after the war. The representatives of the Hungarian Front, who were informed by Horthy of plans for an armistice on 11 October, were able to create a coordinating body with the founding of the Committee of Liberation of the Hungarian National Uprising (*Magyar Nemzeti Felkelés Felszabadító Bizottsága*) on 11 November 1944. Although immediately weakened by the arrest and execution of its leaders, it called for an armed uprising in the German-occupied territories, which, in effect, took the form of limited isolated partisan actions and attacks on German military installations.

The course taken by Hungary's post-war development was decided in December 1944 in Hungary's second biggest town, Szeged, which had been occupied by the Red Army in September 1944. The Social Democratic Party, National Peasants' Party, Bourgeois-Democratic Party, Communists and trade-union representatives formed the Hungarian National Independence Front (*Magyar Nemzeti Függetlenségi Front*) on 2 December. Its programme called for an immediate break with the Third Reich and maximum support for the Red Army. It also demanded a thorough democratisation of public life, a radical land reform to benefit the smallholders and the comprehensive nationalisation of major industries and banks. In the elections held in the eastern part of the country under the auspices of the Red Army the Communists succeeded in winning 71 of the 230 contested seats. The Independent Party of Smallholders won 55 seats, the Social Democrats 38 and the National Peasants' Party 16. The provisional National Assembly, constituted in Debrecen on 22 December 1944, entrusted Colonel Béla Dálnoki Miklós, who had gone over to the Russians on 15 October, with the formation of a government. The new government, which consisted of three generals, three Communists (agriculture, industry and transport, social welfare), two Social Democrats (justice, economics), two Smallholders (foreign affairs and finance) and one representative of the Peasants' Party (interior), revoked all treaties concluded with the Third Reich and declared war on Germany on 28 December. The armistice, which the Hungarians signed with the Allies in Moscow on 20 January 1945, fixed Hungary's borders as they had existed on 31 December 1937, thus renouncing the territorial gains achieved as a result of the Vienna Awards and subsequent military occupations. It was also obliged to play an active role in the war against Germany and pay reparations for damage inflicted by the Hungarian army to the sum of 200 million dollars together with compensation amounting to 100 million US dollars' worth of arms deliveries to both Czechoslovakia and Yugoslavia. The Allied Control Commission for Hungary, which was chaired by a representative of the Soviet High Command, was to monitor the disbanding of fascist organisations and the bringing of war criminals to justice. The most urgent practical political tasks were the creation of a functioning administration, the restoration of public order, feeding the population, reconstructing the worst war damage and introducing the new reforms. The Supreme National Council, formed on 26 January, consisting of the President of the National Assembly, the prime minister and a delegate from the Political Committee of the provisional parliament took over the duties of the head of state. Civilian government was extended to the entire country only after the final withdrawal of German troops at the beginning of April 1945.

Hungary entered the post-war period with a difficult historical legacy. It was still not easy to recognise what effects the Red Army's 'liberation' of the country would have on its political, social and economic structure. However, broad sections of the population recognised as unavoidable the need to eradicate the vestiges of the Horthy era, so strongly shaped by semi-feudal traditions rooted in the nineteenth century, and to give Hungary a modern political and social structure. Since memories of Béla Kun's Soviet dictatorship of a quarter of a century previously were still vivid, there was little desire on the part of most people for Socialist or even revolutionary Communist changes. But they also had no wish to see a restoration of the Horthy system which had rested on the power of the large landowners and urban capitalists, supported by the administration, the judiciary and the army – a system which had held on to power relatively easily through its manipulation of elections and exploitation of revisionist propaganda. Hungary, once more restored to the frontiers laid down in the Trianon Treaty of 1920 and without hope of restoring the historic Kingdom of St Stephen had been once again confined to its territorial heartland. The country, which had suffered badly from the economic effects of the war and the fighting on its territory, had to try as best it could to minimise the consequences of its involvement in Germany's catastrophic defeat. Affected by the rapid collapse of the Allies' wartime coalition, the consolidation of the opposing post-war power blocs and the start of the Cold War, Hungary's path into the post-war world proved much more difficult than expected by the country's patriots and democrats who set about energetically rebuilding the country after the collapse.

CHAPTER FIVE

The Creation of the Hungarian People's Democracy, 1945–56

THE POLITICAL AND ECONOMIC BACKGROUND TO THE GRADUAL COMMUNIST TAKEOVER, 1945–48

With the expulsion of the last Wehrmacht units on Hungarian soil on 4 April 1945 and the country's complete occupation by the Red Army the war had indeed come to an end. Yet it was a long time before the stabilisation necessary to create a democratic order and overcome immense war damage was achieved. In many places the Soviet soldiers had been expected as liberators. Excesses like rapes, indiscriminate arrests and the deportation of over 250,000 persons to forced labour camps in the Soviet Union soon taught the civilian population otherwise. The uncoordinated dismantling of plant and installations to pay for reparations and the unlimited power accrued by the chairman of the Allied Control Commission, Marshall K. E. Vorošilov, made people adopt a more realistic attitude as the character of the new régime appeared in a different light. Around 400,000 Hungarians had been killed in the Second World War. Direct damage to property was estimated at about 22 billion pre-war pengö, a figure which represented about four or five times the national income for 1938 and about 40 per cent of the nation's entire wealth. The destruction of all the bridges over the Danube and the Tisza and the heavy losses in the transport sector, amounting to 35 per cent of Hungary's railway installations, over 80 per cent of its rolling stock and the entire Danube fleet, had a particularly bad effect. A quarter of all dwellings had suffered shelling and bomb damage. The housing stock in Budapest had been particularly badly hit. According to initial estimates, 50 per cent of the country's industrial installations and plant had been totally destroyed. As a result of these losses and the shortages of raw materials, production in May 1945 reached only 30 per cent of its pre-war levels. Agriculture had lost half of its livestock and a third of its machinery, with the result that the grain harvest in 1945, also affected by the radical land reform, produced a yield of only 30 per cent of the pre-war average. Galloping inflation, caused by Germany running up a debt of 1.5 billion Marks by the end of 1944, took off in the spring of 1945. Since Hungary's financial reserves were soon completely exhausted, food could eventually only be obtained by bartering with objects of recognised value.

Under the Soviet occupation the Communists, who had been banned ever since the collapse of the Soviet dictatorship in August 1919, tried immediately – and very successfully – to exploit the collapse of the Horthy régime and its political, social, administrative and judicial institutions. The party leaders returning from Soviet exile in early November 1944 could depend on the support of two to three thousand Hungarian Communists, who were not, however, given any influential positions in the provisional Central Committee of the revived Hungarian Communist Party (*Magyar Kommunista Párt* – MKP) led by its chairman, Ernő Gerő, and his deputy, Imre Nagy. The 'Programme for the Democratic Reconstruction and Future Development of Hungary', published in Debrecen on 30 November 1944, was all but unanimously adopted by the Hungarian National Independence Front (*Magyar Nemzeti Függetlenségi Front*) which had been founded with active Communist assistance and thus became the basis of the Provisional National Government's policies. In this government Communist Party members at first secured only the ministries of agriculture, industry and transport and social welfare. But the interior minister, Ferenc Erdei, who nominally belonged to the National Peasants' Party, which, in the meantime, had been strongly infiltrated by the Communists, was a crypto-Communist who saw to it that the 'Political Police Section' set up in late 1944 (originally ÁVO, later ÁVH) could be used as an instrument of the Communist Party. By exploiting their control of the police, whose economic section was used to intimidate the 'class enemy', assemblies and meetings, the postal and telegraph services, the radio and the traffic in people and goods, together with the granting of material privileges under the guise of 'social welfare' and the implementation of a popular land reform, which created new dependencies, the Communists gained a degree of influence in the country which far outweighed their actual numbers and former political significance.

As dislike of the occupying Red Army grew among the vast majority of Hungarians, the Soviet troops soon did not bother to conceal their open support of the Communists. The preferential support which the Soviet occupation power showed towards the Communists benefited them immediately after the cessation of hostilities when they began taking over control of the administration and local government in the name of the Independence Front in an attempt to replace the old political institutions with national councils at every level. They also benefited from being given places on the councils as equal partners alongside the older-established and more popular Social Democrats and Smallholders, and frequently took over the key position of chairman. The call to safeguard the unity of the working class and join forces in the process of reconstruction was not enough to make the representatives of the older-established Social Democrats and the Trade Union Council agree with the Communists who counted on the support of the National Peasants' Party. The increasingly voiced threat of asking the Soviet occupation power to intervene, together with Communist control of the political tribunals and people's courts, soon achieved the desired effect of discouraging or totally silencing potential opponents.

But it was only when the veteran Communist, Mátyás Rákosi, returned to Hungary in February 1945 with detailed instructions from Moscow that the Hungarian Communist Party became totally committed to Stalin's party line. On 23 February, the Central Committee of the Budapest Communist Party, led by Rákosi, which had come out of illegality on 19 January, merged with the Debrecen party headquarters and Rakosi declared himself General Secretary. The party held a national congress on 20–21 May 1945 at which the Communists employed extremely nationalistic language when it was announced that they were prepared to cooperate with all democratic elements in the task of national reconstruction, seen as the most urgent problem facing the country. The attempt to combine nationalism and Communism by stressing popular national issues, especially territorial ones like northern Transylvania and Slovakia, was justified by the argument that the heightening of nationalist feelings was merely an intermediate stage on the way to true internationalism and any denial of national interests simply meant that the class enemy would be allowed to exploit these for his own political ends.

This direction of policy was a concession to the views held by most of the country's home-based, nationalistically-minded Communists. Unlike those members who had returned from exile in Moscow, they had experienced the war and its accompanying persecutions at first hand and in their own country. They did not view Hungary as a territory occupied by the Red Army and a mere satellite of Moscow, but as a country which would have to undergo a revolution inspired by their own national motivations and carried out by indigenous elements, if necessary with the backing of Soviet troops. They stressed the mobilising of progressive democratic social forces in order to develop Socialism in the framework of a 'new democracy' and geared their domestic political programme to implementing long-overdue political, social and economic reforms. These would not necessarily have to be doctrinaire measures, but should have the effect of depriving their political opponents of their power base. Thus the overriding priority for Hungary's 'home-grown Communists', as they were called, was to create an effective political organisation which would consist of a nucleus of disciplined supporters at the centre of a larger number of affiliated groups which sympathised with most of their short-term aims.

It was to be expected that the 5,000 or so members of the group which made up the Moscow 'Apparatchiks' or 'Muscovites' would seek to establish much closer ties with Stalin and the Soviet Communist Party. The prevailing view amongst this group was that only the powerful backing of the Soviet Union's experienced and purposeful political leaders as well as the presence of the Red Army could prevent the disruptive possibility of foreign intervention before they had time to carry out a national 'revolution'. Only the Soviet leaders could, in their view, obviate the national animosity that existed between Hungary and its neighbours, especially towards Rumania and Czechoslovakia. Stalin had also known how to ensure a high degree of obedience towards the instructions of the Soviet Communist Party because the leaders he designated and made personally responsible to him were a mixture of revolutionary heroes, martyrs and Stalinist bureaucrats who were relatively inexperienced and isolated within the population and even within their circle of party colleagues in Hungary itself. Their insecurity and aggression, which they had developed as a result of their long period of imprisonment, exile or membership of an ethnic minority, their lack of popular support and, despite outward party discipline, often barely concealed personal animosity within the small party leadership, guaranteed that Moscow's instructions would be faithfully carried out. In the ceasefire agreement of 20 January 1945 the USSR had reduced Hungary's sovereignty to a minimum – much more than was the case with Russia's other enemies. This allowed the Kremlin to deploy its own

Soviet experts in the process of government reconstruction and to place Hungarian adherents completely loyal to Moscow in all key positions in the administration, army and police to ensure that the Soviet Communist Party's absolute power to give orders and the Hungarian Party's unconditional subordination to Stalin's personal domination were guaranteed. The growing tensions between individual groups within the Hungarian Communist Party, between the hard core of Hungarian Communists – later called 'national Communists' – the 'Muscovites', Spanish and Chinese civil war veterans, suspected as 'Internationalists', western émigrés and the victims of German concentration camps, were at first politically insignificant.

Thanks to Stalin's backing Mátyás Rákosi (1892–1971) was able to take over the party leadership unopposed. Taken prisoner of war in Russia during the First World War, he had joined the Hungarian Communists after his release and during the Soviet dictatorship had held various posts in the provincial party administration, assuming overall command of the Red Guard in its final phase. He had made his way to the Soviet Union via Vienna and been employed latterly as a party secretary in the executive committee of the Comintern. Entrusted with the task of reconstructing the Hungarian Communist Party, he returned to his homeland in 1924, only to be arrested a year later and eventually sentenced to life imprisonment. It was not until 1940 that he was expelled to the Soviet Union. In February 1945, he returned to Hungary to find Ernő Gerő already there. Gerő had similarly spent a long period in Soviet exile, but, in contrast to Béla Kun who fell victim to the purges in 1939, had survived Stalin's reign of terror and, thanks to his work for the Comintern in France, Belgium and Spain, had a good knowledge of international affairs. Imre Nagy (1896–1958) had also been in exile in Moscow. He, too, had been won over to Bolshevism while a prisoner-of-war in Russia and after years of working underground in Hungary had reached the Soviet Union from Vienna in 1928. During the Second World War he had been put in charge of the Hungarian broadcasts of 'Radio Kossuth' and during his time there had worked alongside József Révai (1898–1959) who was widely regarded as the main ideologue of the Soviet dictatorship in 1919 and who, interrupted by a spell in prison between 1931 and 1934, had tried many times to revive the Communist movement in Hungary. As a political journalist and editor-in-chief of the party newspaper, *Szabad Nép* (A Free People), and finally minister for national education, Révai was given the task of imposing ideological conformity on Hungary.

László Rajk (1908–1949), a former teacher who had been expelled for his Communist activities from the university of Budapest in 1932, had a different experience. As a member of the National Federation of Hungarian Building Workers he had been involved in organising nationwide strikes in 1935 and had taken an active part in the Spanish Civil War as party secretary in the Hungarian Batallion of the International Brigades. After a spell of internment in France he had escaped to Hungary where he was again interned until the end of September 1944. For a short time thereafter he was one of the original organisers of the Hungarian Front. Imprisoned once more and deported to Germany he took no further part in active politics until May 1945 when he built up a very powerful position as secretary of the Budapest party organisation, member of the Central Committee and Politburo, deputy General Secretary of the Communist Party and interior minister. Of the Communists who had spent the war in Hungary only János Kádár, born in 1912, gained prominence. Imprisoned for two years in 1935 following his early involvement in the Communist Youth League, he held an important party post between 1940 and 1941, and, as a Central Committee secretary, had taken part in rebuilding Hungary's banned Communist party from the beginning of 1943 onwards. Although he was promoted to the new Central Committee and Politburo in February 1945 and rose as secretary of the Greater Budapest party organisation to become deputy General Secretary of the Communist Party in 1946, he was unequivocally a second-rank member of a party hierarchy dominated by the 'Muscovites'.

After a highly unscrupulous recruiting campaign the Communist Party was eventually able to win support for its aims from sympathisers and idealists, opportunists and fellow-travellers, fascist converts and frightened civil servants, former Szálasi supporters and members of the lumpenproletariat. Also, some of the mainly Social Democratic workforce and rural poor now joined the party out of conviction. In February 1945, it had 30,000 members and by July of the same year could claim 225,000 members, rising to almost 610,000 by January 1946. Thereafter, membership increased only gradually from 660,000 in December 1947 to 887,472 in June 1948. But, despite these impressive figures the Communists had no hope of coming to power by legal, democratic and parliamentary means, although they were constantly able to extend their sphere of influence thanks to the support and backing they received from the Soviet-dominated Allied Control Commission regardless of objections from the Commission's American and British members.

The main opposition to the Communists came from the Independent Party of Smallholders, Agricultural Workers and Citizens (*Független Kisgazda, Földmunkás és Polgári Párt*) which was refounded in the Soviet-occupied city of Szeged on 23 November 1944. Its Supreme National Council entrusted the Calvinist Reform Church pastor, Zoltán Tildy (party leader), and Ferenc Nagy (chairman), with the party leadership on 19–20 August 1945. This party, which numbered more than 900,000 members by the summer of 1945 and had advocated a greater measure of political democracy, social justice and a 'firm new national policy on land' since 1930, was fully prepared to cooperate with any socially relevant groups within the framework of the Hungarian National Independence Front. However, it saw itself increasingly as a party which stood above social class differences and combined a belief in the bourgeois-democratic way of life, defence of private property and freedom of worship with the aim of creating 'a genuine democracy, which would be built upon Hungary's democratic traditions and imbued with the spirit of Hungary'. Although the Smallholders continued to work within the Provisional Government and the Independence Front, the Communists never tired of denouncing these, their strongest political opponents, as disguised heirs to Horthy's brand of fascism. They attempted to weaken them by provoking secessionist defections and putting pressure on their popular party leaders through slanderous accusations, intimidation or police action.

The Communist Party also manipulated the left wing of the National Peasants' Party which had grown out of the populist movement and had been founded as far back as June 1939 (*Nemzeti Parasztpárt*). Centred on the newspaper *Szabad Szó* (The Free Word), this radical Socialist party led by left-wing intellectuals and representing the agrarian proletariat, first began to be more politically effective within the Hungarian National Independence Front. Its plans for land reform, published on 14 January 1945, called for the breaking up of all estates of more than 100 *hold* (i.e. 57.5 hectares), and formed the basis of the decree issued on 17 March 1945 which abolished the large estates and provided for a redistribution of land for the benefit of the rural poor. All the Smallholders Party's attempts to achieve closer cooperation with the National Peasants' Party, which numbered 170,000 members in the summer of 1945, failed because of opposition from the latter's chairman, Péter Veres, and its leaders who leaned heavily towards the Communists. The efforts of its General Secretary, Imre Kovács, to remove Communist sympathisers from the party's headquarters, also proved unsuccessful, especially after the party's incorporation into the 'Left-Wing Bloc' on 5 March 1946. Thus, the National Peasants' Party drifted more and more into the Communist camp and began to advocate 'the development of a people's democracy', the nationalisation of industry and agricultural collectivisation without being able to prevent its cessation of independent political activity in the autumn of 1948 and self-inflicted dissolution a year later.

The Social Democratic Party, after being driven underground during the Second World War, had been able to reactivate over 350,000 members, mainly industrial workers, by the end of 1945 with its slogan 'Democracy today, Socialism tomorrow'. It supported the idea of a people's republic, far-reaching democratic reforms, the nationalisation of key industries and the confiscation of the great estates. Under Árpád Szakasits, who was elected General Secretary in August 1945, and a majority of leaders on the left of its political spectrum, the Social Democratic Party found it increasingly difficult to resist the Communist call for working-class unity and, as part of the 'Left Bloc', increasingly espoused the latter's aims more openly. The party leadership frustrated both ex-minister, Károly Peyer's attempt early in 1946 to return the party to a more independent line and the negotiations, held in the autumn of 1947, aimed at achieving closer cooperation of all anti-Communist forces under the leadership of the Smallholders' Party. By February 1948, Social Democrats who supported the idea of the party pursuing its own independent policies had been expelled and after a thorough purge the party was forced to merge with the Communists on 12 June 1948 to form the Hungarian Workers' Party (*Magyar Dolgozók Pártja* – MDP).

From early 1946 onwards, differences of opinion occurred with increasing intensity between the unequal partners in this new coalition as to which political direction the country should take and which principles it should adopt in economic and social policy. However, these played only a secondary role in the first months after the war. A large measure of consensus existed between the groups represented in the provisional National Assembly and the Provisional Government. They agreed that the armistice conditions – to strive for Hungary's democratic reconstruction and bring the supporters of Horthy's régime and representatives of Szálasi's rule of terror to justice – should be carried out to the letter. This, together with the payment of reparations, was a precondition for the speedy conclusion of a peace treaty and subsequent withdrawal of an increasingly unwelcome occupying force. There was also unanimous agreement on the need to implement land reform, repair war damage, stimulate the economy and raise the nation's standard of living. However, since there was also considerable disagreement between the political parties as to the practical measures most appropriate to deal with these urgent tasks, their willingness to compromise was increasingly strained. This in turn steadily raised the potential for conflict and encouraged increasingly serious internal quarrels.

Although all the responsible parties recognised the need for a solution to the agrarian problem, agreement on land reform, the first incisive, though somewhat precipitate measure to be carried out, was not easily achieved. At the end of the war almost half of Hungary's 9 million inhabitants still earned their living from agriculture. Of these, about two-thirds, i.e. 3 million people, did not own their land or possessed holdings of less than 5 *hold* (i.e. 2.8 hectares). In contrast, some 10,000 families controlled about half the country's arable land, the 1,000 wealthiest families owning over a quarter of all land under cultivation, and the Catholic Church owned over half a million hectares. Since all previous attempts to redistribute land on a more equitable basis had failed or been sabotaged by the large-scale landowners, it was agreed that the land reform legislation and the principles it would observe regarding the extent of expropriation and redistribution should be prepared thoroughly in advance by a committee of experts. However, correctly estimating the extent of the rural poor's growing impatience, the Communist Party adopted the National Peasants' Party's proposal of 14 January and, by referring to pressure from the Soviet occupying power, forced the other parties to endorse the decrees of 17 March 1945 abolishing the great estates and reallocating the land to the village poor.

Accordingly, land which had been owned by 'traitors to the fatherland' and 'Horthy fascists', including all estates of more than 575 hectares, was expropriated within the space of six weeks. The maximum amount of land allocated to peasants for their individual use was fixed at 115 hectares. Otherwise it was redistributed in parcels of 100 *hold* (i.e. 57.5 hectares). Apart from 11,500 hectares which were spared, land owned by the Church was completely confiscated along with that owned by banks and other enterprises. Forested land of over ten *hold* and orchards and vineyards of over twenty *hold* also had to be handed over. In all, 3.222 million hectares of Hungary's 8.3 million hectares of cultivable land (i.e. 38.8 per cent), was eventually expropriated. The law provided for compensation, but this was paid out only in exceptional cases and was practically worthless in view of the country's rampant inflation. Contrary to the aims of the Smallholders' Party to create small viable farms, the Communists and the National Peasants' Party followed a policy of allocating a share of land, where possible, to all interested parties. Of the 1.874 million hectares earmarked for reallocation (i.e. 22.5 per cent of the all land under cultivation), 642,000 people, including 110,000 former farmhands, 261,000 agricultural labourers, 214,000 dwarfholders, together with smallholders and village tradesmen, received a share of land which generally did not exceed five *hold* (i.e. 2.8 hectares). This meant that about two-thirds of rural households possessed plots of one to five *hold*, making up 23.1 per cent of the country's total arable land. A fifth of the peasants owned between 5 and 10 *hold* (i.e. 18.9 per cent of cultivable land) while just on a tenth owned between 10 and 20 *hold* (i.e. 22.4 per cent). The 3.4 per cent of peasants who owned middle-sized farms of up to 50 *hold* and the 0.6 per cent of richer peasants who owned smallholdings of up to 100 *hold* continued to control a good quarter of the country's arable land (18.3 and 8.9 per cent resp.). Some 1.348 million hectares of expropriated land became state property. After the land reform up to 95 per cent of Hungary's rural population owned small plots of land whose yield was still, however, often insufficient to feed their large families. The *latifundiae* and more profitably productive middle-sized holdings, which had previously satisfied the country's food needs and provided considerable employment, were torn apart. These changes in the structure of ownership also resulted in a complete overturning of the social structure in the countryside.

Helped by the officially appointed Land Redistribution Committees, which were entrusted with implementing the reform at a local level, the Communist Party tried to gain a political foothold in the villages and extend its influence among the National Councils which were the local organs of the National Independence Front. The party activists did not tire of extolling their achievement of having 'given the land to the peasants'. They rejected as a malicious slander any suspicion of wanting eventually to nationalise all available arable land and proclaimed it their intention that the new owners of land would rapidly 'acquire wealth'. When allocating farmland or conveying the live and dead stock of the great estates, or when the Soviet army distributed seeds and fuel, special preference was given to peasants who were willing to cooperate as middlemen and agents. The Communists believed that only by these means could they halt the considerable drift in rural support to the Smallholders' Party. Their approach of appearing as benefactors to the rural poor did win the support of the smallholding peasants at first. But, because cultivation of the redistributed fields had been undertaken with insufficient means and to some extent too late, there was a disastrous harvest already in 1945. Poor yields caused by a drought throughout 1946 and 1947 forced Hungary, a country which had once specialised in agrarian exports, to cover its food needs to a great extent by imports.

Certain of backing from the Soviet-dominated Allied Control Commission, the Communists also called for drastic economic measures to be implemented when their first national congress was held on 20–21 May 1945. The workers' low real wages, which were being steadily eroded by inflation, the shortage of raw materials, the inadequate provision of food to the big cities and the Soviet occupation power's interventions in the economy, demonstrated clearly the necessity of a fundamental transformation of the economy. However, the Smallholders, the right wing of the Social Democrats and the National Peasants' Party had no desire to support the far-reaching measures of nationalisation and state control advocated by the Communists. Ferenc Nagy, who was appointed minister for reconstruction on 11 May 1945, opposed the Communist Party's demands, which were coupled with growing criticism of their coalition partners. Following the resolutions passed by the Supreme National Council of the Smallholders' Party on 19–20 August 1945 the Communists accused their more popular competitor of providing a rallying point for the right-wing opposition and representing capitalist interests, the clergy and the wealthy landowners, citing as evidence the Smallholders' call for an inquiry into the abuses arising from the land reform and for the economy's consolidation on the basis of private capitalism. Among the Social Democrats, in contrast, the upper hand was gained by the faction in the party leadership which was openly sympathetic to the Communist call to defend the unity of the working class in its struggle against reactionary elements and those wishing to restore capitalism.

When Ernő Gerő, on a visit to Moscow on 27 August 1945, signed an agreement pledging economic cooperation with the USSR beyond the guidelines set out by the cabinet, he provoked an internal political crisis. Even the American and British governments intervened, since they saw their own citizens' property interests threatened and wanted to prevent the Soviet domination of Hungarian foreign trade which was beginning to show itself clearly. The unilateral resumption of full diplomatic relations between Budapest and Moscow, announced before the conclusion of a peace settlement on 25 September, and the Soviet foreign minister Molotov's uncooperative attitude at the Conference of Foreign Ministers, which met in London on the 11 September to prepare the peace treaties with the wartime coalition's former enemies, placed an even greater strain on the western Allies' relations with the Soviet Union. Only when the Kremlin agreed to allow the holding of free elections with the participation of all 'democratic' parties, was the American government prepared to establish diplomatic relations with the Provisional Government on 2 November 1945. But the western Allies' realisation that they did not have the means to back up their diplomatic protests to the members of Communist governments or the Allied Control Commission produced a situation in which the American and British governments raised fewer and fewer objections to Stalin's view that Russia's former enemies in eastern Europe had been tacitly handed over to the Soviet sphere of influence at Teheran and Yalta.

But those groups which opposed the Communists with growing reservations and criticism could also claim successes. From the 5 to 13 September 1945 the provisional National Assembly met in Budapest to approve retrospectively the decrees passed by the Provisional Government under General Béla Miklós de Dálnok after the 22 December 1944. The parties of the political centre, strengthened by deputies from the western half of Hungary, were able to achieve the passage of an electoral law based on liberal democratic principles. The large increase in its own membership had led the Communist Party to misjudge the mood of the country and it did not, therefore, raise any fundamental objections. The deputies of the single chamber parliament were to be elected on the basis of a universal and direct, secret suffrage extended to all citizens over the age of 20. Those citizens who faced expropriation proceedings or had been charged by tribunals of enquiry as incriminated or involved in an important capacity in the 25 banned right-wing radical organisations were disenfranchised, as were all of Hungary's ethnic Germans. But in the Budapest municipal elections, held on the 7 October 1945, the single list of Communist and Social Democratic candidates suffered a serious defeat, polling only 42.8 per cent of the vote. In contrast, 50.5 per cent of the electorate supported the Independent Party of Smallholders which had never previously contested an election in the capital. The result, which was more a rejection of the Communists and their Soviet backers than an endorsement of the Smallholders' political views, had a major effect on the national elections held on 7 November 1945. Marshall Vorošilov, the Soviet chairman of the Allied Control Commission once more attempted to propose a single list of candidates which would have given the Smallholders only 40 per cent of the vote and eventually 47.5 of the contested seats. But this move, together with the Communist Party's various efforts to postpone the election failed as a result of the western Allies' objections and the opposition of the other parties. Even the Social Democrats had withdrawn from the single list with the Communists. When the votes were counted after these elections, which were certainly the freest and least rigged of any ever held in Hungary, 57 per cent of the electorate (i.e. 245 seats out of 409) had supported the Smallholders' Party programme. 17.4 per cent (67 seats) had voted for the Social Democrats, 6.9 per cent (2 Seats) for the National Peasants' Party and 1.6 per cent (2 seats) for the Bourgeois-Democratic Party, representing the urban middle class. The Communist Party had won only 797,040 votes, representing 16.9 per cent of the electorate (70 seats), which meant that the Communists had suffered a serious electoral setback. The main reasons for this reverse at the polls were: the widespread anti-Russian feeling caused by the Red Army's excesses and wholesale dismantling of plant and installations as reparations, the growing disillusionment of the smallholding peasantry following a poor harvest, the fear of too radical a transformation of the country's political and socio-economic structures and the Communist Party's inability to present itself as the champion of national interests following the new loss of territories returned to Czechoslovakia and Rumania.

After this clear election result many Magyars expected that Hungary would develop along the lines of a western liberal democracy despite the presence of the occupying Soviet troops who had to be tolerated until a peace treaty had been signed. But Marshall Vorošilov made it plain that the Soviets would stick to their policy of tolerating only a government coalition composed of all parties while safeguarding the gains already made by the Communists. Although the victorious Smallholders, led by Zoltán Tildy, who belonged to the party's left wing and supported closer cooperation with the USSR, supplied the premier and half the government ministers, the Communists, for whom Imre Nagy took over as minister of the interior, were superior in tactical skill and political ruthlessness. Proclaiming the class struggle and the final destruction of the reactionary structures of fascism, the latter began a war of attrition aimed at slowly eroding the power of their political rivals under the cover of 'collective cooperation'. In a phrase which was to gain general currency, Rákosi later described this as 'salami tactics'. Through their use of the 50,000 strong political police to intimidate and eliminate actual or potential opponents the Communists were able to gain ground steadily.

They also benefited from the fact that the 'left-wing' leaders of the Social Democratic Party under the deputy premier, Szakasits, shared many of their short-term aims and developed initiatives which undermined the policies of the majority of parliamentary deputies. Thus, the new parliament, constituted on 6 December 1945, unanimously approved a law introduced by the Communists which placed the mines and power stations under state control – amounting in practice to nationalisation. Apart from the interior ministry, which Lászlo Rajk took over from the ill Imre Nagy, who was averse to illegal radical measures, on 4 February 1946, the Communists provided only the deputy premier (Rákosi) and the ministers of transport and social welfare. Since they, therefore, had no direct possibility of influencing economic policy, they initiated the creation of a Supreme Economic Council on 9 January 1946 which was able to circumvent the cabinet. Empowered to grant loans, distribute raw materials and intervene in the decision-making of large enterprises, this body allowed the Communists to implement their economic views. The workers' committees in the big factories, which were being increasingly infiltrated by Communist Party members, not only tried to influence general trade union policy in order to promote the Communists' aims, but acquired a substantial say in determining wages and price levels. The inflation which had been running at a dizzy pace since December 1945 led to a depreciation of the currency in the first half of 1946 on a scale, unprecedented even in international terms. The result was that by the middle of July a gold pengö was worth 1.4 quadrillion pengö at 1938 values. This allowed the Communists to demand and justify a greater degree of state intervention in the economy. The introduction of a new currency based on the forint (florin) on 1 August 1946 enabled the government eventually to halt the depreciation of the currency. The government's subsequent policy of austerity which aimed at a modest availability of consumer goods and helped stabilise prices encouraged a growth in confidence in the new currency and made a gradual economic recovery possible. In 1946, the government was more or less able to achieve its limited goal of raising the workers' real wages to about a half of their 1938 value and productivity to 60 per cent of its pre-war level in 1939. Under the terms of a reparations agreement signed on 15 June 1945, Hungary was obliged to deliver consigments of goods to the Soviet Union. In 1946, the value of these amounted to 26.4 per cent of the state's total expenditure; in 1947, it was still as high as 17.8 per cent. Comprising 71 per cent of Hungary's total exports, these consign-ments set narrow limits on Hungary's economic recovery. The effective share of goods which had to be produced to meet the country's reparations debt amounted to 82 per cent of its foreign trade with the Soviet Union, 91 per cent of its trade with Yugoslavia and 49 per cent of its trade with Czechoslovakia. Hungary's foreign trade with the West, which had stood at around 90 per cent before the war, fell to just 53 per cent.

The goal of all parties to achieve a high level of production as quickly as possible through a systematic economic recovery and a living standard comparable with that of the pre-war period could only be brought closer by initially encouraging private initiative and the profit motive. The need to reinvest 20 per cent of the national income and limit the production of consumer goods in favour of developing the country's staple products meant that the population still had to put up with sacrifices. The serious damage of the two drought years of 1946 and 1947, the lack of skilled workers, the fail-ures of training programmes, shortages of raw materials and frequent production stoppages caused by a lack of spare parts or energy shortages put a strain on the economy. The Communists used these problems to justify the cabinet decree of 22 November 1946 which placed the country's biggest ironworks (the Rimamurány Ironworks, Ganz & Co., the Manfred Weiss Steel and Metalworks) under state ownership. On 28 May 1947, the Communist-dominated Supreme Economic Council placed all the major banks under state control and these were subsequently formally nationalised on 21 November 1947. The National Assembly decision of 1 July to launch a Three Year Plan for the entire economy by 1 August 1947 subse-quently gave the Communists the opportunity to gain control of the most important areas of production. On 6 February 1948, the National Assembly finally approved legislation which nationalised the bauxite industry and aluminium production and also agreed to the nationalisation of all industrial firms employing more than 100 workers. On 4 April, it also approved the disbanding of the employers' organisation, the National Federation of Factory Owners. A government decree of 18 December 1948 on the organ-isation of cooperatives, the adoption of a Five Year Plan on 10 December 1949 and the law of 28 December nationalising firms of more than ten employees and foreign-owned factories were the outwardly visible signs of the complete assimilation of Hungarian economic life to the obligatory Soviet model.

This was the culmination of a development which had first begun on 27 August 1945 when Hungary had signed a long-term trade agreement with the Soviet Union. Since the volume of Hungarian exports remained relatively small after the end of war and imports were necessary in order to revive industry, the Soviet Union saw the chance of orientating Hungary's national economy more towards the Soviet Union by stepping up deliveries of raw materials and increasing the amount of Hungarian goods for the Russian market. The Russians combined the confiscation of German property, which affected almost all large businesses on account of their multi-faceted involvement with the German banks from 1940 onwards, with the demand that Hungary repay Russia the debts it owed to the defeated German Reich without taking into account the fact that Hungary's credit with the German authorities meant that the balance had been essentially in Hungary's favour. After the initial wholesale dismantling of some branches of industry and the despatch to the Soviet Union of the machinery thus acquired, the Soviet government soon recognised that a reorganisation of the most important enterprises, especially in key industries, into mixed national concerns under Soviet management offered a number of important advantages: they could save on the costs of dismantling, transporting and reinstalling plant, gaining also from its immediate operational use, the more efficient use of Hungarian labour working for Soviet interests and, finally, more effective control of the Hungarian domestic economy. After considerable agreement had been reached in negotiations of 9–18 April 1946 on the question of economic cooperation, the Soviet Union found a way of financing its enterprises more comfortably by investing its share of war spoils in the six mixed-economy companies set up between May and August 1946. Following the creation of a civilian airline, a Danube shipping line (4 May), oil exploration company (23 July) and crude oil refining company (25 July) were also set up, to be followed on 6 August by a company for mining, bauxite extraction and aluminium production as well as a mixed-economic enterprise for the design and construction of plant for the bauxite industry. These companies, which effectively exercised a monopoly in their own branches of industry, were supraterritorial and enjoyed exemption from rates and taxes. The Soviet Union declared their goods to be 'Soviet-produced' and conducted a brisk transit trade which reduced the sales market of those parts of industry related to these enterprises which had remained in Hungarian hands.

The transfer of profits thus acquired enabled the Soviet Union to drain Hungary by over a billion US dollars until 1954 when pressure from Imre Nagy's more self-confident government made the Russians agree to transfer the mixed-ownership companies to Hungarian state ownership for a substantial payment; the only exception being firms mining uranium. These economic practices which aimed at direct exploitation and the fact that before 1948 many prisoners of war and civilian internees were sent to Russia as forced labour stimulated the Hungarian population's latent anti-Russian sentiment and made the work of the Communist Party that much harder.

In contrast, the expulsion of Hungary's ethnic Germans in January 1946 under the terms of the Potsdam agreement met with public approval. By 1948, around 240,000 German Hungarians had been forcibly resettled in the American and Soviet sectors of Germany. A few were also settled in Austria. The emergency measures passed against the remaining 250,000 ethnic Germans in Hungary were revoked in 1950. The Czechoslovak government's intention to repatriate approximately 650,000 Magyars living in Slovakia failed because of the Allies' veto. A treaty between the Prague and Buda-pest governments, signed after lengthy negotiations on 27 February 1946, proposed an exchange of populations between equal numbers of Slovaks settled in Hungary and Magyars resident in Slovakia. Approximately 70,000 people were affected on each side and a further 20,000 may well have left Czechoslovakia voluntarily. As a new and more sympathetic policy towards the national minorities began to emerge, the 50,000 or so Hungarians, who had been forcibly settled in the Sudeten areas abandoned by the Germans in 1945 were allowed to return to their villages once relations between Czechoslovakia and Hungary had returned to normal.

On 1 February 1946, the Hungarian Republic was officially proclaimed following an initiative of the Social Democrats and entirely in line with Communist intentions (Law I of 1946). Tildy, who had been premier up until this point, was made the republic's first president. Thus, the thousand-year-old Kingdom of St Stephen, having survived Turkish rule, revolutions, foreign domination and Horthy's Regency, came to an inglorious end. In the new parlia-mentary republic far wider powers were vested in the president, although Tildy, fearing the Communists and soon worn down by their pressure, made insufficient use of them. On 4 February, the new premier, Ferenc Nagy, a former party official in the wartime Peasant Federation and now chairman of the Independent Party of Smallholders presented his cabinet. The appointment of László Rajk as the new interior minister was to be an especially significant change. As minister for reconstruction and, from November 1945 onwards, also chairman of the National Assembly and National General Council, Nagy had made it clear that he had no thought of giving in to the illegal actions of the Communist Party or the interventions of the Soviet occupying power. He was regarded as a secret sympathiser of the USA and a politician who, while introducing a western-style parliamentary democracy, would even have been prepared to preserve the monarchy.

But Nagy also had to watch helplessly as his interior minister, Rajk, deliberately set out to replace around 50,000 to 60,000 state officials with obedient yes-men within six months. In the 'public meetings' called by the Communists these officials, who had been the pillars of the old system, were forced to resign as a result of the 'people's judgement'. By 1950, probably about 120,000 state employees had lost their jobs. This 'popular movement', which Rákosi praised as 'primitive democracy', helped the Communist Party establish a firmer footing, especially in the countryside and smaller provincial towns. The activities of the People's Courts, which were proceeding against the politically exposed representatives of the Horthy régime, excited the general mood of the country further. On 12 March 1946, Ferenc Szálasi and several members of his Arrow Cross government were executed. They were followed by the former prime ministers Bardossy, Imrédy and Sztójay who were executed as war criminals. In all, 25,000 people may have been sentenced as war criminals by the highly arbitrary People's Courts and the death penalty carried out on about 500 of them. At the same time, between January 1945 and March 1948, there were almost 40,000 political prosecutions which resulted in over 20,000 people being sentenced.

In January and February 1947 a show trial, in which prominent members of the Smallholders' Party were accused of conspiring against the republic with the aim of restoring the Horthy régime, spread fear and terror and helped the Communists accelerate the process of weakening their opponents. Several groups opposed to the régime – Magyar nationalists who deplored the erosion of the old Hungarian Kingdom's traditions, landowners and rich peasant farmers who feared for their economic survival, religious groups which opposed the official atheism of the Communists – provided the excuse the Communists were waiting for by joining forces in a secret organisation called the 'Hungarian People's Community'. Its aim was to establish a coalition government on the western parliamentary model under Horthy's last prime minister, General Géza Lakatos, following the signing of a peace treaty and the subsequent withdrawal of Soviet troops. Since the ministers who belonged to the Smallholders' Party, Albert Bartha (defence) and András Mistéth (reconstruction) and leading right wingers (General Secretary Béla Kovács, Kálmán Saláta, etc.) had known about the planned overthrow of the government, the Communists were able to exploit the affair by denouncing the democratic opposition as a whole and diverting attention from their own violation of civil rights.

The Party of Smallholders had already begun, however, to break up in January 1946. When the Communists introduced draft legislation for a state protection law designed to give a semblance of legality to arbitrary police actions, its critics, led by the lawyer, Deszö Sulyok, were branded as 'reactionaries' and 'fascists'. Threatening to leave the government, the Communists demanded that the larger coalition partner should purge its own ranks. Since the leaders of the Smallholders' Party feared an intervention by the Soviet occupation power if the coalition collapsed just at the point when decisive negotiations on a peace treaty were imminent, they agreed to the Communists' demand and expelled Sulyok and his sympathisers from the party. Thereupon the latter founded the Hungarian Freedom Party (*Magyar Szabadság Párt*) as an 'anti-communist party of national resistance'. The Communist Party's initiative in creating a Left-Wing Bloc (*Baloldali Blokk*) on 5 March 1946, which, alongside the Communists, included Social Democrats, the National Peasants' Party and the Trade Unions Council, and which organised a 400,000-strong demonstration on the main square of Budapest on 7 March, had created a unified counterweight to the weakened Smallholders' Party, which gave growing emphasis to its demands by mobilisng popular support, capitalising on popular sentiment and openly flouting the law.

When the Smallholders' Party's left wing, led by István Dobi and Gyula Ortutay, openly espoused the policy aims of the Left-Wing Bloc and forced the party executive on 12 March 1946 to accept the demands of the Left, which were heavily influenced by the Communists, the party leadership was placed further on the defensive. While they managed to secure some advantages when the coalition was renegotiated through President Tildy's moderation on 5 June 1946, they did not succeed in halting the Communists' advance. The latter were also able to block the Smallholders' intensified efforts in the autumn of 1946 to renew their old wartime alliance with the Social Democrats and bring about a merger with the National Peasants' Party. The Smallholders saw themselves forced to expel several of their deputies who were involved in the alleged conspiracy behind the show trial, whereupon their dynamic General Secretary, Béla Kovács, resigned. On 26 February 1947, he was arrested and abducted by the Soviet security police who charged him with spying for a western intelligence service. The affair finally broke the moral backbone of the Smallholders Party. During the spring of 1947 about another 50 deputies were forced to leave the Independent Party of Smallholders. Led by Zoltán Pfeiffer, they founded the Hungarian Independence Party (*Magyar Függetlenségi Párt*) on 18 July as a rallying point for the conservative-bourgeois, anti-Marxist opposition. Of their former 245 seats in the National Assembly, the Smallholders still held 187, but lost their absolute majority.

The prime minister, Ferenc Nagy, also finally fell victim to the increasingly open attacks on liberal democratic politicians by the state security authorities, who were encouraged and supported by the Communist minister of the interior. Following a cabinet reshuffle which increased the Communist Party's influence, Nagy, who was taking a rest cure in Switzerland at the time and had been officially informed that charges were being made against him in connection with the anti-government conspiracy, announced his resignation on 30 May 1947. Among the other prominent politicans who, like him, chose exile was the President of the National Assembly, the churchman, Béla Varga. The new General Secretary, the Roman Catholic priest, István Balogh, who took over only in February, fell probable victim to Communist blackmail and resigned from his post and that of secretary of state to the prime minister. His resignation, together with the founding of the Independent Hungarian Democratic Party (*Független Magyar Demokrata Párt*) accelerated the collapse of the Smallholders' Party. The Communists could well rejoice, for the fragmentation of their opponents improved their chances of becoming the strongest political force in the country. Although they managed to enhance their position further in the government formed by Lajos Dinnyés, briefly defence minister and Smallholder Party member, on 31 May 1947, they were the most vocal group in calling for the parliament – now again renamed the '*Országház*' – to be dissolved and demanded the holding of fresh elections for 31 August 1947. A new and more restrictive electoral law which denied the franchise to 350,000 of the 5 million citizens previously entitled to vote prepared the way for a Communist victory over opposition groups which lacked funds and were still unfamiliar to the electorate.

But, as in November 1945, the second post-war elections again proved disappointing for the Communists. Despite a massive election campaign and probably also a considerable degree of rigging the results in their favour, the Communist Party won only 22.3 per cent of the vote, giving it only 100 of the 411 available seats in parliament. The Social Democrats won 14.9 per cent of the vote and a representation of 67 seats. Only 8.3 per cent of the electorate voted for the National Peasants' Party which won 36 seats. The Smallholders, now led by the left winger, István Dobi, still managed to attract 15.4 per cent of the vote and returned the second largest parliamentary fraction comprising 68 deputies. Balogh's Independent Hungarian Democratic Party obtained 18 seats from its 5.2 per cent share of the vote, Pfeiffer's Independence Party was rewarded with 49 seats from its 13.4 per cent and the Democratic People's Party (*Demokrata Néppárt*), which had broken its close ties with the Smallholders in the spring of 1946, managed to win as much as 16.4 per cent of the vote and was returned as the biggest opposition party with 60 seats. Splinter groups like the Christian Women's Party, led by mother superior, M. Schlachta (1.4 per cent and 4 seats), the Bourgeois-Democratic Party (1 per cent and 3 seats) and the Hungarian Radical Party (1.7 per cent and 6 seats) were an insignificant factor.

When the anti-Marxist opposition's attempts to form a coalition government with the Independent Party of Smallholders against the Communists and Social Democrats, failed because of opposition from the Smallholders' left wing, the Communist Party did all it could to dispose of its political opponents smartly. Rákosi, who was confirmed as General Secretary at the Third Congress of the Hungarian Communist Party, held between 29 September and 1 October, had a firm grip on the party and had no wish to stage show trials against the leaders of the opposition, preferring instead to adopt a softer approach. By announcing that preparations were in progress to put them on trial and that their parliamentary immunity had been lifted, he encouraged them to flee to the West. Following the departure of D. Sulyok, whose Hungarian Freedom Party had already been dissolved in July 1947, Zóltan Pfeiffer also emigrated to the West on 4 November 1947. His Hungarian Independence Party was subsequently banned on 20 November 1947. After its founder, István Barankovics emigrated, the Democratic People's Party, too, had to dissolve itself, although this did not happen until 4 February 1949. In each case, the parliamentary seats of the outlawed parties were immediately declared to have been vacated. A merger did take place between the Bourgeois-Democratic party and the Hungarian Radical Party to form the Radical Democratic Party Alliance, but this lasted only until 3 March 1949 when the new grouping was then merged into the reorganised Hungarian Independence-Popular Front and, thus, into the Communist government camp. In May 1949, István Balogh's Independent Hungarian Democratic Party also had to cease its activities when it, too, was incorporated into the Popular Front.

With the disappearance of the bourgeois–democratic opposition the majority of Social Democratic party members expected a more determined stand from their traditional organisation against the Communists' dictatorial, totalitarian aspirations. But the party leadership, already heavily infiltrated by Communist supporters, was as little able to organise opposition to the omnipotent Communist Party as the remaining small group of Smallholders, which was torn apart by internal squabbles. On 13 September 1947, its Supreme Council had emphasised the need to continue the coalition with the parties of the Left-Wing Bloc despite its Communist domination which was perceived as a threat. In Dinnyés' second government, re-vamped on 23 September, the Smallholders still provided four ministers, while all the other ministries of any significance were already controlled by the Communists. Alongside Rákosi, who was appointed deputy premier and minister of state, Rajk (interior), Gerő (transport) Erik Molnár (foreign affairs) and Károly Olt (social welfare), the members of the cabinet who nominally belonged to other parties, i.e. Szakasits (deputy premier and minister of state), Erdei (minister of state), József Darvas (public works), Péter Veres (defence) and Gyula Ortutay (education and culture) could be regarded as loyal Communist Party supporters.

On 1 July, the Communist Party won parliamentary approval for a Three Year Plan to be implemented on 1 August. The banks, together with the 264 industrial and commercial enterprises which they controlled, were nationalised on 29 November 1947. This was followed by the nationalisation of almost 600 industrial firms with more than 100 employees on 25 March 1948. Henceforth, 85 per cent of all employees worked in state-controlled enterprises, while many private commercial firms were allowed to continue operating. The Communists attributed the slow rise in living standards, which had been encouraged by a relatively good harvest in 1948 and the slow closing of the gap with industrial production levels of 1938, solely to the decisive measures they had taken in the interests of the country and its workers, the emasculation of profiteering capitalists and the end of the restrictive influence of foreign capital.

The Communists also tried to overcome the population's continued rejection of its arbitrary and coercive measures by stepping up its campaign for working-class unity and a merger of the two Marxist parties, which it saw as inevitable. When the 'right-wing' Social Democrats opposed a merger which would involve the loss of their political independence, their spokesmen, who included the former government ministers, Károly Peyer, A Kéthly, F. Szeder and A. Bán, were expelled following an internal party struggle which lasted until February 1948. At a dubiously convened party meeting at the beginning of March the go-ahead was given for a merger, which was prepared on all levels by a joint political and organisational committee and took place on 12 June 1948 at the Communist Party's Fourth Party Congress and the Social Democratic Party's Thirty-Seventh Congress. At the First Party Congress of the new, united Marxist-Leninist party, held on 13–14 June 1948, the former Social Democrat, Szakasits, was appointed chairman of the new Hungarian Workers' Party (*Magyar Dolgozók Pártja* – MDP) which now numbered over 1.1 million members. Rákosi was made General Secretary and the Communists, János Kádár and Mihály Farkas, were appointed his deputies. The main priorities stressed by the party were: the complete democratisation of the state apparatus, the preparation of a new constitution, an 'improvement in living standards by developing productive forces', the abolition of the 'education monopoly of the propertied classes', state control of church schools, the spread of the class struggle to the countryside, the strengthening of Hungary's international standing and the deepening of relations with the Soviet Union and the new neighbouring 'People's Democracies' of eastern Europe.

The assimilation of the Social Democrats into the system and the destruction of the opposition meant that the Communists had successfully concluded their 'Socialist revolution' in the spring of 1948 and achieved an unchallenged monopoly of political power. They could now set about destroying the last vestiges of freedom and erode the few remaining bastions of anti-Marxism. They could also concentrate on achieving Hungary's assimilation into the 'Eastern Bloc' and force Hungary to emulate an obligatory Soviet model which ran entirely counter to Magyar national traditions. There was now no need to take any account of opponents at home or western public opinion.

The peace treaty, whose main principles had been already laid down in the autumn of 1946, was signed in Paris on 10 February 1947 and became effective on 15 September 1947. With its signing the western Allies surrendered their only means of applying diplomatic pressure to halt or, at least, delay the spread of Socialism in east central Europe and the Soviet Union's incorporation of countries occupied by the Red Army into its direct sphere of influence. To the great disappointment of all Magyar patriots, Hungary was again obliged to accept the frontiers laid down in the Trianon Treaty of 1920 and cede a further 40 square kilometres of territory opposite the Czechoslovak bridgehead city of Bratislava. The country's population of 9 million Magyars had to adjust itself once more to an area of 93,030 square kilometres of territory. The Hungarians felt particularly annoyed that the Soviet foreign minister, Molotov, clearly supported the Rumanians on the question of Transylvania, which was still the object of the rival claims of Budapest and Bucharest, and had defended the Czechoslovak government's drastic policies towards its Magyar minority. The danger posed by the latter was subsequently removed by the forced resettlement of Slovaks, exchange of populations and expulsion of Hungarians regarded as disloyal or incriminated by their wartime activities. Prague's alliance and treaties of friendship with Belgrade and Bucharest had also aroused Hungarian fears of a revival of the Little Entente. Thus, the Hungarian government took a close interest in Tito's initiative to create a Danubian Federation or Balkan Union which they felt would provide better protection for their national interests than a hardening of the old attitudes associated with the idea of the nation state. Most Hungarians were very disappointed in the fact that Hungary's occupation did not end with the signing of the peace treaty. In order to secure its supply routes to Austria's Soviet Zone, the Red Army, which did not shirk from intervening openly on behalf of its Communist protégés, continued to station troops in the country.

After 1945, the Hungarian government also tried to re-establish friendly contacts with the western Allies. However, their diplomats in Budapest and representatives in the Allied Control Commission soon resigned in protest at massive Soviet interference and the illegal actions of the Hungarian Communists. Between 8 and 25 June 1946 a Hungarian government delegation visiting Washington and London had submitted its proposals for peace negotiations and formally requested economic aid. The members of the delegation who belonged to Hungary's democratic parties also asked for moral support. When in January and February 1947, however, the

Communist Party began to destroy the democratic opposition by staging a show trial against members of the Party of Smallholders, a protest by the western Allies and the freezing of a 15 million dollar loan by the US government could no longer halt the Soviet Union's measures to force Hungary's incorporation into their sphere of influence over the eastern European 'People's Democracies'. The Hungarian government's intention to take part in the European Economic Conference, due to be held in Paris on 12 July 1947, at which America's proposed Marshall Plan for Economic Aid and Reconstruction was due to be discussed, had to be withdrawn after the Kremlin had abruptly rejected this programme for European recovery.

Through an economic and loan agreement signed on 15 July 1947 the Soviet government, for its part, undertook to try to tackle Hungary's anticipated economic problems by implementing the Three Year Plan and to guarantee the country's incorporation into the eastern European economic system which was increasingly centred on Moscow. The foreign trade relations of all the eastern European countries were subsequently reduced to a political lever controlled by the Soviet superpower, with the result that, while strengthening its own economic potential, the Soviet Union was able to increase its political domination to the point where it could at least unite those countries which shared its political system and, therefore, its ideological aims into a 'Socialist world empire'. Moscow's direction of the Hungarian economy was a major factor in establishing Soviet political control over the country. In recognition of the good work done by the Hungarian Communists on their takeover of power, but also because, according to Marxism, there can be no exploitation among Socialist states, the Soviet government halved Hungary's remaining reparations debt up to 1 July 1948. Despite this help, Hungary may well have paid compensation to the USSR amounting to a total of at least 250 million US dollars according to world market prices in 1955.

The impetus which came from the first conference of the Communist Information Bureau, which met between 22 and 27 September 1947 at Szklarska Poręba in Poland, was of major importance for the internal political changes imposed on Hungary and its incorporation into the Socialist Bloc. Outwardly, the Cominform was only supposed to support the struggle of the European Communist parties to improve the situation of the working class, maintain peace and defend the independence and sovereignty of its member countries. In legal terms it was not supposed to be an above-party institution, but a forum for coordination which had no coercive power over members. In de facto terms, however, the Cominform became a command headquarters controlled by the Kremlin, against whose decisions there was in practice no possibility of objecting. Like the other leaders of eastern Europe's Communist parties, who, even after the complete emasculation of their opponents, found their dependence on the Kremlin leaders of World Communism increased because of the far-reaching changes imposed upon them in the face of opposition from the majority of their populations and the intensification of conflicts arising from the Cold War, Rakosi generally welcomed the founding of Cominform. For the party faithful, schooled in the USSR, the conformity which Stalin demanded brought with it a certain degree of security. There was no more need in future to disguise the decisive influence of the Soviet Communist Party on the direction taken by the Communist parties of eastern Europe. It was no longer necessary to give the impression that the creation of the Socialist Bloc's monolithic unity, which Stalin henceforth demanded, would be achieved by a joint discussion of the methods and external and internal policy aims of the various Communist parties and the democratic expression of opinions.

When, by invoking Article 53, para. 1 of the United Nations charter, the Soviet government concluded a friendship treaty pledging support for Hungary on 18 February 1948, it was still only a case of legally formalising Hungary's already existing dependence on a treaty which symbolised the purely formal equality of Communist countries on an international level. The signatories to the treaty pledged themselves to support all efforts to maintain world peace and especially to resist any aggressive plans of Germany – which was rearming – and its allies. Beyond this, the treaty also envisaged close economic cooperation. It is doubtful whether Stalin was really prepared to respect the expressly included positive expressions of 'friendship' between the signatories; namely mutual respect of sovereignty, non-intervention in internal affairs and complete equality of status. There was no express mention of the ideologically crucial role of the Soviet Communist Party and the Soviet Union in the treaty, which was soon followed by bilateral agreements with the other members of the Socialist Bloc (Yugoslavia on 8 December 1947, Rumania on 24 January 1948, Poland on 18 June, Bulgaria on 16 July and Czechoslovakia on 16 April 1949). The Soviet and Hungarian Communist party press saw it, at any rate, as embodying a new kind of relationship between Communist states, which confirmed Stalin's argument that a new social structure also demanded new political forms: namely, a community of interests based on the same socio-economic forces and a new approach to international relations.

THE PERSONAL DICTATORSHIP OF MÁTYÁS RÁKOSI

The imposition of a 'united front from below' signalled the 'organic union' of the Communist Party (MKP) with a Social Democratic Party, which had been decimated by purges and expulsions, and resulted in the creation of the new Hungarian Workers' Party (MDP). By the summer of 1948, this development, together with the establishment of extensive Communist Party control at all levels of political, social, economic and cultural life, marked the completion of the Communist takeover in Hungary. The Communist Party's establishment of its monolithic rule was marked by the enunciation of a set of laws, which included intensifying the class struggle and carrying it into the countryside, exposing the remaining opponents of the new system and intensifying relations with the Soviet Union at the expense of Hungary's own national interests. Stress was now placed on transforming the state, society and the economy from within. During this transition from the 'phase of consolidation' to that of 'Socialist construction', Hungary's Communists, while loudly proclaiming their loyalty to the Soviet Union and Stalin, were quickly prepared to demonstrate the doctrinaire uniformity and total conformity expected of them, partly from fear and the need to tow the line, but partly also for the sake of their own careers and personal security. The experiences and political practice of the Soviet Communist Party and the Soviet Union became a sacrosanct dogma. Personal loyalty and devotion towards Soviet desires became the single most important criterion in judging a party functionary or someone's political views at a time when Tito and the Yugoslavian Communist party were successfully opposing this degrading form of subservience and blind obedience. Although some prominent comrades, while acknowledging the need to intensify the class struggle and rapidly change society, held firmly to their conviction that they would have to take national conditions into account in promoting the 'people's democratic revolution', they were branded as political 'deviants' and accused of an apparently inadequate understanding of Stalin's views and the Soviet Union's ideological and political leadership role.

The Communist Party's officials after 1948 were mainly skilled experts at maintaining themselves in power. Those deemed to be the most reliable and most willing in the eyes of the Soviet Communist Party's Central Committee occupied the most important positions in all the executive branches of the state, the management of industry and mass organisations like the trade unions, womens' and youth organisations, cooperatives and cultural organisations. Structured according to the principles of 'democratic centralism', the new MDP claimed to be 'the leading nucleus of all the workers' organisations in the society and state'. Modelling all levels of Hungary's system of training and education on that of the Soviet Union, the Communists aimed at rapidly creating a new intelligentsia schooled in Marxist-Leninist principles, re-educating bureaucrats willing to cooperate with them and strengthening the ideological commitment of the party secretaries. Whereas difficulties were increasingly placed in the way of middle-class citizens, the reformed and standardised school system was designed to ensure positive discrimination for children from workers' and peasant families. The organisation of the press, radio and publishing, all of which had already been the subject of considerable state control since 1945, was restructured. All-embracing censorship measures were further refined and 'Socialist realism' became the artistic norm. In Budapest and the other major cities the monumental Soviet style of architecture met with an enthusiastic reception from architects. Following the nationalisation of Church land, the conflicts which had already been provoked with the Christian churches, especially the Catholic Church, were heightened by the struggle over church schools. The Catholic Church's apparent dependence on the Vatican and its role as the 'vanguard of American imperialism' provided an excuse for interfering in the Church's internal administration and imposing restrictions. The expansion of the planned economy and the forced collectivisation of agriculture were not only necessary to raise the living standard and promote rapid industrialisation; they also served to neutralise politically the peasants who were considered conservative and reactionary, destroy traditional social structures and facilitate social control. Control of the already infiltrated armed forces and ubiquitous secret police fell to party officials who enjoyed the Kremlin's special confidence and were, moreover, often Soviet citizens.

Because of the prevalence in Hungary of traditional anti-Russian attitudes and newer anti-Soviet attitudes which had been reinforced by the experiences of the occupation, the Kremlin thought it vital to allow only those comrades to reach the top echelons of party and government who had long since proved their loyalty towards the Soviet Communist Party, whether as émigrés in Moscow, propagandists of the Comintern or in the service of the NKVD or as keen advocates of Stalinist methods. Stalin's idealised prestige, the myth surrounding his person as the architect of Socialism, victorious field marshall and towering statesman, helped the Kremlin chief to stamp his impression on Communist Hungary's social order and political system. Stalin may well have been comforted by the thought that the leading officials he chose enjoyed no real support among the Hungarian population which the war and the chaos of its aftermath, further destabilised by Communist interference, had left completely demoralised and utterly insecure as a result of additional Communist interference. Despite the existing ties of personal loyalty, which almost assumed the form of a feudal relationship, Stalin always let his place men in Hungary feel a certain degree of insecurity in order to exert an even greater influence on the country's internal development. The psychological element present in their relationship with Stalin, which is not easy to grasp, caused Hungary's Communists to make most of their decisions in anticipation of the possible desires and orders of their Kremlin boss not only out of a sense of devotion and loyalty, but also fear for their lives. However, Stalin's death on 5 March 1953 marked the end of an era in which an individual's decisions had been able to cause abrupt changes in the policy direction of the Socialist countries. His heirs, largely paralysed by the internal Soviet power struggle to find a successor, were forced to witness how Stalin's system of informal and indirect control could no longer function and how the people's democracies, left largely to their own devices, underwent a period of instability during the duration of the power vacuum. The shattering events which befell Hungary in the autumn of 1956 emphatically questioned the Communists' whole range of achievements, and the subsequent 'triumph over counter-revolution' was possible only as a result of the intervention of Soviet troops.

The successful Communist takeover in Czechoslovakia on 25 February 1948 also encouraged the Hungarian Communists to ignore internal protests and press on with their 'Socialist revolution' according to the Kremlin's guidelines. Following the creation of a single Socialist party and the elimination of the parliamentary opposition the Council of Ministers was able to implement the measures required to effect change, mainly by the use of decrees, without encountering any parliamentary objections. On 1 February 1949, the remaining rump parties, now branded the 'reserves of the class enemy', were forced to merge with the newly founded Hungarian Independence-Popular Front (*Magyar Függetlenségi Népfront*), as members of which they were allowed to take part in the coming parliamentary elections held on 15 May 1949 before being forced to dissolve themselves. With the disappearance of the Independent Party of Smallholders, the National Peasants' Party, the Independent Hungarian Democratic Party and the Hungarian Radical Party, the MDP, the 'spearhead of the dictatorship of the proletariat', remained the only organised political force in the country with 71 per cent of the 402 deputies in parliament. Despite the single list of candidates 'only' 95.6 per cent of electors had voted for the Popular Front, a fact which 'clearly' demonstrated the need for strengthening the inculcation of ideological values and purging the party of the working class of its 'unreliable elements'. By January 1950, around 300,000 members had been expelled from the party, reducing its total membership to 828,695.

In December 1948, the former agricultural labourer and Smallholder party politician, István Dobi, took over the new government in place of his party colleague, Dinnyés. Ten of the fifteen members of the new cabinet were Communists, of whom the most prominent were Rakósi, who became deputy prime minister, János Kádár, who took over the interior ministry after August 1948, and László Rajk, who became foreign minister after the same date. Apart from Dobi, the minister for education and culture, Ortutay, and the minister for trade, József Bognár, had been members of the former Party of Smallholders, while the minister for reconstruction, Darvas, and the minister for agriculture, Erdei, had belonged to the National Peasants' Party. The highest office in the land, that of President of the Republic, was filled by the left-wing Social Democrat and Communist fellow-traveller, Árpád Szakasits, who replaced Tildy after the latter's resignation on 30 July 1948 following attacks on him by the Left. Szakasits, however, despite his assumption of high office, was unable to prevent his own arrest and imprisonment in April 1950.

The new régime's encroachment upon legal rights was of great importance in establishing its rule in the Hungarian People's Republic. The country's judicial system had remained essentially intact after 1945, although the creation of new 'People's Courts' to track down war criminals and 'elements hostile to the people' represented an undermining of legal principles. These special courts, which comprised lay-judges supplied by the political parties and trade unions were empowered to pronounce the death sentence. A confession by the accused obviated the necessity to prove his guilt on the part of the court. After the creation of the Left-Wing Bloc and the Communist Party's successful infiltration of the trade unions the People's Courts increasingly became institutions for condemning the 'class enemy'. Introduced in 1947, the Workers' Courts, or 'profiteer courts' as they were called, pronounced sentence on 'crimes' committed by former owners when firms were nationalised or 'economic offences' were committed within private companies. These courts served the political aims of the Communists. A law of March 1948 gave the minister of justice full powers to dismiss judges who had fallen from favour or were deemed politically unreliable and the subsequent dismissal of over 10 per cent of Hungary's judges marked an end to judicial independence. After 1949 more and more 'people's judges' sat in court cases where they gave the content of the judgment, while the formally trained judges remained responsible for seeing that court protocol was observed. This politicisation of the judicial system meant an end to the principle of equality before the law and the courts, and signified the introduction of party-political 'class justice'.

Section VI of the new constitution of 20 August 1949 confirmed the independence of the judiciary and the Supreme Court's control over legal judgements. But since, at the same time, control of the judiciary by the State Prosecutor's Office was laid down and the duty of appointment, accountability and suspension of all judges made subject to the 'guidelines to electors', issued by the party, little remained of judicial independence. The 'control of Socialist law' was brought under the direction of the highest legal authority, namely the State Prosecutor's Office (Law 13 of 1953). Administrative justice had already been transferred in 1948 to the arbitration boards of factories and councils, the parliamentary court and the State Prosecutor's Office. The new criminal law code of 1950, which extensively adopted legal principles applied in the Soviet Union, also introduced the concept of 'Socialist law' in Hungary. In future class justice dealt with the accused and sentenced him primarily according to his social class membership. This resulted in crimes which by definition could be committed only by the class enemy. Under this system a lawyer was permitted only to defend interests which the courts deemed 'just'. The independence of the legal profession was ended and lawyers were placed directly under the minister of justice. In place of the People's Courts special courts attached to the Budapest Criminal Court were eventually entrusted with staging political trials which paid little attention to the official rules or the rights of the accused.

The secret police played a vital role in the process of 'exposing the class enemy' and preparing political trials. From the beginning the Soviets had given it assistance and by training émigrés, defectors and 'turned' prisoners-of-war during the Second World War according to NKVD and NKGB instructions (the People's Commissariats for Internal Affairs, i.e. state security) had prepared the ground for their later use in a Communist takeover. Before 1949, a political department of the Hungarian general staff, under the command of Colonel György Pálffy-Oesterreicher and supported by forty Soviet advisers, fulfilled the functions of a political police. The political department of the gendarmerie (ÁVO) existed alongside this. After 1950, the dynamic Gábor Péter reorganised the various police organisations with the help of Soviet experts. In the new ÁVH he developed a perfect technique of fabricating appropriate conspiracies and confessions at the most opportune moment to exploit a political situation. Thanks to its purges, the secret police, which comprised sixteen departments, kept records on over a million citizens and could rely on some 300,000 informers, was able to remove itself almost entirely from party control during the latter part of the Stalinist era. It became a semi-autonomous institution which eventually only Moscow could directly control. At the same time, the Soviet police kept its own independent secret police apparatus in Hungary. During the period of the great purges and the show trials which offended 'Socialist law', neither the Soviet security service, the MVD, nor Stalin were beyond sending incriminating material about certain officials to the Hungarian party leadership with the instruction that the local security police should follow up the case.

In the armed forces, too, reliable Hungarians, who were pro-Soviet and devoted to the Kremlin, were also given key positions from the time of the country's liberation onwards. The creation of a large army had to wait at first until a cease-fire agreement had been concluded, with the result that in the autumn of 1945 just on 10,000 men were available for the defence of Hungary's frontiers. This force remained poorly equipped, moreover, because of Soviet anxieties concerning their reliability and operational ability. The mass demobilisation carried out immediately after the end of the war had made it possible to dismiss all full-time officers suspected of anti-Communism on the grounds that they had actively supported the war against the Soviet Union. However, a small, superbly trained and politically reliable group of officers had returned home in the wake of the Red Army, most of whom had emigrated to the Soviet Union already in the inter-war period and had proved their commitment in the Rákosi batallion of the International Brigades in Spain or in special units behind the front in the Second World War. The defence minister who initially belonged to the Smallholders' Party could not prevent these 'Muscovites', along with Pálffy-Oesterreicher, Lieutenant General Gusztáv Illy and László Sólyom, from controlling the key positions in the general staff. When, after the signing of the peace treaty which allowed Hungary a standing army of 65,000 men and an air force of 5,000 trained specialists, the government pressed ahead with a build-up of the armed forces, Communist sympathisers, in particular, were given the chance of joining the army as full-time professional officers. The creation of a new officer corps, trained at Soviet military academies or by Soviet military instructors, whose members were recruited from the socially less well-off classes and thus thought less susceptible to bourgeois democratic and pro-western views, resulted in a situation in which by 1954 52.8 per cent of Hungary's officers were of 'proletarian' or 'peasant' origin. As for the generals, 52 per cent had risen from the working class and 21 per cent from the peasantry. The system of political policing and control, emulating the Soviet model and carried out by the 'politruks', i.e. instructors attached to each commanding officer, and the steady increase in political instruction in dialectical materialism of each officer corps intake contributed from the outset to the process of political and ideological re-education. But the modernisation of arms systems led the Kremlin to ensure that only those comrades were put in control of the armed forces whose absolute loyalty to the Soviet Union was in no doubt. The defence minister, Mihály Farkas, and his successor, General István Bata, were Soviet citizens as was the air force chief, Sándor Házi, and the chief of the general staff, János Tóth. Following the Kremlin's instructions, they increased the number of troops to over 100,000 men by 1950, with the result that more than 1 per cent of the entire Hungarian population was permanently under arms.

These major changes were only partly endorsed by the government's new written constitution (Law XX of 1949). Approved by the united Socialist party in parliament on 18 August, the Basic Law, as it was called, came into effect on the 20 August 1949, the traditional national holiday in honour of St Stephen, now referred to as 'constitution day'. Although it was to undergo several significant amendments, it is the same constitution which remains in force to this day. In January 1949, the commission appointed to produce a draft of the new constitution had visited Moscow in order to find inspiration in Stalin's constitution of 1936. Their draft, published on

15 March, was, again following Soviet practice, discussed in the various party organisations. Of the 67 proposed amendments to the constitution, six were incorporated into its final form. According to this constitution, which shows little originality, the 'Hungarian People's Republic' is 'a state of workers and peasants' in which 'the nation's workers' are in the process of gradually abolishing 'the elements of capitalism' and deliberately constructing 'the Socialist economic order'. The constitution created a surrogate parliament in the Presidium (*Elnöki Tanács*) which comprised twenty-one members to be elected and controlled by the country's parliamentary deputies. This functioned not only as a collective head of state, but assumed parliamentary powers during the long periods between the plenary sessions of the wider assembly. Thus, the legislative centre of gravity shifted to official decrees issued by the Presidium. Since the principle of the separation of powers was abolished, the Council of Ministers also had the power to legislate. The constitution also increased the autonomy of the administration and thus prepared the way for the introduction of a system of Soviets which was officially introduced through Law 1 of 1950. These soviets were elected by all citizens entitled to vote following the party's nomination of candidates. In the event of the electorate's wishes being ignored, the voters retained the right to remove from office the new organs of state power who were supervised by the Presidium, the Council of Ministers or the superior soviets at local and regional level. The administration's former independence was abolished and replaced by the principles of 'democratic centralism' and the 'double dependence' on both party control and that of the voters. The Independence Front, which was re-named the 'Patriotic Popular Front' in 1954, was given responsibility for organising elections, thus guaranteeing the continuation of the party's direct leadership and control. Of the 220,000 delegates elected to Soviets for the first time in October 1950, over a third belonged to the MDP.

Many Magyars were particularly offended by the constitution's abolition of the state coat of arms from the Kossuth period, which was replaced by a 'hammer and sickle on a round field of azure, supported on either side by wheatsheafs' with a 'five-cornered red star in the upper half of the field', 'emitting rays on to the field' with 'a folded band of red, white and green underneath'.

After the workers' deprivation of political power within the framework of a united Socialist party, the removal of the democratic parties' scope for activity and the usurpation of the control mechanisms of the state and the economy, the Communists thought the time had come to deal with the last remaining opponent of any significance, namely the 'reactionary' Catholic Church, in particular, its hierarchy. The conflict dated back to the beginning of 1945 when Cardinal József Mindszenty succeeded Cardinal Serédi as Hungarian Primate. This passionate, devout and highly conservative prince of the Church had openly and publicly expressed his rejection of dialectical materialism and Communist aims. When the MKP began to attack the two foundation stones of the Church's influence in Hungary, i.e. landed property and the education of youth, it ruled out the prospect of establishing a modus vivendi between the Catholic bishops and the MKP. Mindszenty, who had been imprisoned by the Arrow Cross while Bishop of Veszprém, openly supported the retention of the monarchy and a cautious approach to any change in Hungary's social and economic order, which he believed could only be achieved by evolutionary means. The Christian Democratic People's Party (*Keresztény Demokrata Néppárt*), which had been founded by Count József Pálffy on 13 October 1944, was able to count at first on the support of broad sections of the clergy. As a broad, conservative Catholic movement, its programme adopted Mindszenty's views, demanding that the creation of a new political, social and economic order be based on natural law, the moral teachings of the gospels and social policy as proclaimed in papal encyclica. On 17 March 1945, it also demanded 'genuine compensation for the Church's confiscated properties' and called for 'the clamour of party-political disagreements to be kept out of the schools'. As a result, the Communists successfully excluded the clergy from participation in the November elections of 1945. The militant Primate took his revenge on 18 October by issuing a committed pastoral letter in which he inveighed against the 'Marxist evil' and called on the faithful to support the Party of Smallholders at the elections. Their subsequent success was almost certainly due to this open intervention by the Church on their behalf. When, despite the Church's protests, the republic was proclaimed on 1 February 1946, Mindszenty defiantly revived his former title of 'Chief Excommunicator of the Realm'.

During 1946 the Communists took revenge by conducting a policy of minor irritation for which the interior minister, Rajk, was chiefly responsible. Church institutions were subjected to petty chicanery, the activities of the church press were obstructed by rationing newsprint and searches carried out in denominational schools, which on more than one occasion resulted in discoveries of 'arms caches'. Church youth organisations and the Catholic Student

Federation, which were accused of involvement in the murder of two Soviet soldiers, were banned. When the Communists also campaigned for the abolition of compulsory religious instruction the conflict escalated. Mindszenty called on all churchgoers to stage mass demonstrations and succeeded in temporarily forcing the MKP to practise restraint. After the rigged elections of August 1947 and the destruction of the democratic opposition the Cardinal forbade the ringing of church bells 'as long as Hungary is ruled by excommunicates'. An attempt at mediation by two prominent laymen, the composer, Zoltán Kodály, and the historian, Gyula Szekfű, proved unsuccessful. It was predictable that the MKP's infuriated leaders would take revenge at the earliest opportunity. In February 1948, attacks against the churches and their denominational schools were stepped up. The Catholics were now joined by the Calvinists and the Lutherans as the targets of government propaganda. Following the government's announcement of its intention bring all denominational schools under state control, Cardinal Mindszenty tried to prevent the carrying out this threat to the Church' activities by a series of petitions, sermons and pastoral letters. The less hierarchically organised protestant churches, on the other hand, which represented about a quarter of the country's practising Christians, did not withstand the pressure for long and handed over their 2,000 schools to state control. On 16 June 1948, the Hungarian parliament, which was unimpressed by the Catholic clergy's vigorous protests, approved the programme to establish state control over all denominational schools. The Catholic Church was dispossessed of some 3,000 educational institutions. As the Cardinal was not, however, prepared to give in, and ordered the 2,500 priests and nuns in the affected schools to stop teaching immediately, the government began a campaign to force the militant cardinal to resign or arrange for his replacement. But since this pressure failed to achieve its objective, Mindszenty was arrested on 23 December 1948 and put on trial between 3 and 8 February 1949, charged with subversion. Although the Cardinal made several confessions under the pressure of psychological torture, his alleged confession of guilt, circulated in a government publication before the trial opened, was a crude forgery. In his skilfully worded, reconciliatory final speech at the trial the Cardinal admitted that the Church had made some mistakes in the pursuit of its political aims. But apart from his illegal contacts with the American ambassador and irregularities in the handing over of foreign aid donations – for which he could hardly be held responsible – the prosecution was unable to furnish proof of any 'crime against the state'.

Nevertheless, he was sentenced to life imprisonment. However, the removal of the Cardinal, who was so much feared by the Communist leadership, did nothing to break the influence of the Catholic Church among its adherents. The party ideologues must have found it disquieting that after religious instruction had been made optional 95 per cent of Hungary's parents still opted for their children to take it, despite the obstacles this placed in their way. The new Hungarian Primate, the Archbishop of Kalocsa, József Grosz, was undoubtedly a much more conciliatory character than Mindszenty, but he, too, showed that he was not prepared to accept any further encroachment upon the Church's rights without a fight. As a result, the government embarked upon a new round in its struggle against the Church in June 1950 by arresting a number of priests and laymen, confiscating most of the monasteries and evicting 12,000 nuns and monks. These measures forced the bishops to sign an 'agreement between the government of the Hungarian People's Republic and the Catholic Church' on 30 August 1950. Under its terms the Council of Bishops was obliged to recognise the régime and the republican constitution. It also agreed to condemn any subversive activity against the people's democracy, to appeal to the faithful to do their utmost in 'the great work which the entire Hungarian people is performing under the leadership of the régime' and to support the aims of the Communist-inspired world peace movement. In return, the government promised to guarantee the Church's 'freedom of action', to return eight Catholic training colleges to Church control and lift the ban on the four orders of Benedictines, Franciscans, Marists and the teaching order of nuns. It also agreed to compensate the Church for its economic expenditure for 18 years until it was again able to maintain itself by its own means. The Hungarian bishops were not allowed to take any disciplinary measures against the so-called 'peace priests' who had sided with the régime. The Calvinist Reformed Church, for its part, had already been obliged to sign an agreement which was similar in content.

Since the internal political climate in Hungary was, however, increasingly deteriorating, the Catholic hierarchy soon found itself subjected to new pressures. The Church's discreet neutrality no longer satisfied the régime which sentenced the interim primate, Grősz, to fifteen years imprisonment in July 1951 after a show trial which ended in the accused making a full confession and incriminating himself to an almost unbelievable degree. Further trials led to heavy sentences being meted out to the Catholic Bishop of Csanád, Msgr Hamvas, the Lutheran bishop, Lajos Ordass and the presbyterian bishop, László Ravasz, although, unlike Mindszenty, they were eventually officially rehabilitated in 1956. From now on the newly created State Office for Church Affairs had little trouble in persuading bishops and priests to take an oath of allegiance to the People's Republic on 21 July 1951. The activities of the 'peace priests', petty harassment and constant secret police surveillance forced the churches to come to terms with the limited scope for action left to them and their increased exclusion from public life.

The establishing of state control over church schools was accompanied by an increasing imitation of Soviet methods and values in the educational sector and cultural life in a way which was completely alien to Magyar traditions and which aroused strong objections. In 1941, 6 per cent of Hungary's population, i.e. 466,180 people over the age of ten were still registered as illiterate. It had therefore been an urgent government priority after the war to overcome this lamentable state of affairs which resulted from the country's backwardness and traditional social structure. By awarding grants the government attempted to increase the number of students from workers' and peasant families, who made up only 5 per cent of the total student population. It also encouraged prospective students to take up the study of the natural sciences. In the period after 1947, an impressive number of higher educational establishments, including vocational and technical schools, universities and technical faculties, were set up in record time in order to train new personnel for the party, the bureaucracy, industry and scientific research. These institutions also offered evening courses and correspondence courses for anyone in full-time employment. In 1951, the selective awarding of grants supported 24,000 students in Hungary, who, however, had to accept, increasing restrictions being placed on their subsequent choice of career.

The proposed increase in student numbers, envisaged in the first Five Year Plan, was greatly exceeded. The number of secondary school pupils, which had been expected to rise by 45,000, rose by 77,000. Instead of the expected figure of 8,000, the number of students matriculating at universities and other higher education establishments showed an increase of 30,000. In 1951 alone, 17,000 new students applied for places, with the result that 33,000 young people in all were involved in acquiring a university education (compared with 11,500 students in 1938). In the same year, 1.25 million children attended elementary school and a further 93,600 pupils were enrolled in further education. The government tried to cope with the unexpected flood of students by bringing forward the completion of the new Technical University for Heavy Industry in Miskolcz, the Agricultural College in Gödöllö and the College for the Chemical Industry in Veszprém. In addition, a Department for Transport Studies was set up in Szeged and a Foreign Languages College established in Budapest.

The party was also able to announce proudly that 57 per cent of students and 68 per cent of secondary school pupils already came from a working-class or peasant background. But when many gave up their studies after a short period owing to adverse external circumstances and major ideological difficulties 'bourgeois' professors were blamed for discouraging the students through their examination system. A great deal of interference in curricular development and training methods in which greater stress was placed on a knowledge of dialectical materialism contributed to a rapid decline in teaching standards and a breakdown in discipline. Although the minister of education, Darvas, admitted to the party newspaper *Szabad Nép* on 29 August 1951, 'Our students are very weak in Mathematics, Hungarian Language and Literature and Physics', adding that 'only all too often proper education is neglected in favour of senseless politicisation', little was done at the height of the Stalinist era to overcome the system's acknowledged inadequacies and free Hungarian education from its Soviet model.

As chief spokesman on cultural affairs during the Rákosi era, József Révai also let it be known on 6 September 1951, that 'the ultimate aim of our national education is to inspire people totally with the truth of the teachings of Marx, Engels, Lenin and Stalin'. Accordingly, those responsible for journalistic and cultural activities were given the task of convincing the adult population of the blessings of the new state ideology through massive attempts at influencing opinion, altering the popular consciousness and disseminating a new ethos. This was accompanied by a cult of the USSR and a drive to promote the learning of the Russian language, carried out principally by the Hungarian-Soviet Friendship Society with its upwards of 1.2 million members. Under the MDP's supervision it pursued its mission of eradicating the Hungarians' deep reservations towards the Soviet Union and of demonstrating the country's close ties with the Soviet people and their great leader, Stalin. In schools and youth organisations, too, a policy of cultural russification was intended to inculcate a spirit of national subordination for as long as it took to instil recognition of the Soviet Union's pre-eminence and of a genuine and voluntary solidarity within the

Socialist bloc. The offical party newspaper *Szabad Nép*, which had a daily print-run of 800,000 copies following the dismantling of Hungary's once varied press, shared the same aim. It sanctified the 'USSR's peace policy' and 'great successes in constructing Socialism', at the same time praising Stalin and his Hungarian 'viceroy', Rákosi. Cultural centres, cinemas, theatres and public libraries, set up at considerable cost throughout the country, were used to promote the party's political aims with considerable educational zeal.

As part of the struggle waged against 'bourgeois objectivism', Hungary's creative artists also found themselves under pressure to tow the official party line. The growing tendency to prescribe dogmatically the subject matter of artistic activity and scientific research produced disastrous results, however, since many intellectuals and artists who opposed Stalinist norms preferred to go to prison or a labour camp rather than serve Socialist realism and do their 'duty to partiality' in the humanities and 'optimistic' art. 'The party demands that our writers supply the nation with positive heroes', Révai stated at the Hungarian Congress of Writers in May 1951. But, despite greatly improved working conditions and considerable social advantages, only mediocre artists were prepared to take up his call. Since the government was not merely content with submission and obedience, but constantly expected enthusiasm, life was increasingly poisoned by deception, cynicism and opportunism.

In order to pre-empt organised opposition, the régime forced about 38,000 citizens, mainly members of the upper classes and intellectuals, including 14,000 citizens of Jewish origin, to leave Budapest in May and June 1951 following the complete confiscation of their property. Throughout the whole of Hungary about 70,000 people may well have been affected by these deportations. According to official information from the time, the forced resettlement included 6 ex-princes, 52 counts, 41 barons, 22 ministers and state secretaries of former governments, 85 generals, 324 staff officers, 30 factory owners, 46 bankers and 250 magnates. Like the others, they were forced to earn a living as agricultural labourers, barred from leaving their allotted place of residence. But the régime did not only act against the 'class enemy'. Following Stalin's call for an 'intensification of the class struggle', it was also ruthless in dealing with its alleged internal enemies. As a result of genuine or feigned Soviet fears of the effects of Titoism in the shape of National-Stalinism, 'left-wing deviance', or its right-wing 'bourgeois' variant, 'revisionism', Stalin had initially allowed purges to be conducted in Albania, Bulgaria and Poland which spilled over in to Hungary in the summer of 1949. Taking the form of a never-ending series of public and secret trials against the opponents of the system they were intended to give the party a monolithic unity and secure the unconditional loyalty of all its members. Those found guilty of minor offences were expelled from the party and often sent to prison camps where they faced high work norms or were allocated to punishment batallions. Veteran Hungarian Communists, who had long served the party, suddenly found themselves accused of being Gestapo agents and Horthy fascists. Men who had fought in Spain and China were suddenly charged with being 'cosmopolitan traitors'. Jews were accused of being 'hirelings of Zionism'. Even some of those who had spent the inter-war period in Moscow were not safe from fabricated charges. László Rajk, who had already been considerably stripped of power when he was transferred from the ministry of the interior to the foreign ministry in August 1948, was arrested in May 1949 at the instigation of the 'Muscovites' around Rákosi, Gerő, Révai and Farkas. At his trial held in May 1949, he, together with his Hungarian and Yugoslav co-defendants, confessed to 'nationalist deviance' and admitted to having fought in Spain as an 'agent of imperialism'. His unbelievable self-deprecation went as far as to confirm the prosecution's fantastic charges aimed at exposing Tito and other National Communists. The trial, which was conducted along the lines of the great Moscow show trials of the 1930s, ended on 22 September 1949 with the pronouncement of death sentences on Rajk, Tibor Szőnyi and András Szalai, who were duly executed on 15 October. The remaining accused were given life sentences or long-term imprisonment. The military who were similarly charged, i.e. Pálffy-Oesterreicher and Korondy, were given a military trial and shot by firing squad.

Protests against the flagrant violation of the conditions on human rights expressly laid down in Article 40 of the peace treaty with Hungary were submitted by the US and British governments as early as 2 April and 31 May 1949. But these were rejected by the Hungarian government and the USSR as interference in the internal affairs of a sovereign state. The United Nations Organisation's condemnation of the show trials on 5 October and 3 November 1950, together with further measures such as the refusal to allow Hungary to join the United Nations (lasting until 1955), could not halt the purges nor prevent the régime's excesses which were later to be euphemistically described as 'contrary to Socialist legality'.

Rákosi and his closest colleagues knew how to use the purges to remove potentially dangerous rivals for power and establish Rákosi's personal dictatorship all the more firmly in Hungary. The political police, the ÁVH, which had been created as the 'shield of revolution' to protect Hungary's people's democracy against any subversion, slipped from party control and established itself as a 'state within the state' which was feared by the population and party officials alike. Among the 4,000 former Social Democrats who fell victim to the purges in early 1950 were leading figures like Szakasits, György Marosán and István Ries. They were followed by about 5,000 trade union officials whose removal provided the régime with the opportunity of reorganising the unions so that they could be used in future primarily to oppress the workers in the interests of fulfilling the government's economic plans.

Disgusted by the mass arrests and campaigns of personal revenge, leading Communists like the 'Muscovite', Imre Nagy, and the celebrated literary theorist, György Lukács withdrew from political life. Others, who, like the interior minister, János Kádár, and the head of the ÁVH, Péter, bore responsibility for the Rajk trial, themselves fell victim to the wave of purges they had initiated. In April 1951 the group of home-based Hungarian Communists, which had been active underground during the war and included foreign minister, Gyula Kállai, secretary of state, Géza Losonczy, and Ferenc Donáth, who had been in charge of Rákosi's personal administration for a time, were arrested along with Kádár and charged on the basis of confessions extorted after severe torture. Kádár was given four years in prison and Donáth two years, while the death penalty passed on Kállai and Losonczy was commuted to life imprisonment by an act of clemency. When the new interior minister, Sándor Zöld, learned that proceedings were being instigated against him personally, he first shot his family and then committed suicide. The purges continued when almost half of all party officials were removed from their positions in October and November 1951. When the party's Central Committee declared war on 'Social Democratism' in June 1952, even the new chairman of the Presidium, Sándor Rónai was removed from office in August. The preparations instigated by Stalin a few weeks before his death, to put the Kremlin's mainly Jewish doctors on trial, caused antisemitism, disguised as 'anti-Zionism, also to spill over to Hungary, despite the fact that Rákosi and most of his circle of party leaders were themselves of Jewish origin. Among the victims of this third wave of purges which lasted until well into 1954 were also such experts in torture and law-breaking as the ÁVH chief, Péter, and the former minister of justice, Gyula Décsi. The exact number of middle and high ranking party officials arrested and sentenced is unknown but, certainly, several thousand may have fallen victim to the purges. In addition, more than 350,000 party members lost their party membership by August 1954, which in most cases meant that those affected were subjected to tangible political and economic disadvantages.

Rákosi, who was, for good or ill, entirely at the mercy of Stalin's pressures and increasingly hated by his own countrymen, had been able to establish his personal dictatorship in Hungary only by spreading fear and terror and building up his own personality cult after the removal of all his rivals. On his 50th birthday, 9 March 1952, he was enthusiastically honoured by both party and state. The public praise and sycophantic fuss accorded him were surpassed only by the Stalin cult. Under Rákosi, the chairman of the National Economic Council, Ernő Gerő, had established a strong position assisted by two other 'Muscovites': the chairman of the State Planning Authority, Zóltan Vas, and the Central Committee Secretary for Economic Affairs, István Friss. His willingness to carry out any order reliably and zealously also allowed the defence minister, Mihály Farkas, to rise in the party hierarchy and the minister of culture and party ideologue, József Révai, also belonged to the party élite for a time. Absolutely loyal to the Soviet Union in the first place and only then to Rákosi, these men took care to follow to the letter the Kremlin's instructions on Hungary's Socialist transformation in their respective spheres of operation. When Rákosi, Gerő and Farkas created a 'Defence Committee' (*Honvédelmi Bizottság*) as a direct result of the Korean War in November 1950, they also created a coordinating authority which became de facto the real centre of power in Hungary, as the Politburo and the party's Central Committee were increasingly stripped of their prerogatives. At the MDP's Second Party Congress held in Budapest between 25 February and 2 March 1951, the leading positions in the party were filled only by those comrades who blindly followed the 'Muscovite' line and accepted Rákosi's position as party leader without question. When Rákosi also assumed the premiership on 14 August 1952, his power seemed complete, even though the economic policies he had pursued had driven Hungary into a profound crisis.

At Stalin's behest, Hungary's national economic development was forced to follow a path of rapid and thorough industrialisation in all sectors. This was accompanied by moves to spread the class struggle to the villages and to tackle the problem of rural poverty at the same time as breaking the opposition of the wealthier peasants. Although the nationalisation of industry and large parts of the service sector had placed almost 90 per cent of the means of production under state ownership by 1948, the legacy of old traditions and Hungary's traditionally evolved social structure had still to be broken up by a programme of forced industrialisation and reduced dependence on the world market. The régime also hoped that industrialisation, public works and the mechanisation of agriculture would remedy the problems of overpopulation, underemployment and a low standard of living in the countryside. The steady growth in agricultural production, required to supply the rapidly growing industrial centres, also appeared to be the best way of reducing the peasants to the level of wage-earners, thereby enabling food distribution to be made subject to state control. Only thus could the régime divert funds needed for industrial investment away from the agricultural sector and exclude the conservative and reactionary peasant farmers from exercising any political influence.

A Three Year Plan, prepared with the help of Soviet experts and inaugurated on 1 August 1947, pursued the overall aim of eradicating the last traces of war damage and increasing production by at least 10 per cent over its 1938 levels. For military reasons maximum emphasis was also placed on developing heavy industry, which received most of the available investment funds, while other sectors were neglected. By 31 December 1949, after almost superhuman efforts and enormous sacrifices, some important sectors had even managed to exceed the plan's quotas, with the result that on 10 December the National Assembly was able to launch the first Five Year Plan as from 1 January 1950. Its main aims were to accelerate the programme of 'Socialist industrialisation' and improve the country's defence capacity. Of the investment target of 35 thousand million forints, 17 thousand million were earmarked for industry. To ensure the plan's success, the Presidium decreed on 29 December 1949 that all firms employing more than ten workers and all foreign-owned firms would be nationalised. At the same time, the workers' productivity norms were increased and their party-controlled trade unions were entrusted with maintaining work discipline in order to meet the plan's targets. Following the Soviet example, economic affairs were regulated by legislation designed to deprive employees of all freeedom of action. State control over the direction of labour was reinforced by the abolition of the right to choose one's place of work and the right to strike. Further nationalisation without compensation, which in February 1952 included, among other things, rights of home ownership (with the exception of small family houses), led to a sharp increase in dissatisfaction among the workers, especially since the leadership's unrealistic revision of the Five Year Plan's schedule contributed to a constantly declining living standard. Although the economy showed all the symptoms of a major economic crisis, the economic Tsar, Ernő Gerő announced self-confidently at the MDP's Second Party Congress that he would transform Hungary from a backward agrarian country to a modern 'country of iron and steel' within four years.

The new direction which nationalisation and industrialisation gave to the economy was also accompanied by the 'Socialist transformation' of rural life. The aim was to collectivise agriculture, thus organising the peasants in a way which would make it easier to exert control over them. This also meant loosening up the existing social structure in such a way that the MDP would in future be the only point of focus and cohesion for the community. In the summer of 1948 the régime began a propaganda war against 'Kulaks', by which it meant peasants who owned more than 25 *hold* (approx. 14 hectares). However, every citizen whom the party deemed politically undesirable could be accused of being a Kulak and subjected to harassment before being sent to a prison camp and having his property confiscated. After this attempt to take the class struggle into the villages proved largely unsuccessful Rákosi launched a recruitment drive in August 1948 to set up agricultural cooperatives on a voluntary basis. In May 1947, he had already promised the small-holding peasants who clung to their land 'that no power in the world will succeed in expropriating land from the beneficiaries of land reform as long as the Communists remain in power'. To persuade them to accept their forced participation in cooperatives, they were initially allowed to hold on to their individual plots. This would be followed by a number of planned stages, at the end of which all land, together with its live and deadstock, would be collectivised. The peasant would eventually retain only a small plot of up to half a hectare for his own private use. By the 1 December 1950, however, only 76,887 families, including 120,000 workers, could be persuaded to join one of the established 2,185 cooperatives.

Because the government still held back at first from imposing compulsory measures, and opened up the market to agricultural produce after rationing had ended in 1949, there was a distinct improvement in the general food situation. But the fact that the national income rapidly outpaced the production of consumer goods led the Soviet economist and theoretician Evgenij Varga, who was of Magyar origin and had been attached to the Hungarian government as an adviser, to demand that the 'consumption fever' should be brought to an end by depressing real wages and forcing collectivisation. In the autumn of 1950, poor harvests, low state-regulated purchase prices and the threat of expropriation caused many peasants to slaughter their livestock and invest their ready cash in consumer goods. Food supplies to the towns were consequently reduced to the point that all foodstuffs had to be rationed again until 30 November 1951 and all meat and animal fat until 30 June 1952. Since over a million workers were already employed in industry and contributed 55 per cent of the national income compared with the agricultural sector's 23.9 per cent, priority had to be given to supplying food to the large cities and industrial concerns. The government also had to introduce coercive measures in order to push ahead with its collectivisation programme.

These measures were at least successful, in as much as some 300,000 families had joined the cooperatives by 30 June 1953. But although the number of collectives had now grown to 5,224, there were still only 375,000 workers engaged in this kind of agricultural production. Many family members devoted themselves exclusively to more profitable private economic activities or moved to industry where there was a marked increase in the number of women workers in particular. A shortage of labour and the limited use of agricultural machinery which was exclusively allocated to the so-called Machine Tractor Stations also led to a series of bad harvests which began as early as 1951 and forced Hungary, once a foremost exporter of agrarian produce, to import foodstuffs in order to cover its domestic needs. Neither the cultivation of fallow land, nor the speeding up of collectivisation, nor the extension of state ownership to take in around 12 per cent of all arable land, fulfilled the government's modest hopes of improving yields. An increase in the supply of artificial fertiliser and more agricultural mechanisation also achieved little, with the result that the agrarian sector continued to be the main constraint preventing the government's fulfilment of its high economic targets.

Although 29 per cent of Hungary's foreign trade was already directly transacted with the Soviet Union. Budapest was greatly disappointed by the modest initial successes of the Council for Mutual Economic Assistance (Comecon) set up in Moscow on 25 January 1949. Despite its undertaking to guarantee 'mutual fraternal aid' on the basis of equality, the Soviet Union, which had virtually achieved autarky, could use Hungary's great dependence on supplies of raw materials and energy, deliberately to fix a low price on goods which Hungary had to supply to the Soviet Union under the terms of Comecon's long-term trade agreements while at the same time steadily increasing its demands for high quality. Since a resumption of Hungary's former trade with the West was inconceivable at the height of the Cold War, there was no alternative but to retreat into the Soviet-dominated economic bloc and continue with the programme of industrialisation demanded by the Soviet Union which solely favoured heavy industry and measured progress in terms of heavy tonnage at the expense of consumer goods production. The West's economic blockade also provided an excuse to blame any economic deficiencies and setbacks on the enmity of western capitalists who were 'envious of Socialist industrialisation and its successes' and to avoid being blamed by the workers for their considerable sacrifices and continually deteriorating living standards.

Since the consolidation of the Soviet Union's east European imperium was central to Stalin's foreign policy, Hungary had no opportunity to develop any of its own diplomatic initiatives. The founding of NATO and the creation of the German Federal Republic was used to increase immeasurably the population's fear of aggressive imperialism. The conflict between Stalin and Tito had resulted in Hungary completely freezing the close relations it had previously had with its southern neighbour and, on the Soviet Union's instructions, responding increasingly aggressively to the Yugoslav Communists' successful attempts to resist pressure from the Kremlin. World opinion's rejection of the persecution of the churches, the terror trials and the purges froze Hungary's minimal contacts with the outside world even further. The outbreak of the Korean War increased fears of a total confrontation of the superpowers almost to the point of hysteria. Hungary's adoption of the Stalinist system of institutional and ideological conformity offered only the possibility of developing bilateral contacts with the other Socialist countries of eastern Europe and sharing in the Soviet Union's initiatives such as the world peace movement. The aims announced at one of the last major conferences of the World Peace Council, held in Budapest in June 1953, that, 'Every nation has the right to determine freely its way of life and must respect that chosen by other peoples' in order to 'facilitate the necessary peaceful co-existence of different systems and allow relations between the nations to be shaped to the advantage of all' still had only limited validity in the Soviet Union's east European sphere of influence.

THE FAILURE OF THE 'NEW COURSE' AND THE POPULAR UPRISING OF OCTOBER 1956

In the final weeks of his life Stalin was increasingly intransigent in demanding ideological conformity and had urged further purges and even closer economic cooperation between the Soviet Union and its east European allies. His unexpected death on 5 March 1953 spared Hungary the incalculable consequences of this intended Soviet interference in its affairs. Because of their weaker position and internal rivalries within the Soviet leadership, Stalin's successors did not dare intervene in the internal affairs of the east European People's Democracies to the same degree of ruthlessness as their predecessor. Despite all attempts to preserve a continuity in relations and to continue using well-tried disciplining methods, the new Soviet leaders were obliged to leave the leading party officials in fellow Socialist countries more to themselves than had previously been the case. Molotov, who had emerged from the leadership struggle still firmly in charge of Soviet foreign policy, supported the retention of Stalin's policies unchanged in form and content. However, after the elimination of the interior minister, Beria, Stalin's actual successors, Malenkov and Krushchev, were able to prevail with their argument that Soviet interests were best served by a policy which would be more flexible in form, but similar in content. Russian domination was no longer to be secured by terror and the methods of the police state nor by the undisguised exploitation of the east European economies, since there was always the danger of a sudden outbreak of open opposition. The National Communist parties, weakened by the purges and internecine struggles of the previous four years, would not be able to deal effectively with such opposition. The view of the new Kremlin leaders that economic concessions would have to be made in order to raise living standards and their recognition of the need to raise the morale and will to succeed of the Communist parties by allowing more autonomy was linked with the hope that the National Communists would thus be able to gain greater recognition and achieve greater popularity in their own countries.

The need to reduce police terror to some extent and remove comrades known to be Stalin's closest disciples out of the firing line aroused the suspicion of Rákosi and his closest colleagues, although, with typical obedience they let themselves be persuaded of the absolute necessity of the 'New Course' which Malenkov advocated. Because of severe food shortages and inadequate housing conditions, the first Five Year Plan's emphasis on encouraging heavy industry and the policy of compulsory agricultural collectivisation had caused general dissatisfaction to rise to boiling point, despite the régime's repressive measures. The arbitrary use of political power prevailed throughout Hungary, as the government tried in vain to reverse the downward economic trend and overcome cultural and spiritual stagnation. The government and administration were over-centralised, the bureaucratic state apparatus entirely subject to the party's directives. Civic rights were trampled upon. Excluding officials responsible for the economy, the inflated bureaucracy had grown to 320,000 civil servants. The party with upwards of 850,000 members was administered by 40,000 senior officials. The state security services may well have employed as many as 10,000 people and over 150,000 soldiers served in the armed forces at any one time. The population, which had grown realistic after campaigns, appeals and compulsory measures designed to educate them to self-responsibility, no longer allowed itself to be conciliated by the party's unbelievable propaganda.

In order to mobilise the population for the parliamentary elections due to be held on 17 May 1953 the largely inactive Popular Front committees were revived as the common organisation linking party members with the politically affiliated, but failed to bridge the gulf which existed between the leadership and the population. A week after the outbreak of the workers' rising in the German Democratic Republic Rákosi, Gerö, Farkas and Imry Nagy, who had meantime become acting deputy prime minister without any real influence, were summoned to the Kremlin. After heated exchanges with their Soviet comrades, Rákosi, who was mocked as the 'Jewish King of Hungary', felt obliged to make do with the post of First Secretary of the MDP and handed over the running of the government to Nagy who had not been implicated in the purges. At the plenary executive meeting of the Central Committee on 27–28 June fierce criticism was levelled at the policies which the régime had pursued up to this point. The personnel of the Politburo and Secretariat was replaced and decisions made on the basic direction to be followed by a new government programme which Nagy submitted to parliament when he presented his new cabinet on 4 July 1953. In order to improve living standards, he announced that consumer goods production would be encouraged at the expense of heavy industry which up until then had been given preferential treatment. Collective farmers were to be allowed to leave the agricultural cooperatives and take their own property with them. He also promised a revision of judicial practices which had abused 'Socialist law', together with the closure of internment camps and an end to arbitrary police methods.

Nagy made it clear in the course of time that he wanted to eradicate what remained of the subordinate role Stalin had imposed on
Hungary and would follow a policy which no longer ran counter
to its interests. He found the idea of a world divided into two
military power blocs and the consequent need of the Socialist countries to defend themselves – which naturally implied the Soviet
Union's leadership – unacceptable because it imposed sacrifices on
Hungary at the expense of its own economic development and social
transformation. In anticipation of the Five Principles of Peaceful
Coexistence, formulated later at the Bandung Conference of the non-
aligned countries, he took the line that respect for national
independence, sovereignty, equality, self-determination and non-
interference in internal affairs had to be applied to the Socialist countries also: 'It is the sovereign right of the Hungarian people to decide
which form of international status is the most favourable for guaranteeing national independence and peaceful development'. Nagy,
the spokesman of a small 'liberal' minority within the MDP was
tolerated by the new Kremlin leadership despite reservations
concerning the practicability of such heretical ideas. The Soviet leaders
hoped that it would be possible to reduce the Hungarian population's
hatred of Rákosi's Communist Party and overcome the country's
economic difficulties. It soon became clear, however, that Rákosi and
his 'dogmatic' followers were not prepared to surrender their
position without a fight, especially since they were able to hold on
to their bastions of power in the planning authorities and economic
administration and could push through Ernő Gerő's appointment as
interior minister. Despite this obstacle, Nagy, who was able to rely
on the support of the intelligentsia, the majority of bureaucrats and
Magyar nationalists, tried very hard to establish control over the
omnipotent state security service, the ÁVH. He hoped essentially to
reduce its status to that of a much smaller state security department
under the interior ministry in order to prevent it from becoming a
political factor in its own right. Most of the 150,000 inmates of
Hungary's prisons and prison camps were released. However, the
process of rehabilitation took a long time and by the end of 1954
had affected only 100 veteran Communist Party members. The
régime's alleged opponents, who had been deported to the countryside, were once more allowed to return to their home towns. By
the end of 1953 more than 500 collectives had been dissolved and
the notorious 'Kulak list' abolished. Only 200,000 peasants continued
to work in the cooperatives which owned just on 18 per cent of the

country's arable land. The redistribution of investment meant that heavy industry was allocated 41.1 per cent fewer funds compared with the previous year. However, the desired speedy economic recovery failed to materialise, since the removal of compulsion was accompanied by a decline in work discipline and, hence, productivity. It soon became apparent that the reform measures which Nagy's political opponents had boycotted were not likely to fulfil the régime's over-exaggerated expectations, even approximately. Nevertheless, in order to fulfil the plan to some extent, increasing pressure was put on the workers to reach their targets by the end of 1954 and the peasants were again called upon to join cooperatives.

Although the Central Committee of the MDP had expressly decided in favour of continuing with the 'New Course' on 31 October 1953, this did not prevent the group around Rákosi from consistently undermining Nagy's policies. The support which the Soviet leaders gave the Hungarian premier on his visit to Moscow in January 1954 and the Kremlin's rejection of Rákosi's policies when the latter addressed them at the beginning of May did nothing to prevent his supporters continuing their delaying and blocking tactics. At the MDP's Third Party Congress, held in Budapest betweeen 24 and 30 May 1954, Rákosi even managed to increase his support among the 70 members of the Central Committee and fill the Politburo, apart from Nagy's post, and the secretariat entirely with his own supporters. The detailed work on the preparation of the second Five Year Plan also provided Rákosi with the opportunity to establish the priorities of national economic development in accordance with his own ideas on the subject. Nagy's attempts in October 1954 to counter the growing influence of his opponents within the party by reviving the Hungarian Independence-Popular Front as part of the Patriotic Popular Front failed to produce the desired effect. After his mentor, Malenkov, was dismissed from his position as chairman to the Council of Ministers of the USSR on the 8 February 1955, he succeeded in remaining in charge of the Hungarian government only until 18 April 1955. Four days previously he and Mihály Farkas, who had up until now supported Rákosi, were stripped of all their party offices. Reduced to the status of a political non-person, Nagy was expelled from the MDP in November 1955 and accused of bearing sole responsibility for all the shortcomings and mistakes of the past.

Rákosi did not enjoy his success for long. Krushchev, who was interested in avoiding an East-West confrontation because of the

Soviet Union's growing economic problems, would no longer tolerate a return to violent Stalinist terror methods. The efforts of the Kremlin's strong man to normalise relations with Yugoslavia as well as eradicate the effects of Stalinism in the Soviet Union increasingly threatened the position of Stalin's most faithful Hungarian paladin who was also mainly responsible for the campaign against Tito. Nagy's brief period in power before handing over the premiership to Rákosi's younger and dependent supporter, András Hegedüs (b. 1922), nevertheless succeeded in reducing the population's fear of intimidation and persecution by the secret police and extending the limits of personal and intellectual freedom. Despite his objections, Rákosi was unable to prevent Cardinal Mindszenty being transferred from prison to a more tolerable form of house arrest in July 1955 or the clergymen sentenced along with Archbishop Grősz from being released from prison in October. When Rajk's widow was also set free, the question as to who should bear political responsibility for the régime's purges and judicial murders could no longer be suppressed. At the plenary executive meeting of the Central Committee, held in June 1953, Rákosi had already admitted once to having set all the ÁVH's operations in motion. Two years later, in mitigation of his offence, all he could do was point out that the actual behind-the-scenes organiser, the ÁVH chief, Péter, had been sentenced to life imprisonment by a military court on 13 March 1954.

Since, under Krushchev, priority was once more given to the expansion of heavy industry, Rákosi did not hesitate to return to the principles of the old Stalinist 'moon economy'. Once again the gap increased between the iron and steel sector, on the one hand, and light industry, consumer goods production and the agricultural sector, on the other. Nevertheless, during Nagy's period in office the Soviet-Hungarian owned companies were returned to full Hungarian ownership. The Soviet government also granted a loan, albeit a modest one, amounting to 25.7 million dollars. On 7 and 8 June 1955, a plenary executive meeting of the Central Committee decided upon the wholesale collectivisation of agriculture in the hope of raising production by 25 per cent. But, despite the government's powers, complete collectivisation could be achieved only gradually, since the peasants, suffering from insecurity and hostile to the policy, offered passive resistance and refused to work on fields managed by the cooperatives. In addition, the hopes of tackling Hungary's economic difficulties more effectively by increasing economic cooperation within the framework of Comecon were only fulfilled to a limited extent. The Kremlin's demand for an increase of 12 per cent in defence expenditure, despite Krushchev's policy of peaceful coexistence, placed yet another heavy burden on the Hungarian economy.

The population was particularly disappointed when the signing of the Austrian State Treaty on 15 May 1955 did not lead to a withdrawal of the Soviet troops still stationed in Hungary for the purpose of securing the Red Army's supply routes. When the Federal Republic of Germany had joined NATO on 6 May, the Soviet Union had used this as the pretext for the People's Democracies to sign a multilateral agreement on friendship, cooperation and mutual support in Warsaw on 14 May, but its terms did not exclude a priori the stationing of Soviet troops on the soil of a signatory country. Since the Soviet leadership showed little interest at first in transforming the Warsaw Pact into a genuine advisory and decision-making body of equal partners, it must have come as a serious blow to the Hungarian 'National' Communists, in particular, to have to come to terms with the loss of part of their sovereignty and freedom of action. In the event of a defensive action against NATO, their armed forces were to be subordinated to a common Supreme Command. They also had to accept the continued presence of Soviet units as a force to preserve internal political order and, hence, the Kremlin's right to intervene militarily. Thus, Hungary's entry to the United Nations on 14 December 1955 did little to raise the nation's sense of injured self-esteem.

Because of its refusal to follow the Soviet example of openly acknowledging its share of responsibility in the anti-Tito campaign and to rehabilitate in any way the victims of the terror trials, the Rákosi régime was increasingly subjected to intensive attacks by Yugoslavia from the summer of 1955 onwards. Krushchev could barely conceal his approval. The result was a slow but steady change in Hungary's internal political climate. Released victims of the purges, younger party officials and activists joined Hungary's intellectuals and artists in demanding a revision of the offical party line. They also wanted those officials guilty for the purges to be exposed and punished. As the gulf deepened between the population and the Stalinist régime, Rákosi felt obliged to make minor concessions in order to prevent any heightening of tensions. Journalists were given a very limited amount of freedom which resulted straight away in more readable newspapers and magazines. When the censor ordered the confiscation of an edition of the weekly newspaper of the Writers' Federation, *Irodalmi Ujság* (Literary Journal) in September

1955 on account of a critical article on the government's cultural policy, the editorial board resigned and 59 well-known writers signed a pointed protest resolution addressed to the Central Committee of the Communist Party. The state security services immediately took disciplinary action. In March 1956, the party leadership felt moved, however, to allow a student discussion circle calling itself the 'Petőfi Club' (after the freedom poet of the 1848–49 Revolution) to meet in Budapest and allowed a limited degree of pluralism, since even the party newspaper *Szabad Nép* spoke out against the rigid imposition of intellectual conformity.

At the Twentieth Party Congress of the Soviet Communist Party, held on 24 and 25 February 1956, Krushchev had denounced some of the crimes of the Stalin era as part of the conflict with his internal party critics and had approved the possibility of different 'national paths towards socialism' as one of Lenin's original principles. For the Soviet Union and the other Communist countries of eastern Europe, the Kremlin leader's denunciation of Stalinism contained a potentially explosive time bomb, although this was unrecognised at the time. Krushchev's blurred formula of a 'limited multiplicity in unity' contained the hope that Communist régimes would emerge which were able to look after their own interests without fundamentally reducing the solidarity of the Socialist Bloc. Closer economic ties and the unifying power of a living ideological discussion would make up for the renunciation of terror and dictatorship. Krushchev's limited understanding of the consequences of this for national political leaderships attempting to gain mass support or, in Hungary's case, facing the population's united opposition, proved as serious a misjudgement as his false estimation of Tito's ambition and the aims of the Chinese Communists.

Krushchev, who also faced growing problems in the other People's Democracies, believed that the First Secretary of the MDP, himself so heavily implicated, should personally press ahead with destalinisation in Hungary. Tito, on the other hand, uncompromisingly demanded that his arch-enemy, Rákosi, be stripped of power. However, a problem arose in that Rákosi's only successor as new party leader was the similarly implicated 'Muscovite', Gerő. The former tried to use the breathing space created by the exchange of views between Moscow and Belgrade by pinning the blame for the violation of 'Socialist legality' exclusively on the secret police, the ÁVH, and its former chief, Gábor Péter. On 27 March 1956, he announced Rajk's posthumous rehabilitation. Only three weeks later, however, he also had to admit publicly to his share of responsibility and complicity. By the beginning of July more than 11,000 people had been released in batches from prison. The cooperation between rebellious intellectuals and dissatisfied workers achieved by the Petőfi Club forced the government to embark upon a limited resumption of the 'New Course' by making material concessions and agreeing to respect legal norms more strictly in future. But when this failed to end the growth of popular discontent, Rákosi believed he could restore calm to the country by reverting to the old methods of repression. In a Central Committee resolution of 30 June he mounted a fierce attack on Nagy and his intellectual sympathisers, and went on to announce 'a complete liquidation of Nagy's conspiracy' at a full meeting of the Central Committee on 12 July. But by now the point had been reached when the Kremlin felt obliged to intervene directly.

The reason for Soviet intervention at this juncture can be found in the riots which broke out among workers in the Polish town of Poznan on 22 June. By 28 June, the unrest had escalated into a political conflict which assumed distinct anti-Soviet tendencies and had to be crushed by regular troops. The affair had made the Soviet leadership aware of the pent-up feelings of bitterness and the extent to which these nurtured the potential for revolution. Thus, Rákosi's untimely actions had conjured up the danger of another, even more dangerous explosion in Hungary. Several Magyar Central Committee members, disturbed by the party leader's blind rage, had, in accordance with the usual procedures, turned to the Soviet ambassador, Yuri V. Andropov, with a request for guidance from the Kremlin. Anastas Mikojan, whom Krushchev used as a 'troubleshooter' during the months that followed, was given the job of bringing the revolutionary outbreaks under control. He arrived in Budapest on 17 July, entrusted with the task of ensuring Rákosi's replacement. On the following day the First Secretary resigned 'for health reasons' and went into Soviet exile where he remained until his death in 1971. His successor, Ernő Gerő, immediately found favour as a loyal spokesman for the pro-Moscow faction. In order to achieve his main aim, which was to put an end to splits within the leadership and maintain Soviet predominance, he wanted to make material concessions to the workers, force the pace of industrialisation even further and continue with the agricultural collectivisation programme. He also wanted to isolate 'subversive and oppositional elements' within and without the party and rehabilitate those party members who had been wrongfully imprisoned. Nagy, whom the Soviets also regarded as a sympathiser of the now deposed Malenkov and the person actually responsible for creating unrest, was not allowed to be reinstated to the MDP leadership. Instead, prominent victims of the Rákosi period, such as J. Kádár, G. Kállai and G. Marosán, were appointed to positions in the party secretariat and Politburo.

This half-hearted Soviet intervention had indeed discredited the Stalinists in Hungary, but could satisfy neither the internal Hungarian opposition nor the sceptical Yugoslavian Communists who at first had no wish to accept the veteran Stalinist, Gerő, as head of the MDP. Reconciliatory gestures, such as the burial with honours of Rajk's mortal remains on 6 October, could not conceal the fact that the new party chief had no clear policy and was unable to stamp out the sparks of revolution. With the continued supported of the once more conspicuous secret police, the army and the Soviet occupation forces, but with only a small basis of support within a party in upheaval, he tried to resist mounting pressures from below. Soviet gestures of support, such as the approval of a loan of 100 million roubles and Tito's willingness, communicated by Krushchev, to boost their prestige by receiving Gerő and his premier, Hegedüs, in Yugoslavia, were no longer sufficient to consolidate his position in any real way. Following lengthy talks in the Kremlin with Mikojan and the party ideologue, Suslov, in early October 1956, Gerő and his companion, Kádár, who accompanied him on the visit, saw the possibility of influencing the course of internal events in Hungary, only if Nagy were allowed to rejoin the party. Whereas the transfer of the party leadership to the rehabilitated National Communist, Władysław Gomułka, in the presence of Krushchev on 19–20 October had stabilised the internal political situation in Poland, the situation in Hungary grew more acute by the hour. From the 20 October, meetings were held at Hungary's universities at which students formulated their ideas in a short programme which consciously imitated the Twelve Point programme of 15 March 1848. They demanded a free press, the immediate withdrawal of Soviet troops, the creation of a genuine multi-party system, guarantees of civic rights and personal freedom, an end to the country's economic exploitation and the punishment of those responsible for the terror of the Stalinist era. When, on the afternoon of 23 October, a demonstration of solidarity with the Poles attracted 100,000 people to the memorial of the Polish general and Hungarian freedom fighter, József Bem, the ÁVH responded with force. The demonstrators flooded into the city centre where, joined by police and soldiers, they set in motion an uprising which soon took on an anti-Soviet character. The helpless party leadership, which had been caught unawares, sought Moscow's permission to appoint Imre Nagy to the premiership, for it was believed that only his personal credibility and moderating influence could help end a general strike which had been called and stop attacks being carried out against the hated security forces and – for the first time – Soviet installations. Marosán, a member of the Politburo, former Social Democrat and an only recently rehabilitated victim of the Rákosi period, turned to the Kremlin for military assistance to put down the 'counter-revolution'. Despite disagreement on which course to adopt, a majority of members in the Presidium of the Central Committee of the Soviet Communist Party agreed to the use of Soviet troops in the hope of being able to nip the disturbances in the bud without creating a sensation. Mikojan and Suslov were also despatched to Budapest in order to repress the popular rising on the spot.

Following the proclamation of a state of emergency the struggle for liberation, which was concentrated mainly on Budapest, was at first quickly brought under control, largely because of the Hungarian army's initial passivity and a massive intervention by Soviet troops which had caused an unnecessary bloodbath. At the same time, the Soviet negotiators put it to Gerő that he should hand over his position as First Secretary of the MDP, by now in complete dissolution, to the popular victim of the Rákosi period, János Kádár, and, like his predecessor, leave Hungary forthwith. The new leadership of Kádár and Nagy appealed to the population to observe law and order in return for a promise to try to persuade the Soviet troops to return to their barracks while negotiating with the Kremlin for their final complete withdrawal from Hungary. The announcement of a new government, including prominent non-Communists, on 27 October, together with the withdrawal of Soviet armoured units beginning on the 28th and Nagy's promise, given over the radio on 31 October 1956, that Hungary would remain Socialist but leave the group of one-party states and pursue a policy of neutrality triggered off a misguided euphoria among the population.

Nagy's utterances reinforced the reservations harboured by Moscow. Not only the Kremlin's emissaries, but ambassador Andropov and the Supreme Commander of the Soviet troops 'provisionally' stationed in Hungary, Grebennik, took the view that the Hungarian Communists could not be given sole responsibility for stabilising the Communist system. Despite its still underdeveloped infrastructure, Hungary's bauxite deposits, uranium resources – regarded as the richest in Europe – together with its geographical situation and population of over 9 million possessed a strategic value which the Soviet leadership was not prepared to surrender, given the incalculable effects such a move would have on the cohesion of the Socialist Bloc. It is probably wrong to assume that the Kremlin only agreed to Nagy's appointment and reform programme because it was in any case intent on military intervention in Hungary and was merely buying time in order to reinforce and regroup its troops stationed there. The first intervention, which the Soviets justified on the basis of Marosán's appeal for help in 'crushing the rebels by using the forces of revolutionary order', made it possible for Nagy to form his government and enabled a change in the party leadership which brought about a normalisation of conditions in Hungary which was optimistically praised by the Soviet press. The Soviets' own contribution to the 'elimination of counter-revolution' was played down. The 'Soviet Government's Declaration of the Principles of Development and Further Consolidation of Friendship and Cooperation between the Soviet Union and other Socialist States', published on 30 October, expressly stated the principle of non-intervention in the internal affairs of fellow Socialist countries, although couched in such terms as to be open to a wide variety of interpretations.

The Hungarian Workers' Party had been deprived of its most prominent Stalinist leaders, but when it continued to show advanced signs of collapse, despite its reorganisation under Kádár and immediate change of name to the Hungarian Socialist Workers' Party (*Magyar Szocialista Munkáspárt* – MSzMP), and Nagy came out in favour of a multi-party system and Hungarian neutrality, the threshold of tolerance which the Kremlin leaders had been hitherto prepared to grant Hungary was crossed. From the evening of 1 November, Soviet units again moved rapidly towards Budapest from their forward bases in the Carpatho-Ukraine where they had been redeployed. Not until 2 November did the Soviet media launch their all-out attacks on Nagy and the 'clique of counter-revolutionaries who had come to power' in Hungary. Therefore, it may be assumed that the Presidium of the Central Committee of the Soviet Communist Party, encouraged by the combined British, French and Israeli attack on the Suez canal, took the decision around All Saint's Day to employ military means finally to force a consolidation of power in their interest. Only after protests to the Soviet ambassador against the Soviet advance on Budapest and the threat that the Hungarian government would terminate its Warsaw Pact membership 'if the new reinforcements were not withdrawn to their previous positions' had proved futile, did Nagy decide to declare Hungarian neutrality on the night of 1–2 November and withdraw from the Warsaw Pact. Thereafter, the Kremlin immediately showed that it was prepared to enter into sham negotiations on the details of troop withdrawals.

While the Soviet Supreme Command dragged its heels in the negotiations on troop withdrawals with a Hungarian delegation led by defence minister, General Pál Maléter, in Tököl near Budapest, Kádár, who as party chief was still a member of the cabinet, tried to form a rival government from Szolnok on the River Tisza. In this he was encouraged by the Soviets and given the active help of ambassador Andropov. On the morning of 4 November, after the Hungarian delegation had been arrested and Soviet troops had begun the fight for Budapest with over 2,500 tanks, Kádár announced that a new government had been formed which had appealed to the Soviet Union for military assistance: 'The Hungarian Government of Revolutionary Workers and Peasants requests the assistance of the Soviet Army Command in helping our nation smash the dark forces of reaction and restore law and order to the country in the interest of our people, the working class and the peasantry'. Nagy, who spoke for the last time on Radio Budapest at 5.20 a.m. on 4 November, reported that the aim of the fighting was, 'to overthrow the legal and democratic government of the Hungarian People's Republic'. Afterwards, he sought political asylum in the Yugoslav embassy along with his closest colleagues, including György Lukács. Almost 200,000 Hungarians escaped across the Austrian border. Despite a general strike and fierce street fighting against superior Soviet armoured units, against which large numbers of Hungarian soldiers also fought, the Soviets' military intervention was effectively over by 10–11 November 1956.

The Hungarian government's official report on the uprising later cited more than 3,000 dead and 13,000 injured as well as over 4,000 destroyed buildings. Actual losses were probably higher. The persecution of the 'counter revolutionaries' which followed, despite the amnesty proclaimed by the Kádár government, may well have resulted in over 20,000 people being sent to prison and thousands to Soviet forced labour camps. Law 4 of 1957, promulgated on 15 January 1957, provided for special courts to sentence participants in the uprising to death without formal charges and speeded up proceedings. Some 2,000 people were accordingly executed. Nagy's attempt to exploit the country's revolutionary atmosphere in order to see a brutal Stalinist dictatorship directly replaced by a national and Social Democratic system had failed and left behind it a heavy trail of blood as well as innumerable painful scars.

The risk to the Kremlin from this second military intervention in Hungary was relatively insignificant. The Red Army was in control of the situation throughout. The West, whose freedom of action was limited by the Suez crisis, made do with protests and verbal threats. The Soviet Union knew how to use its veto in the UN Security Council to block any proposed diplomatic and economic sanctions. The Peoples' Democracies, from the German Democratic Republic to China, did not hesitate to defend publicly the necessity of the Soviet military intervention which even Tito and Gomulka carefully described as unavoidable. The concern expressed, particularly in western Europe and in Communist parties outside the Socialist Bloc, regarding Soviet military intervention against a loyal 'fraternal state' only insisting on its obvious rights of sovereignty, made no impression on the Kremlin. But the warning signs that Soviet prestige might suffer a reverse and the accompanying signs that the hitherto strictly observed power relationships based on Soviet hegemony in eastern Europe were in the process of diosolution, were to cause the Kremlin increasing concern. Its willingness to tolerate 'national paths to socialism' disappeared after Krushchev came under increasing pressure from the Stalinist faction within the Soviet Communist Party. In future, first priority would be given to consolidating the Soviet Union's dominant power position in eastern Europe and maintaining political and economic stability.

CHAPTER SIX
Hungary under Kádár

'HE WHO IS NOT AGAINST US, IS WITH US'

After the crushing of the spontaneous popular uprising of 1956, Hungary's development became inseparably linked with the name of János Kádár. Quite unlike his predecessors, Rákosi and Gerő, he was neither a bloodthirsty Soviet governor nor an inflexible Stalinist. Krushchev's initially docile servant and executor of the the Soviet military administration's instructions soon turned out to be a cautious reformer. Despite granting safe and marginal concessions, he knew how to win the population's grudging approval and toleration of the régime in the course of time and eventually became the affable pioneer of liberalisation. Despite his strict observance of Socialist law, the stiff punishment meted out to prominent participants in the uprising, the start of an efficient and eventually successful collectivisation programme and thorough purges of the party and bureaucracy widened the gulf between the new leadership, heavily dependent on the Soviet military administration and a disappointed, demoralised and disillusioned population. Although a 'revisionist' course along Yugoslav or even Polish lines was as unthinkable as the continuation of Nagy's policy of national autonomy and neutrality, Kádár's personal experiences of the worst forms of Stalinism did, however, rule out a return to the earlier 'dogmatism' of Rákosi's personal dictatorship. The new party chief and prime minister had to pursue an unconventional 'centralist' policy, dictated by the prevailing circumstances, which also took account of national interests. Kádár's brand of 'centrism' was both eclectic and pragmatic. His first aim was to strengthen the régime by putting all his efforts into raising the standard of living, developing the economy and depoliticising many of the country's bureaucratic institutions. Despite limited opportunities to allow more active popular participation in the political decision-making processes, he began dismantling various ideological constraints and supported the population's predisposition to remain apolitical. As a result of the economy's relatively high growth rate, the gradual extinction of the old peasant class with its traditional conservative habits and the accelerated process of urbanisation, Magyar society found itself undergoing a profound process of social transformation during this transitional period, a process which essentially helped Kádár realise his aims.

Kádár was a publicity-shy man who felt an aversion towards any form of personality cult. According to the few known and often contradictory details of his life, he was born János Czermanik, son of a rural labourer, in 1912 in the Adriatic port of Fiume. Soon after completing his apprenticeship as a precision engineer, he joined the Communist Youth League. After a number of years in prison he became one of the co-founders of the illegal Communist Party during the period 1940–41 and after 1943 became Secretary of the Central Committee and editor of the party newspaper *Szabad Nép*. As one of the few Hungarian Communists admitted into the inner ruling circle, dominated by the 'Muscovites', he rose to become deputy General Secretary of the MKP and was made interior minister and head of the state security services in August 1948. In 1951, he was arrested on charges of espionage, state treason and 'Titoism', and after being tortured into confessing was subsequently sentenced to two years' imprisonment. After his rehabilitation he was admitted to the Politburo in July 1956 and given a post as secretary to the Central Committee. In his capacity as First Secretary of the Central Committee, he took over the leadership of the Hungarian Socialist Workers' Party (MSzMP), which he had reorganised, on 25 October 1956, following Gerő's forced resignation. On 4 November 1956, he took over on his own initiative as head of the régime which enjoyed Soviet backing. The opinion of several experts, that after realistically appraising the international situation and the options open to Hungary, Kádár's 'betrayal' of Nagy and the nation's wishes stemmed from a desire to rescue the foundations of the Communist régime through personal intervention and spare Hungary a return to the errors of the Stalinist Rákosi era is, in the light of his subsequent policies, not wholly unjustified.

When, in the early hours of the morning of 7 November 1956, Kádár returned under Soviet escort to the scene of the fighting in

Budapest, he found a completely disintegrated party and an administrative apparatus still barely capable of functioning. The editorial offices and printing presses of the party newspaper – now renamed *Népszabadság* (People's Freedom) – had still to be recaptured from the insurgents. Apart from Kádár, the only members of the provisional Central Committee were initially Antal Apró, István Kossa and Ferenc Münnich. Other members were soon coopted and the Committee called upon all party members to fight against counter-revolution and any attempts to restore capitalism in Hungary. The relative weakness in the size of the new leadership and its organisational support in the Hungarian Socialist Workers' Party (MSzMP) – of its 900,000 members, only 96,000 were admitted to the new party – ruled out the possibility of expelling at a stroke all the party officials implicated in the uprising. Consequently, Kádár was obliged to tolerate supporters of Nagy's policies alongside old Stalinists in the restructured party hierarchy. The new régime did endorse Nagy's decree abolishing the old state security service, the ÁVH, on 3 December, but created a new security department of the state police in its place under the authority of the interior minister and entrusted with the same tasks as its predecessor. How little say Kádár's government and the party had in the running of the country can be seen from the fact that Nagy, who was enticed away from the Yugoslav embassy on 22 November by a guarantee of personal safety, was abducted along with his entourage by a Soviet military escort and 'voluntarily' taken to Rumania. Thereafter, the fight against 'counter-revolutionaries' and 'revisionists' became the main focus of the political debate. The ensuing mass dismissals affected civil servants, teachers, officers, trade union officials, journalists and economic experts just as much as party workers who were judged unreliable. The Writers' Federation was disbanded. Celebrated authors such as Gyula Háy and Tibor Déry, who had described the Soviets' part in the crushing of the revolution as an 'historical mistake', were imprisoned.

Krushchev may well have urged Kádár to take a tougher line when the former visited Budapest early in January 1957. The Hungarian party chief was given a sympathetic hearing when he read out a statement of principle in which he said that the Soviet Union had twice fought on behalf of Hungary's national independence: against Hitler's fascists and the reactionary Horthy régime in 1944–45 and against the 'onslaught of counter-revolutionary imperialism' in 1956. He went on to say that the Red Army was also protecting the country against further imperialist attacks 'in the present tense situation'. Thus, subsequent measures such as the reopening of the internment camps, the proclamation of a state of emergency, the introduction of special courts, the ban on political activities outside the framework of the ruling party, the abolition of the Revolutionary Committee, the creation of workers' vigilante squads as a kind of 'armed wing of the party' and the resumption of censorship may well have been the result of direct Soviet intervention.

Kádár's compliance in what was a difficult situation was rewarded with a series of significant Soviet concessions. A Soviet-Hungarian Pact, signed in Moscow on 28 March 1957, went some of the way to reducing Hungary's hitherto semi-colonial status by giving due consideration to the principles contained in the Soviet declaration of 30 October 1956. New economic agreements allowed for trade between the two states to be developed in future on the basis of world market prices. The Soviet Union not only extended the period of repayments on outstanding debts, but granted a long-term loan of 750 million roubles and consignments of manufactured goods and raw materials to the value of 1.1 billion roubles. Although Kádár's long-term goal of liberalising Hungary's one-party dictatorship and increasing the role of the the individual in shaping public opinion did not accord with the ideological standards set by the Soviet Communist Party, the Kremlin leaders were visibly concerned to improve the credibility of the Hungarian Communists in the eyes of their own people and to strengthen support for a régime which had been imposed on the population only a short time before by the use of Soviet troops. 'The complete equality of relations' between the Soviet and Hungarian Communists and 'the part played by Soviet army units in crushing fascist agitators' actively supported by 'imperialist forces', were praised as a 'noble act of proletarian solidarity'. The 'temporary residence' of Soviet units in Hungary, which was justified by pointing to 'NATO's warmongering' and the arms race, was confirmed on 27 May 1957 when a treaty was signed providing for the stationing of troops on Hungarian soil. After 1958, following a purge of the regular Hungarian armed forces to which Soviet advisers were allocated down to company level, the number of Soviet troops stationed in Hungary was able to be reduced rapidly down to 4 divisions and several air force units, whose total strength of around 80,000 men has remained the same down to the present.

Assured of massive Soviet protection and backing, Kádár also succeeded in pushing back his 'dogmatic' critics. He had decreed the creation of a new Central Committee Secretariat for the party, which had grown to 225,000 members by 1 April 1957. Apart from himself, its members included Jenő Fock, the former leader of the Trade Union Federation, Kállai, Kiss and Marosán. They supported Kádár's rejection of the criticisms made by the earlier party ideologue, József Révai, who had returned from Soviet exile. He called on the régime to give up its relatively 'liberal' course, return to the old Stalinist methods of repression and fully reinstate Rákosi and Gerő. Once Krushchev had defeated the 'anti-party opposition' in the Soviet Communist Party, he did not hesitate to give Kádár his full support, thus pulling the carpet from under the feet of Hungary's internal opposition. At the First Party Congress of the Hungarian Socialist Workers' Party (MSzMP), held on 27–29 June, Kádár, while justifying his own 'centrist' line, attacked both the mistakes of the 'dogmatists', Rákosi and Gerő, and the 'practitioners of counter revolution', Nagy and Losonczy. The refounding of the youth organisation, the Communist Youth League (*Kommunista Ifjusági Szövetség*), the intensified recruitment drive to persuade non-party members to join the Socialist Workers' Party, which offered them improved opportunities for social advancement, the revival of the Patriotic Popular Front and a sensible economic policy were all designed to serve the goals of strengthening the dictatorship of the proletariat and the power of the people while also increasing popular support for the party and the system and securing and maintaining the party's organisational unity.

At this early stage almost all of the country's creative artists, like the vast majority of the population, who had generally lapsed into the doldrums and a mood of resignation, adopted an attitude of passive rejection towards Kádár's régime. But, since Hungary's new political masters did not demand lip-service to Communism or the Soviet Union and kept the use of indoctrinating propaganda within bounds, the political climate began to improve. This was also helped by the fact that the Soviet troops were withdrawn to their barracks from the end of 1957 onwards and the intimidating and provocative presence of 'big brother' thus became less apparent. Although the economy had virtually ground to a halt in November 1956, increased deliveries of goods from fellow Socialist states and the peasant farmers, who were successfully won over to the régime by high prices, assured a sufficient availability of goods. In December 1956, a commission was set up to investigate the economic situation. Led by István Varga, a former member of the Party of Smallholders, it condemned Rákosi's command economy and proposed instead a more rational and less centralised system of economic planning. However, it failed to persuade the government to implement its recommendations of delegating more responsibility to the factories and allowing a controlled element of competition. When, by the middle of 1957, production figures had again reached the levels recorded for September 1956, the government felt justified in reducing wages to their earlier August levels, even though they had been increased as recently as January in order to provide an incentive to productivity. But even at this stage it was clear that there was no likelihood that the targets set by the Second Five Year Plan would be met. As a result, a new Three Year Plan, intended to run until 1960, was introduced in its place on 20 June 1958. When it soon became clear that the new targets could also not be met, the Hungarians introduced the Soviet idea of 'Socialist brigades' in December 1958 in order to boost the economy's insufficent productivity. This form of competition was to be encouraged by the party and the trade unions and was intended to help guarantee the quality of products, together with the maximum exploitation of raw materials, energy resources and machinery. The various economic shortages experienced at the time made the Hungarians keen advocates of Soviet plans for reorganising and integrating Comecon, although they feared that the division of labour written into the treaty signed in Sofia on 14 December 1959, which categorised Hungary as an 'industrialised agrarian country', would, if consistently applied, retard the development of their industrial capacity. However, Comecon initially offered them a closed economic sphere in which they could obtain the raw materials they required relatively cheaply and sell their still relatively uncompetitive products on the world market without too much difficulty. Two-thirds of the country's foreign trade was conducted with Hungary's Comecon partners, whereby the Soviet Union alone absorbed 36.1 per cent of Hungarian exports and produced 95 per cent of Hungary's imported raw iron, 68 per cent of its oil, 51 per cent of its rolled steel, 78 per cent of its wood and 56 per cent of its paper.

The Socialist Worker's Party and the government took special pains to persuade peasants to rejoin the agricultural cooperatives after they had left them en masse during the 1956 uprising. By 31 December 1956, only 2,089 collectives were still operating with approximately 100,000 farmers and 120,000 members cultivating a mere 6.1 per cent of the country's arable land. Ferenc Münnich, who replaced Kádár as prime minister on 28 January 1958, and his agricultural minister, Imre Dögei, were willing to try to win over the peasants by persuasion. By the end of 1958, a total of 143,229 farms were members of the country's 3,507 cooperatives. On 7 December, however, the Central Committee decided to speed up the pace of collectivisation and approved coercive measures against the Kulaks, by which they meant any peasant opposed to the compulsory incorporation of private land into the cooperatives. Although declining productivity made brief pauses for consolidation necessary, the government proudly announced on 30 September 1961 that 1.07 million farms had been organised into 4,546 collectives employing 1,195 million members. In all, 95.6 per cent of all farmland, including 81.1 per cent farmed by cooperatives, had already been incorporated into the 'Socialist sector', while the remaining 16.4 per cent of land managed by collectives remained private farms of about half hectare for the peasants' own use. Thanks to intensive cultivation methods, however, these farms produced a total of 40 per cent of the entire agricultural production of the cooperatives. Thus, 46 per cent of all meat production, 79 per cent of poultry, 90 per cent of eggs, 60 per cent of milk and 80 per cent of fruit was supplied by these individual allotments.

Over the years that followed the government adopted a policy of allowing peasants a part share in labour-intensive and delicate cultures, e.g. viticulture, tobacco-growing and market gardening. Peasants who worked in these areas had their efforts rewarded by being allowed to retain a third of their yield. But despite more intensive mechanisation and the increased use of fertilisers, average yields still lagged behind those recorded in the pre-war years. The summer drought of 1961 and the poor harvests of 1963 and 1964 made it necessary to import large amounts of Canadian maize, which could only be paid for after the Soviet Union was forced to put up some of the necessary foreign exchange. Many young farmers migrated to the towns, preferring to find more regular employment in the factories, with the result that the government was forced to subsidise the collectives over a long period and create additional incentives for the rural population before a noticeable improvement in yields took place towards the end of the 1960s.

The renewed deteriorioration in the Soviet Union's relations with Yugoslavia after the autumn of 1957 also had an effect on Hungary's internal politics. The attacks on 'revisionism' and 'nationalism' at the first World Conference of Communist and Workers' Parties in Moscow in November 1957, together with the call to strictly observe the 'principles of proletarian internationalism', were intended to help Krushchev restore the Soviet Communist Party's leadership claims and the USSR's position of supremacy in the Socialist Bloc. At the same time, they were also designed to prevent the development of 'independent paths to Socialism'. Tito's refusal to accept this political and ideological subordination provoked increasingly sharp criticism of Yugoslavia. On 27–28 March, Kádár tried to mediate with Tito, but failed to close the gap between the Yugoslav and Soviet positions. On a visit of inspection to Hungary from 2 to 9 April 1958 Krushchev made it quite clear that he was not prepared to accept any further deviation from the Moscow party line or attacks on the existence of the Socialist Bloc.

As a result of this 'anti-revisionist campaign', many veteran Stalinists were encouraged to return to Hungary from their Soviet exile and seek readmission to the party and state apparatus from which they had been banned by a Central Committee resolution of February 1958. The wave of purges which was now set in motion against 'revisionists' and 'nationalists' cost several thousand army officers, police officials and many civil servants their party membership and positions. On 16 June 1958 the execution of Imre Nagy, General Pál Maléter and two other leaders of the uprising charged with 'conspiracy and creating a secret organisation aimed at forcibly seizing power and overthrowing the Hungarian People's Democracy' was officially announced in Hungary. These executions, which broke the promises made to the Belgrade government in November 1956 and again in spring 1958 to guarantee the main participants in the uprising free passage out of the country or, at least, spare their lives, not only represented an enormous threat to Tito, but were a brutal act of revenge by Krushchev, a moral setback for Kádár and, thus, a triumph for the 'dogmatists' among his internal party critics.

Despite this loss of credibility, 98.4 per cent of the electorate voted in the elections to the National Assembly and Soviets on 16 November 1958. Of this figure, 99.6 per cent voted for the MDP's single list of candidates. Of the 338 deputies elected, 139 were MDP party officials and 53 were members of the Central Committee. Even Béla Kovács, the former General Secretary of the Party of Smallholders, who had been abducted by the Soviets in February 1947 and first returned to Hungary in 1956, won a seat which illness prevented him from occupying until his death in 1959. The satisfactory election result could not, however, hide the fact that broad sections of the population had remained politically completely passive and felt alienated by the restrictive cultural policy of orthodox Stalinism. Kádár openly acknowledged the population's basic attitude at the MDP's Seventh Party Congress, held between

30 November and 5 December 1959, when he remarked that 'the revolution on the cultural front lags behind the results achieved in the political and economic spheres'.

Since the original Hungarian Communist Party and its successor (from 1948), the Hungarian Workers' Party, had both held three party conferences each up until this point, Kádár did not hesitate to designate the Hungarian Socialist Workers' Party's first congress the 'Seventh' Party Congress, thus legitimising it in terms of the continuity and tradition of Hungary's Communist movement. In all, 669 delegates represented 402,456 party members organised in 17,000 various organisations. The Communist Youth League accounted for a further 380,000 members. The party gave itself a new organisational statute intended to ensure 'democratic centralism' and its implementation. Kádár's foreign policy, aimed at compromise, and Endre Sik, his deputy foreign minister from 1958 onwards, who, despite growing tensions, tried hard to maintain good relations with Peking and Tirana and did not break off relations with Belgrade, was expressly praised by Krushchev, who attended the congress and again emphasised the Soviet Union's willingness to stand by its friends in Hungary at any time against the enemies of Socialism. Kádár's gratitude for the Soviet Union's earlier 'fraternal assistance' and its new offer of support culminated in a request for Soviet troops to remain in Hungary 'as long as the international situation demands it'. It was at this congress that Krushchev developed his theory that many Communist parties obviously had to pull through a type of fever in the period after the Soviet Communist Party's Twentieth Party Congress in order to emerge with a stronger constitution and more resistant to new causes of illness. In his opinion, this had been convincingly demonstrated in the case of Hungary.

Close personal, one might almost say friendly, relations and close political contacts with Krushchev subsequently influenced Kádár's relationship with the Soviet Union. A sense of gratitude and the belief that Hungary's future was closely bound up with that of the Soviet Union, on which it was so economically dependent, encouraged Budapest to pursue a successful policy of cooperation with Moscow. At the same time, the Hungarian régime aimed at achieving the maximum possible freedom in internal politics. Kádár had no hesitation in unreservedly supporting the Soviet position towards the West and supported Moscow in its conflicts with China and Albania after 1961. He was also able to count to a large extent on the loyalty of the seventy-one members of the party's Central Committee as well as that of his colleagues in the Politburo and his five Central Committee Secretaries (Fehér, Fock, Kiss, Marosán and Szirmai). For example, in a government reshuffle in January 1960 he relied on their help in replacing Imre Dögei who had made enemies through his tough collectivisation measures, with the former farm labourer, Pál Losonczi. Dögei was also expelled from the Central Committee. On 12 September 1961, Kádár took over again as head of government in place of Münnich. When Krushchev readopted a policy of de-Stalinisation at the Twenty-Second Congress of the Soviet Communist Party in October 1961 and the Hungarians followed suit, the ideologically inflexible Kiss and Marosán were forced to resign from their party posts in 1962. After fruitless negotiations with his predecessors now living in the USSR, who refused to make a public confession, Kádár was even able to go as far as depriving Rákosi, Gerö and other opponents suspected of 'pseudo-left activities' or 'fractionalism' of their party membership. At the same time, however, the right wing was also warned against failing to pursue the official party line.

These expulsions were intended to mark an end to the Stalinist past and the 'violation of Socialist legality'. At the party's Central Committee's plenary meetings in March and August 1962, responsibilities for the leadership's actions in the Stalinist era were openly admitted – though without mentioning Kádár's and Antal Apró's share in these things. It was decided to rehabilitate and compensate the victims, and offers of clemency for the behind-the-scenes organisers of the show trials were also discussed. Mihály Farkas, Rákosi's right-hand man who died in 1965, and the ex-head of the ÁVH, Péter, were released from prison in 1960, the latter being relegated to a librarian's post. Ernő Gerő, who was by now almost totally blind, was allowed to return to Hungary where he was given the opportunity to live out his final years in peace. Rákosi's repeated requests to be allowed to return to Hungary from Kazakstan, where he managed a paper factory for a time, fell on deaf ears as far as Kádár was concerned. In 1971, the latter eventually allowed Rákosi's mortal remains to be interred in Hungary. However, the régime showed clemency even towards alleged 'counter-revolutionaries', who had been so harshly persecuted after 1957. An initial partial amnesty of 12 April 1959 gave prisoners in the category of those regarded as 'less implicated' in the uprising their freedom. On 31 March 1960, the prison gates swung open for several prominent personalities including Nagy's adviser, Ferenc Donath, Hungary's first President, Zóltan Tildy, and the writers, Tibor Déry and Gyula Háy. Following the closure of the internment camps and the abolition of the summary courts, a further amnesty in March 1963 ensured the release of the last prisoners to be sentenced for their part in the uprising. Kádár was now so firmly in control that he could afford to make these gestures of reconciliation and boost his personal prestige and the party's standing without fear of criticism from the Kremlin or his internal opponents within Hungary.

In January 1962, Kádár had paraphrased a verse from the New Testament (Matthew 12.V.30) when he confidently remarked, 'Whereas the Rákosi regime used to say 'He, who is not for us is against us', we say 'he, who is not against us is with us and welcomed by us'. This maxim also dominated the party's Eighth Party Congress, held between 20 and 24 November 1962 when the party announced that the régime had achieved the realisation of the basic principles of Socialism and that the Hungarian people was now entering a phase of 'complete Socialist construction'. The key economic issue at the congress was how to implement the restructuring of Hungarian industry. Socialist culture would also have to be more strongly developed and contribute to raising the Socialist consciousness of the masses. The 614 delegates at the congress now represented 511,965 party members and candidates, who decided in favour of 'collective leadership as the sine qua non for the further democratisation of political and social life' in a new version of the party's statutes and extended the powers of the Central Committee which now numbered 81 members. The supporters of Kádár's 'centralist' line occupied all the places in the Politburo. The master printer, Rezső Nyers, who had managed to attain the post of finance minister, now joined the Central Committee Secretariat and pushed through a major economic reform. The party had the state apparatus and the administration of the economy so firmly under control that Kádár was able to announce his intention to come some way towards satisfying popular demands for a higher standard of living and for greater personal freedom – though only within certain limits. The leading ideologue and Central Committee Secretary, István Szirmai, began cautiously to satisfy the desire of many Hungarians to travel abroad, which had been stimulated by the increased opportunities to establish contacts and acquire information. The result was that the number of foreign travel permits to the West soared from 35,000 in 1960 to 143,000 within seven years and thereafter leapt to over 3.8 million by 1980. Hungary's foreign exchange earnings also benefited from the steadily growing stream of visitors from the West.

Although bitter memories of the Rákosi period and the bloody crushing of the popular uprising were still very much alive, more and more Hungarians managed to identify with Kádár's cautious pragmatism and relative liberalism. The party had made it a growing priority to mediate between the Kremlin's insistence on conformity within the Socialist Bloc and the expectations and needs of the Hungarian people. Since they had no illusions regarding the true nature of Communist rule and were dependably loyal in national matters, the Hungarians seized the opportunities which Kádár's political system offered them. The leadership realistically appraised the political, strategic and economic realities in order to allow the possibility of a restricted pluralism in internal affairs. A liberal policy on censorship allowed more freedom of speech, the principles of justice were to a large extent observed and totalitarian oppression no longer existed. The programme of Socialist renewal which Kádár purposefully pursued regardless of any setbacks, gave the Hungarians more individual and intellectual freedom, a modest degree of affluence and a satisfactorily functioning economy which had no parallel in the other Communist countries of eastern Europe.

REFORM HUNGARIAN STYLE

The Three Year Plan, launched in 1958 in place of the interrupted Five Year Plan, proved moderately successful in overcoming the economic problems in the wake of the 1956 uprising, but failed to achieve any real economic growth. The accelerated pace of agricultural collectivisation and the economic problems experienced by the other east European Socialist states also had a major affect on Hungary, with the result that the Party Central Committee approved the so-called 'Second' Five Year Plan for the development of Hungary's economy on 12 September 1961. The targets set by the State Planning Office continued to give priority to the encouragement of heavy industry, but also recognised the need for the rapid expansion of the chemicals industry and the provision of machinery, improved seeds and fertilisers for the agricultural sector. As early as 1961, there was a visible shift away from fixing illusory growth targets in favour of relaxing economic planning constraints by giving enterprises more freedom in decision-making, encouraging individual initiative and tolerating the acquisition of private property and pursuit of profit. It was hoped that increased output and improved productivity and technology would raise industrial production by 50 per cent, the GNP by 35 per cent and real income by 16–17 per cent before the end of 1965. Closer cooperation among the member-states of Comecon, the provision of Soviet loans and preferential trading terms with the western industrial countries which granted Hungary the status of 'most favoured' trading partner almost made it possible to fulfil the plan's targets.

The realisation that the Socialist economy would not automatically replace 'outdated individualism' with a 'collective social awareness' also helped the party stimulate the work-effort of ordinary Hungarians and thus increase productivity by allowing a measure of personal gain. In view of Hungary's firmly established membership of the Socialist Bloc, the Soviet leadership was prepared to tolerate initial efforts to develop and apply new forms of economic control. When Kádár visited the Soviet Union between the 10 and 22 July 1963, his echoing of the Soviet demand for closer economic and technological cooperation – aimed primarily at Hungary's neighbour, Rumania, – earned Krushchev's praise and economic concessions in several areas. Stalinism's ruthless exploitation of fellow Socialist countries for the benefit of the Soviet Union had long since given way to a fairer consideration of the mutual advantages to be gained by both sides. On his return visit to Hungary between 31 March and 11 April 1964 Krushchev awarded Kádár the Order of Lenin, bestowing upon him the title of 'Hero of the Soviet Union'. The Kremlin leader's unexpected fall from power on 15 October 1964 did not seriously affect the hitherto much applauded 'special relationship' between Moscow and Budapest, although the party did have to deal with Hungary's growing nationalism and its anti-Soviet undertones during the 'phase of Socialist reconstruction'. The palace revolution which brought Brezhnev and Kosygin to power in the Kremlin came as a surprise to Kádár during a visit to Warsaw, but he paid a warm tribute to his former mentor and assured his countrymen on several occasions that the party would not change its political course. While avoiding any criticism of the wisdom of the decision made by their Soviet colleagues, the Central Committee and the party newspaper *Népszabadság* also praised Krushchev's achievements and his association with Hungarian Socialism during its period of rapid progress.

The small remaining group of Rákosi supporters in Hungary hoped that Krushchev's fall from power would also result in the fall of the pragmatic 'revisionist', Kádár, whose policies they labelled a 'rebirth of Social Democracy'. This, they hoped, would bring about the return of the veteran Stalinist, Rákosi, now living in exile in Kazakstan. To allay fears that the new Kremlin leaders might disturb

Hungary's precarious stability through clumsy actions and cause unrest, Kádár headed a Hungarian delegation which visited Moscow for talks with Brezhnev and Kosygin as early as 8–10 November 1964. From 29 to 31 January 1965, the new First Secretary of the Soviet Communist Party and the Secretary of the Central Committee, Podgornyi, visited Budapest to form their own judgement on the internal political situation in Hungary. The reason for this visit was almost certainly the suspicion that the leaders of the Hungarian Socialist Workers' Party were also not immune to the National Communist virus at loose in Rumania and that Hungary was seeking an alternative to its trade within Comecon by increasing its foreign trade links with the West. On 11 February, Kádár reported to the National Assembly only that the withdrawal of Soviet troops stationed in Hungary had not been discussed at the talks, for although there was no internal political reason for their presence, they remained indispensable for international reasons. However, Hungary's demonstration of its desire to maintain proper diplomatic relations with all countries, the interest shown by foreign minister, János Péter, in western economic strategy and plans for Europe during his visits to Austria and France – especially de Gaulle's vision of a reorganised *Europe des patries* – together with Péter's belief in April 1965 that the countries of Central Europe and the Danube region should increase their contacts with one another in the interest of close regional cooperation, regardless of their different social structures, once more aroused the Kremlin's distrust. In order to avoid disagreement, the Chairman of the Supreme Soviet, A. Mikojan, who as Krushchev's closest colleague and a supporter of Hungarian policy and autonomy for the People's Democracies enjoyed great respect, was despatched to Budapest in April 1965. Since the workers reacted unexpectedly quickly with strike threats to the Stalinist-inspired rumour that Kádár was about to resign, the Kremlin leaders felt obliged to allow the Hungarian party chief to remain in his post while persuading him give up his position as head of government. After a visit to Moscow between the 23 and 29 May 1965, at which a Hungarian delegation conceded to the Soviets their 'full agreement on the most important international problems', together with their support of the Soviet Communist Party in its efforts to maintain the unity of action of all Socialist countries, Kádár handed over his post as prime minister to his deputy, the genial, but somewhat lazy Gyula Kállai on 25 June 1965. In order to counter the popular unrest which it feared would take place, the Central Committee kept its decision secret for three days to give police and military units time to mount a security operation to protect public buildings and let party organisations inform their members of the real reasons behind the decision. Kádár, who henceforth dedicated himself increasingly to party affairs, did, however, recognise how to exploit the opportunity which Krushchev's fall from power opened up for him. From now on he could appear in Hungary with a new sense of self-esteem and not simply as the puppet of the man who had crushed the Hungarian uprising in 1956. In both foreign policy and internal relations within the Socialist Bloc he no longer had to follow Moscow's instructions out of personal loyalty and let Hungary's interests take a back seat. He supported the Kremlin's line on all important issues in a 'calculated alliance', but reserved the right to pursue his own liberalising policies cautiously in internal politics and settle internal party conflicts as soon as they arose. In voting at the United Nations, in granting financial and technical aid to North Vietnam or in freezing economic and cultural contacts with the People's Republic of China, Hungary consistently supported Soviet actions. At the Twenty-Third Party Congress of the Soviet Communist Party in March 1966 Kádár assured the Kremlin that the idea of an anti-Soviet Communism was a contradiction in terms. Nevertheless, the emergence of dangerous nationalist and singularly anti-Soviet tendencies, which provided a marked contrast to the 'Socialist patriotism' the régime wished to inculcate, obliged the Hungarian party to apply countermeasures. The Kremlin, for its part, knew how to reward such efforts to maintain the solidarity of the Socialist Bloc countries. Hungary was allowed to contribute the smallest army and the lowest military expenditure of any of the Warsaw Pact member states and yet was the only country in the 'southern triangle' to send troops to the manoeuvres which took place in southern Bohemia in autumn 1966. From 1968 to the present, the Hungarian army's strength in terms of manpower has remained constant at 102,000 soldiers, who are organised into one armoured division and five motorised infantry divisions, together with a small air force of 140 combat aircraft. Military expenditure, which still amounted to 7.4 per cent of the national budget in 1963, was reduced to 4.6 per cent by 1968 – a figure equivalent to about 2.6 per cent of Hungary's national income.

Even more significant, however, was the fact that the Soviet leadership did not oppose the economic reforms introduced in Hungary under the Third Five Year Plan. The New Economic Mechanism, as it was called, due to come into effect on 1 January 1968, was

235

launched by a Central Committee decree of May 1966. The new plan signalled the introduction of a Socialist market economy which gave producers considerable freedom in fixing prices, determining wages and salaries according to company profits and allowed workers' participation in internal decision-making on production targets and areas of investment. The agricultural cooperatives were also given greater freedom. In September 1965, the Soviet Union introduced a programme of economic reform, which was soon halted, whereby stricter planning controls from above and greater flexibility at the lower level had been designed to secure 'the maximum possible development' of the economy 'in the framework of centralised state planning'. At the same time, the government, within the framework of the NEM which allowed some measure of market forces, aimed at fewer controls, more realistic planning from above and a greater degree of decentralisation in decision-making. The difficulties encountered in the initial phase were greater than expected, because a chronic shortage of capital, disputes over areas of competence and the difficulty of implementing the New Economic Mechanism meant that there was not as rapid an increase in productivity and national income as had been hoped for. Positive effects were, however, noticeable in the agricultural sector since the guarantee of a minimum monthly income slowly closed the gap in earnings between industry and agriculture and halted the population movement away from the land. In view of Hungary's strong economic dependence and its undisputed integration into Comecon, the Soviet Union felt able to allow Hungary more freedom of action in internal policy and even to accept loans from the West. Although the total value of Hungary's trade doubled between 1960 and 1967, the supply of goods nevertheless remained relatively stable. Two-thirds of foreign trade was transacted with the country's Comecon partners, whereby the Soviet Union alone absorbed 36.1 per cent of Hungary's output and supplied 33.3 per cent of its total imports.

Discussion of the New Economic Mechanism also dominated the MSzMP's Ninth Party Congress, held between 28 November and 3 December 1966. The delegates resolved that 'the complete construction of Socialism remained . . . the historic task of the party and people'. The legal rights of the local party branches were also increased in keeping with the aim of furthering the development of Socialist democracy. Industrial democracy was to be strengthened and in particular the National Assembly's participation in the political decision-making process extended. The leadership role of the party, which now numbered 585,000 members, was to be maintained, although its main task was given as the 'scientific analysis and building up of its political control of the masses and their organisation and mobilisation'. At a sitting on 14 April, the parliament, returned on 19 March on the basis of a new electoral law of 11 November 1966, which for the first time provided for more candidates than there were seats, appointed Pál Losonczi as Chairman of the Presidium and Kádár's loyal supporter, Jenő Fock, as the new prime minister in place of Kállai. Socialist Worker party members already comprised 35 per cent workers and 8 per cent peasants. The 'intelligentsia', i.e. members with a completed vocational training or white-collar workers, made up 38 per cent, government employees, civil servants and members of the armed forces 7.9 per cent. A further 9 per cent were retired or in receipt of a pension. Although women accounted for 51.6 per cent of the population, only 22.9 per cent were members of political parties. Between 75 and 80 per cent of the National Assembly deputies, of whom about half gave their occupation as 'worker', were party members, with the result that the Electoral Association of the Patriotic Popular Front was no threat to the party's monopoly of power and the one-party system. Independent initiatives by the Assembly, which, according to Article 19 of the constitution, was 'the supreme organ of state power and representation of the people', was, therefore, narrowly limited, although its sphere of competence was supposed to include legislation, advising on and approving the government's programme, approving the budget, participating in formulating economic planning, ratifying international agreements and electing members to the Presidium and Council of Ministers.

Hungary's leaders, who were fully preoccupied with the economic reforms, followed the Kremlin's lead by distancing themselves from their Yugoslav and Rumanian neighbours and showing little inclination to respond to West German suggestions of establishing full diplomatic relations. This conformist behaviour was no doubt a result of the good, one might even say friendly, ties which developed on the basis of frequent bilateral contacts between the party and government hierarchies in Moscow and Budapest. Brezhnev took the opportunity to extol these relations built on trust when he visited Budapest between the 6 and 9 September 1967 on the occasion of prolonging the Treaty of Friendship and Mutual Support for a further 20 years. The obligation on both sides to increase cooperation within the framework of Comecon and the Warsaw Pact was extended to include military assistance in the event of an attack on either of the signatories 'by any state or group of states' (Article

6). Kádár used the occasion to reiterate his view, 'that no-one in the world has the right to call himself a Communist if he acts against the Soviet Union and holds anti-Soviet opinions'. The Hungarian party chief's behaviour can be understood, only if one considers how Hungary's position in the Socialist Bloc was complicated by its various ethnic and territorial disputes, as well as the half-a-century-old problem of Hungarian minorities in neighbouring states. True, the new Socialist constitutions of Czechoslovakia and Yugoslavia had improved the prospects for their Magyar minorities, but originally made cultural concessions were soon forgotten as a result of latent grievances concerning social and economic discrimination. Budapest was particularly concerned at the forcible abolition of the autonomous rights of the Magyar community in Transylvania from 1958 onwards. The closing down of many cultural establishments, such as the independent Hungarian Bólyai University in Cluj or the forced integration of the Hungarian community's minority schools in 1962 aroused no sympathy in Hungary for the strengthening of Rumanian nationalism under Gheorghe Gheorgiu-Dej and Nicolae Ceaucescu. Although the Hungarian press and government did not politically exploit the Rumanian actions against the Transylvanian Magyars, there was a distinct cooling off in relations between Budapest and Bucharest. Various Soviet initiatives – a conference on European peace and security, efforts to advance the 'process of Socialist integration' in the framework of Comecon and the Warsaw Pact and a new World Conference of Communist and Workers' Parties to condemn the schismatic Chinese leadership – were patronised by Hungary but without any show of deep commitment.

In view of their own painful experience, the Hungarians observed the developments leading up to the 'Prague Spring' of 1968 and the Soviet intervention in Czechoslovakia with considerable interest. Kádár, who met the new Czechoslovak party chief, Dubček, on several occasions and who certainly advised caution, may well have also asked the Kremlin to show understanding, patience and a willingness to compromise with the Czechoslovakian reformers. The decision to mobilise two Hungarian divisions for the military invasion of Czechoslovakia on 21 August 1968 certainly did not come easily to the Hungarian leadership, given that they, too, were trying to develop 'Socialism with a human face', albeit initially only in the cultural and economic spheres. But the spark of revolution could all too easily set Hungary alight by spreading from the neighbouring Magyar minority in Southern Slovakia, thus jeopardising the consolidation of political power which had only just begun and the process of reconciliation between the party and the population. The state authorities managed to keep the lid on demonstrations and meetings held by workers and intellectuals to protest at Hungary's part in the invasion without resorting to a policy of tough repression. The régime justified Hungary's role as 'fulfilling its internationalist duty' and issued a 'recommendation' warning participants in such meetings always to adhere strictly to the party's directives. Hungary's foreign minister, Péter, completely rejected Brezhnev's doctrine of the 'limited sovereignty' of Socialist Bloc members and announced that it would always be 'an ever controversial issue', whether intervention was necessary 'in the interests of peace' or whether it should be avoided if at all possible 'in the interests of Socialist integration'. After 1968, Kádár, whose growing popularity as party chief with all sections of the population was hardly affected by his part in the decision to intervene, also tried successfully to maintain his policy of cautious internal political reform. Despite the reservations of mistrustful 'dogmatists' and opponents of reform, he tried to develop his policies further in practical everyday matters without giving offence or becoming too conspicuous. Kádár's realism, dry pragmatism and instinctive understanding of the realities of power proved to be qualities which were able to dispel the reservations which the Soviets felt towards Hungary's economic and social reforms. In the the first year alone of the NEM's implementation, a reform of the economy which aimed at creating a 'socialist market' in which a considerable number of enterprises would be managed autonomously, had proved so successful despite the undeniable initial problems that the Hungarian economists were able to call all previous attempts at economic coordination unrealistic and propose three alternatives for discussion via the creator of the reform, Politburo member, Reszö Nyers. In the first place, it had to be decided whether cooperation should continue to be developed, as in the past, on the basis of agreements made between states, or whether one should aim more for cooperation of a supranational character built upon 'the economic interests of economic enterprises'; secondly, whether foreign trade in eastern Europe should simply remain a two-way exchange of goods or whether a convertible currency should be introduced as a necessary first step towards a transition to free trade and free currency exchange; thirdly, whether in accordance with initial moves research and production should be coordinated or even integrated.

The Hungarians' desire to find answers to these questions, which would accord with the pace of the country's economic development and the 'principle of national independence', was noted in Moscow with some reservation, although Hungary's economists had been able to show at the end of 1969 that, thanks to the NEM, the growth rate in national income, which had previously been constantly declining, had risen for the first time (from 4.5 per cent in 1968 to 6 per cent in 1969) and the volume of foreign trade had increased by 14 per cent.

The government's reforms in the agricultural sector proved less successful. The law stipulated that the agricultural cooperatives would have to decide themselves how to the use the means of production, develop their own produce and find its market value. They would also have to do the risk-taking and earn their own profits in keeping with their entrepreneurial independence. The collective farms, which had been previously largely subsidised by the state were allowed to increase their prices by 9 per cent in 1966 and by a further 10 per cent between 1968 and 1970. At the same time, the government cancelled the major portion of any losses they had incurred and extended the repayment period of short-term loans. From now on two-thirds of the collectives began to show a profit. But only when they were allowed to indulge in activities outside of horticulture and livestock rearing by taking on the tasks normally associated with industry, transport and trade were they able to raise their incomes on average by 25 per cent, (in exceptional cases, by 60 per cent) and increase their productivity. But with average yields of 32.3 quintals per hectare for maize and 24.3 quintals for wheat, Hungary's yields still fell far behind those of America and western Europe. The high rate of income growth for collective farmers subsequently led doctrinaire critics of reform to curb their entrepreneurial independence and undermine the individual's right to participate in decisions concerning collectively-held property by merging the larger agricultural enterprises into giant economic units. The result was that apathy and a lack of incentive eventually returned at times to the countryside.

In certain Hungarian circles as well as in neighbouring Socialist states and especially in the Kremlin concern was felt at the NEM's unavoidable political side-effects. In order to function properly it required a loosening up of the ossified system of centralised decision-making under the control of the party leadership. The population was to be given improved conditions in the consumer sector and greater individual freedoms, including greater security before the law. While the Soviet leadership refrained from openly criticising the Hungarian Communists, warnings on a personal level and responses designed to calm fears were exchanged on several occasions between 1968 and 1970 without any significant result. After talks with premier Fock and Péter during his visit to Hungary between 14 and 18 November 1968 the Russian foreign minister, Gromyko, emphasised the need to 'develop the unity and security of the Socialist states further'. The 'unity of the Communist movement' was also the main subject of talks which Kádár attended in Moscow between 6 and 10 February 1969 and formed a side issue at the Budapest summit held in March 1969, when a radical reform of the Warsaw Pact's command structure was discussed. Kádár had to dispel the anxieties of his Soviet guests that Hungary might witness the start of a development similar to that which had taken place in Czechoslovakia and an enthusiasm for reform might set in, over which the party might lose control. When, at the invitation of the Soviet Communist Party's Central Committee, Kádár spent a holiday recuperating in the Crimea between 2 and 27 August 1969, where he discussed 'bilateral and multilateral questions of common interest' with the Kremlin leaders, Hungary's internal political situation may well have been placed at the top of the agenda, as was the case during premier Fock's negotiations, held in Moscow on 16–17 March 1970. However, the Hungarian Communists were probably not subjected to too much pressure. Kádár, who had the backing of the entire Hungarian population and no political rival of equal stature to speak of, was the only guarantee of the continuing and contructive development of Communism in Hungary. The 'national traitor', 'Quisling' and 'Judas' of 1956, who been established in power as a result of the Soviets' second intervention had not disappointed his countrymen's hopes for a brand of Communism which was increasingly liberal and tolerable.

Thus, at the Socialist Workers' Party Tenth Party Congress, held in Budapest at the end of November 1970, Brezhnev felt obliged to give his blessing to Hungary's reform programme: 'This principled attempt to solve the most important problems encountered in the development of Socialist society is fully understood by the Communists of the Soviet Union who view it with great respect'. In gratitude for this gesture Kádár made a point of reaffirming his loyalty to the USSR, 'our liberator, ally, true friend and greatest helper in all areas of life'. At the same time, he gave the additional assurance through Central Committee Secretary, Komócsin, that in the event of a conflict of interests Hungary's national interests would always come second to the common interests of the Socialist Bloc.

It was at this conference that Kádár expressed the opinion, 'that the time was not yet ripe to proclaim our country a Socialist republic. We believe that it is preferable to get on with the construction [of Socialism] and worry about the change of name later'. Nevertheless, the government did not hesitate to show that it was prepared to depart from the well-worn path of restrictive Communist internal policy and place its trust in its citizens' political maturity. It introduced a modest measure of local self-government subject to state supervision (Law I of 1971), made spectacular trade deals with the West, raised a long-term loan on the Eurodollar market, improved relations with the Catholic Church and the Vatican and relaxed travel restrictions to all foreign countries. At the same time, emergency measures were required to deal with obvious imbalances in the economic reform. The solutions proposed at a conference in October 1971: the abandonment of disastrous investment projects, the combatting of the shortage of skilled workers and the reduction of the country's growing foreign trade deficit proved so successful that Kádár was able to give the first 'all clear' in February 1972. He promised that the NEM would continue with certain modifications and that greater attention would be paid to achieving social justice.

These economic difficulties resulted in a short-term cooling of relations between the Soviet and Hungarian Communists. The Kremlin appeared to be particularly annoyed by Hungary's efforts to establish normal relations with the People's Republic of China and Albania 'at an official level'. Also, compared with Budapest Moscow had other ideas concerning the pace and aims of Hungary's economic and 'social reforms. Even Kádár, who was summoned to Moscow from 11 to 14 February 1972, could not sweep these differences under the carpet. This was certainly the reason why he made a point of signing a new Treaty of Friendship and Mutual Support during an ensuing visit to Rumania between 24 and 26 February. Its formulation of Hungarian foreign policy went a great way towards accommodating Bucharest's position, but, in an exchange of official greetings Kádár knew how to dilute Ceaucescu's demand to respect the individuality and independence of every nation by adding to it his desire for 'increased cooperation on all levels within the Socialist Bloc'.

The extent of the Kremlin's annoyance at these intensified contacts can be seen from the fact that the Soviet press for the first time made no mention of the obligatory declarations of friendship when Hungary celebrated its liberation on 4 April 1972. Instead, the Hungarian party and government were warned not to 'revert to bourgeois nationalism'. Also, premier Fock's trip to Moscow on

27–28 March 1972, during which he requested additional consignments of Soviet raw materials, produced no conciliatory outcome. But the fears of the 'dogmatists' that a coup by political revisionists was imminent in Hungary, to prevent which an attitude of intransigence was required, proved to have no substance. Kádár was firmly in control and assured his Moscow comrades that his country would contribute to the political and ideological unity of the community of Socialist states as long as his government was allowed to press on as planned with its urgent policy of internal reform.

The Hungarians openly admitted encountering difficulties in implementing their economic reforms and it proved impossible to fulfil the plan's targets. There was a further increase in Hungary's foreign trade deficit with western industrialised countries and the general living standard failed to rise. These factors, together with the fact that Hungary depended greatly on imports of raw materials from the Soviet Union, eventually forced the Hungarian government to improve its strained relations with Moscow and to slow down the pace of reform. The first indication of this change came with the National Assembly's approval on 19 April 1972 of a constitutional amendment (Law I of 1972) which strictly observed the constitutional norms established in the Soviet sphere of hegemony. Although, contrary to expectations, the People's Republic of Hungary was still not transformed into a Socialist republic, it was, however, on account of the prevailing characteristics of its social system, especially property and class relationships, proclaimed a 'Socialist state'. Among the relatively insignificant changes to the re-wording of the text of the 1949 constitution, it was noticeable that the party's claim to a monopoly of leadership extended only to society and no longer to the state: 'The Marxist-Leninist party of the working class is the leading force in society' (para. 3). True, the powers of the Presidium, which functioned as a substitute parliament and collective head of state, and whose decrees had to be ratified by parliament only in retrospect, were only very slightly diminished. Nevertheless, attempts were still made to anchor the position of the Council effectively in the constitution and give more emphasis to the triple function of the local soviets as organs of popular representation, of self-government and of political administration (para. 43). The passage of a law (Law IV of 1972) on the structure of the judiciary introduced after the revision of the constitution, as well as a new law on state prosecutions (Law V of 1972), a new criminal code (Law I of 1973) and a supplementary amendment to the civil Law code (Decree 26 of 1972) amounted to a sweeping legal reform which went a long way towards conceding the citizen full legal rights and guaranteed a proper system of law-courts. The government's apparent tendency to continue with the liberal course it had embarked upon, while fully upholding the necessary principles of a Communist one-party state, was put in perspective by the Central Committee's official publication *Pártélet* (Party Life), when it asserted that the class struggle was by no means over in Hungary. The struggle against both 'right' and 'left'-wing deviance, against the dogmatists, party factions and revisionism, had to be systematically carried on.

This warning was given concrete form in a decree issued by a plenary executive meeting of the Central Committee in November 1972. Despite the country's difficult economic situation, it ordered substantial wage rises for 1.3 million workers in industry and the building trades, while at the same time declaring war on 'bourgeois manifestations' and 'ultra-left views' which were to be eradicated on account of their inherent 'anti-Socialist tendencies'. When on 15 March 1973, the 125th anniversary of the revolt against Habsburg rule, a 'nationalist demonstration' was held in Budapest, the party judged that the time had come to deal with its main critics. The sociologist, András Hegedüs, prime minister in the last phase of the Rákosi era, and the philosophers János Kis and Mihály Vajda were expelled from the party in the middle of May on charges of 'serious errors' and their lack of self criticism. Not long afterwards four more prominent sociologists, Á. Heller, G. and M. Márkus and G. Bencze were forced to leave the party. Artists and scientists, in particular, like the writer, G. Konrad, the sociologist, I. Szelényi, and the poet, T. Szentjóby, had to suffer under an ideologically tougher and more orthodox cultural policy, while the majority of the population and the pampered technocratic intelligentsia were initially spared any major restrictions.

But Hungary's economic problems and the Kremlin's constant warnings that it would not tolerate any developments which might damage the Communist Party's leading role or produce a political climate comparable to Czechoslovakia in 1968 made it necesary to intervene in the NEM reforms. This primarily meant giving the central planning authority wider powers once more, especially in determining prices and incomes policy and investment priorities. On 28 June 1973, a new State Planning Committee was set up, chaired by the then minister of labour, György Lázár. Substantial increases in the cost of food, rents and public transport were accompanied by further wage increases and the reduction of retail prices on selected consumer items in order to keep up the morale of an increasingly disillusioned population.

When Brezhnev visited Budapest at the head of a Soviet party and government delegation between 27 November and 1 December senior Hungarian officials felt obliged to quash rumours that serious Soviet-Hungarian differences had emerged during negotiations on the long-term importation of Soviet raw materials. The Soviet leader's gesture of awarding Kádár the distinction of the Order of Lenin for the second time in honour of his struggle against counter-revolution was intended to dispel once and for all reports of disagreement which were played up in the western press. At any rate, the party felt obliged to agree to the Soviet desire for increased bilateral contacts 'at all levels' in the interest of increasing the imports of raw materials from the USSR and announced that it was entirely willing to increase 'cooperation on economic matters between the ministries, parliaments and political and social organisations'. After the usual meeting of east European party chiefs and heads of government in the Crimea in August 1973, intensified negotiations on matters of economic cooperation and joint agreement on economic strategy for the period 1976–1980 eventually resulted in both sides considerably bridging the gap between them by the late autumn of that year.

However, the Hungarians had to make considerable sacrifices for the Soviets' willingness to compromise on the economic front. On 15 December 1973, Hungary's long-serving foreign minister, János Péter, a trained Calvinist theologian who had often tried to establish greater cooperation between smaller countries regardless of their social system, was replaced by his former secretary of state, Frigyes Puja. Puja's first action as foreign minister was to establish full diplomatic relations with West Germany on 20 December, but of much greater significance was the decision taken by the Central Committee on 27 March 1974. This removed the Central Committee secretary for economic affairs, Rezső Nyers, and the relatively liberal secretary for culture and ideology, György Aczél, from their posts and forced the retirement of the Politburo's number three man, the agricultural expert and deputy prime minister, Lajos Fehér. Nyers' transfer to the post of director of the Institute of Economics of the Academy of Sciences, together with Aczél's effective demotion on being appointed one of the deputy prime ministers, and further personnel changes in the Central Committee Secretariat and the government also appeared to mark a radical departure from the government's economic policy and the end of Hungary's liberal cultural climate.

The party leaders, and Kádár especially, felt compelled to act against widespread fears of an impending return to the 'dogmatism' of the past. Politburo member, Z. Komóscin, launched the new campaign in an article entitled '*Változatlan politikával*' (No change in policy) which appeared in the party newspaper *Népszabadság* on 23 March 1974. In a statement of principle, delivered in a speech in Nyiregyháza on 28 March, Kádár assured his audience that the government would continue with the policy it had pursued up until now, regardless of party personnel changes in several areas: 'Our domestic and foreign policy remain the same. Our tried and tested system of economic planning is being retained, although its practical implementation has to be improved in every area'. Moscow's suspicions that Hungary might travel too far along the road towards becoming a western-orientated consumer society and doubts about the effectiveness of ideological slogans in the lead-up to the negotiations of the Conference on European Security and Cooperation, forced Kádár, who more than ever found himself the central figure in the tensions between ideology and continuity, to give in to Soviet pressure just enough not to have to call a halt to reform Communism.

Although it was already clear by this stage that the unrealistic targets of the Fourth Five Year Plan, due to run until the end of 1975, could not be fulfilled, the population did not have to put up with too much austerity, despite regular, though modest price rises. Enterprises allowed a relatively large measure of freedom in decision-making and interested in signing cooperation agreements with western companies, remained unaffected, even though Hungary was once more closely tied down to working within the framework of Comecon agreements on the common industrial development of eastern Europe and its future economic strategy. The exaggerated expressions of warmth and 'full mutual agreement' at every bilateral meeting of party and government chiefs were not, however, sufficient to allow Kádár – who judged the population's mood exactly – to forget his countrymen's reservations towards Soviet domination. In view of Hungary's great dependence on Russian consignments of raw materials, together with a chronic shortage of foreign exchange and the country's advanced integration into Comecon, Kádár was forced to rule out any possibility of going it alone economically and was prepared to accept certain restrictions in order to avoid even more far-reaching demands, not to mention another Soviet intervention in Hungary's internal affairs. Attempts by Nyers' Politburo successor, Károly Németh, during a visit to Moscow in early September 1974, to convince Soviet economic experts and Brezhnev himself of the need to maintain and even expand Hungary's trade with the industrialised West obviously failed. When three weeks later, a Hungarian party and government delegation led by Kádár and Fock made an official friendly visit to Russia between 25 and 30 September, a communiqué was issued to the effect that opportunities to realise integration would have to be more effectively exploited. It was not difficult to see from its wording that there were still unsolved problems concerning agreement on the economic aspects of cooperation. The Hungarians almost certainly also expressed reservations about Soviet expectations of greater Socialist Bloc integration at the expense of their country's trade with the West.

In his leadership address to the Hungarian Socialist Workers' Eleventh Party Congress, held between 17 and 22 March 1975 in the Ferenc-Rósza Cultural Centre in Budapest, Kádár thought it necessary to make a further pledge of loyalty to Hungarian-Soviet friendship in Brezhnev's presence: 'We regard the strength of our indissoluble fraternal friendship with the Soviet Union as especially important. It gives us the greatest satisfaction that Hungarian-Soviet relations have been deepened and extended to all areas; that they have successfully served the common interests of our countries and their peoples, and strengthened our alliance, cooperation and friendship'. In an express reference to the 30th anniversary of the 'liberation of our homeland by the Soviet army' (4 April), the congress delegates voted unanimously on a new resolution for inclusion in the party programme. This was the 'decree on party work und further tasks', which aimed at a more committed application of ideology not only as regards the party, but government activity and every sphere of public life. Recognition of the workers' importance, their increasing influence on internal management decisions, the appointment of a growing number of manual workers to important positions in the state and party machinery and the step-by-step assimilation of all sections of the population into the working class were proclaimed as the most important goals for the future. Although G. Aczél was re-elected to the new thirteen-man Politburo, the four new members of this leading body: the increasingly prominent deputy prime minister, Lázár, the First Secretary of the Communist Youth League, László Maróthy, Central Committee Secretary, Miklós Óvári, and the Patriotic Popular Front's General Secretary, István Sarlós, ensured that the government's reform policies, though not entirely halted, would not receive any fresh impetus for the time being.

When it was officially announced on 15 May 1975 that the prime minister, Jenő Fock, had resigned on health grounds, there was widespread astonishment. Fock, who had only recently been elected to the Politburo, was replaced by his previous deputy, György Lázár, who had been his permanent representative in Comecon and was regarded as a critic of the liberal NEM policy. In the May 1975 issue of the party's intellectual journal *Társadalmi Szemle* (Social Panorama) Lázár catalogued the NEM's weaknesses, rendered even more acute by the effects of an economic recession in the West, and suggested as a solution 'the more systematic pursuit of the [party's] political and economic line . . . at the same time as raising productivity' and 'participating even more actively [in Comecon's] international division of labour'. The newly elected National Assembly of 15 June 1975, which saw the Patriotic Popular Front candidates returned with the approval of 99.6 per cent of the electorate, unanimously approved Lázár's new government with its many ministerial changes when it was officially announced on 4 July. Two days previously a plenary executive meeting of the Central Committee had appointed two more members to the Politburo: deputy prime minister, István Huzsár, and Presidium chairman, Pál Losonczi.

In the mid-1970s, Hungary's standard of living continued to rise as a result of an annual increase of as much as 6 per cent in real incomes. There was an initial wave of mechanisation, accompanied by a sudden growth in meat consumption and a new spate of building construction, albeit still inadequate to cover needs. However, these developments appeared threatened, as long as the government did not succeed in resolving the 'differences in the method and extent of economic cooperation', repeatedly mentioned in communiqués issued after bilateral meetings with the Soviet government. The prices of raw materials demanded by the Soviet Union for the new period of the Five Year Plan and the small returns produced by Hungarian products threatened Hungary's economic growth and produced the prospect of greater internal social conflict. The party chief, Kádár, who, even in the eyes of the Soviets, was the only guarantee of Hungary's internal political stability, was demonstrably annoyed by frequent party infighting and public discussion of a potential successor and grew increasingly tired of office. On reaching the end of his 65th year in 1977, he indicated his intention of retiring from politics. As a result of this threat, but thanks also to Lázár's proven negotiating skills, the Soviets agreed to sign an agreement on 27 March 1976 which linked the prices to be paid for Soviet raw materials to the profits from Hungary's industrial and agricultural exports for the next decade.

By 1978, the Fifth Five Year Plan, which aimed at increasing Hungary's national income by 30 to 32 per cent, its total industrial production by as much as 35 per cent and the population's real income by 18 to 20 per cent, had resulted in a rapid increase in production. However, the sudden growth in western imports was partly responsible for a worrying deterioration in the balance between the country's external and internal economic performance. In order to check excess demand, consumer prices were subjected to sharp, regular increases, while real incomes remained relatively static. On 1 January 1977, a tax reform was also introduced to help prevent the growth of economic disparities. It allowed considerable exemption from duties paid on profits from agricultural side-line activities, while making the profits of small private firms liable to a strict progressive tax. The same end was served by a reformed prices policy, introduced from the 1980s onwards, which regulated the cost of raw materials according to world market prices and forced state enterprises to operate under the rules of the free market economy – even in the domestic market. However, the overall economic stability which was achieved by these measures restricted economic growth, with the result that the Five Year Plan's quotas could not be fulfilled in every area. For example, the national income rose by only 17 per cent overall and real per capita income by a total of only 8 per cent. For the first time Hungary's debts to the West exceeded 7 billion dollars. The economic cooperation agreements which Hungarian enterprises signed with over 400 West German and approximately 100 Austrian companies led to a considerable expansion in trade with the West and more cooperation in exploiting other markets. Agriculture, the economy's specific problem sector up until the 1970s, did relatively well in terms of production. After 1977 the agricultural collectives were encouraged to merge and eventually numbered 1,338 production units of an average size of 4,000 hectares, a development which helped meet the growing demand for foodstuffs even after a series of moderate harvests. In 1980, for example, Hungary's agricultural exports earned approximately 2 billion dollars. The combination of large-scale state collectives producing on an industrial scale and 1.7 million privately-owned competing farms, mainly comprising fewer than 0.4 hectares and employing several million people producing about 50 per cent of essential foodstuffs on a part-time basis, proved to be an invaluable asset.

This generally positive development in Hungary's national economy, particularly compared with the growing economic problems encountered in other east European Communist countries, was based on a flexibly managed framework of economic planning and independent company initiatives. It was accompanied by surprisingly undoctrinaire measures in both internal and foreign policy. The publicity-shy, soberly realistic and purposeful Kádár increasingly allowed his government greater freedom of action and respected the decisions of organisations and bodies appointed for the purpose of implementing policy. Every official who did not agree with his carefully considered and singularly 'middle course', could expect to be removed from his post. The First Secretary of the party repeatedly declared his willingness to cooperate with anyone, regardless of his views, as long as the latter was 'not hostile' towards Socialism. But he also did not hesitate to carry out his warning to act decisively against those 'who – counting on a deterioration in our situation – wish to undermine our achievements and ignore our laws'. The moderate political reforms which accompanied his economic policy and which were primarily based on his countrymen's material needs gradually gave rise to a more liberal climate. On 18 March 1976, a new military service law was passed which reduced the period of compulsory military service from 36 to 24 months (only 18 for students) and on 19 December 1980, the period of service was universally reduced to 18 months. The decree issued by a plenary executive meeting of the Central Committee on 26 June 1977 proved to be of even greater significance. This permitted more cultural freedom, since Kádár's party did not see its task in terms of imposing opinions, but regarded a measure of pluralism and the freedom of party members to express their opinions as both constructive and necessary. Unlike the other Socialist countries of eastern Europe, Hungary has no official censorship, although the controlling organs of the state and the party does see to it that the guidelines laid down according to the celebrated 'three T's – *tamogatott* (supported), *türt* (tolerated) and *tiltott* (banned) – are followed. Total control of the mass media and the cultural administration's dependence on the party still guarantee that no-one oversteps the permitted threshold of tolerance.

The workers also gained themselves a hearing following the implementation of the second round of NEM reforms. They not only demanded more freedom of information and honest government to help improve their understanding of the political and economic decision-making processes, but pressed for a greater degree of industrial democracy. The ground rules on workers' participation in the management of firms, laid down in a joint resolution of the Council of Ministers and the trade unions' Central Council, essentially limited participation to the signing of collective agreements and social welfare policy. As a result, the power of decision-making on questions of production and type and quality of product still remained entirely in management hands. When the workers were forced to accept a decline in the purchasing power of their real earnings as a result of slower economic growth and the regular fixing of prices according to production costs, the workers began to adopt a more realistic attitude. The leaders of the trade unions and the party reacted swiftly in order to avoid a similar situation arising to that in Poland. At the party's Twelfth Congress, held in Budapest in late March 1980, Sándor Gáspár, the General Secretary of the trade unions' National Council made it clear that his organisation no longer regarded itself as the go-between of party and government, but rather as the representative and protector of the workers' interests. In this connection the trade unions also demanded more dialogue and a greater measure of democracy: 'We can best strengthen the country's economic power, if we rely on democracy, on the clash of opinions and interests, and on the increased participation of the working population'. The tendency to allow the trade unions to represent the workers on specific issues affecting them within the framework of a Socialist system, and thus recognise a certain plurality of interests, emerged clearly in 1980 at the congresses of individual trade unions in different branches of industry held in advance of the Twenty-Sixth Trade Union Congress, which took place between the 12 and 14 December of that year. In speeches made during the congress and in a resolution passed by the delegates, the view was expressed that trade unions possessed a controlling function in a Socialist society, especially the task of protecting the workers' interests independently of party and government. The demand was raised to create machinery to hear workers' grievances against decisions which directly affected their living standards, and the government was called upon to make conditions easier by exercising stricter price controls and introducing a five-day week. After 1 July 1981, steps were taken to make a five-day week a possibility. This was generally introduced after the beginning of 1982 when the average working week was reduced to 42 hours.

This development, which coupled the rewarding of good performance by incentive payments with consistent maintenance of the government's general reform policies, had its critics. But Kádár knew at every stage how to keep the sceptics in check. In April 1977, the head of the Central Committee Secretariat, József Sándor, was forced to make way for István Katona, the former chief editor of the main party newspaper *Népszabadság*, who was replaced in turn by the rector of the Party Academy, Desző Nemes. An even greater stir was caused by the decision of a meeting of the Central Committee on 19 to 20 April 1978 to sack the 57-year-old Central Committee Secretary and Politburo member, Béla Biszku. His duties as head of the influential department in charge of party administration, party cadres and mass organisations were taken over by the economist, Károly Németh. A skilled toolmaker by trade, Biszku, who had been a Politburo member since 1957, Central Committee Secretary for security affairs since 1962 and subsequent head of the influential party cadre in charge of the party's records, was regarded more as Kádár's deputy than as his potential successor. The latter role now seemed to fall to Németh. Born in 1922, he had been a member of the Politburo since 1970 and until 1974 had held a powerful position at the head of the Budapest party organisation. The former deputy prime minister, Ferenc Havasi, assumed responsibility for the continued implementation of economic reforms, because only this former skilled cement worker and long-serving party secretary in the Danube town of Komárom was attributed with the capacity to tackle the effects of the world-wide recession on Hungary's economy. Kádár subsequently made it clear on several occasions that the personnel changes which also took place among the middle and lower ranks of the party were a 'normal development': 'We must ensure a regular change of party personnel appropriate to changing needs while preserving necessary stability. Democracy in our society is also demonstrated by the fact that the leadership is constantly enriched by new personnel.'

Even more sweeping personnel decisions were subsequently taken at the party's Twelfth Congress, held between 24 and 27 March 1980. With the sanction of the 764 delegates, representing 811, 833 party members in all, Kádár took it upon himself immediately to dismiss five of the fifteen Politburo members and to undertake a major shake-out of the 127-man strong Central Committee. As well as Béla Biszku and former premier, Jenő Fock, even the 48-year-old chief of planning and deputy prime minister, István Huszár, had to give up his post. Huszár had shown himself to be a committed economic reformer and had won considerable respect from the Hungarian public as a result of his outspoken criticisms, but lacked a power base within the party. Since Huszár was not made a scapegoat for

Hungary's difficult economic situation, despite planning mistakes, which prime minister Lázár also openly admitted, one may conclude that he was sacrificed mainly in order to appease Hungary's Soviet allies. For, at the same time two dogmatists of the old school, the President of the National Assembly, Antal Apró, and the ideologue, Dezső Nemes, who had, however, always sided with whichever was the stronger faction, were also forced to give up their seats on the Politburo. The three new members – Mihály Korom, who was made Central Committee Secretary in charge of security, Lajos Mehes, the Budapest party chief, and Havasi were regarded as reliable Kádár supporters. Kádár, who was himself confirmed in his position as First Secretary, set about reducing the Central Committee Secretariat from seven to five members.

In addition, a number of important personnel changes took place in the government following the National Assembly elections of 8 June 1980. Although a 'mere' 97 per cent of the electorate cast their vote, 99.3 per cent of unspoiled votes were polled in favour of Patriotic Popular Front candidates. At the same time, the government tried to improve bureaucratic efficiency by merging the ministries into bigger units. As was to be expected, the chairman of the State Planning Council, Huszár, after losing his Politburo membership, had to vacate his government post and was replaced by the former finance minister, Lajos Faluvégi. Apart from Lázár, whose position as premier was unchallenged, his deputy, György Aczél, was the only government minister to hold on to his position in the Politburo. Lázár argued that the tendency to separate the machinery of party and state was in keeping with the government's reforms, since these were intended to liberate economic development from political constraints, especially as regards the selection of personnel. Although Kádár, whose strict Calvinist morality led him to criticise the personal affairs of the defence minister, Lajos Czinege, knew how to prevent this military man, whom Moscow held in high regard, from joining the Politburo, he had to retain him in the government because of Soviet backing. But he was not able to persuade the unpopular and increasingly isolated foreign minister, Puja, who also had Kremlin backers, to give up his post until 7 July 1983. He was replaced by Péter Várkonyi, a former chief editor of *Népszabadság* who, from 1982 onwards, was head of the Central Committee Secretariat with responsibility for international affairs. As early as 23 July 1982, Kádár's loyal supporter, György Aczél, who had been ousted as Central Committee Secretary in 1974 at the Soviets' insistence, replaced the 'dogmatist', András Gyenes, as head of the Central Committee departments responsible for cultivating contacts with other Communist parties.

This office is particularly important, since Hungary's independent path towards Socialism is viewed with extreme suspicion both in Moscow and in the other capitals of the east European Communist countries where it has been commented upon in the past with considerable reservation. Hungary's foreign policy has been entirely directed towards the specific problems of the Socialist Bloc and the country has played a constructive and committed role within Comecon and the Warsaw Pact organisation. It has given its backing to every Soviet initiative and supported, albeit with a certain degree of reservation, the Soviet Union's position within international bodies such as the United Nations. Indeed, Kádár and the Hungarian party attach the greatest importance to Hungary's bilateral relations with the Soviet Union and fellow Socialist countries at both party and governmental level. Thus, it is hardly surprising that several meetings have taken place annually between Brezhnev and Kádár, the Soviet prime ministers Kosygin and Tichonov and Lázár, and the foreign ministers, Gromyko and Puja. Apart from political issues of general interest, the entire problem of European security and agreement on long-term economic strategy and the exchange of the goods have figured prominently in discussions. Hungarian units have played an increasing part in the common Warsaw Pact manoeuvres, which have also taken place on Hungarian territory; the 1979 manoeuvres, code-named 'Shield', being a case in point. Thus, with the possible exception of Rumania, contacts with other Socialist countries are close and are built upon by regular consultations taking place between both party and government officials.

The mistrust which the Socialist Bloc countries have shown towards the Hungarian experiment no doubt arose from the fear that the party might lose its control over the process of gradual liberalisation and a situation might then be created in which its monopoly of power was challenged. The Hungarian Communists were reminded of the events of 1956 and warned against allowing any socio-economic and political climate to arise which would force fellow Socialist states to intervene in order to put the country back on the rails. The internal political freedoms which were granted to Hungary caused both concern and no doubt envy in the other Socialist countries; an example being Kádár's sympathetic remarks on the 'Eurocommunism' of the West European Communists. In the discussion which suddenly emerged in 1976–77 on 'separate paths' towards socialism and the role of the dictatorship of the proletariat, the Hungarian party moved substantially towards adopting the Italian Communist Party's position. A Central Committee resolution of 20 April 1978, expressly stated, 'that the realisation of the different historical tasks faced by each Communist and workers' party in different countries' dmanded that each 'evaluate the concrete circumstances and stipulate the tasks' ahead of them. 'We regard it as natural that the parties decide their own strategy and tactics for themselves'. On 19 November 1978, during the celebrations to mark the 60th anniversary of the founding of the Hungarian Communist Party, Kádár also declared that 'on the basis of our experiences the theory of Marxism-Leninism is an indispensable weapon in the revolutionary struggle of the working class. It is also well known that the theory of Marxism-Leninism is not a dogma but a guide to action and to the concrete analysis of concrete situations'. At its Twelfth Party Congress the First Secretary was nevertheless able to record with satisfaction in his summary address on 24 March 1980, that 'The party's leading role is a reality in the life of our society. Its relationship with the masses is one of mutual trust. The party's policies have the active support of our people'.

On the other hand, it was Kádár's open admissions that 'nationalist, cosmopolitan, revisionist, ultra-left and other dangerous views' still existed in Hungary and his avowals that there was no reason to remain content with the 'Socialist democracy' which had been achieved, that caused the Soviets to reveal their anxieties. Hungary's increased contacts with capitalist countries, the noticeable reserve with which Hungary viewed the Russian intervention in Afghanistan, developments in Budapest's close ally, Poland, Soviet condemnation of China's heretical Communists or the USA's 'warmongering actions', caused the Kremlin to point at every opportunity to Hungary's major economic dependence on imports of Russian raw materials and insist on even closer cooperation within the framework of Comecon. In 1981, the Soviet Union alone absorbed 29.3 per cent of Hungarian exports and Hungary's eastern European trading partners accounted for a further 24.1 per cent. These countries also supplied 27.7 and 21.8 per cent of Hungary's imports respectively. Kádár did not shrink from resisting these massive attempts to apply intimidating pressure. On several occasions, including his final speech to the Twelfth Party Congress, he placed conspicuous emphasis on the sovereignty and independence of Hungary which itself decided all matters concerning policy. At the same time, however, he also made reconciliatory remarks concerning the value 'of close cooperation and the consultation and exchange of views with fellow Socialist countries, especially with the Soviet Union'.

The considerable respect which Kádár has acquired over the years has been demonstrated not least by his visits to western capitals. Talks in Bonn (4–7 July 1977, 26–8 April 1982), Rome (7–9 June 1977) and Paris (15–17 November 1978) have been of major significance in view of the cooperation agreements they have produced. Relations with Austria became mutually profitable and warm for both sides. Not only did the leading politicans of both countries meet for regular consultations, but the abolition of visa requirements also encouraged normal tourist traffic. Even greater satisfaction was felt at President Carter's decision to allow the holy crown of St Stephen, which, together with the royal regalia, had been removed to the USA as a spoil of war, to return to Hungary. This legendary symbol of the concept of a Hungarian state and separate national identity was brought back to Budapest by a delegation headed by the US foreign secretary, Cyrus Vance, on 5 January 1978. The entire nation was also filled with pride when it learnt that Bertalan Farkas had become the first Hungarian cosmonaut to travel in space on board Soyuz 36 between 26 May and 3 June 1980.

On 26 May 1982, the Hungarians celebrated János Kádár's 70th birthday. They felt a sense of gratitude mixed with a certain amount of anxiety about who will eventually succeed him; for the system, characterised by his pragmatism and sense of realism, can scarcely continue in its present liberal form without his moral authority which has remained unchallenged at home. His modest and sober life style and manner of ruling the country, his rejection of any personality cult and capacity to recognise clearly the limits of his reform policies, still only just within the bounds of acceptability so far as the USSR is concerned, have won him the respect, indeed the adulation, of his fellow countrymen. At the present time no successor of similar worth is in sight. Internal power struggles to find a successor or the danger of reopening the gap between the party and the population by a sudden tightening of the reins, can no more be ruled out than a 'corrective' intervention by the Soviets if they think that Hungary's experiment of a 'separate (national) path to Socialism' seriously endangers the solidarity of the Socialist Bloc countries. But even in Hungary itself there are still problem areas which may prove sensitive to any sudden upsets in the overall European balance of power, imbalances in the Socialist Bloc itself, economic shortages or ideologically-imposed changes to Hungary's reformist policies.

HUNGARY IN THE 1980s

On 1 January 1985, Hungary's population, which has recently registered a slight decline, numbered 10.658 million. Of this figure 46.6 per cent, i.e. 4.995 million people, were in employment. Following a reduction in the pensionable age to 60 years for men and 55 for women, 2.131 million Hungarians were eligible for pensions in 1982, although a rapid rise in the cost of living has meant that the value of these has not been generally sufficient to live on and many pensioners have been obliged to take on additional employment for as long as possible. Steady industrial growth, increased agricultural mechanisation and growing urbanisation had helped produce a situation in which approximately 55 per cent of all employees were employed in industry, compared with only 15 per cent in agriculture. About 3 per cent of the population were employed in small private firms. The 'middle class', characterised by its predominantly technocratic character, including those with a higher education or vocational training, white-collar workers, scientists and creative artists already accounts for 24 per cent of the workforce and is still growing. The ruling élite of the party, the government, the military and the security forces accounts for 3 per cent of the working population. Industry in general, including the construction industry in particular, contributed 61.2 per cent of Hungary's national income and 74.8 per cent of its exports in 1981, while agriculture contributed 16 per cent of the national income and 25.2 per cent of export earnings. Whereas industrial employees and agricultural employees could expect to earn an average monthly income of approximately 6,000 forints and 5,500 forints respectively, the monthly average pension amounted to only 2,800 forints. Against a background of an annual average rise of 4.6 per cent on consumer prices, modest increases in wages and pensions over the past few years have failed to compensate adequately for the decline in real purchasing power.

The Sixth Five Year Plan, inaugurated in 1981, aims at consolidating the entire Hungarian economy further by shifting the emphasis of production in favour of more profitable products for which there is an international demand, increasing economic efficiency and, not least, maintaining the present standard of living. However, the government has not succeeded in fulfilling the plan's targets in its first two years of implementation, nor has it succeeded in raising per capita income to the extent it had envisaged. Since less capital has been available for investment, compared with the billion forints invested under the Fifth Five year Plan, it has been possible to achieve an economic equilibrium only by improving profitability, raising productivity and holding down expectations. The unfavourable economic situation in the western industrialised countries, marked by economic recession, high unemployment and a growing protectionism – a development greatly lamented in Hungary – together with broken promises of deliveries from Socialist countries (Poland and Rumania) and a rise in private consumption in excess of the plan's targets, caused Hungary's economic experts particular concern at the beginning of the 1980s.

When, following a visit to Moscow between 18 and 23 July 1983, Kádár won the support of the new Soviet Communist Party leader, Yuri Andropov, for further economic reforms, the Hungarian party leadership and political economists drafted a number of reforms to be implemented during the second half of the 1980s. These won Central Committee approval on 17 April 1984 and were subsequently passed by the Council of Ministers on 10 May. The intention behind the introduction of a 'regulated market' was to combine the advantages of independent private initiative and the economy's operation according to market forces with the necessary central direction of the economy by the state in line with its macro-economic and political aims. Priority was given to restructuring the country's economic institutions and an attempt made to reorganise and redefine the state's various economic functions. State companies were allowed greater autonomy and the scope for ministerial intervention in the planning of business strategy was reduced. Industrial deconcentration was encouraged, competition was intensified and companies were made to bear greater market risks. The government also encouraged the setting up of small businesses under various forms of ownership, while at the same time improving credit and capital facilities to back innovations. The state economic administration's vertical coordination of the economy in almost every area was also removed in favour of a decentralised coordination of the economy which was to be achieved by delegating decision-making to individual concerns. In both Hungary and several neighbouring Socialist countries reservations were immediately expressed concerning the direction being taken by these new Hungarian reforms. As a result of this and the Hungarian government's own present policy of austerity and intervention aimed at achieving economic stability, it seems likely that many of the reforms will be realised only in diluted form, with the result that the gap between intention and reality in the so-called 'Hungarian model' is likely to continue in the years to come.

With a foreign debt amounting to almost 9 billion U.S. dollars in 1982 and an acute shortage of foreign exchange threatening the repayment of interest and capital on loans from the West, the Hungarian government's successful application to join the International Monetary Fund on 6 May 1982 and its membership of the World Bank, announced on 7 July, helped overcome the economy's immediate problems by means of short-term borrowing. But the shock caused by the credit crisis caused the government to take action in late 1982 to reduce Hungary's net debt by means of a further drastic reduction in investment, surplus stockpiling and industrial development funding. These measures were also accompanied by price increases and, more importantly, import restrictions. By massively increasing its exports to Comecon countries by 3 per cent, as well as its exports to developing countries, Hungary managed to achieve a foreign trade surplus of approximately 500 million dollars in 1982. But, since the country's main source of foreign earnings, agricultural production, suffered from a drought in 1983 and since the drastic reductions in imports meant that industrial production rose by only 1.1 per cent, Hungary experienced a marked lowering of living standards in 1983. Against a background of a 7.8 per cent rate of inflation average earnings rose by only 4.4 per cent. Drastic price increases on basic foodstuffs, services and utilities, such as those implemented on 19 September 1983, 23 January 1984 and 19 January 1985, increased transport costs by 60 per cent, energy by 30 per cent and milk by 28 per cent, but still failed to reduce the budget deficit effectively. This stood at 15.7 billion forints in 1985 and could well reach the sum of 23 billion forints in 1986.

The party and the government's insistence on the need to improve Hungary's foreign trade balance and reduce its foreign debt by greatly stimulating exports and the production of substitute products for imported goods at the cost of reducing incomes and private consumption helped reduce Hungary's international debts to only 4.1 billion dollars in 1985. But at the Thirteenth Party Congress, held between 25 and 28 March 1985, Kádár had to admit that the régime's consistent policy of austerity measures had resulted in a general lowering of the standard of living and that real wages, together with the real value of pensions and social benefits, had declined in value. At the same time, industrial production rose by 10.2 per cent between 1981 and 1984, agricultural output by 12.4 per cent and the national income by 8.5 per cent in the same period. The Seventh Five Year Plan, introduced on 1 January 1986, has not yet fulfilled the expectations placed in it, since earnings have risen by 7.2 per cent by the middle of 1986 while industrial production has increased by only 1.2 per cent in the same period, compared with the expected figure of 2.5 per cent. In all, the government hopes by 1990 to achieve an increase of 17 per cent in the national income, 15 per cent in industrial manufacturing and at most 16 to 18 per cent in earnings. In order to achieve these targets it has carried out its threat to consolidate the national economy by closing down unprofitable concerns, reducing the size of the workforce, dividing up large-scale enterprises into more manageable small and middle-sized firms and generally curbing the state's influence on the economy in favour of market forces and private initiative. These policies led Sándor Gáspár, chairman of the Twenty-Fifth Congress of the Hungarian Trade Union Federation and himself a member of the Politburo, to criticise the government on 14 February 1986, when he accused it of encouraging inflation, reducing the population's purchasing power and, in particular, of irresponsibly reducing the status of the formerly highly-valued 200,000 members of the technical intellingentsia, who, although indispensable to the success of the government's reforms, were being forced to supplement their incomes outside their full-time employment. The government had already felt obliged to legalise the so-called 'black economy' in the early 1980s, acknowledging its existence as a viable alternative economy, able to operate independently of bureaucratic controls. Owing to the inadequacies of the state-controlled sector, some 70 per cent of Hungary's workforce supplement their incomes by taking on a second job outside their full-time occupation.

Following the introduction of thirty-two new statutory regulations, approximately 11,000 small private firms were set up in 1982 alone. By the end of 1983 there were about 16,000 such firms employing 130,000 workers mainly in handicrafts. These companies contributed as much as 44.2 per cent of net production in the service sector and 13.4 per cent in the construction industry. According to official estimates, around 16 to 18 per cent of the country's national income, a third of its agricultural output and 40 per cent of its private housing construction are done 'on the side' as part of the semi-legal 'black economy' in both production and services. Since the 20 July 1983 private employers have been allowed to employ up to six employees in private enterprises – twelve, if family members are included. Hungarians with specialist skills can accept employment in the West for a period of up to five years without having to undergo any major formalities, as long as they pay 20 per cent of their earnings in foreign exchange into a Hungarian National Bank account and keep up their Hungarian social insurance contributions by paying in hard currency. One of the most unusual aspects of the Hungarian reform model was the setting up of 'economic labour groups' within companies, whereby workers employed in large state enterprises continue working after normal working hours, using the machines and materials made available by their state employers but privately billing the customer for work done on their employer's behalf. There are now more than 17,000 such groups in Hungary, enabling around 200,000 'spare time workers' to boost their monthly earnings substantially and in exceptional cases even double them.

While the supply of basic provisions has deteriorated in recent years in the Soviet Union and the majority of eastern European countries, the situation in Hungary has steadily improved. In the critical area of meat production Hungary has not only succeeded in covering its domestic needs, but has managed to achieve a stable export surplus and is now the leading meat exporter within Comecon. The agricultural sector, for its part, has recorded wheat and maize yields per hectare, which surpass even those of the American farm belt. Of the 6.5 million hectares presently under cultivation 8 per cent is privately-owned and small-scale producers are responsible for more than 30 per cent of total agricultural production and over 55 per cent of the harvest in particularly labour-intensive sectors (viticulture, tobacco growing, vegetable and potato growing). The 1,450 cooperatives and 160 large state farms, which work 61 per cent and 31 per cent of the land respectively, have their own commercial chain of slaughter-houses, butcher's shops and restaurants and cooperate closely with these small-scale farmers, leaving labour-intensive branches of production, such as seeds and calf-breeding, to the latter while buying up and marketing their produce. It is hardly surprising, therefore, that Andropov's adoption of the positive aspects of Hungarian agricultural policy after 1983, though taken no further under his successor Černenko, has been pushed through by the new General Secretary of the Soviet Communist Party, Gorbachev, who wishes to test the suitability of Hungarian-style reforms on the inefficient agrarian sector of the other eastern European countries. In Hungary, certainly, no-one need starve or queue for any length of time in order to satisfy their basic food requirements.

Despite considerable government efforts, there has still been no significant improvement in the miserable housing situation and the construction of modern flats with adequate living-space. The 1.5 million flats erected before 1980 have provided improved accommodation for over a third of the population. However, the annual target figure of approximately 80,000 new first-time dwellings has not been sufficiently adequate to cover the accommodation needs of the 'baby boom' generation, especially as the continuing decay of many old buildings and lack of funds for extensive renovation programmes are creating an ever growing need to replace old housing stock. According to official estimates, some 360,000 dwellings are in poor condition and a further 100,000 have been condemned as unfit for human habitation. Approximately 350,000 Hungarian families are at present seeking accommodation, since many occupants with children would like to move out of their small one or two-room apartments into larger accommodation. In Budapest in 1985, 60,000 persons were registered on the city's official housing list, 10,000 of whom had little hope of being allocated suitable accommodation in the foreseeable future. Thus, two-fifths of Hungary's citizens have either no accommodation at all or live in accommodation which falls short of their desired requirements. To help overcome the problem, the state makes special funds available to cooperative building societies, as well as state mortgages for the construction of one or two-room family houses. In 1980, 28.6 per cent of housing was state-owned, while 71.4 per cent either belonged to cooperatives or was privately-owned.

Hungary's attraction as a tourist destination can be seen from the number of foreign visitors who are much sought after for the foreign exchange they bring into the country. In 1970, some 6.3 million foreigners visited the country, a figure which rose to 14.8 million in 1981 and 15.4 million in 1982. About 10 million of these visitors spent several days in Hungary as tourists. As a result of simplifying the issuing of visas, abolishing the requirement to change a fixed amount of foreign currency and an improvement in the exchange rate, the number of 'westerners' paying for their holidays in convertible currency also increased to about 15 per cent of all visitors. In 1982, these tourists contributed around 4 per cent of Hungary's foreign exchange earnings. Of the 4 million Hungarians who are allowed to travel abroad each year, around 10 per cent visit capitalist countries.

The contrast between urban and rural life, which was still very apparent in the inter-war period, has now been largely overcome. Apart from Budapest with its 2 million inhabitants there are already five other cities whose population has grown to over 100,000 inhab-

construction of modern flats with adequate living-space. The 1.5 (171,000), Pécs (164,000) and Györ (120,000). In all, 50.4 per cent of the population now lives in towns and between 40 and 60 per cent of the urban working population is employed in industry. In the new industrial centres such as Tatabánya, Salgótarján or Dunaújváros, which have grown up as a result of economic planning, workers comprise nearly 80 per cent of the population. In contrast, 60 per cent of the population in the rural towns of the Great Plain (Alföld) still earn their living from agriculture.

The modernisation and expansion of the education system have always been goals which the Socialist Workers' Party has been especially keen to promote. Compulsory schooling begins at 6 years of age and ends at 16. Free schooling is provided by the elementary school, which children attend for eight years, and four different types of secondary school. Among the 56 institutions ranked as higher education establishments are 9 universities, 9 polytechnics and 13 teacher training colleges, which together have a capacity to train a total of 110,000 students. Scientific research is carried out under the auspices of the celebrated Hungarian Academy of Sciences which has almost 1,500 institutes in which over 30,000 scientists and scholars are employed. While the party has largely succeeded in reconciling the preferentially treated technical intelligentsia to the régime by offering material privileges and favourable opportunities for upward social mobility, social scientists and artists are inclined to view the system with greater detachment and are prepared to criticise it.

At the same time, the party and the government have made a point of cultivating the arts and what has been termed 'human intelligence'. Poets and writers not only receive relatively generous social benefits, but are given sufficient opportunity to publicise their works – as long as they observe the prevailing norms and exercise self-censorship. Gyula Illyés, Miklós Mészöly, Iván Mandy, Miklós Szentkuthy and Géza Ottlik all enjoy considerable respect. The support given to György Konrád for his first two novels ('The Visitor'; 'The Founder of the State') was withdrawn when he collaborated with the sociologist, Iván Szelényi, in producing a report on 'The Intelligentsia on the Road to becoming a Power-Wielding Class'. The subsequent ban on his publications has caused him to turn his back on Hungary in the meantime. Other authors, like the essayist and scriptwriter, Sándor Csoóri, or the poet, György Petri, whose works were denied publication on account of their 'undesirable' subject matter, have, nevertheless, found ways of having their

263

work appear in Hungary. The cultural journals, *Élet es Irodalom* (Life and Literature) and *Mozgó Világ* (World in Action), which are especially popular with the younger generation, provide an important forum for intellectual discussion and push forward the barriers of social and intellectual freedom. In recent years Hungarian filmmakers like Miklós Jancsó ('The Desperate Ones', 'Shimmering Wind'), Károly Makk ('Love'), Péter Gothár ('Time Stands Still') and, above all, István Szabó ('Mephisto') have won international acclaim.

In 1985, the Hungarian Socialist Workers' Party numbered 871,000 members, a figure which represented an increase of 7.3 per cent since the party's Twelfth Party Congress in 1980. Despite the relatively liberal climate the internally strengthened party has experienced little difficulty in maintaining discipline within the country at large and in its own ranks. Fluctuations in its membership have been relatively small. Between 1975 and 1980, 143,000 Hungarians joined the party, compared with 22,000 who left. A total of 7,928 members were expelled and 48,245 had their membership suspended because of their failure to demonstrate an active commitment. Between 1980 and 1985, 28,737 (3.4 per cent) members were censured after undergoing disciplinary proceedings and a further 7,639 were forced to leave the party on account of serious lapses such as a dereliction of duty, irresponsible behaviour towards others, alcoholism and corruption. There has also been an unmistakable rise in the proportion of old to young party members, since only 7.5 per cent of members are younger than 29 years of age and the average age of party members has risen from 45.5 to 46.9 years of age over the past few years. At the last Party Congress in March 1985 it was proudly pointed out that 62.4 per cent of party members were workers and 10.8 per cent peasants. White-collar employees made up a further 16.1 per cent of the membership, those in 'intellectually creative employment' 9.2 per cent and 'others' 1.5 per cent; these last three groups being overproportionately represented. Women, who are entirely unrepresented in the Politburo at present, are greatly underrepresented in the party and comprise only 26.1 per cent of its membership. Over 800,000 young people between the ages of 14 and 28 are organised in the 25,600 branches of the Communist Youth League, while children under the age of 14 are catered for by the Young Pioneers (*Úttörok*).

The Patriotic Popular Front, which includes representatives of the country's churches and national minorities, has 112,400 members, organised into 4,000 local branches, who are mainly involved in canvassing support for the party at elections and helping mobilise popular support for the government's social and political measures. Its long-serving chairman is the former prime minister, Gyula Kállai. The much more politically influential General Secretary of the National Council of the Patriotic Popular Front, István Sarlós, succeeded György Aczél to the post of deputy prime minister on 23 June 1982, but soon moved on to become Chairman of the National Assembly on 19 December 1984. Prior to this the formerly influential, Antal Apró, had retired from this office 'on grounds of age', thus relinquishing his last position of any importance.

The national daily newspapers, like *Népszabadság* (Party), *Magyar Hirlap* (government), *Magyar Nemzet* (Patriotic Popular Front) and *Népszava* (Trade Union) enjoy a press monopoly and exclusively convey the party's ideological and political line. They, together with 1,720 other regional and local newspapers published on a regular basis, have a daily circulation of over 3 million copies. In addition, there are also thirty four weekly newspapers with a circulation of over 7 million copies and sixteen other magazines published by religious groups. A press law of 21 March 1986 confirms the citizen's right to information and directs journalists to convey, alongside coverage of international events, 'a true picture of political, economic, social and cultural life in Hungary'. The law allows for the acceptance of any application to publish a newspaper as long as no violation of human rights or warmongering is involved and chauvinism or discrimination on the grounds of race, sex or creed are avoided. The expectation that publishers will exercise self-censorship and observe the relevant statutory obligations, together with its control over the allocation of newsprint, allows the ruling party to influence both the selection of information and the tenor of its reporting. Television, which now offers over 100 hours of broadcasting on two channels each week, is steadily gaining in importance as a major source of information for the general public.

In 1976, when the stifling of reform was at its height, a general opinion poll was conducted in Hungary. Although it was based on a small sample rather than a representative cross-section of the population (and its findings must therefore be treated with caution) 38 per cent of those interviewed approved of Hungary's Socialist system, while 50 per cent thought that it functioned badly. In the hypothetical event of 'free elections' being held, only 5 per cent expressed a desire to vote for the Socialist Workers' Party. In contrast, 42 per cent said they would vote for a Social Democratic or Socialist party, 27 per cent for a Christian Democratic party, 17 per cent for a peasant party and 6 per cent for a conservative party.

However, despite these findings, it would be wrong to speak of the existence of an 'opposition' as such, far less of any organised resistance against the Kádár régime. The security police, on whose manpower strength no official statistics are available, ensures that no such organised opposition emerges. In an emergency Hungary can call upon its small army of 72,000 soldiers and 21,000 air force troops to join its 20,000-strong border security force and 60,000-strong workers' militia to help the police maintain internal order. In addition, the four Soviet divisions permanently stationed in Hungary exercise an intimidatory effect on the population. Although objections are, nevertheless, sometimes raised against the Communist monopoly of power, they originate from four quite distinct sources: the legacy of traditional populist feelings, the Social Democratic tradition, reformist thinking, which aims at a change of leadership and a new political direction, and popular religious sentiment.

The populist movement, which originally grew out of popular defiance of aristocratic rule, gained fresh impetus during the interwar period and the Second World War, when the ossified oligarchical system blocked every effort towards social, economic and cultural reform. Despite their differing aims, the populists supported the setting up of the Communist régime, only to be subsequently subjected to major persecution between 1949 and 1953. After mid-November 1956 they again became opponents of the system and were denigrated because of their support for a multi-party system. They regained a measure of freedom in the more liberal cultural climate of the late 1960s when they began to highlight the deplorable situation of the persecuted Magyar minorities in Hungary's neighbouring states and, in contrast to the party and the government who had to exercise extreme caution for foreign policy reasons, demanded that the situation be redressed. At present they enjoy the support of the authorities in their attempts to locate the causes of various social and political problems. Their interests range from the reasons behind Hungary's high divorce rate and widespread alcoholism to the causes of the alarming increase in mental illness and large number of suicides.

The groups belonging to the reformist and revisionist opposition first emerged around 1955. Comprising mainly economic reformers, sociologists and representatives of the Lukács school, they remain suspect in the eyes of the party even though they long refrained from criticising official party ideology. Since the late 1970s, however, the party has attempted within the framework of the 'constructive' advancement of Marxism-Leninism the cautious implementation of the modernising innovations called for, in particular, by the Budapest school of sociologists, and has accepted overdue political reforms as a necessary by-product of economic achievements. At the same time, the party tried hard to avoid giving any impression of having succumbed to the 'revisionism' so feared by the Soviet Communists. Against demands for greater democracy and pluralism it has stuck to its official goal of creating a monolithic society by subscribing to the ideal of 'one ideology, one nation'.

Nevertheless, in a series of articles dealing with party ideology and theory, which appeared in *Társadalmi Szemle* in spring 1984, the party announced its willingness to allow 'an even greater measure of Socialist democratisation' and 'self-administration'. Pointing to the 'unsatisfactory development of party democracy', the party's organisational statute was amended with a view to enlarging its social basis and increasing the independence of the party organisation and party members. The new party statute, approved at the Thirteenth Party Congress in March 1985, no longer defines the political function and social basis of its leadership role exclusively in terms of the 'working class'. Together with a new emphasis on specialist knowledge, the value of debate and responsibility for decision-making at a local level, the possibility of developing a 'class position' for the technical intelligentsia, which the party views as increasingly important, seems a genuine prospect. In addition, a fifteen-man-strong Constitutional Committee began work on 6 June 1984, entrusted with helping to 'secure the constitutional social order' and ensure that Hungary's laws, decrees and statutory measures are in harmony with the constitution. The electoral reform, approved by parliament on 23 December 1983, which allows several candidates, who do not necessarily have to belong to the Socialist Workers' Party to stand for election in each of the country's 355 constituencies, was put into effect for the first time on 8 and 22 June 1985. Only thirty-five parliamentary seats were filled on the basis of a central national list of candidates, which secured parliamentary seats for the party chief, Kádár, leading politicians, representatives of the churches and the national minorities, all of whom received over 99 per cent of the votes cast (although only 93.9 per cent of the 7,728 million registered voters actually voted). The much vaunted 'widening of the opportunity for the masses to participate' in the elections only amounted, however, to citizens being allowed to nominate candidates other than the two candidates nominated by the Patriotic Popular Front. The result was that in the first round of the elections twenty-five of the seventy one alternative candidates who stood against the party's official recommendation were elected to the National Assembly and former prominent functionaries like the former prime minister, Jenö Fock, and the former minister of justice, Béla Biszku, were left out in the cold. Since none of the candidates gained an absolute majority in 45 of the constituencies, a second round was necessary. This was held on 22 June, whereby candidates now categorised as 'independent' succeeded in being elected. The relatively free nature of these elections has had no parallel in any of the other Communist states of eastern Europe and has won Hungary considerable respect, despite the limitations and inadequacies which undoubtedly still exist.

On the other hand, the government has done almost everything in its power to obstruct the work of critical intellectuals, who, like the sociologist Ágnes Heller, have tried to investigate the applicability to Hungary of Social Democratic or western democratic ideas of a pluralistic society. The ruling party's desire to avoid, if at all possible, major conflict and changes which might undermine the internal stability of the system has encouraged the emergence of a progressive reformism which no longer basically subscribes to the goals of the Socialist International and western European Social Democracy, but has instead tended to adopt Eurocommunist ideas. But, since this would mean a rejection of Soviet-style Socialism, and since the adoption of a multi-party system would inevitably threaten the ruling party's institutionalised monopoly of power, such speculations have had little appeal within the Socialist Workers' Party.

Up until the present Hungary's opposition groups have made no attempt to join forces, nor have there been any sensational incidents to speak of. Ideas encountered in academic works, magazine articles and smaller discussion circles pose no essential threat to the régime which has a monopoly of power and effectively controls public opinion. While the opposition is, of course, perceived as hostile, the régime is content to keep it under surveillance and rarely employs oppressive measures. Thus, a 'second' culture, which walks a narrow tightrope between being tolerated and being declared illegal, has been able to emerge alongside the official culture encouraged by the state. However, there has still been next to no relaxation in driving illegal *Samizdat* publications underground. These are chiefly scholarly and artistic works, which are either published clandestinely or appear semi-legally. Underground periodicals like *Beszélö* (The Spokesman) or *AB Tájékoztató* (Orientation) provide the opposition at present with its main channels of information and forums for discussion. After the publication of a warning article by the chief editor of *Népszabadság*, Péter Renyi, the security authorities decided to take action against the politically active son of the Rákosi victim Rajk, László Rajk Jnr, whose flat in the centre of Budapest had been used for the regular sale of *Samizdat* literature. On the night of 15 December 1982, the flat was raided and Rajk and several friends interrogated. But, although the law allows the authorities to take action against authors, printers and distributors of underground publications, they have up until now shown great restraint.

Nevertheless, several loosely connected groups have been formed, of which the oldest is *Szeta*, founded by Otilia Solt. This group has set itself the goal of caring for the country's many poor people, such as pensioners, gypsies and unemployed youth, with the help of donations. Other groups of dissidents have formed around the philosopher, János Kiss, who was relieved of his post in the Academy of Sciences at the end of the 1970s, and Gabor Demzsky, whose AB publishing house publishes proscribed books and the monthly magazine *Hormondo* (the Messenger). The group which calls itself MO concerns itself with the events of October 1956, while the circle around the biologist and journalist, János Vargha, has taken up ecological issues and succeeded in halting the construction of two major power stations planned to be built on the Danube, the unforseen consequences of which would have seriously damaged the natural environment of the endangered Auwald forest region. However, their efforts failed to prevent the starting up of the first reactor in the nuclear power station at Paks on 3 November 1983. The dissident groups, whom the government lumps together as the 'opposition', do not attempt to conceal their numerical weakness. While only about 50 people actively organise and promote their various causes, there are some 200 sympathisers who can be described as 'regular workers' and a further 500 people who act as 'occasional helpers'. This '0.1 per cent', as the dissidents like to call themselves, does not claim to be representative, but promotes any sign of non-conformist thinking which is currently spreading rapidly in Hungary and is valued as an essential element and precondition for any further development of Hungarian society.

The relative consideration which the authorities show towards this numerically small 'opposition' has been made easier by the dissidents' own assurance that they will respect Hungary's inherited internal and external situation and campaign primarily for 'important political goals' which appear 'achievable without shaking the foundations of the system'. Arguing that economic reforms can succeed only if they are accompanied by appropriate political changes, the régime's critics call for parliament to play a more significant role and the setting up of an independent council of experts to review the economic situation and redistribute social burdens. They also argue that social groups 'whose very existence' is affected 'to a very considerable degree by the economic crisis' should have the right to form representative bodies and thus view the introduction of a new trade union law as necessary. In future elected shop stewards should be responsible to those who elect them rather than to the party. Arbitration procedures to settle conflicts between employers and employees should be so regulated as to make it possible to 'apply legal forms of pressure'. The government's threat to stop subsidising loss-making concerns has also elicited the opposition suggestion that workers either forsake their wages for a limited period or accept a temporary period of unemployment while receiving appropriate social benefits. Alternatively, the enterprise in question should be run as a cooperative. Of the approximately 300 billion forints which the state made from company profits in 1980, 78 billion forints were used to subsidise loss-making companies and a further 54 million forints to subsidise consumer prices.

Although the proposed major amendments to the civil code of law in 1977 and the new criminal code of law of 1978 introduced a more liberal attitude to the legal system, the reformist opposition demands that the state respect the law more than at present and strictly observe the principle of judicial independence. While recognising the absence of 'statutory censorship restrictions' and acknowledging the 'flexible cooperation' that exists 'between publishers and the authorities', future opportunities for professional bodies, cultural associations and even groups of private citizens to publish their own material are seen as desirable. Yet, despite the realistic approach behind these suggestions and their very careful wording, it would be wrong to expect the party in future to conduct a fruitful discussion with the dissident opposition, since even a dialogue with non-Communists could, in the party's opinion, result in an undermining of its position.

However, the party has not been able to evade such a dialogue with the Catholic Church which has an estimated 6.5 to 7 million members, i.e. 65 per cent of the population. As for the protestant churches, the Calvinist Reformed Church with approximately 2 million members is the largest and four times bigger than the Lutheran Church with its 450,000 members. The Baptists, Unitarians and Methodists represent only a small section of the population and an estimated 3 per cent of Hungarians belong to the Orthodox Church. Of Hungary's estimated 80,000 Jewish citizens, approximately 70,000 live in Budapest. The country's 60 Jewish communities have over 30 synagogues and places of worship, served by 30 rabbis. Apart from a Jewish hospital and several old-people's homes the Jewish community has a rabbinical school consisting of six professors and ten students, as well as several secondary schools.

Following the open conflict between church and state in the early 1950s, the 1956 uprising, which the Catholic hierarchy justified on moral grounds, resulted in strained relations with the party and the government. The intransigent Cardinal Mindszenty, who had been given asylum in the American embassy and refused to leave the country or relinquish his position as Hungarian Primate, forbade any form of contact which might have led to a normalisation of relations. By strictly interpreting agreements signed in 1948 and 1950, the State Office for Religious Affairs inhibited the scope of priests' activities, allowed only a limited amount of pastoral work and especially tried to remove the Church's influence on youth. Petty restrictions regarding the allocation of newsprint, objections to appointments to vacant dioceses, obstacles placed in the way of seminary training and travel restrictions on churchmen became commonplace. Only the stability achieved under Kádár and the party's view that the desired secularisation of society was making good progress as a result of the voluntary acknowledgement of the basis of dialectical materialism – tempered, however, by the realisation that the importance of religion and Catholic ethical norms was still firmly entrenched in much of the population – led to a gradual relaxation of restrictions. Informal contacts were established with the Vatican, with which a partial understanding might even have been reached in 1964, had it not been for Mindszenty's refusal to relinquish his ecclesiastical offices and leave Hungary.

It was not until massive pressure had been applied that the militant cardinal announced that he was prepared to leave for exile in Vienna. In the belief that he was being 'needlessly sacrificed' by the Vatican in its attempts to improve the Church's position in Hungary, he had no desire to give up his ecclesiastical duties, despite numerous appeals by the Pope. As a result, Pope Paul VI eventually removed him from his offices as Primate of Hungary and Archbishop of Esztergom in 1974. His death on 6 May 1975 enabled a return to normal in church–state relations, which had already been prepared by the leading eastern European experts in the Vatican, Archbishops Casaroli and Poggi, and by Cardinal König of Vienna. On 13

November 1975, during an official visit to Italy, prime minister Lázár was granted a private audience with Pope Paul VI, after which both sides announced their intention of developing and improving their contacts with each other. On 12 February 1976, the Vatican officially announced the appointment of László Lékai, who had been Apostolic Administrator of the archdiocese of Esztergom since 1971, to the post of resident Archbishop and Hungarian Primate. Shortly thereafter, Hungary's vacant dioceses were filled and the government and party tried to make their peace with the Catholic bishops in keeping with the spirit of the Helsinki accords of the European Conference for Security and Cooperation. In April 1977, Hungary's bishops were allowed to travel for the first time as a body for their quinquennial ad-limina visit to Pope Paul VI in order to report on the running of their dioceses. But, since there were still complaints and criticism that the government was obstructing the work of the clerical orders and hampering religious instruction, as well as condemnation of the encouragement given to 'movements which challenge the authority of the bishops', the party sought to keep the 'normalising' of relations only within prescribed limits. The new Primate's willingness to follow the state's instructions without protest gave rise to the impression in the Vatican that the Church in Hungary was in danger of becoming an obedient tool in the hands of its rulers, instead of leading a modestly independent life outside the omnipotent control of the state.

Since Kádár's official visit to the Vatican on 9 June 1977, however, the Catholic Church has been subjected to fewer pressures. The new impetus behind the implementation of reforms and the party's willingness to tolerate a certain, albeit limited, degree of pluralism in society, has made it relatively easier for the clergy to carry out its pastoral duties. However, in education and cultural life, the media and publishing the Church has no official say. Although twenty-one new bishops were appointed up to 1978, real influence lay with the diocesan administrations, which were run mainly by vicars-general and curates drawn from the ranks of the priests' peace movement and loyal to the régime. It was also some time before the Bishops' Conference, revived by Cardinal Lékai, appeared as a relatively united body. Since the State Office for Religious Affairs has to vet the filling of important church offices in advance, in practice the bishop has a free hand only in appointing chaplains and assistant priests. The appointment of bishops remains the exclusive prerogative of the collective head of state, the Presidium. Thus, following the death of Cardinal Lékai on 30 June 1986, the appointment of a successor proved extremely difficult until Archbishop László Paskai was appointed in his place on May 3rd, 1987. A ceiling is placed on the number of trainee priests and since 1950 the number of seminaries has been reduced to six with a capacity to train only 300 priests in all. Attempts to reintroduce into Hungary the ecclesiastical orders banned in 1950 have proved unsuccessful. The four teaching orders allowed to carry out their duties – the Benedictines, Franciscans, Piarists and the Sisters of the Poor teaching order of nuns, each of which has about ninety members – are allowed to teach only in the country's eight Catholic grammar schools. Because of the obvious lack of recruits to the priesthood, the 3,500 priests who serve the 2,200 congregations of the country's eleven dioceses find it very difficult to carry out their many duties. The government's control over the allocation of news-print means that editions of the Church's newspapers are limited. *Uj Ember* (The New Man) prints 90,000 copies, *Katolikus Szó* (Catholic Word) 13,800.

It has also become apparent in the course of time that the Communist régime has been able to bring religious instruction in the towns practically to a standstill through various ploys such as limiting the number of pupils to 160 per priest, making parents register their children for religious instruction, the monitoring of instruction by the state authorities and the outright intimidation of children. Only 6 to 7 per cent of all Catholic children, i.e. about 50,000 out of a total school population of 735,000, receive a Catholic education. Since the alumni of the Catholic grammar schools have difficulties placed in their way when it comes to gaining access to higher education, the Church's secondary schools have lost their attractiveness and have to struggle with falling school rolls despite the certification they offer. But Cardinal Lékai, who has only mildly remonstrated against these breaches of the spirit and content of the partial agreement signed in 1964, has thought it more advisable to work constructively within the framework of the Patriotic Popular Front. In order to improve the position of the clergy and ordinary Catholics by means of a dialogue rather than confrontation, he has remarked on several occasions that a considerable measure of agreement exists between the aims of the Catholic faith and those of Socialism. This accommodation to the realities of the Socialist system aroused the suspicion of the Vatican – especially after the papal election of the Polish cardinal, Karol Wojtyła. In a remarkably friendly circular, which was equally intended as a serious warning, John Paul II urged the Hungarian Bishops' Conference on 2 December 1978 to do everything in its power to ensure that 'the

Catholic Church, which has played such an important role in Hungary's history, will also be in a position in future, to mould your country's spiritual countenance'. The rumours which have circulated since Kádár's Vatican visit, that the Hungarian government wants to establish full diplomatic relations with the Curia, have not been denied by the Church, although Vatican sources have pointed out on more than one occasion that the outstanding issues concerning the Church's position in Hungary will have to be resolved before any such major step can be taken.

Addressing the Twelfth Party Congress on 24 March 1980, Kádár somewhat euphemistically announced that 'the faithful participate in the construction of Socialism and the life of the state as citizens with full rights'. The Church's leading representatives recently stated that relations between church and state have been further developed in the last few years to the point where 'it is now no longer a question of ordered relations, but a common effort for the common good'. However, the long-serving head of the State Office for Religious Affairs, Imre Miklos, saw to it that the complaints which the bishops have occasionally voiced concerning the government's inhibiting of the Church's activities were indeed justified. The negotiations conducted in Budapest by the papal nuncio, Poggi, at the end of March 1982, resulted in agreement on procedures regarding the future appointment of bishops, although no concessions from the government on the holding of religious instruction, the readmission of the banned orders or approval for the building of new churches.

The only area in which Church leaders and the government have cooperated closely has been in repressing the so-called 'fundamental congregations', which mainly united young Catholics who, because of the majority of bishops' attitude of support for the régime, no longer saw in Catholicism a corrective to official Communist ideology. These 'fundamental congregations', which were supported at a local level by politically active priests, were denounced as 'hostile to the government' and on several occasions the bishops suspended clergymen who had openly expressed their commitment to this lay work. Even the Vatican felt forced on 16 May 1983 to criticise strongly members of the 'fundamental congregations' who had spoken out against universal conscription and for the creation of alternatives to national service. By criticising the obsequiousness of the bishops and stagnation in the life of the Church and its clergy, the Vatican argued that they were endangering 'the unity of the Catholic Church in Hungary' and would upset the 'good relationship between the government and the faithful'.

Two groups, in particular, deserve to be mentioned in this connection. The Bulányists, named after the Piarist priest, György Bulányi, are an active Catholic youth association based in the capital, whose members are strongly committed on social issues and demand greater freedom and genuine independence for the Church. The Regnumists, whose origins go back to a Catholic youth movement of the inter-war period, insist on the moral and religious education of youth and concentrate mainly on giving private religious instruction. Their markedly uncompromising attitude towards the Communist régime and even the official Church has led to the arrest and imprisonment of their supporters within the priesthood on charges of 'conspiracy and unauthorised religious instruction'. Both groups have links with the unofficial peace movement which is supported by the young, conscientious objectors and priests and seeks closer contacts with like-minded groups in the West.

Hungary's non-Catholic religious denominations, which are very much smaller in numbers, have also made their peace with the state authorities and the Socialist Workers' Party, largely as a result of the fact that the government has been successful in rewarding churchmen who have behaved themselves and been willing to conform. When the World Federation of Lutheran Churches met in Budapest for its Seventh World Congress between 22 and 25 July 1984, the government noted the election of the Hungarian bishop, Zoltán Káldy, as president of this influential organisation of protestant churches with some satisfaction. Complaints about the growing indifference of Hungary's citizens, their unwillingness to make personal and material sacrifices, consumer mentality and spiritual apathy are becoming increasingly common. According to a poll published in the government newspaper *Magyar Hirlap* in July 1980, 50 to 60 per cent of Magyars describe themselves as 'religious', although only a third of these claim to be 'believers', i.e. 20 per cent of the population at most, regularly attend church services. Between 70 and 75 per cent of the country's rural inhabitants and about a third of its townspeople were described as 'believers'. The vast majority of Hungarians, i.e. 80 to 85 per cent of the population, still request church ceremonies for marriages, baptisms and funerals, although, according to the survey, only a quarter of those between the ages of 20 and 29 still believe in God. Since religious instruction in the schools is continually hampered and the clergy would like to preserve their present comforts by cooperating with the régime, it is very unlikely that an open conflict will take place between church and state in Hungary. The reason for this is that believers are to be found at present among all sections of society who are united with the Marxists by what the state sees as a 'long-term and fundamental community of interest'.

The situation of the Magyar minorities among Hungary's neighbours, especially Rumania, may well cause the party and government authorities much greater concern than the problem of co-existence with the churches. According to estimates, about 5 million Hungarians or people of Magyar origin live abroad, including 1.3 million in the West. Their interests are looked after by the 'World League of Hungarians Abroad' and their attitude to their homeland is one of loyalty or, at least, no longer hostile. Contacts with these émigrés are well maintained and intellectuals and scientists of Hungarian background are specifically recruited to represent Hungary's official cultural policy abroad. However, the way in which the political, social and cultural position of the Magyars has developed in fellow Socialist countries has been all the more disappointing in contrast; a fact which caused the influential party official, Aczél, to make the diplomatically cautious statement that 'it transpires that the various Socialist states are not solving their nationalities problem in a similar manner and that the principles of Lenin's policy towards national minorities is not automatically applied. Moreover, while reviving old nationalist aspirations, attempts are also made to curtail the rights of national minorities and force their assimilation'. Of course, it was clear to every informed Hungarian that this comment was an attack on the intolerant nationalities policy of the autocratic Ceauşescu regime in Rumania.

The unsolved problem of the Magyar minority in Rumania and Hungary's demand for the return of Transylvania meant that relations between the two countries in the inter-war period were already so tense that it was impossible to establish any cooperation based on trust. Hungarians who fled Rumania swelled the ranks of the nationalist Right which proclaimed the revision of the border of northern Transylvania as its chief goal. In contrast, many of the Hungarians who remained behind in Rumania joined the then persecuted Rumanian Communist Party, whose 'internationalist' ideology ensured that the interests of all of Rumania's citizens were represented. But this alleged Hungarian 'foreign rule' in the party, which lasted until the late 1940s, is one of the reasons for the Rumanian Communist Party's antagonistic policy towards the Hungarian minority today. Because of their own nationalistic policy, aimed at achieving greater independence from Moscow, the Rumanians fear that the Russians may press for Transylvania's return to

Hungary if they encounter too much obduracy on their part. In 1959, lacking any real support from Budapest, the Hungarian minority, estimated at around 2 million people, had to accept the closure of the Hungarian university in Kolozsvár (Rumanian Cluj). In 1967, the self-governing Magyar region, established fifteen years previously, was replaced by a new administrative region and increasing numbers of Rumanians were settled in predominantly Magyar areas. The number of schools in which Hungarian was taught was systematically reduced and heavy restrictions placed on publications in Hungarian. Since they were denied career advancement opportunities, and since visits by relatives were made difficult and applications to leave the country resulted in the authorities carrying out punitive measures, the Magyars felt that they were being treated as second-class citizens. As far as the Rumanian party and government chief, Ceauşescu, was concerned, he thought that his intolerant minorities policy, which also threatened the existence of the Transylvanian Saxons, would bring his main aim closer. As he put it, 'In the foreseeable future there will be no more national minorities in Rumania: only one Socialist nation'.

For a long time the Kádár régime exercised patience and showed remarkable restraint out of a sense of Socialist solidarity and in the hope of being able to do more for its conationals in the Rumania of the post-Ceauşescu era. Following a bilateral meeting between the two party chiefs on 15 and 16 June 1977, the first for many years, the Rumanians began to show signs of a willingness to compromise. The minorities were still acknowledged as a 'connecting link' between the two countries and reference was made to their protection in keeping with the principles of the United Nations. But, since the solution of the nationalities problem in the Soviet hegemonial sphere was expressly viewed as an 'internal matter' for the host country, the government in Bucharest, concerned at the possible ramifications of the Hungarian reforms, increasingly ignored the interests of its Magyar minority and decisively rejected any interference by the Hungarian government. Thus, neither official statements nor the communiqué issued after premier Lázár's visit to Bucharest on 13 and 14 July 1982 made any mention of the Hungarian minority in Transylvania. However, since the grievances of Rumania's Magyar minority and its harassment increased, the Central Committee Secretaries, Aczél and Várkonyi, conducted 'frank and open talks' at party level in Bucharest on 30 November and 1 December 1982. The only result of these talks was the agreement of both parties to maintain contact. The Hungarian

Samizdat magazine *Ellenpontok* (Counterpoint), which was circulated in Rumania, repeatedly highlighted the dramatically deteriorating situation of the Magyar minority, its staff even directing an appeal by Hungarian dissidents on behalf of their conationals to the European Conference on Security and Cooperation in Madrid. During a visit to Budapest by the Rumanian foreign minister, Ştefan Andrei, between 28 February and 2 March 1983, the authorities were content to issue a statement to the effect 'that the Rumanian national minority in Hungary and the Hungarian national minority in Rumania are factors in the relations between both parties and should contribute to even greater cooperation between Hungary and Rumania'. But since Ceauşescu, attending a meeting of the Councils of Workers of Hungarian and German Nationality on 31 March 1983, stuck to his view that full equality of rights for all citizens of the Rumanian Socialist Republic has been one 'of the great achievements of the Socialist social order', no change can be expected at present in Rumania's intransigent nationalities policy.

The difference between the two governments thus grew more acute, when, on the occasion of the anniversary of the Hungarian state, the Hungarian ambassador to Rumania, Miklós Barity, delivered a speech on Radio Bucharest on 4 April 1984 in which he highlighted the problems of the Hungarian minority and criticised its discrimination, contrasting the Rumanian government's conduct with his own government's much more tolerant nationalities policy. When, on 23 August, the anniversary of Rumania's liberation by the Red Army, Ceauşescu again announced that the problem of Rumania's national minorities had been finally solved, *Népszabadság* replied on 25 August 1984 with a report which criticised actions carried out against Hungarians by Rumanian irregulars in Transylvania in late 1944. Although, following another meeting between the two foreign ministers, Várkonyi and Andrei, on 21 and 22 January 1985 in Bucharest, the official communiqué reported, 'that the Rumanian national minority in Hungary and the Hungarian national minority in Rumania play a leading role in improving the varied cooperation between both countries', the Rumanian authorities increased their restrictions on visits by Hungarians on both sides of the border. Thus, at the Hungarian party's Thirteenth Party Congress Rumania was cautiously criticised without being mentioning by name. When during the summer holiday period in 1985 the Rumanian border formalities were so slow in being carried out that Hungarians had to put up with delays of eight hours on average, the Hungarian press had no hesitation in accusing Rumania of 'openly violating bilateral agreements' and demanded 'retaliation' for this 'harassment'. However, no solution to this growing conflict is at present in sight.

For the 600,000 Hungarians who live along the Hungarian border of Southern Slovakia and make up 4 per cent of the Czech population, conditions, although not ideal, are more favourable. Nevertheless, Hungarian dissidents complain that a 'step-by-step displacement of the [Hungarian] language and culture' is taking place here and that the authorities are demanding loyalty to the host country which will lead to a loss of national identity. Concern was felt when the Czech authorities imprisoned Miklós Duray for a second time because of his activities in defending the rights of Slovakia's Hungarian minority. At regular meetings between Hungarian and Yugoslav leaders the call is repeatedly made for the national minorities of both countries to be granted 'every socio-economic, cultural, educational and other opportunity', and that a responsibility exists to create 'a more balanced position' for them 'in the respective host country'. Having said that, the 504,000 Magyars under Yugoslavian sovereignty, who mainly inhabit the border area of the Voivodina, appear to live under comparatively tolerable conditions. But while Kádár praised the importance of the minorities for the deepening of friendly, neighbourly relations during a visit to Belgrade on 7 and 8 March 1984, after a further visit in late 1985 the Hungarian prime minister, Lázár, and his Yugoslav counterpart, Planinc, expressly spoke of the need to 'improve the situation of the minorities' in order to help intensify and strengthen bilateral contacts between the two governments.

The Hungarian government, for its part, boasts of having made a complete break with the aggressively intolerant nationalities policy of the past and claims to have granted exemplary protection to its minorities. This refers to Hungary's 230,000 Germans, who have, in fact, already been largely assimilated, 130,000 South Slavs, 130,000 Slovaks scattered across the entire country and 25,000 Rumanians. Patient efforts to make the country's 320,000 gypsies settle permanently and integrate into society have not yet been completely succesful.

Concern for the situation of conationals, which has been passionately debated in Hungary, but given little coverage in the media, could lead to a revival of the extremely militant Magyar nationalism of the past and the problem of revising the borders of Trianon Hungary, which dominated the country's history during the inter-war period. The ruling party finds itself in a quandary at present.

Officially, its hands are tied against doing more for the Hungarian minority in Hungary's neighbouring countries. On the other hand, it cannot allow the problem to be exploited solely by the dissidents and nationalists, since a groundswell of nationalism could jeopardise its programme of reforms, against which there are enough reservations as it is in the Socialist Bloc, and thus undermine the domestic stability so far achieved. Faced with the growing problems of implementing the economic reforms and maintaining a more liberal climate, Hungary is especially sensitive and vulnerable to external pressures.

But the danger from this quarter seems less acute at present. Changes in the Kremlin leadership following the death of Brezhnev, who viewed developments in Hungary with considerable scepticism, resulted in the emergence of Yuri V. Andropov as his successor in November 1982. Andropov knew Hungary well from his time as ambassador in Budapest during the crisis of 1956 and was said to appreciate Hungary's cautious policy aimed at improving economic efficiency and raising the standard of living. During an official visit to Moscow by a Hungarian party and government delegation between 18 and 23 July 1983, Kádár was awarded a second Order of Lenin 'for his outstanding services in developing fraternal friendship between Hungary and the Soviet Union and his contribution to peace and the establishment of Socialism'. The new Kremlin leader showed his concrete support for Kádár's avowed commitment 'to advance Socialist economic integration while paying due regard to the most recent know-how in international science and technology' by promising to demonstrate the transferability of the Hungarian NEM model, to specific areas within the Soviet system, acknowledged to be in need of reform – not only in agriculture, but also in industry and the service sector.

However, the hope that the Kremlin's 'period of neutrality' towards Hungary's reform experiment had finally passed, was mistaken. During Andropov's long illness and especially under his successor, K. U. Černenko, who as General Secretary of the Soviet Communist Party, guided Russia's destiny for only a year, the old reservations were revived. The stationing of American medium-range missiles in Europe in response to the hurried deployment of Soviet SS 20s led to a deterioration in East–West relations, already greatly strained as a result of the Soviet invasion of Afghanistan and the suppression of the Solidarity movement in Poland which Hungarians followed with great sympathy. To limit the damage and prevent a breakdown in the dialogue between the superpowers, the Hungarian government, supported by the East

Germans and Rumanians, argued for a policy of compromise and the continuation of the American-Soviet strategic arms limitation talks, for which they were fiercely criticised by the Czech Communists and Kremlin hawks led by foreign minister, Gromyko, and defence minister, Marshall Ustinov. Although, following Gromyko's friendly official visit to Budapest on 17 and 18 April 1984, the communiqué emphasised the 'atmosphere of fraternal friendship, full agreement of views and complete mutual trust', Hungary succeeded at the subsequent meeting of Warsaw Pact foreign ministers in winning sufficient support for its moderate line of avoiding a course likely to lead to confrontation. Attacks in the Czechoslovak Communist Party newspaper, *Rudé Pravo*, in *Kommunist* and in the April edition of *Voprosy istorii* KPSS, which printed a long list of 'revisionist errors' in Hungarian domestic policy and criticised 'right-wing revisionism in foreign policy', failed to shift the Hungarian party and government leadership from its reformist course in domestic policy and pursuit of a dialogue in foreign policy 'despite the stationing of American rockets in Europe'. During the initial phase of the negotiations on the renewal of the Warsaw Pact, Hungary's interest in expanding its trade with the West and difficulties in achieving its economic planning targets resulted in the demand that Hungary in future should no longer have to take part in the costly Siberian or Caucasus manoeuvres or, alternatively, receive financial compensation in return for participating. Concentrating its forces on its own defence needs was thought more sensible. In order to demonstrate goodwill, Hungarian units joined Soviet and Czechoslovak units in taking part in manoeuvres held near the Austrian border in western Hungary in late June 1984 and intensified the training of recruits. When the commander-in-chief of the Warsaw Pact allies, Marshall Kulikov, and his chief of the general staff, General Gribkov, met Kádár on 3 January 1985, the Hungarian leadership subsequently announced its full support for a prologation of the east European military alliance.

In contrast, the dynamic new General Secretary of the Soviet Communist Party, Mikhail Gorbachev, takes an unprejudiced view of the Hungarian 'model', since he himself is looking for ways to stimulate and improve the efficiency of the stultified Soviet economy. After a meeting between Gorbachev and Kádár on 25 September 1985 the official communiqué stressed the 'importance in principle of the course adopted to accelerate socio-economic development in both countries'. The Hungarians were obliged to accept that the 'all-round raising of production' can only be achieved through 'better use of the historical advantages of Socialism and all the possibilities of the Socialist planned economy', and by 'actively emphasising the social, ideological and spiritual values of Socialist construction, acknowledging . . . what is involved in Socialist construction'. They dare not throw this advice to the wind, for Hungary obtains in rapidly increasing supplies approximately 90 per cent of its oil, 40 per cent of its coal imports, 96 per cent of its natural gas, 90 per cent of its imported iron ore and 90 per cent of timber imports from the USSR. At the conference of the Political Advisory Committee of the Warsaw Pact States, held in Budapest on 10 and 11 June 1986, Gorbachev was given his first opportunity to form his own judgement on the present state of Hungary's reform measures and Kádár's unchallenged position as party chief.

It is not yet clear whether the present Kremlin leadership is prepared to tolerate the continuation of the Hungarian 'experiment' only under János Kádár or whether it will show his successor that it is prepared to make the same allowances. In many ways, Kádár, who celebrated his 75th birthday in May 1987, has grown tired of office and has indicated his wish to retire and enjoy his old age after many exhausting years of fulfilling his official duties in an exemplary manner. As yet there is no sign of any potential successor who would be acceptable to a consensus of opinion. Those who over the years have been named as possible successors have fallen by the wayside. György Aczél, who was for a long time Kádár's close colleague and loyal servant, is 66 years old and not much younger than Kádár himself. Moreover, as the initiator and protector of the liberal cultural climate, he remains suspect in the eyes of the doctrinaire Communists and conservative provincial party officials. Following the dismissal of the influential chief of planning and deputy prime minister, Károly Huszár, at the Twelfth Party Congress, younger economic specialists, like the Politburo members and Central Committee Secretaries, Károly Németh and Ferenc Havasi, who can be trusted to continue with the cautious programme of reform, have risen to occupy high positions. At present the 64-year-old Németh appears to have the best prospects as a potential successor, since the Thirteenth Party Congress, held in 1985, appointed him deputy General Secretary. But the Budapest party secretary, Károly Grosz, a Kádár protégé, who has risen rapidly in the last few years to become a full member of the Politburo, and who was appointed prime minister in June 1987, is also still in the running at the age of 56.

The small, but still present, orthodox wing of the party, which is beginning to warn against the 'harmful effects' of the reforms through the head of the party's Control Commission and ex-Central Committee Secretary, András Genyes, might be able to influence the direction of Hungary's domestic policy, but only in the event of receiving unqualified Soviet backing. A government reshuffle of 6 December 1984 resulted in the emergence of Lajos Czinege as deputy prime minister. Although highly regarded in Moscow, Czinege is extremely unpopular in Hungary on account of several scandals and his appointment can be seen primarily as a gesture to the Kremlin to assert 'the party's leadership role in all areas of Socialist community life', alongside the attempt to give the armed forces a dynamic new leadership more open to reforms. But, since the new defence minister, István Olah, suffered a heart attack on 15 December 1985 and was replaced by the chief of the political administration of the armed forces, colonel-in-chief Ferenc Karpati, it is impossible to say at present whether and in what direction the army will think of intervening in the debate on Kádár's successor. In the Party Central Committee, recently reduced to 105 members and including 41 first-time delegates, in the thirteen-man-strong Politburo, to which, as well as Grosz, the Youth Association functionary, Csabo Homori, and the chairman of the National Council of National Cooperatives, István Szabó, have also been newly appointed, and in the influential Central Committee Secretariat, the advocates of reform and Kádár's personal supporters have a comfortable majority, In view of this, it is unlikely that the Hungarian model will come to an abrupt end, even after the departure of the present party chief. In his three decades in office Kádár has become the guarantor of his country's relative autonomy and liberality. Whereas after the defeated Hungarian uprising of 1956 his name was synonymous with savage repression, oppression and voluntary subordination to the power of the Soviet military, today he commands the respect even of the former opponents he once mercilessly suppressed and consigned to political oblivion.

Despite wishful thinking in the West that a parliamentary system along western democratic lines will eventually establish itself in Hungary, the country's firm ties with the Socialist Bloc rule out any political development which would challenge the ruling party's monopoly of power. The hegemonial power, the Soviet Union, has sufficient informal and direct control mechanisms at its disposal to block any potentially dangerous Hungarian initiative in good time. The various levels of Hungary's political and economic dependence on the Soviet Union, which have now been established for almost forty years, are so numerous that these ties, which affect every area of public life, can be used to stabilise relations at any time. Given Comecon, the Warsaw pact, Soviet troops stationed in Hungary and political and moral pressure from fellow Socialist countries, the Soviet Communist Party has important elements of control at its disposal which can be systematically employed if, in its estimation, Hungary's reform policies infringe upon the Marxist-Leninist Party's sole right to wield power, or if conditions in Hungary threaten to destabilise Communist rule in neighbouring countries and harm the security interests of the Soviet Union within its east central European satellites. On the other hand, Hungary can serve as a model for the Communist system's capacity for reform and self-renewal: decentralisation allowing concerns to make their own decisions, cooperation with western companies, the greater availability of consumer goods, support for private initiatives in the service sector, restricted press censorship and the opportunity of allowing people to travel to capitalist countries. Hungary's exemplary raising of economic efficiency and general living standards, which can serve to pacify a population, which of all the east European nations, is growing more and more dissatisfied with economic conditions, is certainly something which also lies in the interest of the Soviet leadership.

The Hungarians have learnt certain lessons from their own history. Realistically appraising the conditions imposed on them by the general European political situation in the past fifteen years, they have managed to create considerable freedoms in every area of life by adopting a pragmatic approach to their country's development. Hungary's pluralism, although limited in comparison with western countries, offers the Magyars the maximum possible benefits at the least possible risk, and stands out in marked contrast to the grey monotony, resignation and almost total withdrawal of the population into the individual sphere encountered elsewhere in eastern Europe. Hungary's political structure is characterised by the same flexibility which has been seen in its social, economic and intellectual development. The level of autonomy which has so far been achieved has been accepted, firmly established and is still capable of further development. So long as those in power understand how to balance Hungarian society's rising expectations against the growing vigilance of the Soviet hegemonial power over the Hungarian experiment, so long as the population is wise enough to be content with the cautious realisation of modest reforms and so long as the Kremlin does not provoke Magyar national pride by interfering on a major scale in Hungarian affairs – one need have no fears for Hungary's future.

Chronology

285

	independent principality under Habsburg overlordship
1699	26 January. Following the military victories of Prince Eugene of Savoy, the Peace of Karlowitz ends Ottoman rule over Hungary
1703–11	Uprising led by Prince Ferenc II (Rákóczi) of Transylvania
1707	The Diet of Ónod proclaims the dethronement of the House of Habsburg
1711	30 April. The Peace of Szatmár effects a compromise between the Hungarian estates and the absolutist Habsburg monarchy
1722–23	Hungary agrees to the Pragmatic Sanction and accepts the principle of the female line of succession to the Habsburg throne
1731	*Carolina Resolutio*: restrictions on non-Catholics openly practising their religion are accompanied by their exclusion from public office
1740–80	Habsburg Empress Maria Theresia, Queen of Hungary
1780–90	Habsburg Emperor Joseph II, King of Hungary – greater centralisation of the state administration with German as the official language
1781	The Tolerance Edict allows non-Catholics freedom of worship and the right to hold to public office
1785	Reorganisation of Hungary's administration. Hereditary serfdom abolished
1825	3 November. Founding of the Academy of Hungarian Sciences
1848–1916	Emperor Francis Joseph I
1848	15 March. Revolutionary outbreaks in Pest. 7 April–10 September. Count Lajos Batthyányi forms Hungary's first autonomous government with responsible ministers 15 September. Creation of the National Defence Committee under Lajos Kossuth
1849	14 April. Dethronement of the House of Habsburg and proclamation of an independent Hungary 13 August. Surrender of the *Honvéd* at Világos October–November. Introduction of the neo-absolutist administration in Hungary
1853	2 March. Urbarial Decree abolishing feudal dues
1855	18 August. Concordat signed between the Vatican and

	the Habsburg monarchy
1860	20 October. The October Diploma
1861	26 February. The February Patent
1866	3 July. Prussia defeats Austria in the Battle of Königgrätz (Sadowa)
1867	17 February–14 November 1871. Count Gyula Andrássy's government
1868	25 June Hungarian–Croat Compromise
1871	14 November–30 November 1872. Count Menyhért Lónyai's government
1873	1 January. Pest, Buda and Óbuda merge to form Budapest
1875	20 October–13 March 1890. Count Kálmán Tisza's government
1878	12 April. Formation of a 'United Opposition'
1879	7 October. Signing of the Dual Alliance between Austro-Hungarian Monarchy and the German Empire
1882	20 May. Signing of the Triple Alliance between Austria-Hungary, Germany and Italy.
1884	Founding of the Independence and 1848 Party
1890	13 March–17 November 1892. Count Gyula Szápáry's government
	7 December. Founding of the Hungarian Social Democratic Party
1892	17 November–14 January 1895. Sándor Wekerle's first government
1894	10 December. Passing of the anti-church laws
1895	14 January–26 February 1899. Baron Dezső Bánffy's government
1896	Millenium Celebration
1899	26 February–27 June 1903. Kálmán Széll's government
1903	27 June–3 November. Count Károly Khuen-Héderváry's first government
	17 September. Emperor Francis Joseph I's army order (from Chlopy) stressing the unity of the imperial army
	3 November–18 June 1905. Count István Tisza's first government
1905	January. Liberal Party's electoral defeat
	18 June–8 April 1906. Baron Géza Fejérváry's government
1906	8 April–17 January 1910. Sándor Wekerle's second government

1909	11 November. The Independence Party splits
1910	17 January–22 April 1912. Count Károly Khuen-Héderváry's second government
	19 February. Founding of the National Party of Work
1912	22 April–10 June 1913. László Lukács' government
1913	10 June–5 June 1917. Count István Tisza's second government
	14 June. Founding of the United Independence and 1848 Party led by Count Mihály Károlyi
1914	28 June. Archduke Francis Ferdinand, heir apparent to the throne of Austria, murdered in Sarajevo
	28 July. Austria-Hungary declares war on Serbia
1916	21 November. Death of Emperor Francis Joseph I
1916–18/22	Emperor Charles I, King Charles IV of Hungary
1917	15 June–18 August. Count Móric Esterházy's government
	18 August–24 October 1918. Sándor Wekerle's third government
1918	16 October. The Emperor Charles issues the October Manifesto promising a federal structure for Austria
	25 October. Formation of the Hungarian National Council under the chairmanship of Count Mihály Károlyi
	29 October. Croatia secedes from Hungary
	30–31 October. The bourgeois-democratic (Chrysanthenum) revolution
	31 October–8 January 1919. Count Mihály Károlyi's government
	3 November. Cease-fire agreed in Padua between Austria-Hungary and the Entente Powers
	16 November. Proclamation of the Hungarian Republic
	24 November. Founding of the Hungarian Communist Party
1919	11 January. Count Mihály Károlyi elected President of the Hungarian Republic
	18 January–20 March. Dénes Berinkey's government
	16 February. Land reform law
	21 March. Proclamation of the Soviet Republic and creation of the Revolutionary Governing Council led by the Communist Béla Kun

	2 April. Promulgation of the provisional constitution and a new electoral law
	5 May. Formation of a rival government in Arad led by Count Gyula Károlyi
	1 August. Removal of the Revolutionary Governing Council. End of Soviet Rule in Hungary
	6 August. István Friedrich's government
	16 November. Admiral Miklós Horthy marches on Budapest at the head of the National Army
	25 November–13 March 1920. Károly Huszár's government
1920	1 March. Horthy elected Regent
	14 March–27 June. Sándor Simonyi-Semadam's government
	4 June. Trianon Peace Treaty
	19 July–13 April 1921. Count Pál Teleki's government
1921	26–30 March. King Charles IV's first restoration attempt
	14 April–18 August 1931. Count István Bethlen's government
	20–24 October. King Charles IV's second restoration attempt
	6 November. Dethronement of the House of Habsburg.
1922	18 September. Hungary accepted as member of the League of Nations and joins on 31 January 1923
1926	11 November. Reconstitution of the Upper House of the Hungarian parliament
1930	13 October. Founding of the Independent Party of Smallholders
1931	14 June. Collapse of the Hungarian banks
	24 August–21 September 1932. Count Gyula Károlyi's government
1932	1 October–12 October 1936. Gyula Gömbös' government
1934	16 March. Rome Protocol on Hungarian, Italian and Austrian cooperation
1936	12 October–13 May 1938. Kálmán Darányi's government
1937	1 July. The Regent's powers increased
1938	14 May–16 February 1939. Béla Imrédy's government
	2 November. First Vienna Award restores Southern

Slovakia and the southern Carpatho-Ukraine to Hungary

1939   13 January. Hungary joins the Anti-Comintern Pact

12 February–3 April 1941. Count Pál Teleki's government

15 March. Hungary occupies the remainder of the Carpatho-Ukraine

11 April. Hungary leaves the League of Nations

1940   30 August. Second Vienna Award restores northern Transylvania to Hungary

20 November. Hungary joins the Three Powers Pact

1941   4 April–9 March 1942. László Bárdossy's government

11 April. Hungary attacks Yugoslavia

27 June. Hungary declares war on the USSR

1942   9 March–19 March 1944. Miklós Kállay's government

1943   September. Secret negotiations with the western Allies

1944   19 March. Hungary occupied by German troops

22 March–24 August. Döme Sztójay's government

29 August–15 October. Géza Lakatos' government

12 September. Refounding of the Hungarian Communist Party

11 October. Signing of a provisional cease-fire in Moscow

15 October. Horthy's proclamation calling for an end to the fighting; Arrow Cross stages coup

16 October. Horthy appoints Arrow Cross leader, Ferenc Szálasi, prime minister

11 November. Formation of the Liberation Committee of Hungary's National Rising

21 December. Creation of a Provisional National Assembly and formation of a Provisional National Government led by Béla Dálnoki Miklós

1945   20 January. Signing of the armistice agreement between the Allies and Hungary in Moscow

15 March. Government decree on expropriation and redistribution of land

4 April. Cessation of hostilities in Hungary

4 November. Parliamentary elections; the Smallholders win 57 per cent of the vote

1946   9 January. Creation of the Supreme Economic Council

1 February. Proclamation of the Hungarian Republic; Zoltán Tildy becomes first President

	4 February–30 May 1947. Ferenc Nagy's government
	5 March. Creation of the Left-Wing Bloc
	1 August. Currency reform halts inflation; new forint coinage introduced
1947	January. Exposure of 'counter-revolutionary conspiracy' of Hungarian Unity
	10 February. Signing of the Paris Peace Treaty
	31 May–10 December 1948. Lajos Dinnyés' government
	1 August. Three Year Plan introduced
1948	10 February. Signing of Treaty of Friendship, Co-operation and Mutual Support between Hungary and the USSR
	12–4 June. Day of Party Unity: the Hungarian Communist Party merges with the Social Democratic Party to form the Hungarian Workers' Party (MDP)
1949	3–8 February. Trial of Cardinal József Mindszenty, sentenced to life imprisonment on charges of anti-state activities
	15 March. Reorganisation of the National Independence Front into the new Hungarian Popular Front for Independence
	18 August. Acceptance of the constitution of the Hungarian People's Republic
1950	2 January. First Five Year Plan introduced
	30 August. Agreement between the government and the Catholic prelates
1951	25 February–2 March. MDP Second Party Congress
1952	14 August. Mátyás Rákosi, MDP First Secretary replaces István Dobi as prime minister
1953	27–28 June. MDP Central Committee meets in full session; decree on new official party line
	3 July. Imre Nagy forms a government
1954	24–30 May. MDP Third Party Congress
	23–24 October. Founding congress of the Patriotic Popular Front
1955	14 April. Nagy relieved of all party offices
	18 April. András Hegedüs replaces Nagy as prime minister
	11–14 May. Hungary becomes a founder member of the Warsaw Pact Organisation
1956	14–25 February. Twentieth Party Congress of the Soviet Communist Party

18–21 July. M. Rákosi replaced by Ernő Gerő as First Secretary of the MDP

1 November. Founding of the Hungarian Socialist Workers' Party (MSzMP)

4 November. Creation of the Revolutionary Workers' and Peasants' Government under János Kádár in Szolnok

By 10–11 November the 'counter-revolution' is crushed by the massive deployment of Soviet troops

1957   20–28 March. A party and government delegation led by Kádár signs an agreement in Moscow on the stationing of Soviet troops in Hungary

1958   2 January. Introduction of the Second Three Year Plan

28 January–12 September 1961. Ferenc Münnich's government

1959   30 November–5 December. MSzMP Seventh Party Congress

1960   12 February. Party Central Committee decree on the socialisation of agriculture

1961   2 January. Introduction of the Second Five Year Plan

13 September–25 June 1965. János Kádár's government

1962   30 March. Central Committee announces the completion of the socialisation of agriculture

20–24 November. Eighth Party Congress announces the construction of Socialism in Hungary

1963   10 November. Trade and currency agreement with the Federal Republic of Germany; trade missions established

1964   15 September. Talks between the Hungarian government and the Vatican

1965   30 June–14 April 1967. Gyula Kállai's government

1966   23 November–3 December. Ninth Party Congress decides to introduce the New Economic Mechanism (NEM) on 1 January 1968

1967   14 April–15 May 1975. Jenő Fock's government

6–9 September. Prolongation of the Treaty of Friendship, Cooperation and Mutual Support with the Soviet Union

1968   1 January. Implementation of the Economic Reform decree (NEM)

1970   23–28 November. Tenth Party Congress

1971   3 November. Party Central Committee decides to

	extend role of the party organisation in the state apparatus
1972	19 April. Decision to amend the constitution
1973	28 June. Setting up of a State Planning Commission chaired by György Lázár
	20 December. Establishment of diplomatic relations with the Federal Republic of Germany
1974	21 March. Dismissal of Central Committee secretary for economic affairs, Reszõ Nyers
1975	17–22 March. Eleventh Party Congress programme on the creation of an advanced Socialist society
	15 May. György Lázár replaces Jenõ Fock as prime minister
	13 November. Lázár is given a Vatican audience with Pope Paul VI
1976	12 February László Lékai appointed Archbishop of Esztergom and Cardinal-Primate of the Catholic Church in Hungary
1980	24–27 March. Twelfth Party Congress
1981	2 January. Introduction of the Sixth Five Year Plan
1982	6 May. Hungary joins the International Monetary Fund
	7 July. Hungary becomes a member of the World Bank
1985	25–28 March. Thirteenth Party Congress. Introduction of new Party Statute
	8–22 July. Parliamentary elections including, for the first time, independent constituency candidates
1986	2 January. Introduction of the Seventh Five Year Plan 30 June. Death of the Catholic Cardinal–Primate, László Lekai
1987	25 May. Kádár's 75th birthday
	June. Changes within the MSzMP and the government: Károly Grosz replaces György Lázár as prime minister and apparently improves his chances to succeed Kádár; Ferenc Havari loses responsibility for economic affairs and is promoted to deputy General Secretary of the party; János Berecz, CC–Secretary for information and propaganda, achieves full membership in the politbureau

Select bibliography

Aczél, György, *Szocialista kultúra – közösségi ember (Socialist Culture – Man in Community)*. Budapest 1975.

Aczél, Tamás und Tibor Méray, *The Revolt of the Mind: a Case History of Intellectual Resistance Behind the Iron Curtain*. New York 1960.

Adám, Mágda et al. (eds), *Allianz Hitler-Horthy-Mussolini. Dokumente zur ungarischen Außenpolitik (1933–1944)*. Budapest 1966.

Adonyi-Naredy, Franz von, *Ungarns Armee im Zweiten Weltkrieg: Deutschlands letzter Verbündeter*. Neckargemünd 1971.

Alden, Percy (ed.), *Hungary of To-day. By Members of the Hungarian Government*. London 1909.

Andics, Hellmut, *Der Staat, den keiner wollte. Österreich 1918–1938*. Vienna 1962.

András, Emmerich und Julius Morel (eds), *Kirche im Übergang*. Die Katholische Kirche Ungarns 1945–1982. Gesammelte Studien des Ungarischen Kirchensoziologischen Institutes. Vienna 1982.

Andrássy, Graf Julius (Gyula), *Ungarns Ausgleich mit Österreich vom Jahre 1867*. Leipzig 1897.

Andritsch, Johann (ed.), *Ungarische Geisteswelt von der Landnahme bis Babits*. Gütersloh 1960.

Antal, Endre, *Grundlagen und reformpolitische Einordnung des ungarischen Wirtschaftssystems*. Berlin 1978.

Antalffy, György, *L'Etat socialiste et la théorie marxiste de l'état et du droit*. Szeged 1965.

Apponyi, Count Albert, *Justice for Hungary: Review and Criticism of the Effect of the Treaty of Trianon*. London 1928.

Bakó, Elemér (ed.), *Guide to Hungarian Studies*. Stanford, Cal. 1973.

Balla, Bálint, *Soziologie und Gesellschaft in Ungarn Vol I*. Stuttgart 1974.

Balogh, Sándor et al., Magyarorszáq a XX. században (Hungary in the Twentieth Century). Budapest 1986.

Bangó, Jenő, Das neue ungarische Dorf. Berne 1974.

Baranyi, George, Stephen Széchenyi and the Awakening of Hungarian Nationalism, 1791–1841. Princeton, N. J. 1968.

Bardy, Roland, 1919 – La Commune de Budapest. Paris 1972.

Baross, Gábor, Hungary and Hitler. Astor, Fla. 1970.

Bartsch, Günther, Revolution und Gegenrevolution in Osteuropa, 1948–1968. Bonn 1971.

Batkay, W. M. Authoritarian Politics in a Transitional State: István Bethlen and the United Party in Hungary 1919–1926. New York 1982.

Benoschofsky, Ilona und Elek Karsai (eds), Vádirat a nácizmus ellen: Dokumentumok a magyarországi zsidóüldözék történetéhez (Indictments against Nazism: Documents on the History of the Persecution of the Jews in Hungary). 3 Vols. Budapest 1958–1967.

Berend, Iván and György Ránki, The Development of the Manufacturing Industry in Hungary (1900–1944). Budapest 1960.

Berend, Iván and György Ránki, Hungary: A Century of Economic Development. New York 1974.

Berger, Peter (ed.), Der Österreichisch-Ungarische Ausgleich von 1867. Vorgeschichte und Wirkungen. Vienna, Munich, 1967.

Bernatzik, Edmund, Das staatsrechtliche Verhältnis zu Ungarn. Vienna 1911.

Bernath, Mathias und Felix von Schröder (eds), Biographisches Lexikon zur Geschichte Südosteuropas. 74 Vols. Munich 1970–81.

Bödy, Paul, Joseph Eötvös and the Modernization of Hungary, 1840–1870, A Study of Ideas of Individuality and Social Pluralism in Modern Politics. Philadelphia, Pa. 1972.

Bogyay, Thomas, Grundzüge der Geschichte Ungarns. Darmstadt 1977.

Borbándi, Gyula, Der ungarische Populismus. Mainz 1976.

Borsányi, György, Kun Béla (Béla Kun's biography). Budapest 1974.

Braham, Randolph L., The Hungarian Jewish Catastrophe: A Selected and Annotated Bibliography. New York 1962.

Braham, Randolph L., The Politics of Genocide: The Holocaust in Hungary. 2 Vols. New York 1981.

Bridge, Francis Roy, From Sadowa to Sarajevo. The Foreign Policy of Austria-Hungary, 1866–1914. London, Boston 1972.

Brook-Shepherd, Gordon, The Last Habsburg (the biography of the Emperor Charles). London 1968.

Brunner, Georg and Boris Meissner (eds), *Verfassungen der kommunistischen Staaten*. Paderborn usw. 1979.

Bucsay, Mihály, *Geschichte des Protestantismus in Ungarn*. Stuttgart 1959.

Bunzel, Julius, *Studien zur Sozial- und Wirtschaftspolitik Ungarns*. Leipzig 1902.

Carsten, Francis L., *Revolution in Central Europe, 1918–1919*. London 1972.

Concha, Victor M., *La Gentry, sa génèse et son rôle en Hongrie*. Budapest 1913.

Csáky, Moritz, *Von der Aufklärung zum Liberalismus. Studien zum Frühliberalismus in Ungarn*. Vienna 1981.

Csáky, Moritz, *Der Kulturkampf in Ungarn. Die kirchenpolitische Gesetzgebung der Jahre 1894/95*. Graz usw. 1967.

Csatari, D., *Dans la tourmente. Les relations hungaro-roumaines de 1940 à 1945*. Budapest 1974.

Csizmadia, Ernő, *Socialist Agriculture in Hungary*. Budapest 1979.

Czebe, Jenő and Tibor Pethö, *Hungary in World War II. A Military History of the Years of War*. Budapest 1946.

Deák, Francis, *Hungary at the Paris Peace Conference: the Diplomatic History of the Treaty of Trianon*. New York 1942.

Deák, István, *The Lawful Revolution. Louis Kossuth and the Hungarians, 1848–1849*. New York 1979.

Decsy, János, *Prime Minister Gyula Andrássy's Influence on Habsburg Foreign Policy during the Franco-German War of 1870–1871*. New York 1979.

Delaney, Robert F., *This is Communist Hungary*. Chicago, Ill. 1958.

Diószegi, István, *Die Aussenpolitik der Österreichisch-Ungarischen Monarchie 1871–1877*. Vienna 1985.

Dióiszegi, István, *Hungarians in the Ballhausplatz. Studies in Austro-Hungarian Common Foreign Policy*. Budapest 1983.

Door, Rochus, *Neueste Geschichte Ungarns. Von 1917 bis zur Gegenwart*. Berlin/DDR 1982.

Dreisziger, Nándor A. F., *Hungary's Way to World War II*. Astor Park, Fla, 1968.

Engel-Janosi, Friedrich and Helmut Rumpler (eds), *Probleme der franzisko-josephinischen Zeit 1848–1916*. München 1967.

Enyedi, György, *Hungary: An Economic Geography*. Boulder, Col. 1976.

Erdey, Ferenc (ed.), *Information Hungary*. Budapest 1968.

Erdey-Grúz, Tibor and Imre Trencsény-Waldapfel (eds), *Science in Hungary*. Budapest 1965.

Farkas, Julius von, *Der Freiheitskampf des ungarischen Geistes 1867–1914. Ein Kapitel aus der Geschichte der neueren ungarischen Literatur.* Berlin 1940.

Farkas, Julius von, *Ungarns Geschichte und Kultur in Dokumenten.* Wiesbaden 1955.

Fázsy, Rudolf, *Die Geschichte der Ungarn.* Munich 1960.

Fejtő, François, *A History of the People's Democracies.* London 1974.

Feketekúthy, László, *Ungarn vom Heiligen Stephan bis Kardinal Mindszenty.* Zürich 1950.

Fenyo, Marion D., *Hitler, Horthy and Hungary. German-Hungarian Relations 1941–1944.* New Haven, Conn. 1972.

Fischer, Holger, *Politik und Geschichtswissenschaft in Ungarn: die ungarische Geschichte von 1918 bis zur Gegenwart in der Historiographie seit 1956.* Munich, Vienna 1982.

Fischer, Lewis A. und Philip E. Uren, *The New Hungarian Agriculture.* Montreal 1973.

Flachbart, Ernst, *A History of Hungary's Nationalities.* Budapest 1944.

Fournier, August, *Österreich-Ungarns Neubau unter Kaiser Franz-Joseph I. Eine Historische Skizze.* Berlin 1917.

Frank, Tibor, *The British Image of Hungary 1865–1870.* Budapest 1976.

Franzel, Emil, *Der Donauraum im Zeitalter des Nationalitätenprinzips 1789–1918.* Bern 1958.

Frauendienst, Werner (ed.), *Ungarn – zehn Jahre danach, 1956–1966.* Mainz 1966.

Friss, István (ed.), *Essays on Economic Policy and Planning in Hungary.* Budapest 1978.

Friss, István (ed.), *Reform of the Economic Mechanism in Hungary. Nine Studies.* Budapest 1971.

Futaky, István (ed.), *Ungarn–ein kommunistisches Wunderland?* Reinbek 1983.

Gadó, Ottó (ed.), *Reform of the Economic Mechanism in Hungary.* Budapest 1972.

Galàntai, József, *Die Osterreichisch – Ungarische Monarchie und der Weltkrieg.* Budapest 1979.

Glettler, Monika, *Pittsburg–Wien–Budapest. Programm und Praxis der Nationalitätenpolitik bei der Auswanderung der ungarischen Slowaken nach Amerika um 1900.* Vienna 1980.

Görlich, Ernst Joseph, *Ungarn.* Nuremberg 1965.

Gosztony, Péter, *Miklós von Horthy.* Göttingen 1973.

Gottas, Friedrich, *Ungarn im Zeitalter des Hochliberalismus. Studien zur Tisza-Ära (1875–1890).* Vienna 1976.

Gratz, Gusztáv, *A dualizmus kora. Magyarország története 1867–1918* (*The Age of Dualism. The History of Hungary 1867–1918*). 2 Vols. Budapest 1934.

Grothusen, Klans-Defler (ed.), *Ungarn. Süd–arteuropa–Handbuch vol. 5*. Göttingen 1987.

Hainbuch, Friedrich, *Kirche und Staat in Ungarn nach dem Zweiten Weltkrieg*. Munich 1982.

Hajdú, János and Béla C. Tóth, *The 'Volksbund' in Hungary*. Budapest 1962.

Hajdú, Tibor, *The Hungarian Soviet Republic*. Budapest 1979.

Halász, Zoltán (ed.), *Ungarn. Geographie, Geschichte* . . . Budapest 1964.

Hanák, Péter *et al.*, *Magyarország története 1848–1918* (*The History of Hungary 1848–1918*). 2 Vols Budapest 1978.

Hanák, Péter (ed.), *Die nationale Frage in der Österreichisch-Ungarischen Monarchie 1900–1918*. Budapest 1966.

Hanák, Péter (ed.), *Studien zur Geschichte der Österreichisch-Ungarischen Monarchie*. Budapest 1961.

Hanák, Péter, *Ungarn und die Donaumonarchie*. Munich, Vienna 1984.

Hanák, Tibor, *Die marxistische Philosophie und Soziologie in Ungarn*. Stuttgart 1976.

Hantsch, Hugo, *Die Geschichte Österreichs. Vol. 2: 1648–1918*. Graz, Vienna 1950.

Hartl, Hans, *Nationalitätenprobleme im heutigen Südosteuropa*. Cologne 1973.

Hefty, Georg P., *Schwerpunkte der Außenpolitik Ungarns 1945–1973. Vorgeschichte, Infrastruktur, Orientierung, Interaktionsprozesse*. Munich 1980.

Hegedüs, András *et al.*, *Die neue Linke in Ungarn*. Berlin 1974.

Heller, Ágnes and Ferenc Fehér, *Ungarn '56. Geschichte einer anti-stalinistischen Revolution*. Hamburg 1982.

Helmerich, Ernst C. (ed.), *Hungary*. New York 1957.

Hennyey, Gustav, *Ungarns Schicksal zwischen Ost und West*. Mainz 1975.

Hillgruber, Andreas, 'Deutschland und Ungarn 1933–1944. Ein Überblick über die politischen und militärischen Beziehungen im Rahmen der europäischen Politik.' In: *Wehrwissenschaftliche Rundschau* 9 (1959), pp. 651–676.

Hitchins, Keith, 'Hungarica 1961–1974. Literaturbericht über Neuerscheinungen zur Geschichte Ungarns von den Arpaden bis 1970.' In: *Sonderheft 9 der Historischen Zeitschrift*. Munich, Vienna 1981.

Hoensch, Jörg K., *Der ungarische Revisionismus und die Zerschlagung der Tschechoslowakei.* Tübingen 1967.

Hóman, Bálint and Gyula Szekfű, *Magyar történet* (*History of Hungary*). 5 Vols. Budapest 1941–1943.

Horthy, Miklós, *Confidential Papers.* Budapest 1965.

Horthy, Nikolaus, *Memoirs.* London 1956.

Horváth, Zoltán, *Die Jahrhundertwende in Ungarn. Geschichte der zweiten Reformgeneration 1896–1914.* Neuwied 1966.

Hungarian National Commission for UNESCO (ed.), *Cultural Policy in Hungary.* Paris 1974.

Huszár, Tibor *et al.* (eds), *Hungarian Society and Marxist Sociology in the Nineteen-seventies.* Budapest 1978.

Ignotus, Paul, *Hungary.* New York 1972.

Il'ičev, F. L. *et al.* (eds), *Sovetsko-vengerskie otnošenija 1945–1948 gg. Dokumenty i materialy.* Moscow 1969.

Illyés, Gyula, *Vie de Petőfi.* Paris 1962.

Islamov, Muslim Tofik, *Političeskaja bor'ba v Vengrii nakanune pervoj mirovoj vojny 1906–1914.* Moscow 1972.

Israeljan, Viktor Levonovič, *133 geroičeskich dnja. Vengerskaja Sovetskaja Respublika 1919 g..* Moscow 1959.

Istorija Vengrii v trech tomach. Moscow 1972.

János, Andrew C., *The Politics of Backwardness in Hungary, 1825–1945.* Princeton, N. J. 1982.

János, Andrew C. und William B. Slottman (eds), *Revolution in Perspective: Essays on the Hungarian Soviet Republic of 1919.* Berkeley, Cal. 1971.

Jaray, Gabriel L., *La question sociale et le socialisme en Hongrie.* Paris 1909.

Jászi, Oszkár, *The Dissolution of the Habsburg Monarchy.* Chicago, Ill. 1929.

Jászi, Oskar, *Revolution and Counter-revolution in Hungary.* London 1924.

Juhász, Gyula *et al.* (eds), *Diplomáciai iratok Magyarország külpolitikajához, 1936–1945* (*Diplomatic Documents on Hungarian Foreign Policy*). 6 Vols. Budapest 1962 ff.

Juhász, Gyula, *Hungarian Foreign Policy 1919–1945.* Budapest 1979.

Kabdebo, Thomas, *Diplomat in Exile. Francis Pulszky's Political Activities in England,* 1859–60. New York 1979.

Kabdebo, Thomas, *Hungary.* Oxford 1980.

Kádár, Imre, *The Church in the Storm of Time., The History of the Hungarian Reformed Church During the Two World Wars, Revolutions and Counter-Revolutions.* Budapest 1958.

Kádár, János, *Eine starke Volksmacht bedeutet ein unabhängiges Ungarn.* *Reden und Artikel – Auswahl 1957–1959.* Berlin/DDR 1961.

Kádár, János, *Reden und Schriften 1964–1971.* Berlin/DDR 1972.

Kádár János, *Vorwärts auf dem Wege des Sozialismus. Reden und Schriften 1960–1966.* Berlin/DDR 1967.

Kállai, Gyula, *A magyar függetlenségi mozgalom, 1936–45 (The Hungarian Independence Movement 1936–1945).* Budapest 1965.

Kállay, Nicholas (Miklós), *Hungarian Premier. A Personal Account of a Nation's Struggle in the Second World War.* New York 1954.

Kampis, Antal, *The History of Art in Hungary.* Budapest 1966.

Kann, Robert A., *Das Nationalitätenproblem der Habsburgermonarchie. Geschichte und Ideengehalt vom Vormärz bis zur Auflösung des Reiches im Jahre 1918.* 2 Vols. Graz. Vienna 1964. (N.B. earlier English version, *The Multinational Empire, Nationalism and National reform in the Habsburg Monarchy 1848–1918.* New York, 1950)

Kann, Robert A. *The Habsburg Empire. A study in Integration and Disintegration.* New York 1957.

Károlyi, Mihály, *Memoirs. Faith Without Illusion.* London 1956.

Katus, László, 'Die Magyaren'. In: A. Wandruszka and P. Urbanitsch eds., *Die Habsburgermonarchie, vol. 3, Die Völker des Reiches.* Vienna 1980, pp. 410–488.

Katzburg, Nathaniel, *Hungary and the Jews: Policy and Legislation, 1920–1943.* Ramat-Gan 1981.

Kecskeméti, Paul, *The Unexpected Revolution. Social Forces in the Hungarian Uprising.* Stanford, Cal. 1961.

Kenyeres, Agnes *et al.* (eds), *Magyar életrajzi lexikon (Hungarian Biographical Dictionary).* 2 Vols. Budapest 1967, 1969.

Kertész, Stephen D., *Diplomacy in a Whirlpool: Hungary Between Nazi Germany and Soviet Russia.* Notre Dame, Ind. 1953.

Kessler, Joseph, 'Turanism and Pan-Turanism in Hungary, 1890–1945.' Phil. Diss. Berkeley, Cal. 1967.

King, Robert R., *Minorities and Communism: Nationalities as a Source of Tension among Balkan Communist States.* Cambridge, Mass. 1973.

Király, Béla K., *Ferenc Deák.* Boston 1975.

Király, Béla K. *et al.* (eds), *The First War Between Socialist States: The Hungarian Revolution of 1956 and Its Impact.* New York 1983.

Király, Béla K. und Paul Jónás (ed.), *The Hungarian Revolution of 1956 in Retrospect.* New York 1978.

Kirchen im Sozialismus. Kirche und Staat in den osteuropäischen sozialistischen Republiken. Frankfurt 1977.

Kiszling, Rudolf *et al.*, *Die Revolution im Kaisertum Österreich 1848–1849.* 2 Vols, Vienna 1948.

Klaniczay, Tibor *et al. Geschichte der ungarischen Literatur.* Budapest 1963.

Klein, Bernát, 'Hungarian Politics from Bethlen to Gömbös. The Decline of Liberal-Conservatism and the Rise of Right Radicalism.' Phil. Diss. New York 1962.

Die konterrevolutionäre Verschworung von Imre Nagy und Komplizen. Vols 1–5, Budapest 1956–1957.

Kopácsi, Sándor, *Die ungarische Tragödie. Wie der Aufstand von 1956 liquidiert wurde.* Stuttgart 1979.

Köpeczi, Béla, *Kulturrevolution in Ungarn.* Budapest 1978.

Kosáry, Domokos, G., *A History of Hungary.* Cleveland, New York 1941.

Kovrig, Béla, *Hungarian Social Policies, 1920–1945.* New York 1954.

Kovrig, Bennett, *Communism in Hungary. From Kun to Kádár.* Stanford, Cal. 1979.

Kovrig, Bennett, *The Hungarian People's Republic.* Baltimore 1970.

Közi, Horváth, *József Kardinal Mindszenty.* Königstein n.d.

Kühl, Joachim, 'Das ungarländische Deutschtum zwischen Horthy und Hitler. Außenpolitik und Volksgruppenfragen 1919–1944.' In: *Südostdeutsche Heimatblätter* **4** (1955), pp. 117–147.

Lackó, Miklós, *Arrow-Cross Men, National Socialists, 1934–1944.* Budapest 1969.

Lades, Hans, *Die Nationalitätenfrage im Karpatenraum. Der österreichische Ordnungsversuch 1848/49.* Vienna, Leipzig 1941.

László, Ervin, *The Communist Ideology in Hungary. Handbook for Basic Research.* Dordrecht 1966.

László Rajk und Komplizen vor dem Volksgericht. Berlin/DDR 1949.

Lehár, Anton, *Erinnerungen. Gegenrevolution und Restaurationsversuche in Ungarn 1918–1921.* (ed.) Peter Broucek. Vienna 1973.

Lehmann, Hans Georg, *Der Reichsverweser-Stellvertreter. Horthys gescheiterte Planung einer Dynastie.* Mainz 1975.

Levai, Jenő (ed.), *Eichmann in Hungary. Documents.* Budapest 1961.

Lomax, Bill, *Hungary 1956.* London 1976.

Lorenz, Reinhold, *Kaiser Karl und der Untergang der Donaumonarchie.* Vienna 1959.

Low, Alfred D., *The Soviet Hungarian Republic and the Paris Peace Conference.* Philadelphia, Pa. 1963.

Lukács Lajos (ed.), *The Vatican and Hungary 1846–1878. Reports and Correspondence on Hungary of the Apostolic Nuncius in Vienna.* Budapest 1981.

Macartney, C. A., *The Habsburg Empire 1790–1918*. New York 1969.

Macartney, C. A., *Hungary and Her Successors. The Treaty of Trianon and its Consequences 1919–1937*. London 1937.

Macartney, C. A., *October Fifteenth. A History of Modern Hungary, 1929–1945*. 2 Vols. Edinburgh 1956, 1957.

Magyar nemzeti bibliográfia. Bibliographia Hungarica. Budapest 1946 ff.

Marczali, Heinrich, *Ungarische Verfassungsgeschichte*. Tübingen 1910.

May, Arthur J., *The Passing of the Habsburg Monarchy, 1914–1918*. Philadelphia, Pa. 1966.

Mayer, Arno J., *The Politics and Diplomacy of Peacemaking: Containment and Counterrevolution at Versailles, 1918–1919*. New York 1967.

McCagg, William O. *Jewish Nobles and Geniuses in Modern Hungary*. New York 1972.

Mercator (*Pseudonym*), *Die Nationalitätenfrage und die ungarische Reichsidee*. Budapest 1908.

Mindszenty, Kardinal József, *Erinnerungen*. Frankfurt 1974.

Miskolczy, Julius, *Ungarn in der Habsburger-Monarchie*. Vienna 1959.

Mocsy, István I., *The Effects of World War I: The Uprooted. Hungarian Refugees and Their Impact on Hungarian Domestic Politics, 1918–1921*. New York 1983.

Molnár, Miklós, *Budapest 1956. A History of the Hungarian Revolution*. London 1971.

Molnár, Miklós, *A Short History of the Hungarian Communist Party*. Boulder, Col. 1978.

Montgomery, John F., *Hungary: the Unwilling Satellite*. New York 1947.

Mucs, Sándor and Ernő Zágori, *Geschichte der Ungarischen Volksarmee*. Berlin/DDR 1982.

Nagy, Ferenc, *The Struggle Behind the Iron Curtain*. New York 1948.

Nagy, Imre, *Politisches Testament*. Munich 1959.

Nagy, Zsuzsa, *The Liberal Opposition in Hungary 1919–1945*. Budapest 1983.

Nagy-Talavera, Nicholas M., *The Green Shirts and the Others: A History of Fascism in Hungary and Rumania*. Stanford, Cal. 1970.

Nemes, Dezső, *History of the Revolutionary Workers Movement in Hungary, 1944–1962*. Budapest 1973.

Nyers, Rezső, *The Cooperative Movement in Hungary*. Budapest 1963.

Ortutay, Gyula, *Kleine ungarische Volkskunde*. Budapest 1963.

Der Österreichisch-Ungarische Ausgleich von 1867. Materialien (Referate und Diskussion) der internationalen Konferenz in Bratislava 28.8.–1.9. 1967. Bratislava 1971.

Österreich-Ungarn in der Weltpolitik 1900–1918. Berlin/DDR 1965.

Orbán, Sándor, *Egyház és állam 1945–1950 (Church and State 1945–1950).* Budapest 1962.

Paál, Job and Antal Radó (eds), *A debreceni feltámadás (Resurrection in Debrecen).* Debrecen 1947.

Paikert, Géza Charles, 'Hungary's National Minority Policies, 1920–1945'. In: *Slavic and East European Review* 12 (1953), pp. 201–218.

Pamlényi, Erwin (ed.), *A History of Hungary.* Budapest 1971.

Pastor, Peter, *Hungary Between Wilson and Lenin. The Hungarian Revolution of 1918–1919 and the Big Three.* New York 1976.

Pécsi, Márton and Béla Sárfalvi, *The Geography of Hungary.* London 1964.

Pintér I., *Hungarian Anti-Fascism and Resistance 1941–1945.* Budapest 1986.

Plaschka, Richard Georg and Karlheinz Mack (eds.), *Die Auflösung des Habsburgerreiches. Zusammenbruch und Neuorientierung im Donauraum.* Munich 1970.

Pollak, Walter, *1848: Revolution auf halbem Wege.* Vienna 1974.

Pölöskei Ferenc, *Hungary after Two Revolutions (1919–1922).* Budapest 1980.

Pryce-Jones, David, *The Hungarian Revolution.* New York 1970.

Puškaš, Andrej Ivanovič, *Vnešnjaja politika Vengrii. Nojabr' 1918–aprel' 1927 g.* Moscow 1981.

Puškás, Juliana, *From Hungary to the United States (1880–1914).* Budapest 1982.

Radó, Sándor, *Ökonomische Geographie der Ungarischen Volksrepublik.* Berlin/DDR 1963.

Ránki, György, *Economy and Foreign Policy. The Struggle of the Great Powers for Hegemony in the Danube Valley 1919–1939.* New York 1983.

Ránki, György, *Unternehm– Margarethe. Die deutsche Besetzung Ungarns (The German Occupation of Hungary).* Budapest 1984.

Ránki, György et al. (eds), *Magyarország Története 1918–1945, (A History of Hungary 1918–1945)* Budapest 1976.

Reinert-Tárnoky, Ilona, 'Die ungarische Innenpolitik und das Agrarproblem in der Zeit des Dualismus.' In: *Südost-Forschungen* 23 (1964), pp. 215–283.

Reitlinger, Gerald, *Die Endlösung. Die Ausrottung der Juden Europas 1934–1945.* Munich 1964.

Révész, László, *Die Anfänge des ungarischen Parlamentarismus.* Munich 1968.

Rob, Gerda, *Unbekannter Nachbar Ungarn.* Aarau, Stuttgart 1983.

Robinson, William F., *The Pattern of Reform in Hungary. A Political, Economic and Cultural Analysis.* New York 1973.

Rodionov, N. N. (ed.), *Sovetsko-vengerskie otnošenija 1948–1970 gg. Dokumenty i materialy.* Moscow 1974.

Rothenberg, Gunter A., *The Army of Francis Joseph.* West Lafayette, Ind. 1976.

Rothermere, Viscount, *My Campaign for Hungary.* London 1939.

Rutter, Owen, *Regent of Hungary. The Authorized Life of Admiral Nicholas Horthy.* London n.d.

Sagvari, Agnes (ed.), *Budapest. The History of a Capital.* Budapest 1975.

Sándor, Vilmos, *Die Hauptmerkmale der industriellen Entwicklung in Ungarn zur Zeit des Absolutismus (1849–1867).* Budapest 1960.

Savarius, Vincent (Pseudonym of Béla Sándor Szász), *Freiwillige für den Galgen: die Geschichte eines Schauprozesses.* Cologne 1963.

Schmidt-Pauli, Edgar von, *Nikolaus von Horthy. Admiral, Volksheld und Reichsverweser.* Hamburg n.d.

Schöpflin, George, *Hungarians in Romania.* London 1979.

Seton-Watson, R. W., *Corruption and Reform in Hungary: a Study of Electoral Practice.* London 1911.

Seton-Watson, Robert W., *Racial Problems in Hungary.* London 1908.

Seton-Watson, Robert W., *Treaty Revision and the Hungarian Frontiers.* London 1934.

Shawcross, William, *Crime and Compromise: János Kádár and the Politics of Hungary Since Revolution.* London 1974.

Siegel, Jacob S., *The Population of Hungary.* Washington, D.C. 1958.

Silagi, Denis, *Ungarn – Geschichte und Gegenwart.* Hanover 1972.

Sinor, Denis, *History of Hungary.* New York 1959.

Sipos, Péter, *Imrédy Béla és a Magyar Megujulás Pártja (Béla Imrédy and the Party of Hungarian Revival).* Budapest 1970.

Spohr, Ludwig, *Die geistigen Grundlagen des ungarischen Nationalismus.* Berlin, Leipzig 1936.

Statistical Pocket Book of Hungary. Budapest 1958ff.

Stehle, Hansjakob, *Die Ostpolitik des Vatikans, 1917–1975.* Munich. 1975.

Strassenreiter, Erszébet and Péter Sipos, *Rajk László.* Budapest 1974.

Süle, Tibor, *Sozialdemokratie in Ungarn. Zur Rolle der Intelligenz in der Arbeiterbewegung 1899–1910.* Cologne Graz 1967.

Surányi, Miklós, *Bethlen.* Budapest 1927.

Das System der Lenkung der Volkswirtschaft der Ungarischen Volksre-publik. Budapest 1972.

Szabad, György, *Hungarian Political Trends Between the Revolution and the Compromise (1849–1867).* Budapest 1977.

Szabó, István, *Ungarisches Volk. Geschichte und Wandlungen.* Budapest 1944.

Szabolcsi, Bence, *Geschichte der ungarischen Musik.* Leipzig 1965.

Székely, András, *Illustrierte Kulturgeschichte Ungarns.* Leipzig, Jena 1978.

Székely, András, *Kleine ungarische Geschichte.* Budapest 1974.

Szlovák, Alexander, 'Kollektivierung der ungarischen Landwirt-schaft, 1949–1959.' Diss. München 1964.

Taylor, A. J. P., *The Habsburg Monarchy 1809–1918. A History of the Austrian Empire and Austria-Hungary.* London 1948.

Teleki, Pál, *The Evolution of Hungary and its Place in European History.* New York 1923.

Tilkovszky, Loránt, *Nationalitätenpolitische Richtungen in Ungarn in der gegenrevolutionären Epoche 1919–1945.* Budapest 1975.

Tilkovszky, Loránt, *Pál Teleki (1879–1941): A Biographical Sketch.* Budapest 1974.

Tilkovszky, Loránt, *Ungarn und die deutsche 'Volksgruppenpolitik; 1938–1945.* Cologne, Vienna 1981.

Timár, Mátyás, *Reflections on the Economic Development of Hungary, 1967–1973.* Leyden 1976.

Tőkes, Rudolf L., *Béla Kun and the Hungarian Soviet Republic.* New York 1967.

Toma, Peter, A. und Iván Völgyes, *Politics in Hungary.* San Francisco 1977.

Tóth, Adalbert, *Parteien und Reichstagswahlen in Ungarn 1848–1892.* Munich 1973.

Tschuppik, Karl, *The Reign of Emperor Francis Joseph, 1848–1916.* London 1930.

Új magyar lexikon (New Hungarian Dictionary). 6 Vols., Budapest 1959–1962.

Ullein Reviczky, Antal, *Guerre allemande, paix russe: le drame hongrois.* Neufchâtel, Paris 1947.

Unger, Mátyás and Ottó Szabolcs, *Magyarország története (The History of Hungary).* Budapest 1973.

Vágó, Béla and George L. Mosse (eds), *Jews and Non-Jews in Eastern Europe, 1918–1945.* New York 1974.

Váli, Ferenc A. *Rift and Revolt in Hungary. Nationalism versus Communism.* Cambridge, Mass. 1961.

Valiani, Leo, *The End of Austria-Hungary*. London 1973.

Valjavec, Fritz and Gertraud Krallert-Sattler (eds), *Südosteuropa-Bibliographie*. Munich 1956 ff.

Varga, Jańos, *Typen und Probleme des bäuerlichen Grundbesitzes in Ungarn, 1967–1849*. Budapest 1965.

Varga, Laśzló, *Human Rights in Hungary*. Gainsville, Fla. 1967.

Vasari, Emilio, *Ein Königsdrama im Schatten Hitlers. Die Versuche des Reichsverwesers Horthy zur Gründung einer Dynastie*. Vienna 1976.

Vasari, Emilio, *Die ungarische Revolution 1956. Ursachen, Verlauf, Folgen*. Stuttgart 1981.

Vasari, Emilio, *Der verbannte Kardinal*. Vienna 1977.

Vass, Henrik, *Les caractéristiques principales du développement des conditions sociales en Hongrie (1956–1966)*. Budapest 1967.

Vass, Henrik (ed.), *Studies on the History of the Hungarian Working Class Movement (1867–1966)*. Budapest 1975.

Vécsey, József, *Kardinal Mindszenty*. Munich 1962.

Vécsey, József and Johann Schwendemann (eds and trans.), *Mindszenty-Dokumentation*. Vienna 1956.

Vécsey, József and Johann Schwendemann (eds and trans.), *Der Prozeß gegen den Kardinal. Reden, Hirtenbriefe, Presseerklärungen, Einkerkerung, Gefangenschaft, Befreiung 1947–1956*. St. Pölten 1957.

Vermes, Gabor, *István Tisza. The Liberal Vision and Conservative Statecraft of a Magyar Nationalist*. New York 1985.

Vinaver, Vuk, *Jugoslavija i Mad'arska 1918–1933*. Beograd 1971.

Vogl, Ferenc, *Theater in Ungarn 1945–1965*. Cologne 1966.

Völgyes, Iván, *The Hungarian Soviet Republic, 1919: An Evaluation and a Bibliography*. Stanford, Cal. 1970.

Völgyes, Iván, *Hungary. A Nation of Contradictions*. Boulder, Col. 1982.

Völgyes, Iván (ed.), *Hungary in Revolution, 1918–1919. Nine Essays*. Lincoln, Neb. 1971.

Walter, Friedrich and Harold Steinacker, *Die Nationalitätenfrage im alten Ungarn und die Südostpolitik Wiens*. Munich 1959.

Wandruszka, Adam and Peter Urbanitsch (eds), *Die Habsburgermonarchie 1848–1918*. 5 Vols. Vienna 1973–1987.

Weber, Johann, *Eötvös und die ungarische Nationalitätenfrage*. Munich 1966.

Weidlein, Johann, *Geschichte der Ungarndeutschen in Dokumenten*. Schorndorf 1959.

Wertheimer, Eduard von, *Graf Julius Andrássy, Sein Leben und Seine Zeit nach ungedruckten Quellen*. 3 Vols. Stuttgart 1910–1913.

Zeman, Zbyněk A. B., *The Break-Up of the Habsburg Empire*

1914–1918. A Study in National and Social Revolution. London 1961.

Zinner, Paul E., *National Communism and Popular Revolt in Eastern Europe.* New York 1957.

Zinner, Paul E., *Revolution in Hungary.* New York 1962.

Zitta, Victor, *Georg Lukács' Marxism.* The Hague 1964.

Zsigmond, László, *Die Zerschlagung der Österreichisch-Ungarischen Monarchie und die internationalen Kräfteverhältnisse.* Budapest 1960.

Zsoldos, László, ·*The Economic Integration of Hungary Into the Soviet Bloc: Foreign Trade Experience.* Columbus, Ohio 1963.

Index